Keep this book. You will need it and use it throughout your career.

About the American Hotel & Lodging Association (AH&LA)

Founded in 1910, AH&LA is the trade association representing the lodging industry in the United States. AH&LA is a federation of state lodging associations throughout the United States with 11,000 lodging properties worldwide as members. The association offers its members assistance with governmental affairs representation, communications, marketing, hospitality operations, training and education, technology issues, and more. For information, call 202-289-3100.

LODGING, the management magazine of AH&LA, is a "living textbook" for hospitality students that provides timely features, industry news, and vital lodging information.

About the Educational Institute of AH&LA (EI)

An affiliate of AH&LA, the Educational Institute is the world's largest source of quality training and educational materials for the lodging industry. EI develops textbooks and courses that are used in more than 1,200 colleges and universities worldwide, and also offers courses to individuals through its Distance Learning program. Hotels worldwide rely on EI for training resources that focus on every aspect of lodging operations. Industry-tested videos, CD-ROMs, seminars, and skills guides prepare employees at every skill level. EI also offers professional certification for the industry's top performers. For information about EI's products and services, call 800-349-0299 or 407-999-8100.

About the American Hotel & Lodging Educational Foundation (AH&LEF)

An affiliate of AH&LA, the American Hotel & Lodging Educational Foundation provides financial support that enhances the stability, prosperity, and growth of the lodging industry through educational and research programs. AH&LEF has awarded hundreds of thousands of dollars in scholarship funds for students pursuing higher education in hospitality management. AH&LEF has also funded research projects on topics important to the industry, including occupational safety and health, turnover and diversity, and best practices in the U.S. lodging industry. For information, call 202-289-3180.

BASIC HOTEL AND RESTAURANT ACCOUNTING

Educational Institute Books

UNIFORM SYSTEM OF ACCOUNTS FOR THE LODGING INDUSTRY
Ninth Revised Edition

RESORT DEVELOPMENT AND MANAGEMENT
Second Edition
Chuck Y. Gee

PLANNING AND CONTROL FOR FOOD AND BEVERAGE OPERATIONS
Fifth Edition
Jack D. Ninemeier

TRAINING FOR THE HOSPITALITY INDUSTRY
Second Edition
Lewis C. Forrest, Jr.

UNDERSTANDING HOSPITALITY LAW
Fourth Edition
Jack P. Jefferies/Banks Brown

SUPERVISION IN THE HOSPITALITY INDUSTRY
Third Edition
Raphael R. Kavanaugh/Jack D. Ninemeier

ENERGY AND WATER RESOURCE MANAGEMENT
Second Edition
Robert E. Aulbach

MANAGEMENT OF FOOD AND BEVERAGE OPERATIONS
Third Edition
Jack D. Ninemeier

MANAGING FRONT OFFICE OPERATIONS
Sixth Edition
Michael L. Kasavana/Richard M. Brooks

STRATEGIC HOTEL/MOTEL MARKETING
Revised Edition
Christopher W. L. Hart/David A. Troy

MANAGING SERVICE IN FOOD AND BEVERAGE OPERATIONS
Second Edition
Ronald F. Cichy/Paul E. Wise

THE LODGING AND FOOD SERVICE INDUSTRY
Fifth Edition
Gerald W. Lattin

SECURITY AND LOSS PREVENTION MANAGEMENT
Second Edition
Raymond C. Ellis, Jr./David M. Stipanuk

HOSPITALITY INDUSTRY MANAGERIAL ACCOUNTING
Fifth Edition
Raymond S. Schmidgall

PURCHASING FOR HOSPITALITY OPERATIONS
William B. Virts

THE ART AND SCIENCE OF HOSPITALITY MANAGEMENT
Jerome J. Vallen/James R. Abbey

MANAGING TECHNOLOGY IN THE HOSPITALITY INDUSTRY
Fourth Edition
Michael L. Kasavana/John J. Cahill

MANAGING HOSPITALITY ENGINEERING SYSTEMS
Michael H. Redlin/David M. Stipanuk

BASIC HOTEL AND RESTAURANT ACCOUNTING
Fifth Edition
Raymond Cote

ACCOUNTING FOR HOSPITALITY MANAGERS
Fourth Edition
Raymond Cote

CONVENTION MANAGEMENT AND SERVICE
Sixth Edition
Milton T. Astroff/James R. Abbey

HOSPITALITY SALES AND MARKETING
Fourth Edition
James R. Abbey

MANAGING HOUSEKEEPING OPERATIONS
Second Edition
Margaret M. Kappa/Aleta Nitschke/Patricia B. Schappert

DIMENSIONS OF TOURISM
Joseph D. Fridgen

HOSPITALITY TODAY: AN INTRODUCTION
Fourth Edition
Rocco M. Angelo/Andrew N. Vladimir

MANAGING BAR AND BEVERAGE OPERATIONS
Lendal H. Kotschevar/Mary L. Tanke

ETHICS IN HOSPITALITY MANAGEMENT: A BOOK OF READINGS
Edited by Stephen S. J. Hall

HOSPITALITY FACILITIES MANAGEMENT AND DESIGN
Second Edition
David M. Stipanuk

MANAGING HOSPITALITY HUMAN RESOURCES
Third Edition
Robert H. Woods

FINANCIAL MANAGEMENT FOR THE HOSPITALITY INDUSTRY
William P. Andrew/Raymond S. Schmidgall

HOSPITALITY INDUSTRY FINANCIAL ACCOUNTING
Second Edition
Raymond S. Schmidgall/James W. Damitio

INTERNATIONAL HOTEL MANAGEMENT
Chuck Y. Gee

QUALITY SANITATION MANAGEMENT
Ronald F. Cichy

HOTEL INVESTMENTS: ISSUES & PERSPECTIVES
Third Edition
Edited by Lori E. Raleigh and Rachel J. Roginsky

LEADERSHIP AND MANAGEMENT IN THE HOSPITALITY INDUSTRY
Second Edition
Robert H. Woods/Judy Z. King

MARKETING IN THE HOSPITALITY INDUSTRY
Fourth Edition
Ronald A. Nykiel

CONTEMPORARY HOSPITALITY MARKETING
William Lazer/Roger Layton

UNIFORM SYSTEM OF ACCOUNTS FOR THE HEALTH, RACQUET AND SPORTSCLUB INDUSTRY

CONTEMPORARY CLUB MANAGEMENT
Edited by Joe Perdue for the Club Managers Association of America

RESORT CONDOMINIUM AND VACATION OWNERSHIP MANAGEMENT: A HOSPITALITY PERSPECTIVE
Robert A. Gentry/Pedro Mandoki/Jack Rush

ACCOUNTING FOR CLUB OPERATIONS
Raymond S. Schmidgall/James W. Damitio

TRAINING AND DEVELOPMENT FOR THE HOSPITALITY INDUSTRY
Debra F. Cannon/Catherine M. Gustafson

08/03

BASIC HOTEL AND RESTAURANT ACCOUNTING

Fifth Edition

Raymond Cote, CPA, CCP

EDUCATIONAL INSTITUTE
American Hotel & Lodging Association

Disclaimer

This publication is designed to provide accurate and authoritative information in regard to the subject matter covered. It is sold with the understanding that the publisher is not engaged in rendering legal, accounting, or other professional service. If legal advice or other expert assistance is required, the services of a competent professional person should be sought.

—*From the Declaration of Principles jointly adopted by the American Bar Association and a Committee of Publishers and Associations*

The author, Raymond Cote, is solely responsible for the contents of this publication. All views expressed herein are solely those of the author and do not necessarily reflect the views of the Educational Institute of the American Hotel & Lodging Association (the Institute) or the American Hotel & Lodging Association (AH&LA).

Nothing contained in this publication shall constitute a standard, an endorsement, or a recommendation of the Institute or AH&LA. The Institute and AH&LA disclaim any liability with respect to the use of any information, procedure, or product, or reliance thereon by any member of the hospitality industry.

2113 N. High Street
Lansing, Michigan 48906

The Educational Institute of the American Hotel & Lodging Association is a nonprofit educational foundation.

Printed in the United States of America
2 3 4 5 6 7 8 9 10 07 06 05 04 03

ISBN 0-86612-236-2

Editors: Donald Peterson
Timothy J. Eaton

Contents

About the Author

Raymond Cote

RAYMOND COTE is a Certified Public Accountant (CPA) and a Certified Computer Professional (CCP). His professional credentials also include Accreditation in Accountancy by the American Council for Accountancy. He has been an Enrolled Agent (EA) authorized to practice before the Internal Revenue Service and has held positions as President of a local Chamber of Commerce and Vice President and Director of Education for the Florida Accountants Association.

For eighteen years, Professor Cote taught undergraduate and graduate courses in accounting and financial management in the United States and abroad. In the private sector, he has been the chief accountant for a major food and lodging corporation and the controller and vice president of leading companies. His entrepreneurial endeavors include a food and beverage operation in Florida, a retail and service conglomerate, and a consulting/certified public accounting firm.

Professor Cote holds a M.S.B.A. and B.S.B.A. from Suffolk University in Boston, Massachusetts, and an Accounting Degree from Burdett College in Boston. He has written four hospitality accounting textbooks for the Educational Institute: *Basic Hotel and Restaurant Accounting, Accounting for Hospitality Managers,* and the prior versions of these two books, *Understanding Hospitality Accounting I* and *Understanding Hospitality Accounting II.* His past writings include another text, *College Business Math* (1984–1988, PAR, Inc.), and numerous training manuals for private industry.

Preface

THIS NEW EDITION of *Basic Hotel and Restaurant Accounting* represents a substantial revision of the previous edition, which was titled *Understanding Hospitality Accounting I.* Hospitality schools throughout the world have used this book's predecessor to teach students the basics of accounting. In keeping with the needs of these schools, we have retained the philosophy that hospitality students and managers are rarely accountants by profession. This means that they need an authoritative, reader-friendly text that incorporates practical topics encountered in the real world. To that end, we have updated and reorganized much of the earlier edition's content and incorporated many new topics and several new chapters that characterize 21st century accounting. Concluding each chapter is a brief ethics case that describes a scenario about which the student is asked to answer specific questions and make ethical determinations.

Basic Hotel and Restaurant Accounting also retains its predecessor's style of addressing the needs of the industry in a manner that is both understandable and comprehensive and that provides the reader with the professional business vocabulary and financial skills to be successful in the hospitality industry.

This new edition addresses the major changes taking place in the processing of financial information. These changes affect the way managers, bookkeepers, and accountants do their jobs. Journals are no longer manually posted. Account balances are not manually calculated. Nor are documents such as worksheets and financial statements prepared manually. Advances in accounting procedures and technology have brought new levels of speed and accuracy to the accounting profession. But today's hospitality student must be technologically prepared. This text introduces these issues.

Chapter 1 presents an introduction that defines accounting, identifies the various users of accounting information, briefly describes several organizations that are pertinent to hospitality accounting, and discusses generally accepted accounting practices. Chapter 2 looks at the various forms of business organization and at how business format affects taxation. Chapters 3, 4, and 5 introduce the financial statements and address the individual line items of the balance sheet and income statement.

The question of whether to teach debits and credits is controversial among hospitality faculty. To address this conflict, debits and credits are presented in their entirety in chapter 6, making it easier for those instructors wishing to avoid the topic to do so. (Note, however, that if you are using this text as part of the Educational Institute's course, this chapter will be covered on the Final Exam.)

Chapters 7 and 8 introduce the student to the procedural aspects of accounting that are now automated. Because these routine functions are now computerized, the reader is spared the tedious clerical procedures that long have been the bane of accounting courses.

The specific needs of modern hospitality accounting call for texts that take more than a generalized approach; they need to focus on instruction that addresses the unique issues of the industry. To this end, we have devoted separate chapters to restaurant accounting and hotel accounting. In Chapter 9, the food and beverage aspects of hospitality accounting are addressed in conformance with the *Uniform System of Accounts for Restaurants,* published by the National Restaurant Association. Chapter 10 focuses on accounting issues as they pertain to the lodging function of hospitality. This chapter is in conformity with the *Uniform System of Accounts for the Lodging Industry,* published by the American Hotel & Lodging Association. The hotel accounting chapter also covers hotels with casino operations.

Chapter 11 covers the critical topic of cash handling and accounting and thoroughly explains the purpose and preparation of the important daily cashiers report and bank reconciliation. Special attention is given to credit card commissions and credit card "cash float."

Chapter 12 is a capstone chapter that first shows students how to read the income statement, balance sheet, and statement of cash flows and then shows students how to perform meaningful analysis of the data. Important to the student's real-world experience following formal study, this chapter responds to the hospitality industry's demand that today's graduates be proficient in reading and analyzing financial statements.

The Appendix concludes the text by reproducing excerpts from the 2001 Annual Report issued by Dave & Buster's, Inc. These excerpts present the financial statements, notes, and auditor report to give readers an opportunity to see a real case of financial reporting.

For use with this book, a Student Workbook is available that contains several assignments and problems per chapter. The Solutions Manual for instructors provides not just the answers to the workbook problems, but comprehensive and fully worked out solutions that demonstrate how the solution is achieved.

I dedicate this work to the cherished memory of my mother and father, Alice and Raymond Cote, with love, honor, and gratitude.

Chapter 1 Outline

What Is Business Accounting?
- Fundamental Purpose
- Bookkeeping
- Accounting
- The "Bean Counter" Myth

Users of Accounting Information
Why Study Accounting?
The Corporate Accounting Department
The Accounting Profession
The Certified Public Accountant
- Audit and Attest Function

Influence of Government and Professional Organizations
- Securities and Exchange Commission
- Internal Revenue Service
- American Institute of Certified Public Accountants
- Financial Accounting Standards Board
- Hospitality Financial & Technology Professionals
- American Hotel & Lodging Association
- Educational Institute of AH&LA
- National Restaurant Association

Generally Accepted Accounting Principles
- Unit of Measurement
- Historical Cost
- Going-Concern
- Conservatism
- Objectivity
- Time Period
- Realization
- Matching
- Materiality
- Consistency
- Full Disclosure

Business Transactions
Accounting Income vs. Taxable Income
The Accounting Equation

Competencies

1. Define and describe the purpose of accounting. (pp. 4–6)
2. Identify the various users of accounting information and explain why the study of accounting is important to a hospitality career. (pp. 6–7)
3. Describe briefly the various types of accounting positions and responsibilities found in private and public accounting. (pp. 7–10)
4. Identify various governmental and professional organizations that influence the field of hospitality accounting. (pp. 10–13)
5. Explain the purpose of, and define several, generally accepted accounting principles. (pp. 13–17)
6. Describe how business transactions are recorded in double-entry accounting system. (pp. 18–20)
7. Explain why accounting income and taxable income can be different. (pp. 20–21)
8. Identify the five account classifications and the fundamental accounting equation. (pp. 22–23)

1

Introduction to Accounting

Accounting is often referred to as "the language of business." Executives, investors, bankers, creditors, and governmental officials use this language in their day-to-day activities. In order to effectively communicate in today's business world, a fundamental grasp of the theory and practice of accounting is required.

Accounting, like any other profession, has its own technical symbols, terminology, and principles. In accounting, these elements form the "vocabulary" used to convey financial information, especially that information presented in the form of financial statements.

Many of those presently employed within the hospitality industry and many students new to the field of hospitality sometimes feel that the language of business is understood only by specialists who seem to thrive on "number crunching." This misconception arises from an unfamiliarity with the fundamental purpose of accounting and the logic that lies behind basic accounting activities.

This introductory chapter dispels many misconceptions about basic accounting activities, while providing answers to such questions as:

1. What functions do bookkeeping and accounting perform?
2. Why should hospitality students study accounting?
3. What is the composition of a corporate accounting department?
4. What is a certified public accountant?
5. Which organizations influence accounting?
6. What fundamental principles of accounting apply to all businesses?
7. What is a business transaction?
8. How is accounting income different from taxable income?
9. What is the significance of the accounting equation?

This chapter addresses the importance of accounting to all professionals in the field of hospitality. The functions of a corporate accounting department and the role of an independent certified public accountant are examined. Attention is given to *generally accepted accounting principles* that form the basis for producing financial statements. An examination of business transactions provides insight into accounting logic and business terminology. The chapter explains why accounting income can be different from taxable income and closes with a look at account classes and the basic accounting equation.

What Is Business Accounting?

Though there are many fanciful and technical definitions of accounting, all fall short in conveying in understandable terms what it is that accounting exactly does. In this text, we do not repeat or attempt to add yet another academic definition that is difficult, if not impossible, to understand. Rather, we attempt to clarify just what accounting is.

Fundamental Purpose

The fundamental purpose of **accounting** is to provide accurate, useful, and timely financial information. This information may take the form of financial statements, forecasts, budgets, and many types of reports that can be used to measure the financial position and operating performance of a hospitality business.

A full and comprehensible sense of the accounting profession is captured in the following practical, workable, and unsophisticated definition:

> Accounting involves recording business transactions, analyzing business records and reports, and producing reliable information.

The American Institute of Certified Public Accountants provides a definition of accounting based on the **accounting function**:

> Its function is to provide quantitative information, primarily financial in nature, about economic entities that is intended to be useful in making economic decisions. [1]

Bookkeeping

Bookkeeping is the initial phase of accounting and is only part of the overall function of accounting. Accountants supervise bookkeepers whose primary function is to record business transactions in the accounting records. An accountant analyzes the accounting records for accuracy and compliance with accepted accounting practices and company rules. After the accounting records are judged satisfactory, the financial statements are prepared.

Accounting

It is impossible to produce a full description of the profession of accounting in a single statement because the field is varied and extensive. This chapter attempts to clarify the issue by examining the different tasks an accountant performs, analyzing a corporate accounting department, and describing the specialization of an independent certified public accountant.

Accounting data is used to produce several different kinds of reports, such as formal financial statements, one-line messages (i.e., cash balance, receivables), graphs, and statistical data. Exhibit 1 shows how accounting data is used to depict what happens to the U.S. lodging industry dollar.

The "Bean Counter" Myth

When companies cut jobs or expenses, the blame is often placed on the "bean counters," an incorrect and undeserved reference to accountants. Accountants are

Exhibit 1 U.S. Lodging Industry Dollar

ALL HOTELS — 2000

Source and Disposition of the Industry Dollar

Revenues

Costs and Expenses

Source: *Trends in the Hotel Industry—USA Edition 2001* (San Francisco: PKF Consulting, 2001), p. 64.

not responsible for staff cuts. They process and report information produced from real business transactions; accountants do not fabricate drops in sales or profits, they merely report actual conditions. Nor do accountants make decisions to eliminate jobs or reduce expenses; such actions are not within their purview.

The management of a company makes the decision to cut jobs and expenses.

Users of Accounting Information

Financial information is used by management, investors, potential investors, creditors, governmental agencies, and many other constituencies. The fundamental principles applied in preparing this information are basically uniform for all of these users.

A business entity is an organization that provides products or services and conducts other profit-motivated economic activities. A business entity has many users interested in its financial data. These users can be classified as external users and internal users.

External users are those outside of the business who require accounting and financial information. Suppliers want financial information before extending credit to the hospitality operation. Bankers require financial statements before lending funds for building, remodeling, or making major purchases. Investors or stockholders make decisions to buy, sell, or hold based on information in the financial statements. Various governmental agencies, such as the Internal Revenue Service, also require specific kinds of financial information. Labor unions make decisions based on an employer's financial information.

Internal users include those inside the hospitality business such as the board of directors, the general manager, departmental managers, and other staff involved in the day-to-day and long-range analysis, planning, and control of the hospitality operation. Hospitality managers require much more detailed information regarding day-to-day operations than is provided by the major financial statements. For this reason, an accounting department generally prepares an assortment of reports for various levels of management.

Why Study Accounting?

Your professional career will require you to make economic decisions. All economic decisions require financial information. Accounting is the service that provides financial data. Your career might not require you to prepare financial data, but you will be a user of this information. For this reason, you need to know how the data is processed and how the reports are prepared so that you better understand the information on the financial statements. With this knowledge, you can make intelligent economic decisions and succeed in this extremely competitive business environment.

Knowledge of the basic theory and practice of accounting is a valuable tool with which to achieve success not only in the hospitality industry but in the management of your personal finances as well. However, students planning careers in the hospitality industry often tend to neglect the accounting aspects of their field of study. Some believe that they will be able to "pick up" the essentials of accounting once they are out of school and on the job. But, once on the job, many find that day-to-day responsibilities confine them to specific areas of a property's operation. Increased specialization within the hospitality industry at times creates a situation in which relatively few, outside of those actually employed within accounting departments, have opportunities to learn the theory and practice of accounting at a level required by the demands of today's business world.

Most colleges and universities require accounting as part of a business curriculum because the future managers of any type of business need to grasp the essentials of accounting in order to make sound business decisions. Managers need to understand how basic decisions regarding operational matters (such as replacing equipment or changing policy regarding the extension of credit to customers) will affect the financial statements of the business.

Managers and supervisors working in the hospitality industry recognize the importance of understanding the basic theory and practice of accounting. In the highly competitive field of hospitality, successful careers often depend on an ability to make daily operating decisions based upon analyses of financial information. In order to achieve satisfactory profit objectives for their areas of responsibility, managers must thoroughly understand how the accounting system accumulates and processes financial information. The increasing use of computers to record accounting information and to prepare financial statements has not diminished the necessity of mastering this business language.

Some individuals are reluctant to learn the fundamentals of accounting because they mistakenly believe that accounting is "numbers oriented," requiring a sophisticated background in mathematics. Accounting theory and practice is not based on complicated mathematics; it is based on *logic* and emphasizes basic terminology, fundamental concepts, and relatively straightforward procedures. Applying the logic of accounting requires only the most basic math skills—addition, subtraction, multiplication, and division. Once the terminology, concepts, and procedures of accounting are mastered, accounting practices are not as difficult to understand as some people tend to believe.

The Corporate Accounting Department

With the availability to small business of inexpensive computers, the clerical function of accounting has changed. Because the records are maintained in computerized files, bookkeepers no longer have to perform the tedious process of manually recording to individual bookkeeping records and computing a balance for each record. Accountants no longer prepare manual listings of individual records with balances (called trial balances) because these trial balances are computer-generated.

However, as useful as the computer has become, there still are processes that require human intervention. Bookkeepers must still determine how a business transaction is to be recorded, and the accountant must continue to analyze those records. Even though computers can easily print the financial statements, the accountant must carefully review them for accuracy. Because computers have taken over much of the number crunching, accountants have become analyzers, financial interpreters, and consultants.

The management structure of the accounting function (in descending order) is typically:

- Chief financial officer (CFO)
- Vice-president of finance
- Treasurer
- Controller
- Chief accountant
- Accounting supervisor

Bookkeepers and various levels of skilled accountants form the staff of the accounting department. The departments of larger companies separate the duties of the staff into two divisions of responsibility: financial accounting and managerial accounting.

Financial accounting is concerned primarily with recording and accumulating accounting information to be used in the preparation of financial statements for external users. Financial accounting involves the basic accounting processes of recording, classifying, and summarizing business transactions. It also includes accounting for assets, liabilities, equity, revenue, and expenses. The focus of this book is primarily directed toward financial accounting.

Managerial accounting is concerned primarily with recording and accumulating information so that financial statements and reports can be prepared for internal users. Managerial accounting provides various management levels of a hospitality organization with detailed information, such as performance reports that compare the actual results of operations with budget plans. Since managerial and financial accounting are closely connected branches of accounting, this text will, at times, address various managerial accounting activities, but only as they relate to the basic functions of financial accounting. This author's *Accounting for Hospitality Managers*, published by the Educational Institute of the American Hotel & Lodging Association, offers interested readers a detailed approach to managerial aspects of accounting.[2]

The Accounting Profession

One reason it is difficult to give a simple definition of accounting is that the field encompasses many different disciplines requiring various levels of education and experience. Accountants can be employed in any of a number of broadly-defined specialties, namely not-for-profit accounting, public accounting, and private accounting.

Not-for-profit accountants serve such organizations as schools, hospitals, and government agencies.

Public accountants provide services such as taxation accounting, management consulting, and auditing of financial statements to the general public and business enterprises. The qualifications and work of the certified public accountant are discussed later in this chapter.

Private accountants are employed by a business enterprise. The following is just a small representation of the many and varied types of specialized accounting positions in a corporate accounting department of a business enterprise:

- Budgeting and forecasting
- Cost accounting
- Tax accounting
- Internal auditing
- Accounting systems design

Budgeting and forecasting deals with estimating (forecasting) a company's future performance in the form of a plan called the budget. Accountants who work in this area develop forecasts, then compare the predicted results with actual results in order to determine any variances from the forecast. These accountants also analyze the variances and their causes and report them to management for any corrective action.

Cost accounting relates to the recording, classification, allocation, and reporting of current and prospective costs. Cost accountants determine costs in relation to products and services offered by a hospitality business and in relation to the operation of individual departments within the property. One of the primary purposes of cost accounting is to assist management in controlling operations.

Tax accounting is the discipline of preparing and filing tax forms required by various governmental agencies. A significant part of the tax accountant's work involves tax planning to minimize the amount of taxes that must be paid by a business. Although the emphasis of tax accounting lies in minimizing income tax payments at the federal, state, and local levels, this branch of accounting also involves other areas such as sales, excise, payroll, and property taxes.

Internal auditing focuses on the review of company operations to determine compliance with management policies. Internal auditors also review accounting records to determine whether these records have been processed according to proper accounting procedures. Another important responsibility within this area of expertise is the internal auditor's design and review of internal control policies and systems.

Internal auditing in the private sector should not be confused with the audit and the attest function performed by independent certified public accountants. Internal auditors are employees of a company, but generally do not report to the company's chief accounting officer; this arrangement allows them to maintain their independence. Usually they report to the company's board of directors or an audit committee.

Accounting systems design focuses primarily on the information system of a hospitality organization. This information system includes not only accounting, but other areas as well, such as reservations. As more and more hospitality operations become computerized, accounting systems experts will necessarily become electronic data processing specialists, such as programmers and systems analysts.

The Certified Public Accountant

A **certified public accountant** (CPA) is an individual who has met educational and experience requirements prescribed by state licensing laws and who has passed the national Uniform CPA Examination.

To qualify for certification, the applicant must meet rigid academic standards. Many states now require an applicant to have 150 credit hours of college education to qualify just to sit for the exam. In addition, a certain number of these hours must be in accounting and business courses as specified by the state's board of accountancy.

The CPA examination is a multiple-day examination covering topics such as financial accounting and reporting, auditing, and business law. The financial accounting area includes federal income taxes, managerial accounting, and governmental accounting. The examination not only tests an applicant's problem-solving skills and knowledge of theory, it also evaluates the individual's writing skills by means of essay questions.

Passing the CPA exam is only the beginning. Before being licensed to practice, an individual may be required to complete an internship period under the supervision of experienced CPAs. But the process doesn't end there. Once a CPA is licensed, both the state licensing board and the American Institute of Certified Public Accountants require that a program of continuing professional education be maintained under standards established by these organizations.

Audit and Attest Function

An audit is a comprehensive investigation by an independent CPA of a company's records and financial statements. An independent CPA is one who is neither employed by that company nor related to any officer of the company. The investigation involves an examination of the financial records and evidential matter, confirmation of receivables and payables, and observation of the physical inventory.

The objective of an audit is the **attest function**, which involves issuing an **opinion**. The word "opinion" in accounting has a very special meaning. Contained in a letter accompanying the financial statements, this opinion expresses a conclusion on the reliability and fairness of the statements and states whether the financial statements were prepared in accordance with generally accepted accounting principles.

Influence of Government and Professional Organizations

A number of governmental and private organizations influence the field of accounting. Even though all have similar interests and seek timely and reliable financial information, each has specialized interests demanded by the accounting profession. Bankers, investors, stockholders, trade organizations, government, and business enterprises influence the practice of accounting in the public, private, and governmental sectors. The accountant is deluged by regulations and recommended guidelines from government agencies, professional organizations, and accounting organizations such as:

- The Securities and Exchange Commission
- The Internal Revenue Service
- The American Institute of Certified Public Accountants
- The Financial Accounting Standards Board
- Hospitality Financial & Technology Professionals
- The American Hotel & Lodging Association
- The Educational Institute of AH&LA
- The National Restaurant Association

Securities and Exchange Commission

The **Securities and Exchange Commission** (SEC) is concerned primarily with promoting disclosure of important information, enforcing securities laws, and protecting investors by maintaining the integrity of the securities markets. The SEC requires public companies to disclose meaningful financial and other information to the public. The SEC also oversees other key participants in the securities world, including stock exchanges, broker-dealers, investment advisers, mutual funds managers, and public utility holding companies.

The SEC's effectiveness derives from its enforcement authority. The SEC can bring civil enforcement actions against individuals and companies that break the securities laws. Typical infractions include insider trading, accounting fraud, and providing false or misleading information about securities and the companies that issue them. Though it is the primary overseer and regulator of the U.S. securities markets, the SEC works closely with many other institutions, including Congress, other federal departments and agencies, the stock exchanges, state securities regulators, and various private sector organizations.

Internal Revenue Service

The **Internal Revenue Service** (IRS), an agency of the U.S. Department of the Treasury, is responsible for enforcing the internal revenue laws and intervening when necessary. Revenues are collected through individual income taxes; corporation taxes; excise, estate, and gift taxes; and social security/retirement taxes. The IRS is structured into functional areas such as collection of taxes, investigation of violations of internal revenue laws, legal enforcement, taxpayer services, returns processing, compliance, information systems, and criminal investigation.

Congress enacts the tax laws. After a statute is enacted, the IRS issues regulations to help interpret and apply the law. The **Internal Revenue Code (IRC)** is a codification of the tax laws and regulations. The taxation of income is a major consideration of individuals, investors, business management, and the accounting profession.

American Institute of Certified Public Accountants

The **American Institute of Certified Public Accountants** (AICPA) is the national professional organization for all Certified Public Accountants. Its mission is to provide members with the resources, information, and leadership to enable them to provide valuable services in the highest professional manner to benefit the public as well as employers and clients. In fulfilling its mission, the AICPA works with state CPA organizations and assigns priority to those areas where public reliance on CPA skills is most significant.

To achieve its mission, the AICPA seeks the highest possible level of uniform certification and licensing standards and promotes and protects the CPA designation. It establishes professional standards and assists members in continually improving their professional conduct, performance, and expertise. The AICPA monitors the performance of its members in enforcing current standards and requirements.

Financial Accounting Standards Board

The mission of the **Financial Accounting Standards Board** (FASB) is to establish and improve standards of financial accounting and reporting for the guidance and education of the public, including issuers, auditors, and users of financial information. FASB is the designated organization in the private sector for establishing standards of financial accounting and reporting. Those standards govern the preparation of financial reports and are officially recognized as authoritative by the Securities and Exchange Commission.

Hospitality Financial & Technology Professionals

The **Hospitality Financial & Technology Professionals** (HFTP) is the society for financial and MIS professionals in the hospitality industry. HFTP offers numerous training sessions on hospitality accounting and technology, as well as professional development seminars for clubs, gaming, and other areas of special interest.

American Hotel & Lodging Association

The **American Hotel & Lodging Association** (AH&LA), formerly the American Hotel & Motel Association (AH&MA), is the largest national trade association for the U.S. hotel and lodging industry. AH&LA provides its members with resources to operate more efficiently and more profitably; these resources cover the lodging, hospitality, and travel and tourism fields. Educational resources are produced by the organization's Educational Institute.

The Educational Institute of AH&LA

The **Educational Institute of AH&LA**, referred to as EI, is the world's leading provider of industry-tested, research-driven training resources. EI succeeds in meeting its education and training mission by publishing videos, textbooks, courseware, seminars, multi-media CD-ROM programs, and self-paced learning courses on the Internet to reach all levels of hospitality personnel. EI is the certifying body for hospitality industry personnel. EI's academic division develops course materials for two-year and four-year hospitality schools worldwide and offers distance learning programs of college level hospitality courses on a home-study basis via the Internet and by mail. In addition to publishing world-leading hospitality textbooks, EI publishes the *Uniform System of Accounts for the Lodging Industry.*

National Restaurant Association

The **National Restaurant Association** (NRA) is the leading business association for the restaurant industry. The NRA and its Educational Foundation share a mission to represent, educate, and promote the rapidly growing food and beverage industry.

Generally Accepted Accounting Principles

For almost every profession, there are guidelines and rules to ensure that members carry out their responsibilities in accordance with accepted quality standards. Professional accounting standards have evolved from commonly adopted practices and in response to changes in the business environment. These accounting standards are known within the profession as **generally accepted accounting principles,** and are commonly referred to by the acronym GAAP. GAAP encompasses not only standards, but also conventions and principles from which specific technical rules and procedures are developed.

These generally accepted accounting principles have received substantial authoritative support and approval from professional accounting associations such as AICPA and HFTP, from the FASB through its Statements on Financial Accounting Standards (SFAS), and from governmental agencies such as the Securities and Exchange Commission. Additionally, the AICPA publishes Statements of Position and industry practice and audit guides.

The application of these generally accepted accounting principles ensures that consistent accounting procedures are followed in recording the events created by business transactions and in preparing financial statements. This consistency makes it possible for internal and external users of financial statements to make reasonable judgments regarding the overall financial condition of a business and the success of business operations from period to period.

Unit of Measurement

Since the value exchanged in a business transaction is expressed in monetary terms, the prevailing monetary unit is used to record the results of business transactions. For businesses in the United States, the common unit of measurement is the U.S. dollar.

A common unit of measurement permits the users of accounting data to make meaningful comparisons between current and past business transactions. Imagine the difficulties that would arise if the accounting records of a hospitality operation recorded food purchases in terms of the British pound and food sales in terms of the U.S. dollar!

Historical Cost

The principle of **historical cost** states that the value of merchandise or services obtained through business transactions should be recorded in terms of actual costs, not current market values.

For example, assume that a truck having a market value of $15,000 is purchased from a distressed seller for $12,800. The amount recorded as the cost of the truck is $12,800. As long as the truck is owned, the value (cost) shown in the accounting records and on the financial statements will be $12,800.

Going-Concern

The principle of **going-concern**, also known as continuity of the business unit, states that financial statements should be prepared under the assumption that the business will continue indefinitely and thus carry out its commitments. Normally, a business is assumed to be a going-concern unless there is objective evidence to the contrary.

The going-concern assumption can be used to defend the use of historical costs in the presentation of financial statements. Since there is no evidence of liquidation of the business in the near future, the use of liquidating or market values would not be appropriate unless the principle of conservatism applies.

Conservatism

The principle of **conservatism** serves to guide the decisions of accountants in areas that involve estimates and other areas that may call for professional judgment. However, it is important to stress that this principle is applied only when there is uncertainty in reporting factual results of business transactions.

FASB states that assets and income should be fairly presented and not overstated. This does not in any way suggest that income or assets should be deliberately understated. The purpose of the principle of conservatism is to provide the accountant with a practical alternative for situations which involve doubt. When doubt is involved, the solution or method that will not overstate assets or income should be selected.

For example, if a hotel is the plaintiff in a lawsuit and its legal counsel indicates that the case will be won and estimates the amount that may be awarded to the hotel, the amount is not recorded until a judgment is rendered.

Other examples of the principle of conservatism involve the valuation of inventories, marketable securities, and accounts receivable. Determining the net realizable value of these items requires professional judgment. Following the principle of conservatism, inventories and marketable securities are presented in the financial statements at either cost or market value, whichever is lower. Accounts receivable are presented along with an offsetting account (contra account) that provides for accounts that are judged to be uncollectible:

Accounts Receivable	$255,000
Less: Allowance for Doubtful Accounts	5,000
Accounts Receivable (Net)	$250,000

Objectivity

The principle of **objectivity** states that all business transactions must be supported by objective evidence proving that the transactions did in fact occur. Obtaining objective evidence is not always a simple matter. For example, a canceled check serves as objective evidence that cash was paid. However, it is not evidence of the reason for which the check was issued. An invoice or other form of independent evidence is necessary to prove the reason for the expenditure.

When independent evidence is not available to document the results of a business transaction, estimates must be made. In these cases, the choice of the best estimate should be guided by the principle of objectivity. Consider the case of the owner of a restaurant who contributes equipment, purchased several years before for personal use, to the business in exchange for 100 shares of company stock. Let's further assume that there is no known market value of the restaurant corporation's stock. Ambiguity arises as the owner believes that the equipment is worth $1,200, while the catalog used by the owner when the equipment was purchased several years ago shows the cost to have been $1,400, and an appraiser estimates the current value of the equipment at $850. In this case, the principle of objectivity determines the amount to record. The most objective estimate of the current value of the equipment is the appraiser's estimate of $850.

Time Period

This generally accepted accounting principle, also known as the *periodicity assumption,* recognizes that users of financial statements need timely information for decision-making purposes. Therefore, accountants are charged with preparing more than just annual financial statements.

The accounting departments of many hospitality operations prepare financial statements not only on an annual basis, but quarterly and monthly as well. Financial statements which are prepared during the business year are referred to as *interim financial statements.* Because accountants may not have all the information at hand in order to complete accurate interim financial statements, they must often proceed on the basis of assumptions and make estimates based on their professional judgment.

Realization

The **realization** principle states that revenue resulting from business transactions should be recorded only when a sale has been made *and* earned. The simplest example of the principle of realization involves a customer paying cash for services rendered. When a hotel receives cash from a guest served in the dining room, a sale has been made and earned. The results of the transaction are recorded in the proper accounts.

What about the guest served in the dining room who charges the bill to an open account maintained by the hotel? In this case, even though cash is not received at the time of performance, a sale has been made *and* earned. The revenue and the account receivable are recorded at the time of the sale. However, according to the principle of realization, if a hotel receives cash for services that has not yet been earned, then the transaction cannot be classified as a sale. For example, if a hotel receives an advance deposit of $500 for a wedding banquet to be held two months later, the cash received must be recorded—but the event cannot be classified as a sale. This is because the business has not yet earned the revenue; services have not been performed or delivered. In this case, receiving cash creates a liability account called Unearned Revenue. The full amount of the advance deposit is recorded in this account.

Matching

The **matching** principle states that all expenses must be recorded in the same accounting period as the revenue they helped to generate. When expenses are matched with the revenue they helped to produce, external and internal users of financial statements and reports are able to make better judgments regarding the financial position and operating performance of the hospitality business. Two accounting methods—cash accounting and accrual accounting—are used to determine when to record the results of a business transaction.

Cash Accounting. The **cash accounting** method records the results of business transactions only when cash is received or paid out. Small businesses usually follow cash accounting procedures in their day-to-day bookkeeping activities. However, financial statements that are prepared solely on a cash accounting basis may not necessarily comply with generally accepted accounting principles. If expenses are recorded on the basis of cash disbursements, then expenses will not necessarily match the revenue they helped to generate. This may occur for any number of reasons.

For example, assume that each month begins a new accounting period for a particular restaurant. During each month, the restaurant follows the principle of realization and records revenue only as sales are made and earned. The restaurant also records expenses only as cash payments (which include payments by check) are made to various suppliers and vendors. This cash accounting method will not ensure that expenses will match the revenue generated during the month because many expenses will be incurred during each month but not paid until the following month. These expenses include utility bills, laundry bills, and telephone bills that the restaurant may not even receive until the first week of the following month.

The Internal Revenue Service generally will accept financial statements prepared on a cash accounting basis only if the business does not sell inventory products and meets other criteria. Since food and beverage operations sell inventory products, these establishments must use the accrual method.

Accrual Accounting. In order to conform to the matching principle, most hospitality operations use the accrual method of accounting. The **accrual accounting** method adjusts the accounting records by recording expenses that are incurred during an accounting period but that (for any number of reasons) are not actually paid until the following period. Once the adjusting entries have been recorded, financial statements and reports for the accounting period will provide a reasonable basis for evaluating the financial position and operating performance of the hospitality business.

Materiality

The generally accepted accounting principle of **materiality** states that material events must be accounted for according to accounting rules; however, insignificant events may be treated in an expeditious manner. Decisions concerning the materiality of events vary. Most of these decisions call for professional judgment on the part of the accountant.

In general, an event (or information) is material depending on its magnitude and the surrounding circumstances. The general criterion is based on whether, in the judgment of a reasonable person, that person would be affected by its omission. Information is material if it can make a difference in the decision process of a reasonable user of the financial statements. For example, a pending lawsuit for $150 against a million-dollar corporation would not be considered a material item.

Consistency

Several accounting methods are available to determine certain values that are used as accounting data. For example, there are various methods for determining inventory values and for depreciating fixed assets. The choice of which method to use is the responsibility of high-level management officials of the hospitality operation.

The generally accepted accounting principle of **consistency** states that once an accounting method has been adopted, it should be consistently followed from period to period. In order for accounting information to be comparable, there must be a consistent application of accounting methods and principles. When circumstances warrant a change in the method of accounting for a specific kind of transaction, the change must be reported along with an explanation of how this change affects other items shown on the operation's financial statements.

Full Disclosure

The generally accepted accounting principle of **full disclosure** states that the financial statements of a hospitality operation should be accompanied by explanatory notes. These notes should describe all significant accounting policies adopted by the operation and should also report all significant conditions or events that materially affect the interpretation of information presented in the financial statements.

Commonly required disclosures include, but are not limited to, policies regarding the accounting method used to depreciate fixed assets and the methods used to determine the value of inventory and marketable securities. Commonly disclosed items that affect the interpretation of information reported in financial statements include, but are not limited to, changes in accounting methods, extraordinary items of income or expense, and significant long-term commitments. Exhibit 2 presents examples of the types of disclosures that may be found in notes accompanying the financial statements of a hospitality property.

Exhibit 2 Types of Disclosure and Examples

Types of Disclosure	Example
Accounting methods used	Straight-line method of depreciation
Change in the accounting methods	A change from depreciating a fixed asset using the straight-line method to using the double declining balance method
Contingent liability	A lawsuit against the company for alleged failure to provide adequate security for a guest who suffered personal injury
Events occurring subsequent to the financial statement date	A fire destroys significant uninsured assets of the hotel company one week after the end of the year
Unusual and nonrecurring items	A hotel firm in Michigan suffers significant losses due to an earthquake

Business Transactions

Business transactions initiate the accounting process. A **business transaction** can be defined as the exchange of merchandise, property, or services for cash or a promise to pay. Specific accounts are set up to record the results of business transactions that involve promises to pay.

For example, if a restaurant buys merchandise or supplies on open account, this promise to pay is classified as an **account payable.** If a guest purchases food and beverage items from the restaurant on open account, the guest's promise to pay is classified as an **account receivable.** Exhibit 3 shows the effect on cash and receivables when goods are sold and the effect on cash and payables when goods are purchased.

Promises to pay may also involve the use of legal documents. If, in order to purchase certain equipment, a restaurant obtains funds by signing a promissory note, the liability is classified as a note payable. If realty (land or buildings) is involved, the liability is classified as a **mortgage payable.**

A business transaction creates events that affect two or more bookkeeping accounts in the accounting records. The following examples present very basic business transactions, describe the events created by those transactions, and identify the bookkeeping accounts that are affected by those events.

Example #1. When a guest enjoys a dinner at a restaurant and pays for the meal with cash, the business transaction that occurs is the exchange of food and services for cash. This business transaction creates the following events that affect the restaurant:

1. The cash received increases the assets of the restaurant.
2. A sale is made, thus increasing the sales volume (revenue).

Exhibit 3 Cash, Payables, and Receivables Transactions

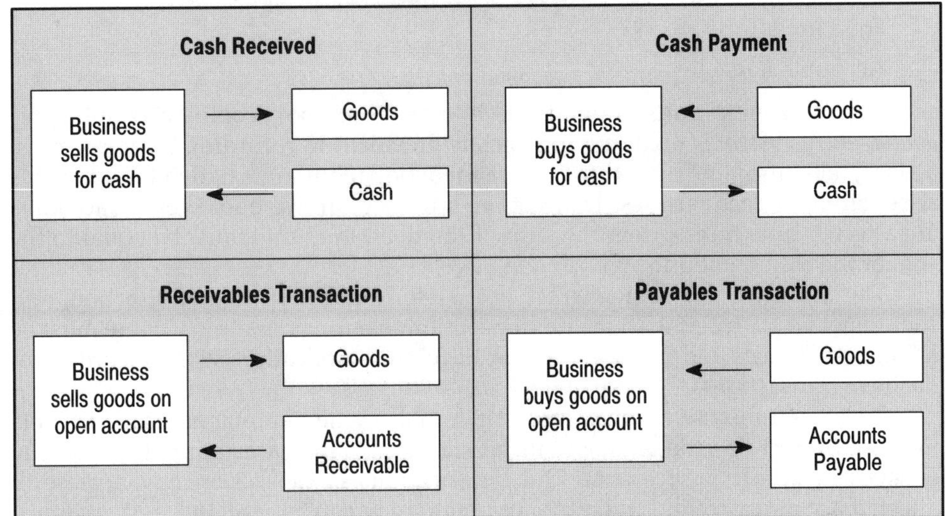

These events affect the following bookkeeping accounts:

1. Cash
2. Food Sales

Example #2. When a guest enjoys a dinner at a restaurant and pays for the meal by charging the amount of the guest check to an open account maintained for him or her by the restaurant (no credit card is involved), the business transaction that occurs is similar to the previous example. However, in this case, food and services are exchanged not for cash, but for a promise to pay. The change in the method of payment does not affect the basic events created by the business transaction:

1. The guest's promise to pay increases the assets of the restaurant.
2. A sale is made, thus increasing the sales volume (revenue).

However, the change in the method of payment does change one of the accounts affected by the events. The promise to pay and the sale affect the following bookkeeping accounts:

1. Accounts Receivable
2. Food Sales

Example #3. When a restaurant buys food provisions on open account from a supplier, the business transaction that occurs is also an exchange of food and services for a promise to pay. However, the events created by this transaction that affect the restaurant are as follows:

1. The increase in food provisions increases the assets of the restaurant.
2. The restaurant's promise to pay increases the liabilities of the restaurant.

The bookkeeping accounts affected by these events are as follows:

1. Food Inventory
2. Accounts Payable

Every business transaction affects two or more bookkeeping accounts. This *double-entry system of accounting,* which is prevalent in recording business transactions, takes its name from the fact that equal dollar amounts of debits and credits are entered for each business transaction. If more than two bookkeeping accounts are affected by a transaction, the sum of the debit amounts must be equal to the sum of the credit amounts.

The **double-entry system** does not relate to addition and subtraction, and should not be confused with the misconception that for every "plus" there must be a "minus." Pluses and minuses do not have any application in the recording of business transactions.

Business transactions are recorded in terms of whether their associated events increase or decrease the affected business accounts. Increases are not necessarily offset by decreases, or vice versa. One type of business transaction may increase all affected accounts; another type of transaction may decrease all affected accounts; yet another type may produce a combination of increases and decreases.

Most people know that accountants are concerned with debits and credits, which, indeed, play an important role in accounting. To apply debits and credits correctly, however, it is first necessary to learn the different types of accounts and understand the increase/decrease effect of business transactions.

It is a mistaken conclusion that a debit will add and a credit will subtract. Such a conclusion is in error and will make it difficult to comprehend debits and credits.

The foundation for debits and credits is the increase/decrease effect that is based on the types of accounts affected by a particular business transaction. It is more important to understand the effect and content of business transactions than to learn how to record them in an accounting format. This approach enables the student to analyze how a business transaction affects the bookkeeping accounts.

Accounting Income vs. Taxable Income

Not all generally accepted accounting principles are used in determining the amount of income tax that a business must pay. Differences arise because the objectives of financial accounting under generally accepted accounting principles are not the same as the objectives that may lie behind the Internal Revenue Code (IRC).

The objectives of financial accounting are:

- To provide accurate, timely, and relevant information to help users of financial information make economic, financial, and operational decisions regarding the business.
- To satisfy the common interests of the many users of financial statements, rather than satisfying the specific interests of any single group.
- To select from various accounting alternatives those methods that will present fairly the financial condition of the business and the results of business operations.

These objectives focus solely on the interests and needs of internal and external users of financial information. The generally accepted accounting principles do not attempt to influence business transactions. The overall objective is to ensure that the results of business transactions are fairly presented in the financial statements of a business.

The objectives of the IRC, on the other hand, are guided by large-scale political, economic, and social concerns. Some of the major objectives of the IRC could be:

- To influence change in the economy.
- To promote policies that are in the public interest.
- To achieve social objectives.

These political, economic, and social objectives can powerfully influence business activities. For example, governmental economic policy may lower taxes during an economic recession in an attempt to increase consumer demand for products and services, which eventually may increase production and decrease unemployment. Or, governmental economic policy may raise taxes during a period of high inflation in an attempt to decrease consumer spending and eventually reduce spiraling prices. Political policy may direct legislators to grant tax credits during an energy crisis in an attempt to stimulate purchases of energy-saving equipment. Social policy may legislate tax incentives for private businesses to hire the elderly, the disabled, or individuals from disadvantaged social groups.

An important practical result of the difference in objectives is that the method of accounting for revenue and expenses under generally accepted accounting principles differs from procedures dictated by income tax law. Consequently, the income shown on a business's financial statements *(income before income taxes)* may not be the same figure that appears as *taxable income* on the business's income tax return.

Differences among depreciation methods used for financial reporting and tax reporting are not uncommon. This allowable practice will result in a temporary difference between the income before income taxes reported on the financial statements and on the income tax return, as shown in the following hypothetical comparison:

	Financial Statement	Tax Return
Sales	$100,000	$100,000
Depreciation	20,000	30,000
Other expenses	60,000	60,000
Income before income taxes	$ 20,000	$ 10,000
	↑ Accounting Income	↑ Taxable Income

Exhibit 4 Accounting Equation

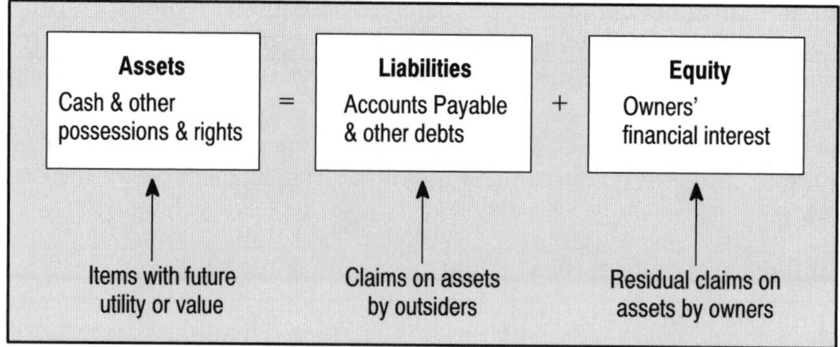

The Accounting Equation

All the bookkeeping accounts in any accounting system for all businesses consist of the following five classifications:

- Assets
- Liabilities
- Equity
- Revenue
- Expenses

Understanding accounting can be simplified if one takes the time and effort to learn these five account classifications and the types of accounts that compose these classifications.

These five classifications also play an important part in the logic of accounting and its system of checks and balances. One such factor is the **accounting equation** which is:

Assets = Liabilities + Equity

Assets are cash, possessions, and purchased rights; liabilities are the debts of the business; and equity represents the owner's financial interest in the business. Exhibit 4 illustrates the relationship of these three account classifications. Exhibit 5 shows the accounting equation for a company that has assets of $100,000, liabilities of $60,000, and equity of $40,000.

The accounting equation becomes more important to a business manager or creditor if its intent is viewed as a financial equation. From a finance perspective, assets are the sum total of any company, liabilities are a claim on those assets by creditors (outsiders), and equity is the leftover (residual) claim on those assets by owners.

At this point, the question might arise, "What happened to the other two classifications of Revenue and Expenses?" Disregarding accounting technicalities for the present, the result of revenue and expense accounts produces a profit or loss

Exhibit 5 Accounting Equation with Amounts

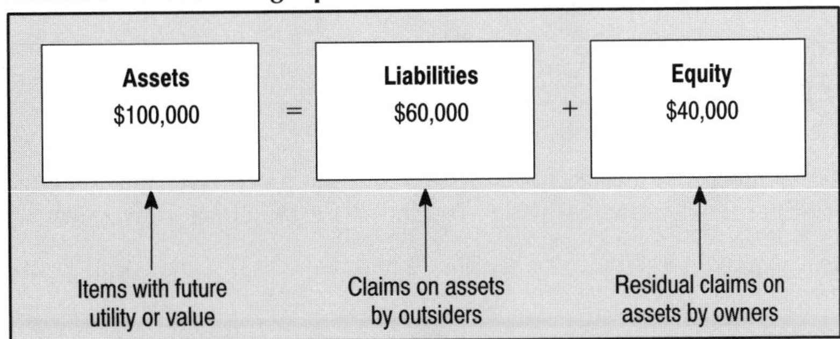

that is transferred to an account in the equity classification in the accounting process. Thus, while there are five account classifications, the accounting equation is still correctly stated as:

$$\text{Assets} = \text{Liabilities} + \text{Equity}$$

or in its abbreviated form:

$$A = L + EQ$$

Endnotes

1. Statements of the Accounting Principles Board, No. 4, "Basic Concepts and Accounting Principles Underlying Financial Statements of Business Enterprises" (New York: American Institute of Certified Public Accountants, 1970), par. 40.
2. Raymond Cote, *Accounting for Hospitality Managers,* 4th ed. (Lansing, Mich.: Educational Institute of the American Hotel & Lodging Association, 2001).

Key Terms

accounting—Accounting involves recording business transactions, analyzing business records and reports, and producing reliable information. However, no single definition can fully describe this profession because of its varied fields of specialization.

accounting equation—Assets = liabilities + equity. The accounting equation plays an important role in the logic of accounting and its system of checks and balances.

accounting function—Accounting's function is to provide quantitative information, primarily financial in nature, about economic entities that is intended to be useful in making economic decisions.

accounting systems design—The architecture of a hospitality organization's information system. The system includes not only accounting, but other functional areas, such as reservations.

accounts payable—The amount owed to a supplier for purchases on open account.

accounts receivable—The amount due from customers for sales of goods and services on open account.

accrual accounting—An accounting method that adjusts the accounting records by recording expenses that are incurred during an accounting period but which are not actually paid until the following period.

AH&LA—American Hotel & Lodging Association. Formerly called the American Hotel & Motel Association. A trade association for the U.S. lodging industry.

AICPA—American Institute of Public Accountants. The national professional organization for CPAs.

assets—The total of cash, possessions, and purchased rights of a hospitality operation.

attest function—The result of comprehensive investigation by an independent CPA, called an audit. The attest function involves issuing a professional auditor's *opinion.*

bookkeeping—The initial phase of accounting; its primary function is to record business transactions.

budgeting and forecasting—Estimating a company's future performance in the form of a plan called the budget.

business transaction—The exchange of merchandise, property, or services for cash or a promise to pay.

cash accounting—An accounting method that records the results of business transactions only when cash is received or paid out.

cost accounting—The recording, classification, allocation, and reporting of current and prospective costs.

CPA—Certified Public Accountant. A designation for a professional who has passed a national exam and also has qualifying academic and experience credentials.

conservatism—An accounting principle that serves to guide the decisions of accountants in areas that involve estimates and other areas that may call for professional judgment.

consistency—An accounting principle that states that once an accounting method has been adopted, it should be consistently followed from period to period.

double-entry system—A bookkeeping system in which every business transaction affects two or more accounts and total debits must equal total credits.

Educational Institute of AH&LA—A world leader in the publication of texts, courses, and other educational materials for the hospitality industry.

equity—An owner's financial interest in a business. Equity represents the assets remaining after an operation's liability claims have been satisfied.

FASB—Financial Accounting Standards Board. An organization having the authority to enact and enforce accounting standards.

financial accounting—A branch of accounting concerned with preparation of financial statements for external users.

full disclosure—An accounting principle that states that the financial statements of a hospitality operation should be accompanied by explanatory notes.

GAAP—Generally Accepted Accounting Principles. The conventions from which specific technical rules and procedures are developed.

going-concern—An accounting principle that states that financial statements should be prepared under the assumption that the business will continue indefinitely and thus carry out its commitments.

HFTP—The Hospitality Financial & Technology Professionals, a society for financial and MIS professionals in the hospitality industry.

historical cost—An accounting principle that states that the value of merchandise or services obtained through business transactions should be recorded in terms of actual costs, not current market values.

internal auditing—The review of a company's operations to determine compliance with management policies.

IRS—Internal Revenue Service. A governmental agency with the authority to enforce tax regulations and collection of income tax revenues.

liabilities—The total debts of an operation.

managerial accounting—A branch of accounting concerned with preparation of financial information for internal users.

matching—An accounting principle that states that all expenses must be recorded in the same accounting period as the revenue they helped to generate.

materiality—An accounting principle that states that material events must be accounted for according to accounting rules; however, insignificant events may be treated in an expeditious manner. Decisions as to the materiality of the event or information calls for professional judgment on the part of the accountant.

mortgage payable—A liability related to realty (land and buildings).

NRA—The National Restaurant Association, the leading business association for the restaurant industry.

objectivity—An accounting principle that states that all business transactions must be supported by objective evidence proving that the transactions did in fact occur.

opinion—The result of an audit and attest procedure. The auditor's opinion is contained in a letter accompanying the financial statements and expresses a conclusion on the reliability and fairness of the statements.

realization—An accounting principle that states that revenue resulting from business transactions should be recorded only when a sale has been made *and* earned.

SEC—Securities and Exchange Commission. A governmental agency having the authority to enact and enforce laws relating to the securities markets.

tax accounting—The discipline of preparing and filing tax forms required by various governmental agencies.

Review Questions

1. What is the fundamental purpose of accounting?
2. What are some examples of external and internal users of financial statements?
3. What is the definition of a business transaction?
4. What is the definition of accounting based on its function?
5. What is the difference between accounting and bookkeeping?
6. How is financial accounting different from managerial accounting?
7. How do generally accepted accounting principles serve the accounting profession?
8. What are the eleven generally accepted accounting principles presented in this chapter? Identify and describe them.
9. What are the definitions of the terms *accounts receivable* and *accounts payable*?
10. What is the attest function as performed by a certified public accountant?

Problems

Problem 1

Specify whether each of the following statements is true (T) or false (F).

1. The receipt of cash or payment of cash must be present for a business transaction to occur.
2. Accounting and bookkeeping are identical.
3. A check is not evidence of a business transaction because it only shows that cash was paid; it is not evidence of the reason for the payment.
4. Financial accounting is primarily concerned with external users.
5. FASB is a hospitality trade association.
6. Managerial accounting is primarily concerned with internal users.
7. The concept of materiality is difficult to quantify because an amount that is significant for one company may not be material for another company.
8. A building that cost $60,000 is now appraised for $85,000. The appraised value will appear on the financial statements.
9. The accounting equation can also be viewed as a financial equation.
10. The five classifications of accounts are assets, liabilities, equity, revenue, and expenses.

Problem 2

A restaurant's cash register shows sales of $1,400 for the day. Of this amount, $600 was cash sales. The restaurant does not accept any credit cards. What amount represents the sales to be recorded to Accounts Receivable?

Problem 3

Land and building were purchased by a restaurant for $225,000. The down payment was $75,000, and the balance was financed by a mortgage. What amount will be recorded to Mortgage Payable?

Problem 4

A restaurant makes the following food purchases which will go directly to the stockroom: Vendor A for $50 cash and Vendor B for $450 on Accounts Payable. What total amount will be recorded to Food Inventory?

Problem 5

A hospitality corporation is preparing its annual reports. The accounting records show sales of $250,000 and expenses excluding depreciation at $175,000. The company elects to use different depreciation methods for financial and tax reporting purposes. Depreciation for accounting purposes is $40,000, and for tax purposes the depreciation expense is $65,000. Compute the income before income taxes on the financial statements and the taxable income on the income tax return.

Problem 6

A guest books a banquet to be held six months from today. The price of the banquet is $9,000, and the guest pays 10% of that amount today. What amount will be recorded as a sale today?

Problem 7

A lodging operation purchases a parcel of land with cash. What bookkeeping accounts are affected?

Problem 8

A restaurant purchases land and buildings with a cash down payment and the balance financed by a mortgage. What bookkeeping accounts are affected?

Problem 9

Match the following situations with the accounting principle that best applies. In some cases, more than one principle may apply.

A. Unit of Measurement
B. Historical Cost
C. Going-Concern
D. Conservatism
E. Objectivity
F. Time Period

G. Realization
H. Matching
I. Materiality
J. Consistency
K. Full Disclosure

1. A large hotel corporation is preparing its year-end financial statements. Management has informed the certified public accountant that in two months it will begin closing 15 of its hotel properties. The accountant will provide information of this future event on the current year-end financial statements because of the __________ principle and the __________ principle.
2. A hotel purchases a van for $5,000 from a distressed rental agency. Due to the __________ principle, it is recorded at $5,000, even though the hotel could resell it for $6,500.
3. A motel receives an advance deposit of $150 for reserving guestrooms and meeting-room space. This transaction cannot be classified as a sale because of the __________ principle.
4. A resort hotel has used the straight-line method to depreciate its recreation equipment. This year it decides to use another type of depreciation method on these same assets. This violates the __________ principle.
5. A medium-size hotel with an extensive food and beverage operation records business transactions on a cash accounting basis. This violates the __________ principle.

Problem 10

A company has assets of $150,000. The liabilities of the company total $45,000. What amount is the owner's equity?

Ethics Case

Tom Daring had been employed by a national CPA firm for the last several years. Recently, Tom was discharged for failing to pass the CPA exam after several attempts. The CPA firm was satisfied with his performance, but company policy prohibited the retention of anyone who could not be licensed as a certified public accountant.

Tom holds a degree in accounting and was an honors graduate from a well-known university. For several months he has been searching for employment in private industry where the CPA designation is not always a requirement. He has been to dozens of unsuccessful interviews. He was fully qualified for these positions, but other applicants who are CPAs were selected to fill the openings.

To improve his chances of finding employment, Tom has decided to declare that he is a CPA on his résumé.

1. Identify the stakeholders in this case. (Stakeholders are those parties who are affected beneficially or negatively.)

2. Describe the legal and moral issues involved in this situation.
3. Assume that Tom has been hired by a new employer who is unaware that Tom has falsified his CPA credential. Tom's performance is outstanding, and he has contributed many profit-improving suggestions. Now Tom is being considered for promotion. Should he continue to deceive his employer?

Chapter 2 Outline

- Initial Planning Strategy
  - Business Checklist
  - Business Plan
  - Business Licenses
  - Credit and Debit Cards
- Business Formation
  - Proprietorship
  - Partnership
  - Corporation
  - Limited Liability Company
- Taxation of Business Income
  - Proprietorship
  - Partnership
  - Corporation
  - Limited Liability Company
- Insuring the Business
  - Liability Insurance
  - Crime Insurance
  - Property Damage Insurance
  - Business Interruption Insurance
  - Multi-Peril Insurance

Competencies

1. Describe the use of and need for business checklists, plans, and licenses when purchasing or expanding an existing business. (pp. 31–35)
2. Explain why it is important for hospitality operations to install customer credit/debit card systems. (pp. 35–37)
3. Describe the major forms of business organization and the advantages and disadvantages of each. (pp. 37–44)
4. Outline the taxation of business income for the major forms of business organization. (pp. 44–46)
5. Describe the broad forms of insurance coverage and their use in the hospitality industry. (pp. 46–49)

2

Business Formation, Taxation, and Insurance

THE LODGING INDUSTRY was traditionally composed of properties operated by individual owners called proprietors. Since the average hotel was small, a sole proprietor (or a partnership of two or more owners) was usually able to own and manage the operation. However, properties have increased in size, and more and more hotels and motels are owned or franchised by corporations. In some cases, independent management firms operate the property for absentee owners or at the direction of corporate executives.

For those with managerial, executive, and ownership aspirations, the hospitality industry ranks high in opportunity among all American businesses. The modern hotel represents a sophisticated array of management, financial, and operating systems. Students and entrepreneurs interested in this field are concerned with answers to such questions as:

1. What are some of the preliminary considerations in starting a business?
2. What are the various forms of legal business organization?
3. What is the federal income tax impact on the different business organizations?
4. What kinds of business insurance should be considered?

Owning a business is the ultimate goal of many hospitality professionals and students. Even those students who do not presently plan to be business owners might change their thinking after several years in the work field; therefore, the concepts presented in this chapter apply not just to aspiring entrepreneurs. Any business executive must understand the legal forms of business, taxation of business, and general insurance requirements. These topics and others in this chapter provide the fundamental knowledge necessary for any manager, executive, or business owner to succeed in the competitive hospitality business. The impact of choosing one form of business organization over another is evaluated in each case.

No single reference or individual can provide all of the specific assistance needed to start a business. A developing business should make full use of qualified and expert professionals. The cost of such advice is small compared with the substantial risks and potential benefits involved.

Initial Planning Strategy

Successful entrepreneurs, executives, and managers all share a common modus operandi; namely, they investigate before undertaking a venture and establish realistic, practical plans to achieve an objective. These entrepreneurs realize that the advice of professionals might be required in certain areas such as law, taxation, and insurance. This advice, though expensive, may eliminate more costly complications later. The principles in this chapter apply to both the start-up of a new business and the expansion of an existing business. Some of the factors to be considered for any business success are:

- Business checklist.
- Business plan.
- Business licenses.
- Credit cards.
- Legal form of business.
- Taxation of income.
- Insurance.

Business Checklist

The federal government and many states publish guides designed to help the beginning business. For example, the Michigan Department of Commerce publication *Guide to Starting a Business in Michigan* contains general information as well as information specific to Michigan. It includes such topics as establishing a basic business plan; securing adequate financial support; complying with federal, state, and local tax obligations; and obtaining necessary licenses and permits.

For entrepreneurs starting a business, the preparation of a checklist helps to arrange in an orderly fashion those items requiring research and action. A thorough checklist can form the basis for discussing business plans with an attorney, accountant, banker, or insurance agent. Exhibit 1 is a checklist from the *Guide to Starting a Business in Michigan.*

Business Plan

A **business plan** is a strategic management tool that is extremely useful in defining and assessing:

- Products and services.
- Market study and analysis.
- Competition.
- Sales forecasts and expense budgets.
- Equipment requirements.
- Cash flow and financing requirements.

The plan helps management and financial institutions assess the strengths and weaknesses of a business. Unfortunately, the business plan is too often not prepared until it is necessary to obtain financing for a new or existing company. The successful business executive develops a business plan up front because it serves as a guide in making intelligent and proper business decisions.

Exhibit 1 Checklist for Starting a Business

This checklist is designed to be used as "helpful hints" for beginning businesses. Frequently, when the decision to start a business moves from an idea to reality, everything seems to demand immediate attention. Important steps may be overlooked. Completing the essential steps included in the checklist will increase the efficiency and organization of a new business.

1. Personal Assessment

_______ Motivation and energy. Willingness to put in long hours with an unpredictable financial return.

_______ Business experience, background and training for the operation.

_______ Leadership and organizational abilities. Willingness to assume decision-making responsibilities.

_______ Interest in working with many different types of people.

2. Planning

_______ Determine and define the products or service to be provided.

_______ Develop a business plan.

_______ Develop a financial plan.

_______ Develop a marketing and/or promotion plan.

3. Establishment

_______ Secure financing.

_______ Contact the Office of the Michigan Business Ombudsman and/or federal, state and local agencies for regulatory information and permit and license applications.

_______ Review federal, state and local tax laws.

_______ Obtain management assistance from resource organizations such as Small Business Centers (SBC), Small Business Development Centers (SBDC) and/or Service Corps of Retired Executives (SCORE).

_______ Get necessary professional advice and assistance from attorneys and accountants.

_______ Complete all forms and pay all fees.

4. Implementation

_______ Register the business name.

_______ Obtain adequate insurance coverage.

_______ Hire and train employees.

_______ Initiate marketing plan.

Source: *Guide to Starting a Business in Michigan,* Michigan Department of Commerce, p. iv.

A business plan must be customized to fit a particular business and the management that is to run the business; no two plans are identical. Yet, a prototype or template is a useful guideline to tailor a business plan for any business. Exhibit 2 is a business plan framework from the *Guide to Starting a Business in Michigan.*

Exhibit 2 Business Plan

One of the most important steps in starting a business is the development of a business plan. Not only will the plan provide much needed direction to help guide the business owner, it will also serve as an essential introduction to the business for financial investors and others who must be informed about its operation and convinced of its prospects. A business plan should always be tailored to the specific circumstances of the business, emphasizing the strengths of the venture and addressing the problems.

1. **Cover Sheet**
   Name of business, address and telephone number, and the name(s) of principal(s).
2. **Statement of Purpose**
   A summary of the business covering at least the following items: business concept; product information; current stage of business (start-up, developing or existing); and anticipated financial results and other benefits.
3. **Table of Contents**
4. **The Business**
   a. Description of business: What product or service will you provide?
   b. Historical development: List the name, date of formation, legal structure, subsidiaries and degrees of ownership of your business.
   c. Product/service lines: What is the relative importance of each product/service? Include sales projections if possible.
   d. Market segment: Who will buy your product?
   e. Competition: Describe competing companies and how your business compares.
   f. Location: Where will you locate; why is it the best location?
   g. Marketing: What marketing methods will you use?
5. **Management**
   a. Business format: Is your business a proprietorship, partnership or corporation?
   b. Organizational chart: What is the personnel structure and who are the key individuals and planned staff additions?
   c. Personnel: What are the responsibilities and past experiences of partners and employees?
6. **Finance**
   a. Funding: What are your sources of financing and percentage from each source?
   b. Advisors: What are the names and addresses of accountant, legal counselor, banker, insurance agent and financial advisor?
   c. Cash requirements: What are your initial cash requirements, and what will they be over the next five years?
   d. Controls: What budget and cost systems do you/will you use?
   e. Sales and profit picture: What is your historical financial statement and/or financial projection?
7. **Production**
   a. Description: How will production or delivery of services be accomplished?
   b. Capacities: What physical facilities, suppliers, patents, labor and technology do you have or will you use?
   c. Capital equipment: What type and amount of machinery and durable equipment will you need to operate your business?
   d. Supplies: Where and how will you obtain your components and day-to-day supplies and services?
8. **Supporting Documents**
   Include personal resumes, personal financial statements, cost of living budget, letters of reference, job descriptions, letter of intent, copies of leases, contracts and other legal documents that you believe convey an accurate picture of your business.

Source: *Guide to Starting a Business in Michigan,* Michigan Department of Commerce, p. 1.

Business Licenses

Before starting any business, an entrepreneur needs to know about the particular local, state, and federal requirements for that type of business. While states and municipalities have their own specific requirements for businesses, it is possible to make general statements about the types of basic licenses, permits, and registrations most new businesses require.

Local. It may be necessary to obtain a business license from the city, town, or county in which the business is located. In addition, the business must comply with applicable zoning laws and building codes.

State. Unless the business is specifically exempt, most state governments require the business to file for a "sales and use tax" number associated with a sales tax permit. Particular types of businesses (for instance, liquor stores, barber shops, real estate agencies, restaurants, and hotels) may require certain additional licenses granted by the state.

Sometimes, a business operates under a name that is different from the legal name of its corporation or owner. In such a case, the company's business name may require registration under a state's "fictitious name" statute.

Federal. An Employer Identification Number (EIN) is required for all corporations, partnerships, and limited liability companies. An EIN is required for a proprietorship if wages are paid to one or more employees. An entrepreneur must apply for an EIN by completing IRS Form SS-4—Application for Employer Identification Number (see Exhibit 3).

Credit and Debit Cards

The planning stage of a new business should address the installation of a customer credit card system. In the current business environment, customers expect to be able to pay by credit card or debit card. The hospitality business that does not offer this convenience is at a major disadvantage with its competitors. Customers enjoy using credit and debit cards because these cards eliminate check-writing hassles, reduce the amount of cash the customers need to carry, and produce an expense tracking record.

Credit cards and debit cards are a major element of commerce in the hospitality industry. Credit cards and debit cards offer benefits to the hospitality business in the areas of:

- Customer convenience: Credit cards are a common medium of exchange and customers expect an established business to accept credit cards. A business that does not offer this convenience is subject to lost sales.
- Increased customer spending: Customers are not limited by the cash on hand and generally spend more using credit cards.
- Greater cash flow: Credit cards greatly reduce the necessity of house charges. Instead of waiting 30 or more days to collect on a sale, cash is either instantly available or available within two or three days.

Exhibit 3 IRS Form SS-4, Request for EIN

Form **SS-4**
(Rev. December 2001)
Department of the Treasury
Internal Revenue Service

Application for Employer Identification Number
(For use by employers, corporations, partnerships, trusts, estates, churches, government agencies, Indian tribal entities, certain individuals, and others.)
▶ **See separate instructions for each line.** ▶ **Keep a copy for your records.**

EIN
OMB No. 1545-0003

Type or print clearly.

1 Legal name of entity (or individual) for whom the EIN is being requested

2 Trade name of business (if different from name on line 1) | 3 Executor, trustee, "care of" name

4a Mailing address (room, apt., suite no. and street, or P.O. box) | 5a Street address (if different) (Do not enter a P.O. box.)

4b City, state, and ZIP code | 5b City, state, and ZIP code

6 County and state where principal business is located

7a Name of principal officer, general partner, grantor, owner, or trustor | 7b SSN, ITIN, or EIN

8a Type of entity (check only one box)
☐ Sole proprietor (SSN)
☐ Partnership
☐ Corporation (enter form number to be filed) ▶
☐ Personal service corp.
☐ Church or church-controlled organization
☐ Other nonprofit organization (specify) ▶
☐ Other (specify) ▶
☐ Estate (SSN of decedent)
☐ Plan administrator (SSN)
☐ Trust (SSN of grantor)
☐ National Guard ☐ State/local government
☐ Farmers' cooperative ☐ Federal government/military
☐ REMIC ☐ Indian tribal governments/enterprises
Group Exemption Number (GEN) ▶

8b If a corporation, name the state or foreign country (if applicable) where incorporated | State | Foreign country

9 Reason for applying (check only one box)
☐ Started new business (specify type) ▶
☐ Hired employees (Check the box and see line 12.)
☐ Compliance with IRS withholding regulations
☐ Other (specify) ▶
☐ Banking purpose (specify purpose) ▶
☐ Changed type of organization (specify new type) ▶
☐ Purchased going business
☐ Created a trust (specify type) ▶
☐ Created a pension plan (specify type) ▶

10 Date business started or acquired (month, day, year) | **11** Closing month of accounting year

12 First date wages or annuities were paid or will be paid (month, day, year). **Note:** *If applicant is a withholding agent, enter date income will first be paid to nonresident alien. (month, day, year)* . . . . ▶

13 Highest number of employees expected in the next 12 months. **Note:** *If the applicant does not expect to have any employees during the period, enter "-0-."* . . . . ▶ | Agricultural | Household | Other

14 Check **one** box that best describes the principal activity of your business.
☐ Construction ☐ Rental & leasing ☐ Transportation & warehousing ☐ Health care & social assistance ☐ Wholesale–agent/broker
☐ Real estate ☐ Manufacturing ☐ Finance & insurance ☐ Accommodation & food service ☐ Wholesale–other ☐ Retail
☐ Other (specify)

15 Indicate principal line of merchandise sold; specific construction work done; products produced; or services provided.

16a Has the applicant ever applied for an employer identification number for this or any other business? . . . . ☐ **Yes** ☐ **No**
Note: *If "Yes," please complete lines 16b and 16c.*

16b If you checked "Yes" on line 16a, give applicant's legal name and trade name shown on prior application if different from line 1 or 2 above.
Legal name ▶ Trade name ▶

16c Approximate date when, and city and state where, the application was filed. Enter previous employer identification number if known.
Approximate date when filed (mo., day, year) | City and state where filed | Previous EIN

Third Party Designee
Complete this section **only** if you want to authorize the named individual to receive the entity's EIN and answer questions about the completion of this form.
Designee's name | Designee's telephone number (include area code) ( )
Address and ZIP code | Designee's fax number (include area code) ( )

Under penalties of perjury, I declare that I have examined this application, and to the best of my knowledge and belief, it is true, correct, and complete.

Name and title (type or print clearly) ▶ | Applicant's telephone number (include area code) ( )

Signature ▶ Date ▶ | Applicant's fax number (include area code) ( )

For Privacy Act and Paperwork Reduction Act Notice, see separate instructions. Cat. No. 16055N Form **SS-4** (Rev. 12-2001)

A hospitality business (merchant) has many options when implementing credit card transactions. The choice is made based on a combination of credit card processing fees and timeliness in converting the credit card into cash. The most basic system is to manually prepare the credit cards; but this approach presents internal control problems and obvious transaction delays. The availability of stand-alone credit card readers (card-swipe equipment) and adaptability of electronic cash registers (ECR) and point-of-sale (POS) devices have simplified the processing time between customer and merchant. Card-swipe equipment electronically processes the credit card for approval and can print the credit card voucher (credit card receipt).

To establish credit card commerce, a merchant normally contacts a merchant services provider who processes the credit cards and then electronically makes a deposit in the merchant's checking account at a designated bank. The merchant services provider charges an up-front fee for this processing service. For example, if a merchant (the hospitality business) processes $5,000 of credit card business with a merchant services provider and the fee is one percent, the merchant services provider transmits a deposit of $4,950 to the designated bank account of the hospitality business.

VISA and MasterCard credit cards are called bankcards because they are issued by banking organizations. Merchant services providers can set up a hospitality business to process these bank cards and other credit cards such as Discover, American Express, and Carte Blanche. Arrangements can be made with a local bank to accept manual credit vouchers as a deposit in a checking account. These are treated the same as a cash deposit. Generally, this service incurs a much higher fee than electronically processing credit cards through a merchant services provider.

From a merchant's perspective, there is one significant difference between credit cards and debit cards: credit cards incur both transaction and commission fees, while debit cards incur only transaction fees. There is also a significant difference to the consumer. When a consumer uses a credit card, payment is not due until receipt of the bank statement; at that time, a check is issued to the credit card company. When a consumer uses a debit card, the amount processed by the merchant is instantly deducted from the consumer's bank account.

Business Formation

The formation of a business requires selecting its legal form of business organization. The various types of legal business forms (organization) are discussed later in this chapter. The form of business selected affects:

- Start-up organizational costs.
- Personal liability.
- Government regulation.
- Accounting and legal fees.
- Independence of owner.

- Complexity of the accounting system.
- Business year.
- Income taxes.

The choice is not simple because each has unique advantages and disadvantages that can affect profits. In most cases, the choice of an inappropriate legal form of business organization can be expensive and difficult to correct.

Many individuals select the corporate form of business because someone carelessly makes a hasty statement that it is the best legal form of business organization. In fact, it may be the most inflexible and expensive form of business. The predominant reason for selecting the corporate form is the exaggerated claim of *no personal liability*. This is a misleading claim because (1) government can hold owners of a corporation personally liable for unpaid income and payroll taxes, and (2) any business form can be protected by liability insurance

It is essential that the hospitality student become familiar with the various kinds of legal forms of business. The decision of which legal form of business to choose requires the assistance of a lawyer and accountant because legal, accounting, and governmental regulations have a bearing on this issue and are complex to decipher.

The following legal forms of business organization are examined here:

- Proprietorship
- Partnership
- Corporation
- Limited liability company

Proprietorship

A **proprietorship** business form is distinguished in that the business is not legally incorporated, and the business is owned by a single individual.

The owner of a proprietorship is a self-employed individual. A significant advantage of this unincorporated form of business is that it is the easiest, quickest, and least expensive form of business to legally establish.

Exhibit 4 compares the distinguishing features of a proprietorship to those of a partnership and a corporation. A significant *disadvantage* is that the owner has unlimited personal liability for any debts or uninsured claims against the business because from a legal perspective, the owner and business are the same party and inseparable. However, from an accounting point of view, the business and owner are separate entities; therefore, the financial statements of the business cannot include assets or liabilities of the owner.

No Wages for Owner. A self-employed individual (owner of a proprietorship) cannot be legally paid a salary or wage from the business because the law interprets the owner and business as a one-in-the-same legal entity. A self-employed individual can withdraw funds at his or her pleasure providing such funds are available

Exhibit 4 Legal Forms of Business Organization

	Human Resources			Initial Funding			Government Regulation	Revenue	
	Management Control	Personnel and Expertise	Continuity/ Transferability	Requirements and Costs	Ability to Raise Capital	Losses/Debts		Profits	Growth Potential
Proprietorship	One owner in total control	Depends mainly on owner's skills; hard to obtain quality employees	Ends on death of owner; free to sell or transfer	Costs are lowest (filing fee required if business held under name other than owner's)	Limited—all equity (funding) must come from proprietor; loans based on credit-worthiness of owner	Owner liable for all debts	Little regulation; few records needed	All profits to owner	Limited options —reinvest profits, obtain loans on owner's line-of-credit
Partnership	Divided among two or more partners; decisions made by majority or prearranged agreement (limited partner cannot manage the business)	Depends mainly on partners' skills; hard to find suitable employees	Ends on death of partner (unless otherwise agreed in writing); transfer conditions vary with agreement	Costs low; general partnership agreement optional but recommended (limited means that agreement stating liabilities and responsibilities of each partner is required)	Limited to resources of each of the partners and the ability of each to acquire loans and/or investors	Partners liable for all debts (limited partner has restricted liability and involvement per partnership agreement)	Subject to limited regulation; few records needed; articles of partnership should be drawn up	Divided among partners	Limited options —reinvest profits, obtain loans on owners' lines-of-credit
Corporation	Corporation acts as one person, but Board of Directors holds legal, formal control; working control held by those who manage the business day-to-day	Allows for flexible management; easier to secure quality employees with the necessary expertise	Continues with overlapping; most flexible in terms of transfer of interest (i.e., ownership) from one shareholder to another	Costs are highest; legal forms, documents, professional fees required	Greatest equity potential—can sell new stock; loans based on corporate financial strength and expertise, thus providing larger borrowing base	Corporation liable for all debts (i.e., shareholders are liable only for amount invested; are liable for more only if personal guarantees were given)	Extensive record-keeping required; must have articles of incorporation, by-laws and filing fees	Retained in corporation; shareholders receive dividends	Flexible—can reinvest profits (at discretion of Board of Directors); sell additional shares; obtain loans on corporate credit

Source: *Minding Your Own Small Business: An Introductory Curriculum,* Department of Health, Education, and Welfare 1979. Contract Number 300-7000330.

in the business. These withdrawals are not a deductible business expense. The owner does not pay any income tax on these withdrawals.

No Income Taxes for Business. The business does not directly pay income taxes. Since the business and owner are legally viewed as one entity, the profits of the business are declared on the owner's *personal* income tax return (IRS Form 1040, Schedule C). Because the owner pays an income tax on the profits of the business, his or her withdrawals are not taxed.

Partnership

A **partnership** has many similarities to a proprietorship, except for the number of owners (see Exhibit 4). A partnership is distinguished in that the business form is not legally incorporated, and the business is owned by two or more individuals.

This type of unincorporated business carries many risks: each partner is responsible for the debts of and claims against the business, and each partner is responsible for the business actions of the other partner(s).

A partnership is a very complex form of business and should not be organized without a formal document called a partnership agreement that specifies the allocation of profits or losses and other items such as responsibilities and the investment of each partner. Because of the risks involved, legal and accounting services prior to the formation of a partnership are vital.

Similarities to Proprietorship. The partnership form of business is arguably the most difficult to comprehend. The legal, accounting, and tax issues are substantial even for the experienced professional. The following list of similarities between a partnership and a proprietorship helps to clarify the issue.

- Neither form is legally incorporated.
- Both incur unlimited liability for partners (except for limited partners, described below).
- Income taxes of the business are paid by the proprietor or each of the partners.
- Partners are not paid a salary or wage.

While the partnership does not pay income taxes, it does file an information return (IRS Form 1065). This return shows the income or loss of the partnership allocated to each partner on the basis of the partnership agreement. Each partner then reports his or her share of the income or loss on IRS Form 1040, using Schedule E.

General vs. Limited Partners. Every partnership must have at least one **general partner** responsible for the management and control of the business. A partnership may have any number of **limited partners,** who do not and legally may not participate in the active management of the business. General partners have unlimited personal liability, while limited partners enjoy the freedom of not being personally liable for the acts of the general partners or any debts or claims against the business.

Corporation

A **corporation** is distinguished by the facts that the business form is legally incorporated and the business is owned by one or more individuals. Refer again to Exhibit 4.

The owners of a corporation are called shareholders or stockholders. From a legal, tax, and accounting perspective, the owners of a corporation and the business are *not* related; each is a separate entity. The following is a list of some of the characteristics of a corporation.

- It is legally incorporated.
- The assets are owned by the business, not the shareholders.
- Shareholders have only limited liability.
- Income taxes are paid by the corporation (except see Subchapter S corporation later in this chapter).
- The owners may be paid a salary or wage.

Articles of Incorporation. Unlike many nations, the United States does not have a single, national law governing the formation and governance of corporations. Although there are federal laws relating to taxation, disclosure, and trading of securities, the formation of corporations is left to state law. Forming a corporation involves an incorporation process that is a legal procedure performed by filing *articles of incorporation* with the secretary of corporation's office in the state in which the corporation's home office is located. Each state has its own incorporation laws. In general, the articles of incorporation (also called the *certificate of incorporation*) identify the incorporator and describe the corporation and its stock. The incorporator need not be an expected owner or officer of the corporation.

Description of Corporation. The secretary of corporation's office must approve the corporate name to avoid duplication with other corporations in that state. The articles of incorporation must state the business purpose of the corporation. Stating a single purpose such as "food and beverage operation" may limit future business activities. To avoid filing an amendment to the articles of incorporation (incurring legal and state fees), a broader definition of the corporation's business is generally used. For example, the nature or purpose of the business might be stated as "the corporation may engage in any lawful act or activity for which corporations may be incorporated under the general corporation law."

Authorized Stock. The kind of stock and number of shares the corporation might intend to issue must be stated in the articles of incorporation. One should not confuse stock authorized and **stock issued**. The number of shares of stock the corporation may legally issue (sell) is its **authorized stock;** the shares actually issued later are called stock *issued*. A corporation is not required to sell all of its authorized stock. The state incorporation fees are generally based on the number of authorized shares, the number being in a range such as one to 1,000 and progressing to larger number ranges. If the corporation later requires more authorized shares, a simple amendment to the articles of incorporation is all that is required. Describing the authorized stock also involves terms like par value, capital stock, common stock, and preferred stock.

Par Value. Some states base their incorporation fees on par value per share or a combination of par value and number of authorized shares. Par value is one of the most misunderstood terms regarding corporate stock. For an equity security, par is usually a very small amount that bears no relationship to its market price, except for preferred stock, in which case par is used to calculate dividend payments. **Par value** is a legal term and its relevance generally is that corporate stock cannot be originally issued below its par value per share. Corporations generally select a low par value of one cent, five cents, or ten cents. For example, the par value of Wendy's stock is ten cents per share, which has no relationship to its market value. To give corporations greater flexibility, many states allow the use of *no par* value stock.

Capital Stock. The term **capital stock** does not designate any one type of stock; instead, the term represents a generic reference to all types of stock. Corporations may issue a single class of stock or multiple classes of stock, as the certificate of incorporation provides. Stock may be voting or non-voting, and shares of one class may be given a greater or lesser number of votes per share than shares of another class. Ownership of stock is generally evidenced by a stock certificate such as that illustrated in Exhibit 5; however, it is not necessary to issue a stock certificate. A corporation may plan to issue common stock and preferred stock. Generally, common stock must be issued because it gives shareholders a voting privilege.

Common Stock. Common stock is one type of capital stock. Common stock stands last in line for dividends and proceeds in the event of liquidation. The advantage of **common stock** is that it generally gives the stockholders a voting privilege. This voting right gives stockholders the decisive power to *elect* a board of directors who set corporate policy. The board of directors then *appoints* the officers of the corporation to carry out these policies. This line of command and hierarchy is illustrated in Exhibit 6.

Common stock is attractive because of its potential for significant increase in its market value. There are many success stories of stockholders who became wealthy individuals because they bought IBM, Microsoft, Wal-Mart, or any of a number of other growth companies.

Preferred Stock. Preferred stock is another type of capital stock. The advantage of **preferred stock** is that preferred stockholders receive dividends before the common stockholders and in the event of liquidation, the preferred stockholders receive liquidating dividends before the common stockholders. However, in the event of liquidation, creditors receive liquidation proceeds first, and last in line are the preferred and common stockholders; this "leftover" claim is referred to as a **residual claim**. Disadvantages of preferred stock are:

- The annual dividend (usually paid on a quarterly basis) is fixed for the life of the stock.
- The market value of preferred stock does not enjoy the potential growth value of common stock.

Exhibit 5 Stock Certificate

BN 55320

LESS THAN 100 SHARES

NUMBER

SHARES

COMMON STOCK

INCORPORATED UNDER THE LAWS OF THE STATE OF DELAWARE

Loews Corporation

THIS IS TO CERTIFY THAT

IS THE OWNER OF

SEE REVERSE FOR CERTAIN DEFINITIONS

CUSIP 540424 10 8

FULL PAID AND NON-ASSESSABLE SHARES OF THE COMMON STOCK OF THE PAR VALUE OF ONE DOLLAR ($1.00) PER SHARE OF *Loews Corporation (hereinafter called the Corporation) transferable on the books of the Corporation in person or by duly authorized attorney upon surrender of this certificate properly endorsed. This certificate and the shares represented hereby are issued and shall be held subject to all of the provisions of the Certificate of Incorporation and the amendments thereto (copies of which are on file with the Transfer Agent) to all of which the holder by acceptance hereof assents. This certificate is not valid until countersigned by the Transfer Agent and registered by the Registrar.*

Witness the seal of the Corporation and the signatures of its duly authorized officers.

Dated

CERTIFICATE OF STOCK

CORPORATE SEAL 1969 DELAWARE LOEWS CORPORATION

SPECIMEN

SECRETARY

CHAIRMAN OF THE BOARD

COUNTERSIGNED AND REGISTERED: CITIBANK, N.A. (NEW YORK) TRANSFER AGENT AND REGISTRAR

BY

AUTHORIZED OFFICER

05 10 80

TENS | UNITS 1 2 3 4 5 6 7 8 9 0

© SECURITY-COLUMBIAN BANKNOTE COMPANY

Courtesy of Loews Corporation

Exhibit 6 Organization Chart for a Corporation

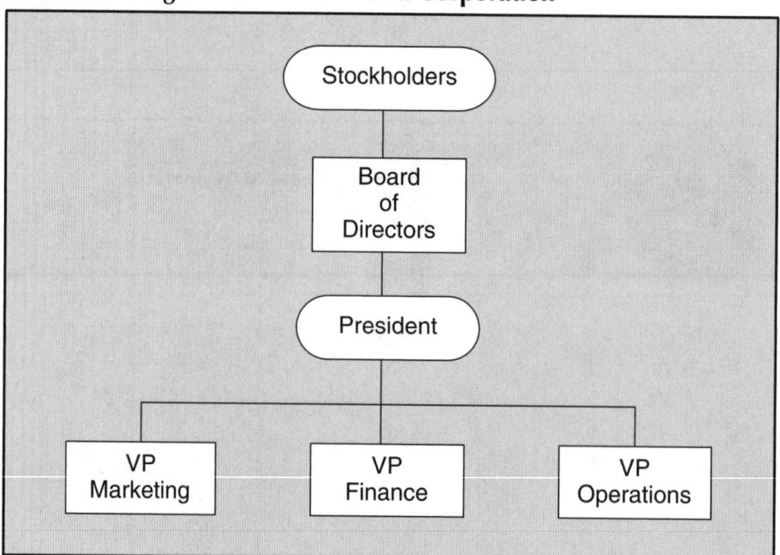

- The right to vote often is not granted to preferred stockholders.
- Preferred stock is often **callable**, meaning that the company can repurchase its preferred stock at a predetermined price.

To overcome some of these disadvantages, preferred stock may be issued as **convertible** preferred stock, which allows the stockholder to convert the preferred stock to common stock at a predetermined exchange ratio.

Limited Liability Company

All states now have enacted **limited liability company** (LLC) statutes. An LLC is a separate legal entity formed by filing articles of organization with the secretary of state. The LLC is a relatively new form of business entity; it is neither a partnership nor a corporation, but it combines the major advantages of both forms of doing business. For example, the members of an LLC may enjoy the limited liability of a corporation but yet be taxed as a partnership.

Taxation of Business Income

The taxation of business income is a complex process requiring the expertise of a qualified tax preparer. It is important to retain the services of a qualified professional during the initial business-planning phase because the legal form of business organization has a major impact on the taxation of business income. A certified public accountant (CPA) or enrolled agent (EA) authorized to practice before the Internal Revenue Service has demonstrated knowledge in the field of taxation by virtue of having completed professional examinations.

The federal government and most states tax business income. A few cities also tax business income. The income tax is computed on **taxable income** multiplied by an applicable tax rate. Taxable income is the result of business sales and all other taxable revenue minus deductible business expenses allowed by tax law. Taxable income and accounting income may not be identical because of the difference between income tax accounting rules and generally accepted accounting principles.

The following analysis of income taxation for the various forms of business organizations pertains only to federal income taxation. There is no uniformity of state income taxation.

Proprietorship

A proprietorship does not directly pay income taxes. Instead, the owner of a proprietorship pays the tax with his or her personal tax return. The income and deductions of the business are entered on IRS Schedule C—Profit or Loss From Business and attached to Form 1040—U.S. Individual Tax Return. A qualifying small business may instead use Schedule C-EZ, which is a condensed version of Schedule C.

The **self-employment tax** (SE tax) is a social security and Medicare tax for owners of proprietorships. It is similar to the social security and Medicare tax withheld from the pay of wage earners. Because a proprietor does not withhold these taxes from employees' earnings, the SE tax is generally at double the rate that would be withheld from employee wages. The SE tax is computed on IRS Form SE—Self-Employment Tax, which is also attached to Form 1040.

Partnership

A partnership does not directly pay income taxes, but it does file Form 1065—U.S. Return of Partnership Income (which is an information return) with the Internal Revenue Service. Each partner receives notice of his or her share of taxable income from the partnership. This income is reported on Schedule E—Supplemental Income and Loss and is attached to Form 1040. Each partner is also liable for any self-employment tax.

Corporation

From a legal perspective, a corporation is a legal entity that is separate and distinct from its owners (stockholders). From a federal income tax perspective, the taxation of corporations has two possible alternatives.

Under the general rule whereby the corporation is separate from its owners, a corporation files a tax return and pays its own income tax. These corporations are called **C corporations** because they are taxed under Subchapter C of the Internal Revenue Code (IRC). However, qualifying small business corporations may elect to be treated as a partnership for federal income tax purposes. Thus, the income is "passed through" (allocated) to the stockholders who will pay the tax. These pass-through entities are called **S corporations** because they are taxed under Subchapter S of the IRC. Election to be taxed as a Subchapter S corporation must be filed in a timely manner by qualified small business corporations on IRS Form 2553.

Subchapter C Corporation. A corporation that is taxed as a Subchapter C corporation files Form 1120—U.S. Corporation Income Tax Return and pays its own income tax. Large corporations, especially those listed on a major stock exchange, file as a Subchapter C corporation because they cannot meet the qualifying factors to be taxed as a Subchapter S corporation. A small business corporation will file as a Subchapter C corporation if it fails to qualify as a Subchapter S corporation or does not make such election.

Subchapter S Corporation. A Subchapter S corporation generally does not pay tax on its income. It files Form 1120S—U.S. Income Tax Return for an S Corporation, an information return, with the Internal Revenue Service. Each stockholder receives a notice of his or her share of taxable income from the Subchapter S corporation; this income is reported on Schedule E—Supplemental Income and Loss and is attached to his or her Form 1040.

Limited Liability Company

The Internal Revenue Service coverage of limited liability companies (LLC) is limited and very complex. Adding to the intricacy of taxation of limited liability companies is that the IRC does not specifically address LLC issues. The Internal Revenue Service generally treats an LLC as a partnership. However, under certain circumstances, it is possible for an LLC to elect and qualify to be taxed as a corporation. Under certain conditions, members of an LLC could be liable for self-employment taxes. For example, if the member has personal liability for the debts of the LLC or has management authority, that member is responsible for the self-employment tax on his or her share of allocable taxable income.

Those business entities that cannot initially qualify as a Subchapter S corporation may satisfy the requirements to qualify as an LLC. For example, a Subchapter S corporation has a limitation on the number of shareholders and a stipulation that all stockholders must be U.S. citizens or resident aliens.

Insuring the Business

Without proper protection, a hospitality business could be subject to financial ruin due to casualty losses and legal claims resulting from its activities. Insurance can help shield a business from risks that carry the most potential for a damaging loss.

When considering insurance, owners should prioritize their insurance needs and determine the types of coverage needed. For example, some insurance may be considered imperative to protect the property from catastrophic loss. At the same time, lower and upper limits should be established to determine whether the operation has the right amount of coverage.

The types of insurance required by a hotel or restaurant are complex and the assistance of a qualified insurance consultant is typically needed. The four broad classes of insurance coverage that a hospitality operation needs to consider are:

- Liability.
- Crime.
- Property damage.
- Business interruption.

We conclude this section with a discussion of multi-peril insurance—a special-purpose coverage that combines elements of these broad classes under a single policy.

Liability Insurance

Liability insurance provides a hospitality business with coverage for property damage or personal injury claims arising from guests, employees, and others. It does not insure the business against damages to its property and other assets.

A lawsuit involving a liability claim could mean a catastrophic loss to an uninsured business. Therefore, it is vital that a business consider carrying some form of liability protection in the event of lawsuits. A liability policy generally will provide for the policyholder's legal defense and pay claims up to the limits of the policy.

Several different types of liability coverage may be necessary to protect the hospitality business from property or injury claims made by others. Exhibit 7 lists and describes a number of important types of liability coverage that lodging operations may carry. Some types (particularly **automobile liability insurance** and **workers' compensation**) may be required by law.

Crime Insurance

A hospitality business always runs the risk of losses brought about by a criminal act such as robbery, burglary, employee embezzlement, or theft.

Several different types of crime insurance policies may be necessary to protect the hospitality business from these and other criminal activities. Exhibit 7 describes three different types: **fidelity bonds**, money and securities insurance, and innkeeper's liability insurance.

Instead of providing separate policies for each type of crime, insurance companies may provide optional crime coverage packages to policyholders. Crime insurance can be expensive, so most policies have a "deductible" in order to keep costs down; for each claim by a policyholder (insured), an insurance company (insurer) would be liable only for the loss in excess of a stated deductible amount. For example, assume a hotel has an insurance policy with a $500 deductible clause and it files a loss claim for $1,200. The insurance company would pay only $700 on this claim—the actual loss claimed less the deductible amount.

Property Damage Insurance

Property damage insurance protects the insured business against direct losses to its property (such as buildings, contents, and vehicles) due to fire, theft, accidents, and other types of casualties. Other casualties covered by such policies may include lightning, windstorms, hail storms, aircraft crashes, riots, and actions associated with strikes and civil disturbances.

Exhibit 7 Specific Types of Insurance Policies

Class/Policy	Description of Coverage
Liability Insurance	
Automobile Liability Insurance	Claims from guests or the general public for bodily injury or property damage resulting from the operation of business vehicles; may be expanded to include coverage for the use of employees' cars for business purposes.
Workers' Compensation Insurance	Claims involving personal injury or death incurred by employees in the course of their employment; mandatory in most states; compensation amounts are prescribed by law.
General Liability Insurance	Claims of others (employees excluded) for injuries sustained on the premises or resulting from activities of the business (automobiles excluded).
Product Liability Insurance	Claims for bodily injury or property damage caused by the consumption of food, beverages, or other products of the business.
Garage Coverage	Claims involving bodily injury or property damage on premises of public or guest garage or parking lot.
Garage Keeper's Legal Liability	Liabilities for fire or theft of vehicles on premises of public or guest garage or parking lot.
Crime Insurance	
Fidelity Bonds	Losses of cash due to theft by employees.
Money & Securities Insurance	Losses due to theft or other reasons caused by persons other than employees.
Innkeeper's Liability Insurance	Claims for damage or destruction of guest property on the premises.
Property Damage Insurance	
(General)	Property losses due to fire, theft, accidents and other types of casualties; may be expanded to include buildings, contents and vehicles.
Business Interruption Insurance	
(General)	Reimbursement for loss of earnings and continuing charges and expenses when an operation is forced to interrupt business; payrolls may be covered or excluded.

It is important to carefully read a property damage policy to determine exactly what is covered and what is excluded from coverage. A given policy cannot reasonably be expected to cover all possible losses. "Riders" are special provisions added to the policy to extend coverage. Such provisions may be needed to protect against *indirect property losses;* for instance, damage caused by smoke or water from a fire in a building adjacent to (but not owned by) the hospitality property.

Business Interruption Insurance

In the event of fire or other disasters, a property may be forced to interrupt its business while repairs are being made. Strikes or civil disturbances may prevent the hospitality business from conducting its normal business activities. Business interruption insurance provides the insured with coverage for loss of earnings and continuing expenses until the business can resume operations. Depending on the policy, payroll may be covered or excluded.

Restoration of the business activities should proceed with the same concern as if no insurance was involved. It is better to earn business revenue than to collect business interruption insurance.

Multi-Peril Insurance

A single business operation could purchase many separate insurance policies to cover its insurance requirements. Rather than shopping for each type of insurance needed, a business may secure coverage by purchasing a multi-peril policy. Under this policy, the owner has the benefit of broad coverage for losses arising from on-site conditions relating to ownership, maintenance, or use of the property. However, the standard multi-peril package provides no coverage for problems that occur off the property or that arise from contract obligations.

Key Terms

authorized stock—The kind of stock and number of shares a corporation is allowed to issue as described in its articles of incorporation.

automobile liability insurance—Coverage for claims from guests or general public for bodily injury or property damage from a vehicle.

business plan—A strategic management tool to assess strengths and weaknesses.

callable—An option giving a corporation the right to buy back its stock from shareholders at a predetermined price.

capital stock—A term representing the classes of stock, namely common and preferred.

common stock—A type of capital stock with voting privileges.

convertible—An option giving shareholders the right to convert their preferred stock or bonds to common stock at a predetermined exchange basis.

corporation—An incorporated business owned by one or more individuals.

fidelity bonds—Insurance coverage for losses of cash due to employee theft.

general partner—Partner with authority in the management of a partnership. General partners have personal liability.

liability insurance—Coverage for claims of others (employees excluded) for injuries on the premises (autos excluded).

limited liability company—A form of business organization that may be taxed as a partnership but enjoy the limited liability of a corporation.

limited partner—Partner with no management authority and no personal liability.

partnership—A business form owned by two or more individuals and not incorporated.

par value—Another descriptive label to identify a corporation's authorized stock as described in its articles of incorporation.

preferred stock—A type of capital stock preferred as to dividends but whose owners generally do not have voting privileges.

property damage insurance—Coverage for property losses (building and contents, vehicles) due to fire, theft, and other casualties.

proprietorship—A business form owned by one individual and not incorporated.

residual claim—A leftover claim, being last in line for any proceeds.

self-employment tax—A combination of social security and Medicare taxes payable by self-employed individuals such as owners of proprietorships and partnerships.

stock issued—The actual number of shares issued by a corporation from its authorized stock.

Subchapter C corporation—A corporation taxed under Subchapter C of the IRC that must pay its own income taxes.

Subchapter S corporation—A corporation taxed under Subchapter S of the IRC and passes its taxable income to its shareholders who in turn pay the income tax.

taxable income—Sales plus other taxable revenue minus deductible business expenses.

workers' compensation insurance—Coverage for injuries or death incurred by employees in the course of their employment.

Review Questions

1. What are the six items defined and assessed in a business plan?
2. Under what conditions is an EIN required?
3. What are the three major benefits to the merchant of credit cards and debit cards?

4. From the consumer's perspective, what is the significant difference between credit cards and debit cards?
5. What is the most significant advantage of a proprietorship?
6. What is the most significant disadvantage of a proprietorship?
7. What is the difference between a general partner and a limited partner?
8. What is the difference between authorized stock and issued stock?
9. What is capital stock?
10. What is taxable income?
11. What is the self-employment tax?
12. What is the legal difference between a Subchapter C corporation and a Subchapter S corporation?
13. What is the difference in federal income tax treatment between a Subchapter C corporation and a Subchapter S corporation?
14. What is the major difference between liability insurance and property damage insurance?

Problems

Problem 1

Which of the following require a federal employer identification number?

Proprietorship with no employees	_______
Corporation with no employees	_______
Corporation with one employee	_______
Corporation with ten or more employees	_______

Problem 2

Which of the following apply to a proprietorship?

Limited liability of owner	_______
In accounting, owner and business are separate	_______
By law, owner and business are not separate	_______
Owner can be paid a wage or salary	_______
Income tax on business profits are paid by the owner	_______
Owner must pay income tax on withdrawal of $90,000	_______
Business profit is reported on Form 1040, Schedule C	_______
Owner pays a self-employment tax on business profit	_______

Problem 3

An incorporator files articles of incorporation with the state's secretary of state office. The stock entries on the form are 50,000 shares of common stock and 10,000 shares of preferred stock. What is the number of shares for each of the following items?

Capital stock	________
Common stock authorized	________
Preferred stock authorized	________
Common stock issued	________
Preferred stock issued	________

Problem 4

A corporation has the following business results: Sales $100,000; nontaxable dividend income $20,000; rental income $10,000; business expenses of $60,000. What is its taxable income?

Problem 5

Which of the following owners will pay income tax on the profits of a business?

Corporation qualified under Subchapter C	________
Corporation qualified under Subchapter S	________
General partner	________
Limited partner	________
Proprietorship	________

Problem 6

What *specific type* of insurance policy is needed to cover the following casualties?

Company auto injuring guest	____________
Fire damage to company auto	____________
Guest injured due to broken stair	____________
Employee injured due to broken stair	____________
Fire damage to hotel building	____________
Loss of profits due to fire	____________
Loss of cash due to employee theft	____________

Ethics Case

Finer Foods, Inc., is applying for a bank loan of $250,000. Fred Helendona is the president and only shareholder of the corporation. The corporation is very profitable, and the loan will be used for expansion of facilities to accommodate customer demand.

The real estate (land and building) is not owned by the corporation; it is leased from Fred Helendona, who owns it as an individual. This rental arrangement is not unusual and was recommended by Fred's accountant before the business was started.

Because the corporation does not own any real estate, its balance sheet appears weak when its assets are compared to its liabilities. As company president, Fred instructs the accountant to enter the value of the real estate on the company's balance sheet in order to improve its assets picture. This balance sheet will be used to apply for the bank loan.

1. Identify the stakeholders in this case.
2. Comment on the legal and accounting issues involved in this deception.
3. What other alternative is available to the president to help the company get a bank loan?

Chapter 3 Outline

Basic Financial Statements
Statement of Income
- Revenue
- Cost of Sales
- Gross Profit
- Operating Expenses
- Income Before Fixed Charges and Income Taxes
- Fixed Charges
- Income Before Income Taxes
- Income Taxes
- Net Income (or Loss)

Equity Statements
- Statement of Owner's Equity
- Statement of Retained Earnings

Balance Sheet
- Current Assets
- Property and Equipment
- Other Assets
- Current Liabilities
- Long-Term Liabilities
- Equity Section

Statement of Cash Flows
- Operating Activities
- Investing Activities
- Financing Activities

Competencies

1. Identify the major financial statements and explain when they are issued. (pp. 55–56)
2. Define the purpose and describe the contents of the income statement, balance sheet, statement of owner's equity, statement of retained earnings, and the statement of cash flows. (pp. 56–69)

3

Introduction to Financial Statements

THE PURPOSE OF FINANCIAL STATEMENTS is to present in monetary terms what a business has accomplished, its financial well-being, and the sources and uses of its cash during the period examined. The income statement presents what a company has accomplished, the balance sheet shows its well-being, and the statement of cash flows explains where cash came from and how the cash was spent.

Statements are important to stockholders, investors, management, creditors, and other interested parties who need to evaluate a company's financial accomplishment. A company may have the best product or services, but it cannot stay in business unless it is properly managed, achieves a status of profitability, and is able to pay its bills. While financial statements by nature are historical, professional analysis can render an opinion as to the outlook for a company.

This chapter provides the reader with a comparison of statements issued for both a corporation and a proprietorship, using the same financial data. The chapter answers such questions as:

1. What are annual and interim financial statements?
2. What is the purpose and content of the income statement?
3. What is the purpose and content of the statement of owner's equity?
4. What is the purpose and content of the statement of retained earnings?
5. What is the purpose and content of the balance sheet?
6. What is the purpose and content of the statement of cash flows?

Basic Financial Statements

The basic financial statements prepared by hospitality businesses are the statement of income, the equity statement (the name of which varies by business form), the balance sheet, and the statement of cash flows. These four statements present independent information, yet have a relationship to each other. For example, the income (or loss) from the income statement is transferred to the equity statement; the result of the equity statement is carried over to the balance sheet; the statement of cash flows is prepared from information on the income statement and balance sheet.

Annual financial statements are issued at the end of a company's business year, also called a fiscal year. A **fiscal year** might be a calendar year or a year consisting of twelve consecutive months starting in any month other than January. It is customary for companies whose stock is publicly traded to issue an elegant packet containing the financial statements, a president's letter to stockholders, and glossy pictures of products, people, and services. Management, stockholders, investors, creditors, and other interested parties are eager to obtain the annual statements of businesses so that they can properly examine and evaluate the companies' performances.

The best-run companies also issue monthly financial statements to management. Those companies whose stock is publicly traded also issue quarterly financial statements to their stockholders. Such statements issued during the business year are called **interim financial statements**.

Statement of Income

The **statement of income** shows revenue and expenses and provides information about the *results of operations* for a stated period of time. This is the financial statement that tells if a business operated at a profit or loss for the period of time covered by the statement. The time period may be one month or longer, but does not exceed one business year. Since the owners of proprietorships or partnerships pay personal income taxes on the net income from their operations, their fiscal years generally begin on the first of January. However, the fiscal year of certain corporate forms of business organization may be any twelve consecutive months.

Since the statement of income reveals the results of operations for a period of time, it is an important measure of the effectiveness and efficiency of management. Understanding how the statement is used to evaluate management is the key to understanding the logic behind the sequence of categories that appears on the statement. The major categories that appear on the statement of income are:

- Revenue.
- Cost of Sales.
- Gross Profit.
- Operating Expenses.
- Fixed Charges.
- Net Income (or Loss).

The following sections discuss these categories in some detail and provide a brief explanation of the line items appearing within them. Exhibits 1 and 2 point out the differences between statements of income prepared for proprietorships and those prepared for corporations.

Revenue

Revenue results when products and services are sold to guests. The total revenue figure on the statement of income indicates the actual dollar amount that guests have been billed for products and services offered by the hospitality property.

Exhibit 1 Statement of Income for a Proprietorship

Deb's Steakhouse
Statement of Income
For the Year Ended December 31, 20X2

REVENUE		
Food Sales	$120,000	
Liquor Sales	50,000	
Total Revenue		$170,000
COST OF SALES		
Food	42,000	
Liquor	11,000	
Total Cost of Sales		53,000
GROSS PROFIT		117,000
OPERATING EXPENSES		
Salaries and Wages	36,000	
Employee Benefits	6,900	
China, Glassware, and Silverware	300	
Kitchen Fuel	900	
Laundry and Dry Cleaning	2,100	
Credit Card Fees	1,500	
Operating Supplies	5,000	
Advertising	2,000	
Utilities	3,800	
Repairs and Maintenance	1,900	
Total Operating Expenses		60,400
INCOME BEFORE FIXED CHARGES		56,600
FIXED CHARGES		
Rent	6,000	
Property Taxes	1,500	
Insurance	3,600	
Interest Expense	3,000	
Depreciation and Amortization	5,500	
Total Fixed Charges		19,600
NET INCOME		$ 37,000

Note: The net income figure is transferred to the Statement of Owner's Equity illustrated in Exhibit 3

Exhibit 2 Statement of Income for a Corporation

Deb's Steakhouse, Inc.
Statement of Income
For the Year Ended December 31, 20X2

REVENUE		
Food Sales	$120,000	
Liquor Sales	50,000	
Total Revenue		$170,000
COST OF SALES		
Food	42,000	
Liquor	11,000	
Total Cost of Sales		53,000
GROSS PROFIT		117,000
OPERATING EXPENSES		
Salaries and Wages	55,000	
Employee Benefits	7,900	
China, Glassware, and Silverware	300	
Kitchen Fuel	900	
Laundry and Dry Cleaning	2,100	
Credit Card Fees	1,500	
Operating Supplies	5,000	
Advertising	2,000	
Utilities	3,800	
Repairs and Maintenance	1,900	
Total Operating Expenses		80,400
INCOME BEFORE FIXED CHARGES AND INCOME TAXES		36,600
FIXED CHARGES		
Rent	6,000	
Property Taxes	1,500	
Insurance	3,600	
Interest Expense	3,000	
Depreciation and Amortization	5,500	
Total Fixed Charges		19,600
INCOME BEFORE INCOME TAXES		17,000
INCOME TAXES		2,000
NET INCOME		$ 15,000

Note: The net income figure is transferred to the Statement of Retained Earnings illustrated in Exhibit 4

Revenue is *not* income. Revenue appears at the top of the statement of income; net income (or loss) appears at the bottom. Income results when total revenue exceeds total expenses. A loss results when total expenses exceed total revenue.

Exhibits 1 and 2 show the total revenue figure for Deb's Steakhouse at $170,000. Note that revenue generated by food sales ($120,000) is listed separately from revenue generated by beverage sales ($50,000). Distinguishing the major sources of revenue allows management to identify the separate contributions of the food operation and the beverage operation to the total gross profit of the establishment.

Cost of Sales

The **cost of sales** section of the statement of income shows the cost of merchandise used in the selling process; it does not contain any cost for labor or employee meals. Since the revenue appearing on the income statement for Deb's Steakhouse resulted from sales of food and beverages to guests, the cost of sales figure ($53,000) represents *the cost of food and beverage merchandise served to guests.* Cost of sales can also be called **cost of goods sold**.

Gross Profit

Gross profit is calculated by subtracting cost of sales from net revenue (net sales). Gross profit is sometimes referred to as gross margin or gross margin on sales.

Gross profit is an intermediate income amount from which operating expenses and fixed charges are deducted to arrive at net income. Gross profit must be large enough to cover all of these expenses for the business to earn a net income.

Operating Expenses

The **operating expenses** section of the statement of income lists expenses that are most directly influenced by operating policy and management efficiency. If the statement of income showed these expenses as a single line item, this would not communicate much information to the users of the statement. Breaking out each of the significant operating expenses allows management and others to readily identify expense areas that may be excessive and that call for further analysis and possible corrective action. A brief explanation of the line items included under operating expenses on the statements of income for Deb's Steakhouse follows.

Salaries and Wages. This line item includes the regular salaries and wages, extra wages, overtime pay, vacation pay, and any commission or bonus payments to employees. Note that the figure shown as salaries and wages for the corporate form of Deb's Steakhouse is greater than the salaries and wages figure shown for the proprietorship form of Deb's Steakhouse. This difference results from the fact that the owner of a proprietorship cannot be paid a salary or wage.

Employee Benefits. This line item includes the cost of free employee meals, social security and Medicare taxes (FICA), federal and state unemployment taxes, union and nonunion insurance premiums, state health insurance, union and nonunion pension fund contributions, medical expenses, workers' compensation insurance, and other similar expenses. Expenses related to employee benefits can be significant for restaurant operations. Note that the amount for employee benefits shown for Deb's Steakhouse, Inc., is greater than that shown for Deb's Steakhouse (proprietorship). This difference arises because: (a) an owner of a proprietorship cannot deduct benefits on his or her behalf, and (b) there are no payroll taxes on behalf of the owner, since wages cannot be paid to an owner.

China, Glassware, and Silverware. These items are generally considered direct service expenses rather than repair and maintenance expenses. Therefore, replacement costs for china, glassware, and silverware appear here as a separate item under Operating Expenses. This line item also includes the depreciation expense for china, glassware, and silverware.

Kitchen Fuel. This line item includes only the cost of fuel used for cooking, such as gas, coal, charcoal briquettes, steam, electricity, or hickory chips.

Laundry and Dry Cleaning. This line item includes the cost of laundering table linens and uniforms; contracting for napkin, towel, and apron service; and cleaning uniforms, wall and window hangings, and floor coverings.

Credit Card Fees. This item includes the amount paid to credit card organizations for central billing and collection of credit card accounts.

Operating Supplies. This item represents supplies that have been used and are not includable as inventory. These include cleaning supplies, paper supplies, guest supplies, and bar supplies. The statements of income for Deb's Steakhouse list operating supplies as a single line item. However, large operations may list the categories of operating supplies separately on the statement of income.

Advertising. *Marketing* is the more general term used to describe the varied expenses incurred in promoting a restaurant operation to the public. Items listed under marketing vary with the needs and requirements of individual properties. Deb's Steakhouse is a relatively small operation, so its marketing expenses consistently include only advertising costs such as newspaper ads, circulars, and brochures. Therefore, it is more appropriate and informative for that operation to list advertising instead of marketing as the operating expense item on the statement of income. Large restaurant operations, on the other hand, may incur significant marketing expenses in such areas as sales, advertising, and public relations. It would be appropriate for these properties to list the term *marketing* as a direct expense line item on the statement of income.

Utilities. This line item includes the cost of electricity, fuel, water, ice and refrigeration supplies, waste removal, and engineer's supplies. Note, however, that the utilities item does not include fuel used for cooking purposes. The cost of energy used for cooking purposes appears as a separate line item. If electricity or gas is used as kitchen fuel and for heating and lighting, it is necessary to use meter readings or estimate usage in order to isolate kitchen fuel expense.

Repairs and Maintenance. This line item includes the cost of plastering, painting, decorating, repairing dining room furniture and kitchen equipment, plumbing and heating repairs, and other maintenance and repair expenses.

Income Before Fixed Charges and Income Taxes

The figure for income before fixed charges and income taxes is used to measure the success of operations and the effectiveness and efficiency of management. Therefore, this section of the statement of income is extremely important to management. This figure is calculated by subtracting total operating expenses from the gross profit figure.

Note in Exhibit 1 that for a proprietorship form of business organization this section of the statement of income reads as "Income Before Fixed Charges." Income taxes are not mentioned because a proprietorship does not pay income taxes—the owner does. A proprietorship's business income is reported on the owner's personal income tax return.

Fixed Charges

The **fixed charges** section of the statement of income includes rent, property taxes, property insurance, interest expense, and depreciation. Fixed charges are those expenses that are incurred regardless of whether the business is open or closed, and they remain relatively constant even with changes in sales volume.

Income Before Income Taxes

For a corporation, fixed charges are subtracted from income before fixed charges and income taxes to arrive at the amount of income before income taxes.

Note that the statement of income for a proprietorship (Exhibit 1) does not include this line item. Again, this is because a business organized as a proprietorship does not pay income taxes—the owner does.

Income Taxes

The income taxes section of the statement of income includes federal and other government income taxes. Again, note that this line item does not appear on the statement of income for a proprietorship.

Net Income (or Loss)

The bottom line of the statement of income reveals the net income (or loss) of the operation for a stated period. This figure will indicate the overall success of operations for the period of time covered by the statement of income. The amount of net income shown for the corporate form of Deb's Steakhouse differs from that of the proprietorship form of business organization because:

- The owner of a proprietorship cannot be paid a salary or wage; thus there are also no applicable payroll taxes on that salary or wage.
- The owner of a proprietorship is not entitled to deductible benefits.
- The owner of a proprietorship pays the income taxes of the business on his or her personal income tax return.

Exhibit 3 Statement of Owner's Equity for a Proprietorship

Deb's Steakhouse
Statement of Owner's Equity
For the Year Ended December 31, 20X2

Deb Barry, Capital—January 1, 20X2	$ 91,000
Add Owner's Investments during the year	0
Add Net Income for the year ended December 31, 20X2	37,000
Total	128,000
Less Withdrawals during the year	30,000
Deb Barry, Capital—December 31, 20X2	$ 98,000

Notes:

1. The net income figure is from the Statement of Income illustrated in Exhibit 1.
2. The ending capital amount is transferred to the Balance Sheet illustrated in Exhibit 5.

Exhibit 4 Statement of Retained Earnings for a Corporation

Deb's Steakhouse, Inc.
Statement of Retained Earnings
For the Year Ended December 31, 20X2

Retained Earnings, January 1, 20X2	$43,000
Add Net Income for the year ended December 31, 20X2	15,000
Total	58,000
Less Dividends Declared during the year	0
Retained Earnings, December 31, 20X2	$58,000

Notes:

1. The net income figure is from the Statement of Income illustrated in Exhibit 2.
2. The ending retained earnings amount is transferred to the Balance Sheet illustrated in Exhibit 6.

Equity Statements

Equity statements reflect changes in equity that occurred during an accounting period. Exhibit 3 illustrates a statement of owner's equity prepared for a proprietorship and Exhibit 4 depicts a statement of retained earnings prepared for a corporation. The following sections explain the line items that appear on these equity statements.

Statement of Owner's Equity

The **statement of owner's equity** is prepared for a proprietorship form of business organization. The owner's capital account reflects the owner's residual claims to the assets of the business. The owner's claims are residual because they follow any claims to assets that creditors may have, as represented by the liabilities section of the balance sheet.

Exhibit 3 shows the statement of owner's equity for Deb's Steakhouse. Deb Barry's equity for the period just ended is calculated by adding net income and subtracting withdrawals from the amount of owner's equity shown on the previous statement of owner's equity prepared for the prior period. (Normally, the owner's investments are also added; however, the proprietor in this example did not make such investments in her business during the current year.) The net income figure is the same figure that appears on the bottom line of the statement of income in Exhibit 1.

Statement of Retained Earnings

The **statement of retained earnings** is prepared for the corporate form of business organization. Its purpose is to compute the amount of earnings retained by the corporation. *Retained Earnings* represents the lifetime profits of the business that have not been declared as dividends to the shareholders.

Exhibit 4 illustrates the statement of retained earnings for Deb's Steakhouse, Inc. Note that the amount of retained earnings for the period just ended is calculated by adding net income and subtracting dividends declared from the amount of retained earnings shown on the previous statement of retained earnings prepared for the prior period. The net income figure is the same as that appearing on the bottom line of the statement of income in Exhibit 2. *Dividends Declared* includes all dividends declared during the current accounting year regardless of whether they are paid or unpaid.

Balance Sheet

The **balance sheet** shows assets, liabilities, and equity, revealing the *financial position* of a business. This information is presented as of the close of business on a certain date. The expression used by accountants is that the balance sheet provides information *on a given date.* The phrase "on a given date" has an entirely different meaning from the phrase "for a stated period of time," which is used to describe the time period covered by an income statement.

For example, a balance sheet dated March 31 would present the status of financial information as of the close of business on that particular day. If you were counting the cash you presently have, you would state a dollar amount as it exists on the date you performed the count. All amounts shown on the balance sheet represent a status of existence on a certain day.

The balance sheet is composed of three major sections:

- Assets

- Liabilities
- Equity

Assets represent cash, receivables, inventories, equipment, property, and rights acquired by the business either by purchase or stockholder investment. Assets are items that are not used up at present; they have future utility or value.

Liabilities represent the debts of the business. Liabilities represent claims on assets by outsiders.

Equity represents the owner's financial interest in the business. Equity also represents a claim on the assets; however, this claim is by the owners, and it is a residual claim to those of the creditors.

Another way of looking at the balance sheet is that the assets represent the resources of the business and the liabilities and equity represent the claims on those resources. This pragmatic relationship is represented in the accounting equation:

Assets = Liabilities + Equity

The following sections discuss the assets, liabilities, and equity sections of the proprietorship and corporate balance sheets for Deb's Steakhouse as illustrated by Exhibits 5 and 6, respectively. A brief explanation of the line items appearing under the basic balance sheet categories is also provided. The only significant difference between balance sheets prepared for proprietorships and those prepared for corporations is in the equity section.

Current Assets

Current assets are defined as those assets that are convertible to cash within twelve months of the balance sheet date. Items appearing as current assets are usually listed in the order of their liquidity—that is, the ease with which they can be converted to cash.

Cash. Cash consists of cash in house banks, cash in checking and savings accounts, and certificates of deposit.

Accounts Receivable. This line item includes all amounts due from customers carried by the restaurant on open accounts.

Inventories. This line item includes merchandise held for resale, such as food provisions and liquor stock. Inventories also include operating supplies such as guest supplies, office supplies, and cleaning supplies.

Prepaid Expenses. This line item shows the value of prepayments whose benefits will expire within twelve months of the balance sheet date. Prepaid expense items may include prepaid interest, rent, taxes, and licenses.

Property and Equipment

The property and equipment portion of the balance sheet lists noncurrent assets. The major noncurrent assets are land, buildings, and equipment. The costs for Building and for Furniture and Equipment that appear on the balance sheets for Deb's Steakhouse are decreased by amounts shown as Accumulated Depreciation.

Exhibit 5 Balance Sheet for a Proprietorship

Deb's Steakhouse
Balance Sheet
December 31, 20X2

		ASSETS		
CURRENT ASSETS				
Cash			$34,000	
Accounts Receivable			4,000	
Inventories			5,000	
Prepaid Expenses			2,000	
Total Current Assets				$ 45,000
PROPERTY AND EQUIPMENT				
	Cost	Accumulated Depreciation		
Land	$ 30,000			
Building	60,000	$15,000		
Furniture and Equipment	52,000	25,000		
China, Glassware, Silver	8,000			
Total	150,000	40,000		110,000
OTHER ASSETS				
Security Deposits			1,500	
Preopening Expenses			2,500	
Total Other Assets				4,000
TOTAL ASSETS				$159,000
		LIABILITIES		
CURRENT LIABILITIES				
Accounts Payable			$11,000	
Sales Tax Payable			1,000	
Accrued Expenses			9,000	
Current Portion of Long-Term Debt			6,000	
Total Current Liabilities				$ 27,000
LONG-TERM LIABILITIES				
Mortgage Payable			40,000	
Less Current Portion of Long-Term Debt			6,000	
Net Long-Term Liabilities				34,000
TOTAL LIABILITIES				61,000
		OWNER'S EQUITY		
Capital, Deb Barry—December 31, 20X2				98,000
TOTAL LIABILITIES AND OWNER'S EQUITY				$159,000

Exhibit 6 Balance Sheet for a Corporation

Deb's Steakhouse, Inc.
Balance Sheet
December 31, 20X2

	Cost	Accumulated Depreciation		
ASSETS				
CURRENT ASSETS				
Cash			$34,000	
Accounts Receivable			4,000	
Inventories			5,000	
Prepaid Expenses			2,000	
Total Current Assets				$ 45,000
PROPERTY AND EQUIPMENT				
Land	$ 30,000			
Building	60,000	$15,000		
Furniture and Equipment	52,000	25,000		
China, Glassware, Silver	8,000			
Total	150,000	40,000		110,000
OTHER ASSETS				
Security Deposits			1,500	
Preopening Expenses			2,500	
Total Other Assets				4,000
TOTAL ASSETS				$159,000
LIABILITIES				
CURRENT LIABILITIES				
Accounts Payable			$11,000	
Sales Tax Payable			1,000	
Accrued Expenses			9,000	
Current Portion of Long-Term Debt			6,000	
Total Current Liabilities				$ 27,000
LONG-TERM LIABILITIES				
Mortgage Payable			40,000	
Less Current Portion of Long-Term Debt			6,000	
Net Long-Term Liabilities				34,000
TOTAL LIABILITIES				61,000
STOCKHOLDERS' EQUITY				
Common Stock				
Par Value $1				
Authorized 50,000 shares				
Issued 25,000 shares			25,000	
Additional Paid-In Capital			15,000	
Total Paid-In Capital				40,000
Retained Earnings, December 31, 20X2				58,000
TOTAL STOCKHOLDERS' EQUITY				98,000
TOTAL LIABILITIES AND STOCKHOLDERS' EQUITY				$159,000

Depreciation spreads the cost of an asset over the term of its useful life. **Depreciation expense** is the cost of depreciation for only the current accounting period; it is shown on the income statement. **Accumulated depreciation** is the sum of all depreciation from prior years to the present and is shown on the balance sheet. It is important to stress that this procedure is not an attempt to establish the market values of assets. The cost of the asset minus the amount of its accumulated depreciation leaves the net asset value, or what is sometimes called the "book value." This should not be confused with market value—the value that the asset could bring if sold on the open market.

Accumulated depreciation does not affect the noncurrent asset Land because land does not wear out *in the normal course of business.* Accumulated depreciation also does not affect China, Glassware, and Silver on the balance sheet because amounts for deterioration, breakage, and loss have already been deducted directly from this asset account.

Other Assets

The other assets portion of the balance sheet includes assets that do not apply to line items previously discussed. Security deposits include funds deposited with public utility companies (for instance, telephone, water, electric, and gas companies) and other funds used for similar types of deposits. Preopening expenses include capitalized expenses incurred before the opening of the property.

Current Liabilities

Current liabilities are obligations that will require settlement within twelve months of the balance sheet date. The total current liabilities alerts the restaurant operator to cash requirements of the operation and is often compared with the total figure for current assets.

Accounts Payable. This line item shows the total of unpaid invoices due to creditors from whom the restaurant receives merchandise or services in the ordinary course of business.

Sales Tax Payable. This line item includes all sales taxes collected from customers that are payable to federal or local governmental agencies.

Accrued Expenses. This line item lists the total amount of expenses incurred for the period up to the balance sheet date but that are not payable until after the balance sheet date and have not been shown elsewhere as a current liability.

Current Portion of Long-Term Debt. Since the total figure for current liabilities includes all obligations that will require an outlay of cash within twelve months of the balance sheet date, this line item includes the principal portion of long-term debt that is due within one year of the balance sheet date.

Long-Term Liabilities

A long-term liability (also called long-term debt) is any debt *not* due within twelve months of the balance sheet date. Any portion of long-term debt that is due within twelve months of the balance sheet date is subtracted from the total outstanding obligation and is shown in the current liabilities portion of the balance sheet.

Equity Section

Exhibit 5 shows the equity section of the balance sheet prepared for a proprietorship. The Owner's Equity line item shows the interests of the sole owner in the assets of Deb's Steakhouse. The figure for Deb Barry's Capital account in Exhibit 5 is the same figure that appears as the current balance on the statement of owner's equity in Exhibit 3. If the balance sheet were prepared for a partnership, the interests of each partner would be shown as line items under Partners' Equity. Changes in equity accounts of the partners would be shown in a statement of partners' equity whose format would be similar to that of the statement of owner's equity.

Exhibit 6 shows the equity section of the balance sheet prepared for a corporate form of business organization. *Common Stock* shows the par value, the number of shares authorized, and the number of shares issued. *Additional Paid-In Capital* shows the total amount for cash, property, and other capital contributed by stockholders in excess of the par value of the common stock. *Retained Earnings* includes that portion of net income earned by the corporation that is not distributed as dividends, but is retained in the business. The figure for Retained Earnings in Exhibit 6 is the same as that shown at the bottom of the statement of retained earnings in Exhibit 4.

Statement of Cash Flows

The major purpose of the **statement of cash flows (SCF)** is to provide information about where a company's cash came from and where that cash was spent. Its focus is on **cash provided** or **cash used** and not on profit or loss. Cash flow is the net result of cash receipts minus cash payments. If cash receipts exceed cash payments, the cash flow is positive, also called a cash inflow, meaning cash has been *provided* by an activity. If the cash payments exceed the cash receipts, the cash flow is negative, also called a cash outflow, meaning cash has been *used* by an activity. The statement of cash flows is shown in Exhibit 7; note that there are three major sections:

- Operating activities
- Investing activities
- Financing activities

The ending cash shown on the SCF must reconcile with the cash shown on the balance sheet. Note that the ending cash of $34,000 on the SCF in Exhibit 7 is equal to the cash amount on the balance sheet in Exhibit 6.

Operating Activities

The **operating activities** section shows either the cash provided or cash used from the primary day-to-day operating activity of a business. For a restaurant, the primary day-to-day operating activity is cash generated from sales of food and

Exhibit 7 Statement of Cash Flows

Deb's Steakhouse, Inc.
Statement of Cash Flows
December 31, 20X2

Cash Flows from Operating Activities:		
Cash provided from operations		$ 27,000
Cash Flows from Investing Activities:		
Cash proceeds from sale of equipment	$ 5,000	
Deposit on vehicles	(20,000)	
Cash used by investing activities		(15,000)
Cash Flows from Financing Activities:		
Issuance of 1,000 shares of common stock	11,000	
Payment of 20X1 dividends declared	(1,000)	
Cash provided from financing activities		10,000
Increase (decrease) in cash for the year		$ 22,000
Cash at the beginning of the year		12,000
Cash at the end of the year		$ 34,000

beverages. For a hotel, the primary day-to-day operating activity is cash generated from rooms, dining room, gift shop, and other departments of the hotel. The generation of cash will be different from income because not all sales result in an immediate cash receipt and not all expenses require an immediate cash payment.

Investing Activities

The **investing activities** section shows the cash provided from the sale of or cash used for the purchase of:

- Short-term and other investments.
- Land, buildings, and other property.
- Equipment.

For example, if a hotel purchased several vehicles with a $20,000 cash deposit and a $75,000 bank loan; the cash *used* is $20,000; this amount would appear in the investing activities section of the statement of cash flows.

Financing Activities

The **financing activities** section shows the cash provided from activities such as issuance of capital stock or bonds and cash borrowings.

The financing activities section also shows cash used from activities such as payment of dividends and payment on the debt portion of cash borrowings.

Key Terms

accumulated depreciation—The sum of all depreciation from prior years to the present. It is recorded on the balance sheet.

annual financial statements—Statements issued at the end of a business year.

assets—Cash, receivables, inventories, equipment, property, and other rights of a business.

balance sheet—A financial statement showing a business's financial position on a given date in terms of assets, liabilities, and equity.

cash provided—A positive cash flow situation in which cash receipts exceed cash payments; also called cash inflow.

cash used—A negative cash flow situation in which cash payments exceed cash receipts; also called cash outflow.

cost of goods sold—See cost of sales.

cost of sales—A term that shows the cost of merchandise used in the sales process.

current assets—Cash and other assets that can be converted to cash within twelve months of the balance sheet date.

current liabilities—Debts of the business that must be settled within twelve months of the balance sheet date.

depreciation—A term defining the practice of spreading the cost of an asset over the term of its useful life.

depreciated expense—The cost of depreciation for only the current accounting period. It is recorded on the income statement.

financing activities—A section of the SCF that shows either the cash provided or cash used in transactions involving capital stock, cash loans, payment of dividends and on the debt portion of cash borrowings.

fiscal year—Business year. Can be any twelve consecutive months.

fixed charges—Expenses incurred regardless of sales volume. Also referred to as occupancy costs.

gross profit—The result of net sales minus cost of sales.

interim financial statements—Statements issued during the business year.

investing activities—A section of the SCF that shows either the cash provided or cash used in transactions involving investments, property, and equipment.

liabilities—The debts of a business.

operating expenses—A section of the statement of income that lists expenses that are most directly influenced by operating policy and management efficiency.

operating activities—A section of the SCF that shows either the cash provided or cash used by the primary day-to-day business activity.

revenue—The amounts billed for sales of merchandise and services.

SCF—See statement of cash flows.

statement of cash flows—A financial statement showing where cash came from and how it was spent.

statement of income—A financial statement showing revenue and expenses for the purpose of reporting on the results of operations.

statement of owner's equity—A financial statement prepared for a proprietorship that shows the owner's capital interest, which is the sum of his or her investments and income or assets not withdrawn for personal use.

statement of retained earnings—A financial statement prepared for a corporation that shows the lifetime earnings of the business that have not been declared as dividends.

Review Questions

1. What is the purpose of the statement of income?
2. What are the basic categories that appear on the statement of income?
3. What is the difference between revenue and net income?
4. What is the purpose of the statement of owner's equity and the statement of retained earnings?
5. What is the purpose of the balance sheet?
6. What are the major categories that appear on the balance sheet?
7. What is the definition of current assets? Give examples.
8. What is the definition of property and equipment? Give examples.
9. What is the purpose of the statement of cash flows?
10. What are the three activities sections and their purpose on the statement of cash flows?

Problems

Problem 1

Compute the cost of sales from the following information.

Food Sales	$80,000
Cost of Food Used	23,000
Employee Meals Served	500

Problem 2

Compute the gross profit from the following information:

Sales	$100,000
Cost of Sales	33,000
Payroll	30,000
Operating Expenses	12,000

Problem 3

Compute the total assets from the following information.

Cash	$15,000
Food Inventory	4,000
Food Sales	100,000
Common Stock Issued	26,000
Accounts Receivable	5,000
Land	30,000
Retained Earnings	32,000
Building	80,000
Furniture & Equipment	22,000
Accounts Payable	2,500
Additional Paid-In Capital	8,000

Problem 4

On which financial statements would the following items be presented?

Cash	______________
Accounts Payable	______________
Food Sales	______________
Withdrawals	______________
Common Stock Issued	______________
Dividends Payable	______________
Payroll Expense	______________
Food Inventory	______________
Prepaid Expenses	______________
Cost of Sales	______________
Land	______________
Accounts Receivable	______________
Advertising Expense	______________
Prepaid Advertising	______________
Mortgage Payable	______________

Problem 5

Sales are $50,000; cost of sales is $15,000; and all other expenses total $40,000. Determine the amount of revenue based on this information.

Problem 6

Compute the ending cash balance if the beginning cash balance was $40,000 and the SCF shows the following:

Cash Used by Operating Activities	$10,000
Cash Used by Investing Activities	20,000
Cash Provided by Financing Activities	25,000

Problem 7

Specify whether each of the following statements is true (T) or false (F).

_______ 1. The income statement represents the financial position of a business.

_______ 2. Retained earnings represent the lifetime profits of the business that have not been declared as dividends to the shareholders.

_______ 3. The proper way to write a date for a balance sheet as of the year ended December 31, 20XX is as follows: December 31, 20XX.

_______ 4. *Fiscal year* is another term for *business year.*

_______ 5. *Accumulated depreciation* is another term for *depreciation expense.*

_______ 6. *Dividends declared* is another term for *dividends payable.*

_______ 7. *Cost of goods sold* is another term for *cost of sales.*

_______ 8. *Sales* is another term for *revenue.*

_______ 9. Land is not depreciated in hospitality industry accounting.

_______ 10. The balance sheet shows revenue and expenses.

Problem 8

Use the following information to prepare an income statement for Wings Diner, Inc., for the year ended March 31, 20XX. Use the proper statement heading and a format similar to that used in the textbook for Deb's Steakhouse, Inc.

Payroll	$ 50,000
Employee Benefits	9,500
Cost of Food Sold	30,000
Cost of Liquor Sold	15,000
Food Sales	$100,000
Utilities	5,000
Depreciation	10,000
Income Taxes	300
Property Insurance	6,000
Supplies Expense	3,000
Rent	8,750
Liquor Sales	50,000
Interest	7,000
Advertising	2,250
Property Taxes	2,000

Problem 9

An analysis of the financial information provided by a business shows that its debts total $307,000 and that the owner's equity in the business is $182,000. From this information, determine the total assets of this company.

Problem 10

Curfew Inn is a proprietorship owned by Susan Plies. For the year ended December 31, 20X2, the net income of the lodging operation was $38,500. During that year, Susan invested $20,000 and withdrew $27,000. The financial records show that the bookkeeping account called *Capital, Susan Plies* had a balance of $12,750 on December 31, 20X1.

Prepare a statement of owner's equity for the year ended December 31, 20X2.

Problem 11

For the year ended December 31, 20X9, the net income of National Motels, Inc., was $85,900. The Retained Earnings account on January 1, 20X9, showed a balance of $62,000. During the year 20X9 the board of directors declared the following dividends to its stockholders:

May 21:	$8,500
November 28	$8,500

The dividends declared on November 28 have not been paid as of December 31, 20X9. Prepare a statement of retained earnings for the year ended December 31, 20X9.

Problem 12

Using the following information, prepare a balance sheet on December 31, 20X7, for the Summer Resort, a proprietorship owned by Stan Robins. The statement of owner's equity prepared for the year ended December 31, 20X7, shows a total of $97,000. The asset and liability bookkeeping accounts show the following balances on December 31, 20X7:

Accumulated Depreciation on Equipment	$ 5,000
Accounts Receivable	9,000
Cost of Furniture	40,000
Cost of Equipment	10,000
Accumulated Depreciation on Building	20,000
Accumulated Depreciation on Furniture	20,000
Cost of Building	$182,000
Cash	16,500
Land	20,000
Accounts Payable	8,000
Accrued Expenses	9,700
Prepaid Expenses	2,500
Wages Payable	4,100
Inventories	3,800

Mortgage Payable is $120,000, of which $15,000 is due currently.

Problem 13

Prepare the statement of cash flows from the following information.

Cash At Beginning of Year	$45,000
Cash Provided from Operations	30,000
Cash Proceeds from Sale of Equipment	10,000
Deposit on New Equipment	12,000
Issuance of Capital Stock	15,000
Payment of Dividends Declared	7,000

Ethics Case

Dekkon Foods & Lodging, Inc., is managed by executives who understand the value of ethics in the hospitality industry. They want to sharpen their own ideological ethical attitudes and foster those of their supervisory employees in order to benefit the company's customers, employees, and other stakeholders.

To accomplish this purpose, management has hired a consultant to conduct several seminars on ethics. The first seminar covered the following three basic principles involved in ethical decision-making:

- The Principle of Utilitarianism. This principle asks "What decision will provide the greatest amount of good for the greatest amount of people?"
- The Principle of Rights. This principle states that human beings have certain moral rights that must be respected at all times regardless of factors such as race, religion, or economic status.
- The Principle of Justice. This principle means that everyone should be treated fairly in matters that involve administration of rules, assignment of job duties, promotions, and compensation.

1. Which principle(s) is/are involved when management is considering the administration of lie detector tests to employees? Discuss any controversial elements or constraints involved in evaluating this action.
2. Which principle(s) is/are involved when management is writing policies for promotion? Discuss any controversial elements or constraints involved in evaluating this action.
3. Which principle(s) is/are involved when management is estimating the staffing levels required to serve guests? Discuss any controversial elements or constraints involved in evaluating this action.

Chapter 4 Outline

- Asset Classification
- Current Asset Accounts
  - Cash
  - Short-Term Investments
  - Accounts Receivable
  - Inventories
  - Prepaid Expenses
- Noncurrent Asset Accounts
  - Investments
  - Property and Equipment
  - Other Assets
- Liability Classification
- Current Liability Accounts
  - Accounts Payable
  - Sales Tax Payable
  - Income Taxes Payable
  - Accrued Payables
  - Advance Deposits
  - Current Maturities of Long-Term Debt
- Long-Term Liability Accounts
  - Reclassification Example
- Bonds
  - Types of Bonds
  - Bond Prices
  - Bonds Issued at a Discount
  - Bonds Issued at a Premium
  - Bond Sinking Fund
- Equity Classification
- Proprietorship Equity Accounts
  - Capital
  - Withdrawals
- Partnership Equity Accounts
- Corporation Equity Accounts
  - Common Stock Issued
  - Additional Paid-In Capital
  - Retained Earnings
  - Preferred Stock Issued
  - Donated Capital
  - Treasury Stock
  - Stockholders' Equity on the Balance Sheet
- Limited Liability Company Equity Accounts

Competencies

1. Identify and describe the asset accounts. (pp. 78–85)
2. Identify and describe the liability accounts. (pp. 85–89)
3. Identify the types of, and describe the accounting for, bonds. (pp. 89–91)
4. Identify and describe the equity accounts. (pp. 91–99)

4

Analysis of Balance Sheet Accounts

THE THREE MAJOR FINANCIAL STATEMENTS are the balance sheet, income statement, and statement of cash flows. Of these three, there is an inclination to give the least attention to the balance sheet because of its lackluster content and complexity. The balance sheet reports on the financial position of a company; this is another way of saying that the balance sheet shows the financial health of a company. Instead of looking at where a company has been (income statement), the financial data on the balance sheet reports on the *present status* of a company. This status can give an indication of inherent future difficulties for the company to operate as a going concern.

The balance sheet is prepared from the *assets, liabilities,* and *equity* account classifications, collectively referred to as **balance sheet accounts**. The specific balance sheet accounts used by any company depend on its size and industry. However, a representative listing of the balance sheet accounts found in most companies is shown in Exhibit 1.

The structure and composition of the balance sheet results in a factual portrayal of the accounting equation:

Assets = Liabilities + Equity

The arrangement of these accounts on the balance sheet can be in either an *account* format or a *report* format. The account format is a two-column document that lists the assets on the left side of the report and the liabilities and equity on the right side. The report format shows all the accounts in a single column. A preponderance of the business community prefers the report format.

Every business has assets, liabilities, and equity. The balance sheet content and format is similar for all types of industries—hotels, restaurants, travel agencies, retail, and manufacturing.

This chapter gives an in-depth description of the balance sheet accounts and provides answers to such questions as:

1. Which accounts are current assets, investments, property and equipment, and other assets?
2. Which accounts are current liabilities and long-term liabilities?
3. What are bonds payable, types of bonds, bond prices, and sinking fund?
4. What are the components of equity for a proprietorship, partnership, and corporation?

Exhibit 1 Balance Sheet Accounts

ASSET ACCOUNTS

Cash	Land
Short-Term Investments	Building
Accounts Receivable	Furniture & Eqiupment
Food Inventory	China, Glassware, Silver
Beverage Inventory	Linen
Office Supplies Inventory	Uniforms
Operating Supplies Inventory	Organization Costs
Prepaid Insurance	Security Deposits
Prepaid Rent	

LIABILITY ACCOUNTS

Accounts Payable	Accrued Interest
Sales Tax Payable	Advance Deposits
Income Taxes Payable	Current Maturities of Long-Term Debt
Accrued Payroll	Notes Payable
Accrued Payroll Taxes	Mortgage Payable
Accrued Property Taxes	

EQUITY ACCOUNTS

For Corporations:	**For Proprietorships or Partnerships**
Common Stock Issued	Capital, (owner's name)
Additional Paid-In Capital	Withdrawals, (owner's name)
Retained Earnings	

Asset Classification

Assets are items owned by the business that have a commercial or exchange value and are expected to provide a future use or benefit to the business. Ownership in this case refers to possession of legal title and, thus, applies to assets purchased on credit or financed by borrowings, in addition to those assets purchased with cash.

If the balance sheet simply listed all of these assets under one grouping, it would be difficult for the reader to easily perform analyses regarding the financial position of the company. For this reason, these assets are further divided into the following meaningful groups:

- Current assets
- Investments
- Property and equipment
- Other assets

The following sections define each of these categories and discuss individual accounts in some detail.

Current Asset Accounts

Current assets consist of cash or assets that are convertible to cash within twelve months of the balance sheet date. To be considered a current asset, an asset must be available without restriction for use in payment of current liabilities.

Among the major categories of current assets are the following accounts, listed here in order of liquidity:

- Cash
- Short-term investments
- Accounts receivable
- Inventories
- Prepaid expenses

Cash

Cash refers to currency, personal checks, travelers checks, and possibly credit and debit cards. Credit and debit card transactions are treated as cash if the cash is instantly available upon depositing the credit card vouchers with a local bank or processing through a merchant credit card services provider. Credit and debit cards are subject to credit card fees (also called commissions) that are an expense of doing business. If credit card volume is significant, these fees should be monitored and recorded daily. If they are not, the cash balance will be inflated.

For example, if a merchant (hospitality business) processes $5,000 of credit cards with a merchant services provider and the fee is one percent, then the merchant services provider transmits a deposit of $4,950 to the designated bank account of the hospitality business.

The bankcards (MasterCard and VISA) offer merchants a direct deposit service if a manual credit card voucher system is used. Under this direct bank deposit arrangement, the merchant receives funds for credit card deposits faster than if the merchant were on an electronic system with a credit card services provider. The retailer manually deposits the credit card vouchers at the retailer's bank and the deposit is treated similar to a cash deposit; there is no wait for a third party (credit card service provider) to transmit the deposit. The disadvantage of using credit card vouchers for manual direct deposit is that the credit card fee is generally higher.

Manual credit card preparation is not prevalent in the hospitality industry. Most hospitality operations use a credit card swipe machine as shown in Exhibit 2 that produces a credit card receipt voucher. These electronic swipe machines can be used as stand-alone units integrated with an electronic cash register (ECR) or point-of-sale (POS) system.

Any cash that is restricted for current use must be disclosed as such in the financial statements and a determination made whether the cash is to show under current assets or noncurrent assets. Two examples of restricted cash funds are *compensating balances* and *special-purpose funds.*

Exhibit 2 Credit Card Swipe Device

Courtesy Hypercom Corporation

A compensating balance usually takes the form of a minimum amount that must be maintained in a checking account as a stipulation of a borrowing arrangement with a bank. These compensating balances may be includable under current assets if the arrangement is short-term. Compensating balances required by long-term borrowing arrangements should be included under noncurrent assets, preferably Investments.

Special-purpose funds may be deposited in a special bank account and set aside by management for a specific purpose, such as acquisition of property or equipment. Cash that is earmarked, either voluntarily or by contract, for a special purpose relating to long-term needs should be included under noncurrent assets, preferably Investments.

Short-Term Investments

Short-term investments, known also as **marketable securities,** are trading securities (stocks, bonds) that meet the conditions of (1) being readily marketable and (2) earmarked by management for conversion into cash should the need arise.

Accounts Receivable

The most common receivable is **accounts receivable**, which represents the amounts owed to a firm by its customers.

Credit cards that do not have banking arrangements for converting the vouchers to immediate cash are treated as accounts receivable.

A hospitality business may issue its own credit cards (usually referred to as in-house credit cards) to the public. Any transactions on these cards are included in accounts receivable because the firm directly invoices and collects from the customer.

Allowance for Doubtful Accounts. A bookkeeping account called **Allowance for Doubtful Accounts** represents an estimate of potential receivables that may become uncollectible. Historical analysis and aging of the receivables are used to compute the estimated doubtful accounts. The allowance for doubtful accounts is a contra-asset account because it reduces a related asset, in this case, the receivables.

Notes Receivable. A promissory note (see Exhibit 3) is a written promise to pay a definite sum of money at some future date. When a promissory note is made payable to the hospitality company, the company is called the *payee* of the note. Promissory notes have two characteristics not normally associated with accounts receivable. First, they are negotiable instruments because they are legally transferable among parties by endorsement. Second, these notes generally involve the payment of interest in addition to the principal (amount of loan).

Notes receivable that are collectible within one year of the balance sheet date can be included under current assets. Long-term notes receivable should be included with the noncurrent assets under Investments.

Inventories

This current asset account includes stocks of food and beverage merchandise held for resale; stocks of operating supplies such as guest supplies, office supplies, cleaning supplies, and engineering supplies; and other supplies held for future use. **Inventories** are recorded in such bookkeeping accounts as Food Inventory, Beverage Inventory (Liquor Inventory), Gift Shop Inventory, Operating Supplies, Cleaning Supplies, Office Supplies, and Restaurant Supplies. Supplies of china, glassware, and silver are not current assets; these items are not intended to be consumed in the short term. They are longer-lived assets and properly belong in the Property and Equipment category.

Prepaid Expenses

Prepaid expenses are expenditures, usually recurring, that produce a measurable benefit that will affect more than one accounting period, but no more than twelve months. Examples of prepaid expenses include prepaid rent (excluding security deposits) and prepaid insurance premiums, both of which are paid in advance and benefit future accounting periods.

Prepaid expenses are commonly shown in separate accounts such as:

- Prepaid rent.
- Prepaid insurance.

Exhibit 3 Explanation of a Promissory Note Form

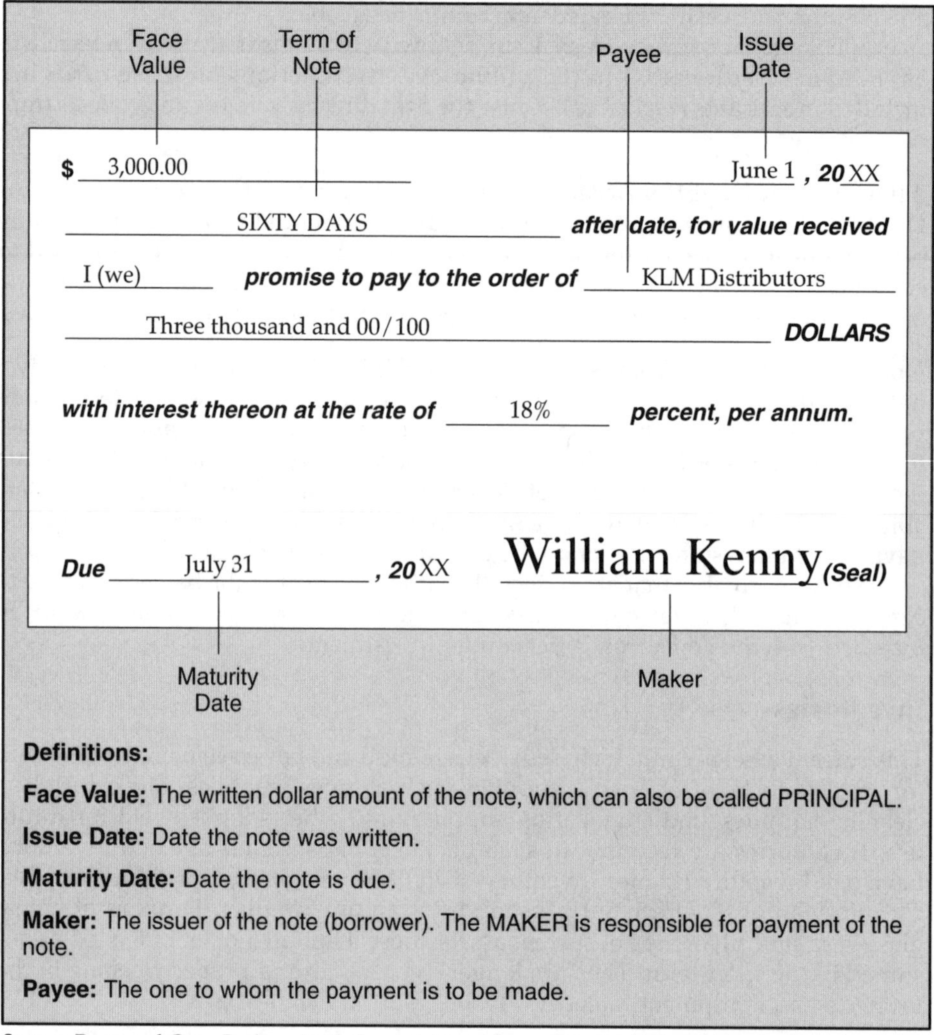

Definitions:

Face Value: The written dollar amount of the note, which can also be called PRINCIPAL.

Issue Date: Date the note was written.

Maturity Date: Date the note is due.

Maker: The issuer of the note (borrower). The MAKER is responsible for payment of the note.

Payee: The one to whom the payment is to be made.

Source: Raymond Cote, *Business Math Concepts* (Providence, R.I.: P.A.R. Inc., 1985), p. 54.

- Prepaid interest.
- Prepaid service contracts.

Technically, prepaid expenses are unexpired costs that will benefit future periods but are expected to expire within a relatively short period, usually within twelve months of the current accounting period.

For example, payment of the current month's rent on the first of the month or after is *not* a prepaid expense because it is for the current month of the accounting period. However, if the rent for July is paid in June, the payment of the July rent is recorded as prepaid rent in June.

Noncurrent Asset Accounts

Current assets are those assets that are convertible to cash within twelve months of the balance sheet date. By contrast, noncurrent assets are those assets that are *not* to be converted to cash within twelve months of the balance sheet date.

There are three major categories of noncurrent assets:

- Investments
- Property and Equipment
- Other Assets

The following sections discuss these three categories in more detail, providing definitions for some noncurrent asset accounts found in most businesses.

Investments

The Investments category can be bewildering because it has a different meaning in accounting and finance. In accounting, the term **investments** is a balance sheet category that does *not* include short-term investments. Instead, Investments is used to indicate noncurrent assets.

The most likely item to appear under Investments is the purchased corporate stock of affiliated companies or other companies for the purpose of influence or control. Other items that can appear under Investments are those securities that failed the short-term investment test, land held for expansion or future sale, and restricted cash accounts that are not readily available for use.

Property and Equipment

The noncurrent asset category of **Property and Equipment** includes those assets of a relatively permanent nature that are **tangible** (possess physical substance) and are used in the business operation to generate sales. These **long-lived assets** (assets with a life expectancy of more than one year) are also referred to as plant assets or **fixed assets**.

Property and Equipment accounts include such noncurrent assets as land, buildings, furniture, fixtures, vehicles, ovens, dishwashing machines, and other similar long-lived assets.

Typical fixed-asset accounts are:

- Land.
- Buildings.
- Furniture and Equipment.
- Transportation Equipment.
- China, Glassware, Silver, Linen, and Uniforms.

The preferred accounting treatment for china, glassware, silver, linens, and uniforms is to capitalize the cost of the initial purchase or complete replacement of these items.

Accumulated Depreciation. Depreciation is a method for allocating the cost of an asset over its useful life. The bookkeeping account **accumulated depreciation** contains the sum of these depreciation allocations for all prior years up to the present period. Accumulated depreciation is a contra-asset account because it reduces a related asset. The following do not have a related accumulated depreciation account:

- Land
- China, glassware, silver
- Linen
- Uniforms

In hospitality, as in most industries, land is not depreciated because it does not "wear out" or become consumed. (Land *can* be depreciated in such industries as mining and forestry; such depreciation is called *depletion*.) China, glassware, silver, linen, and uniforms use a different method of accounting for their limited life. Instead of using an accumulated deprecation account, the cost of these assets is directly reduced by a *depreciation factor*. The *Uniform System of Accounts for the Lodging Industry* recommends a life not to exceed three years and expensing any replacements.

Other Assets

The noncurrent asset category **other assets** consists of purchased **intangible assets** that are long-lived but have no physical substance; their ownership conveys certain rights and privileges to their owner.

Intangible assets are also depreciated, except that accounting uses the term *amortization* to represent the cost allocation of an intangible asset over its useful life. Another difference is that the amortization calculation is not set up in an accumulated account; instead, the calculation directly reduces the cost of the intangible assets.

The following discusses some of the more common intangible assets.

Security Deposits. Security deposits include funds deposited to secure occupancy or utility services (such as telephone, water, electricity, and gas) and any similar types of deposits.

Preopening Expenses. The *Uniform System of Accounts for the Lodging Industry* now recommends that preopening expenses should no longer be capitalized (recorded as an asset), but rather should be expensed in the year incurred. Those companies who previously capitalized preopening expenses may continue to show the remaining unamortized cost as an asset until it reaches zero. For that reason, we will present a discussion of preopening expenses as an asset. Importantly, it is acceptable for companies outside the United States to continue capitalizing and amortizing preopening expenses.

Organization Costs. Organization costs are expenditures incurred while legally forming the corporation and include such items as legal fees, stock certificate costs, accounting fees, promotional fees, incorporator's expenses, and underwriting fees to issue publicly held stock.

Trademarks and Trade Names. The federal government provides legal protection for trademarks and trade names if they are registered with the U.S. Patent Office. Material costs associated with their purchase are recorded as Trademarks and Trade Names, a noncurrent asset account.

Franchise Right. Franchising involves a long-term contract wherein the franchisor agrees to lend its name, goodwill, and back-up support to the franchisee. For these benefits, the franchisee agrees to maintain required quality standards and follow certain operating procedures. In addition, the franchisee pays the franchisor in the form of initial costs and annual fees.

An account called *Franchise Right* may be used to record the initial franchise cost, if material. Annual payments under a franchise agreement should be "expensed" by recording these expenditures to an expense account such as Franchise Fees Expense or Royalties Expense.

Goodwill. Goodwill has a different meaning in the fields of marketing and finance (accounting). A company may enjoy a superior product or reputation that obviously generates goodwill. However, any value for this goodwill would be arbitrary and cannot appear on the balance sheet of such company.

Goodwill *can* be recorded if it is the result of the purchase of a business and the price paid for the assets is in excess of the fair market value (FMV) of those assets. For example, a business purchased for $875,000 as shown below results in goodwill of $75,000:

	FMV
Land	$ 200,000
Building	500,000
Furniture & Equipment	100,000
Total FMV of assets purchased	$ 800,000
Price paid for the assets	875,000

Goodwill = Excess over FMV $ 75,000

Liability Classification

Liabilities are the debts of the business (what the business owes its creditors). Liabilities represent the claims of creditors on the assets of a business and are sometimes referred to as *creditors' equities.*

Liability is important because it reflects a present and future demand on the cash flow of a company. For this reason, the liabilities section of the balance sheet is divided into current liabilities and long-term liabilities.

Current Liability Accounts

Current liabilities are those liabilities that are due within twelve months of the balance sheet date. The settlement of current liabilities can be achieved by the payment of cash, the exchange of another current asset, replacement by another current liability, or other new financing.

The customary current liability accounts are:

- Accounts Payable.
- Sales Tax Payable.
- Income Taxes Payable.
- Accrued Payables.
- Advance Deposits.
- Current Maturities of Long-Term Debt.

Accounts Payable

Accounts payable result from verbal or implied promises to pay at some short-term future date. Such transactions usually arise when food, beverages, supplies, services, or utilities are purchased from vendors (also called suppliers or purveyors) *on credit.* Accounts payable are sometimes referred to as trade payables.

Sales Tax Payable

Taxes on retail sales are levied by many states and some cities. Usually the sales tax is imposed on the consumer; however, it is the seller who must collect the tax from the buyer, file the appropriate sales tax return, and remit the sales tax collected. Essentially, the seller acts as a collection agent for the taxing authority. Thus, sales taxes collected are a liability and are excluded from revenue (sales).

Income Taxes Payable

This account generally applies only to corporations as previously discussed. The federal government, most states, and some municipalities impose taxes on the taxable income of a corporation. A corporation might have three accounts as follows:

- Federal Income Tax Payable
- State Income Tax Payable
- Municipal Income Tax Payable

Accrued Payables

Accrued payables represent unrecorded expenses that, at the end of an accounting period, have been incurred but not yet paid. These unpaid expenses often require estimates, which may be computed by reference to historical data or by prescribed analytical procedures. The accrual of expenses is performed to comply with the matching principle—that is, to record expenses to the period in which they are incurred. Typical examples are:

- Accrued payroll.
- Accrued payroll taxes.

- Accrued property taxes.
- Accrued interest expense.

Advance Deposits

Advance deposits are customer payments to the business for goods and services that have not yet been provided. Advance deposits are customary for reservations for banquets and rooms. Advance deposits cannot be treated as revenue because the sale has not been earned; instead, the cash received is treated as a liability.

Current Maturities of Long-Term Debt

This is not a bookkeeping account. Instead, it is an amount transferred from long-term liabilities that is due within twelve months of the balance sheet date. These current maturities are also called **current portion of long-term debt**. A thorough explanation of current portion of long-term debt is provided in the following discussion of long-term liabilities.

Long-Term Liability Accounts

Long-term liabilities can consist of:

- Notes payable.
- Mortgages payable.
- Bonds payable.

Long-term liabilities are a **hybrid liability** because part of the liability can be a current liability and the remainder a long-term liability. A note or mortgage payable usually has monthly payment provisions and special attention is required for proper placement on the balance sheet. Each payment due within twelve months of the balance sheet date is reclassified and the sum is shown under current liabilities; the amount due after this 12-month period is shown under long-term liabilities.

Bonds are a major form of financing and are discussed later in this chapter.

Reclassification Example

We will use a 14-month note to illustrate how *reclassification* of long-term debt is performed. Assume that on February 15, 20X1, a business executed a 14-month loan for $14,000, with payment terms of $1,000 per month plus interest at a specified rate. Exhibit 4 shows the debt structure of this loan on the day the funds were borrowed.

The $14,000 debt requires monthly payments; therefore, the next twelve monthly payments of $1,000 represent a current liability called *current portion of long-term debt,* and the balance is classified as long-term debt. Since no payments have yet been made, the balance sheet at the end of the month will appear as follows:

Exhibit 4 Status of Note at Time of Loan: 2/15/X1

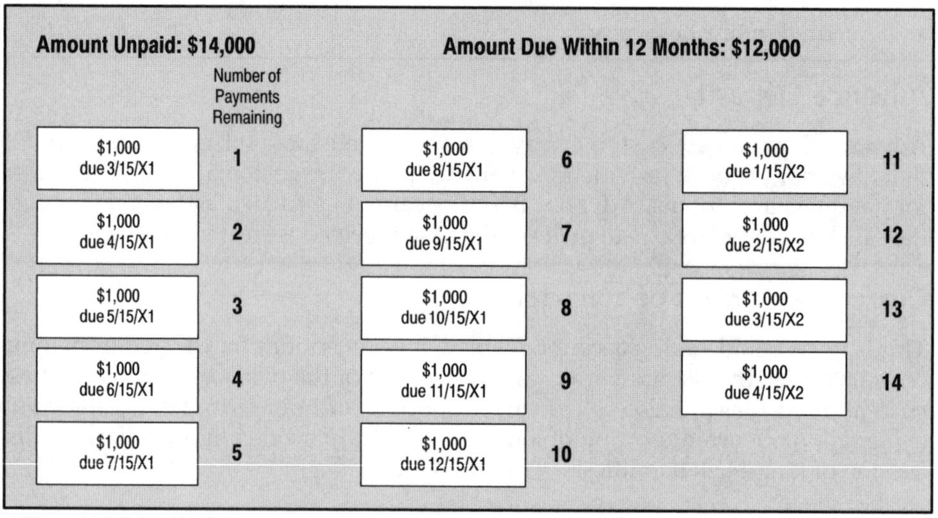

Amount Unpaid: $14,000 | **Amount Due Within 12 Months: $12,000**

Payment	Number of Payments Remaining	Payment	Number	Payment	Number
$1,000 due 3/15/X1	1	$1,000 due 8/15/X1	6	$1,000 due 1/15/X2	11
$1,000 due 4/15/X1	2	$1,000 due 9/15/X1	7	$1,000 due 2/15/X2	12
$1,000 due 5/15/X1	3	$1,000 due 10/15/X1	8	$1,000 due 3/15/X2	13
$1,000 due 6/15/X1	4	$1,000 due 11/15/X1	9	$1,000 due 4/15/X2	14
$1,000 due 7/15/X1	5	$1,000 due 12/15/X1	10		

Balance Sheet
February 28, 20X1

Current Liabilities:		
Current portion of long-term debt		$12,000
Long-Term Liabilities:		
Note Payable	$14,000	
Less current portion due	12,000	
Long-term debt		2,000

On March 15, a payment of $1,000 plus interest is made on the loan. Now the unpaid balance is $13,000. Exhibit 5 shows the debt structure of this loan after the first payment has been made.

The $13,000 unpaid balance requires monthly payments; therefore, the next twelve monthly payments of $1,000 represent a current liability, and the balance is classified as long-term debt. The balance sheet at the end of the month will appear as follows:

Balance Sheet
March 31, 20X1

Current Liabilities:		
Current portion of long-term debt		$12,000
Long-Term Liabilities:		
Note Payable	$13,000	
Less current portion due	12,000	
Long-term debt		1,000

On April 15, another payment of $1,000 plus interest is made on the loan. Now the unpaid balance is $12,000. Exhibit 6 shows the debt structure of this loan after the second payment has been made.

Exhibit 5 Status of Note After First Payment: 3/16/X1

Amount Unpaid: $13,000 **Amount Due Within 12 Months: $12,000**

Payment	Number of Payments Remaining	Payment	Number of Payments Remaining	Payment	Number of Payments Remaining
$1,000 due 4/15/X1	1	$1,000 due 8/15/X1	5	$1,000 due 1/15/X2	10
$1,000 due 5/15/X1	2	$1,000 due 9/15/X1	6	$1,000 due 2/15/X2	11
$1,000 due 6/15/X1	3	$1,000 due 10/15/X1	7	$1,000 due 3/15/X2	12
$1,000 due 7/15/X1	4	$1,000 due 11/15/X1	8	$1,000 due 4/15/X2	13
		$1,000 due 12/15/X1	9		

Exhibit 6 Status of Note After Second Payment: 4/16/X1

Amount Unpaid: $12,000 **Amount Due Within 12 Months: $12,000**

Payment	Number of Payments Remaining	Payment	Number of Payments Remaining	Payment	Number of Payments Remaining
		$1,000 due 8/15/X1	4	$1,000 due 1/15/X2	9
		$1,000 due 9/15/X1	5	$1,000 due 2/15/X2	10
$1,000 due 5/15/X1	1	$1,000 due 10/15/X1	6	$1,000 due 3/15/X2	11
$1,000 due 6/15/X1	2	$1,000 due 11/15/X1	7	$1,000 due 4/15/X2	12
$1,000 due 7/15/X1	3	$1,000 due 12/15/X1	8		

At this phase of the loan, there are only twelve monthly payments remaining. Therefore, the complete unpaid balance of $12,000 represents a current liability. The balance sheet at the end of the month will appear as follows:

Balance Sheet
April 30, 20X1

Current Liabilities:	
Note Payable	$12,000

Bonds

Bonds are a long-term liability and another form of notes payable. Companies might find it more attractive to raise large amounts of cash by issuing bonds than by taking out a commercial loan. Well-known companies can issue bonds with a lower interest rate than they would pay on a commercial loan. Bonds are typically sold in units of $1,000 (the **face value** or maturity value). Bonds generally pay interest twice a year to the bondholders. The issuing company is obligated to pay the holder of the bond its face value at a specified future date called the **maturity date.**

A **bond certificate** is evidence of ownership. A supporting legal document called a **bond indenture** explains the rights and privileges of the owner and any special terms and features.

Types of Bonds

The types of bonds are defined by their maturity dates, collateral, registration, and other properties. A bond may have one or more of these features.

Term and Serial Bonds. A bond that matures at a specified maturity date at its full face value is a **term bond**. A **serial bond** spreads the payment of its face value over several maturity dates.

Secured and Unsecured Bonds. Bonds backed with collateral of specific assets are **secured bonds**, also called mortgage bonds. **Debenture bonds** are unsecured bonds backed only by the good faith of the issuer.

Registered and Bearer Bonds. Bonds issued in the name of the owner are **registered bonds**. Bonds not registered in any name are called **bearer bonds** or coupon bonds because the holder must send in coupons to receive interest payments. Most bonds issued are registered bonds.

Convertible and Callable Bonds. Bonds that can be converted into common stock are **convertible bonds.** Bonds that can be called in and paid before the maturity date are **callable bonds.**

Bond Prices

Bonds, like stock, are traded on national markets and are attractive to many investors. A bond might not necessarily sell in these markets at its face value. If a bond bears an interest rate more attractive than current offerings or money market rates, that bond could sell for more than its face value. Conversely, if money market rates are more attractive than a bond's stated rate, it might sell at less than its face value. Bond prices are quoted at a percentage of their maturity value. A bond quoted at 100 means its price is $1,000 (100% × $1,000) and a bond quoted at 95 means its price is $950 (95% × $1,000). A bond may be originally issued at a discount or a premium from its face value. Many factors influence the price of bonds—the trend of interest rates, the reputation of the issuer, and market conditions.

Bonds Issued at a Discount

At original issue, a bond might sell at less than its face value because of the issuer's reputation or because the bond's stated interest rate is less than market rates. For example, a company may issue $3,000,000 of face value bonds but sell them at $2,700,000. The $300,000 is called a **discount** and is an expense that will be

Exhibit 7 Financial Structure of a Proprietorship

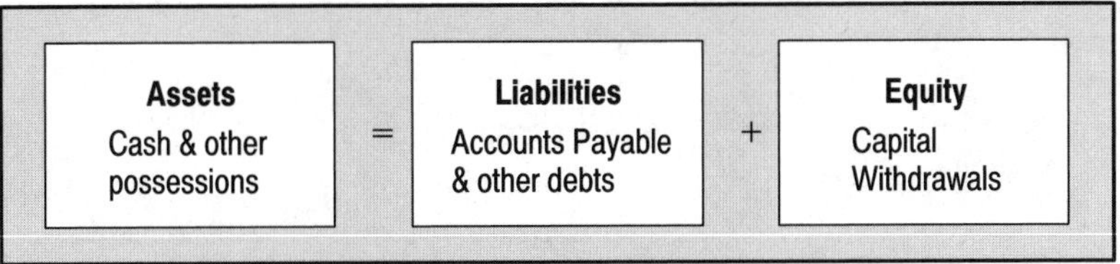

amortized over the life of the bond because, at maturity, the issuing company must pay the $3,000,000 face value.

Bonds Issued at a Premium

At original issue, a bond might sell at more than its face value because the bond's stated interest rate is more than market rates. For example, a company may issue $3,000,000 of face value bonds but sell them at $3,200,000. The $200,000 is called a **premium**; it is treated as a reduction of interest expense and the premium will be amortized over the life of the bond because at maturity, the issuing company need only pay the $3,000,000 face value.

Bond Sinking Fund

To make a bond more attractive, a **sinking fund** provision under the control of a trustee such as a bank or trust company is used. A sinking fund is cash (or other assets) periodically put aside specifically to retire the bond debt. This cash can be invested and it is expected that the sinking fund payments and any interest or other income will be sufficient to pay the face value at maturity date. The sinking fund is reported in the investment section of the balance sheet.

Equity Classification

The **equity accounts** represent the claims of the owner(s) on the assets of the business. By contrast, the liability accounts represent creditors' claims on the assets. Taken together, these accounts support the fundamental accounting equation:

Assets = Liabilities + Equity

This equation can be restated as:

Assets = Claims of Creditors + Claims of Owners

The types of equity accounts depend upon whether the company is a proprietorship, partnership, corporation, or limited liability company.

Proprietorship Equity Accounts

A proprietorship requires only two equity accounts: a *capital account* to represent the owner's financial interest in the business and a *withdrawals account* to accumulate the cash drawings or other assets withdrawn from the business by the owner. Exhibit 7 illustrates the financial structure and the components of the equity section

Exhibit 8 Effect of Equity Transactions in a Proprietorship

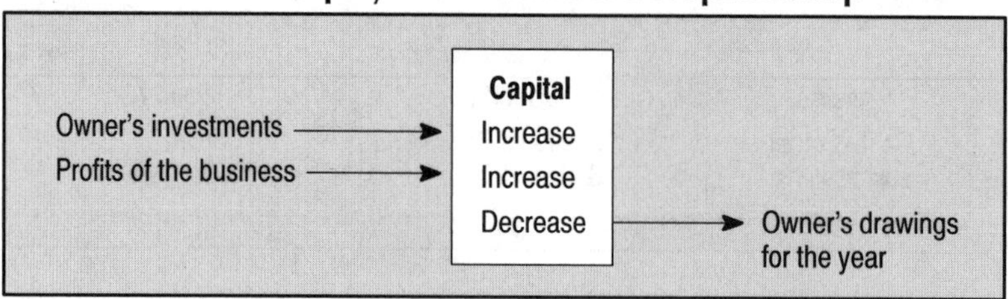

of a proprietorship. The two bookkeeping accounts used to record equity transactions are capital (owner's name) and withdrawals (owner's name).

The types of equity transactions that may occur for a proprietorship form of business organization include:

- The owner investing personal cash or property in the business.
- The owner withdrawing cash or property from the business for personal use.
- The business records either an operating profit or loss for the accounting period.

Exhibit 8 illustrates how the equity section of a proprietorship is affected by the various equity transactions.

Capital

The **capital account** represents the owner's financial interest in the business. It reflects the equity transactions between the business and its owner.

An owner's financial interest in the proprietorship is increased whenever the owner makes personal investments in the business. These personal investments can be in the form of cash, equipment, or property.

The capital account is also increased by the profits of the business because the profits belong to the owner of a proprietorship. These profits increase the capital account regardless of the amount of withdrawals made by the owner.

Withdrawals

The **withdrawals account** is a temporary bookkeeping account used to accumulate the owner's drawings from the proprietorship. Some accountants refer to this account as the *drawings* account.

An owner may withdraw cash, inventory, or other assets from the business. The effect of these drawings is to reduce his or her financial interest (equity) in the proprietorship. The sum in the withdrawals account is used to reduce the capital account.

Partnership Equity Accounts

Accounting for a partnership is similar to that of a proprietorship, with the exception that the transactions of two or more owners are involved. Therefore, each

Exhibit 9 Financial Structure of a Partnership

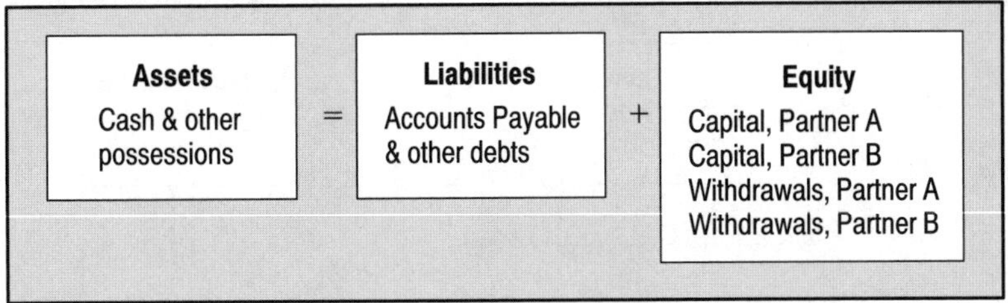

Exhibit 10 Financial Structure of a Corporation

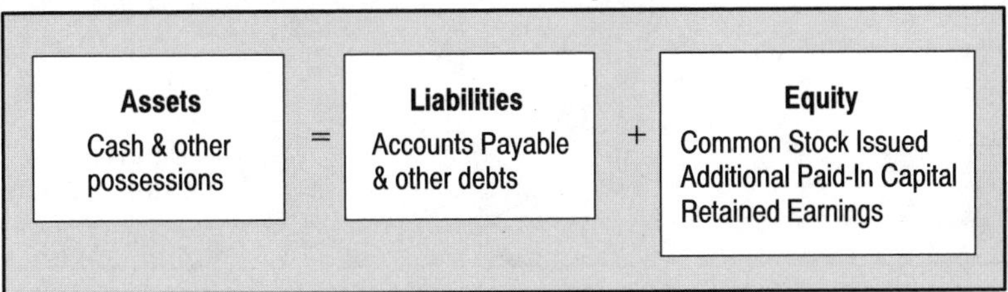

owner requires individual capital and withdrawals accounts. The partnership's net income or loss is allocated to each partner in accordance with the division of profits as specified in the partnership agreement. In the absence of an agreement, the income (or loss) of the partnership is divided equally among the partners.

Exhibit 9 illustrates the financial structure and the components of the equity section of a partnership having two partners. Notice that each partner has his or her own capital and withdrawals account.

Corporation Equity Accounts

The equity section for a corporation may be labeled Stockholders' Equity or Shareholders' Equity; the terms are interchangeable. The equity section of a corporation is more involved than that for a proprietorship or partnership because the corporation is a legal entity separate from its owners.

A simple corporate structure, as shown in Exhibit 10, includes the following equity accounts:

- Common Stock Issued
- Additional Paid-In Capital
- Retained Earnings

A more complex corporate structure might include these equity accounts:

- Preferred Stock Issued
- Donated Capital
- Treasury Stock

Exhibit 11 Effect of Equity Transactions in a Corporation

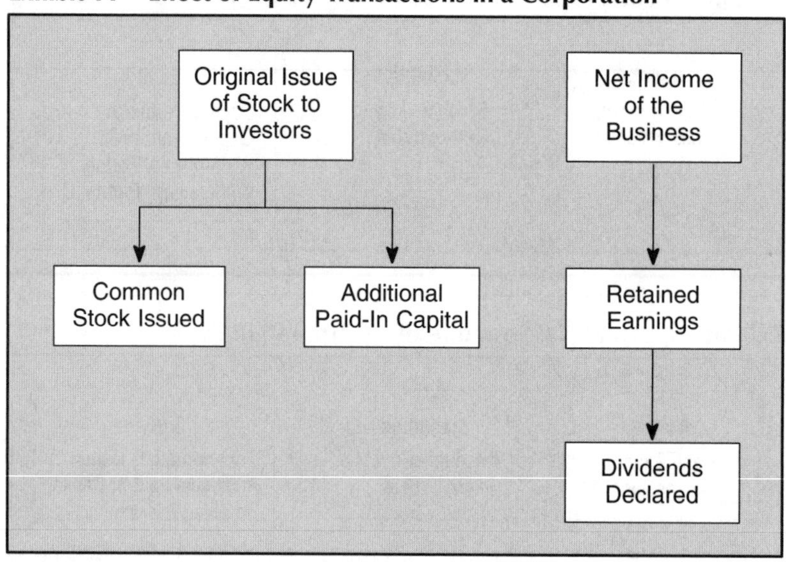

A corporation owns its assets, owes its liabilities, and has legal claim to its earnings. Earnings may be distributed to stockholders in the form of dividends. These dividends first must be declared by the corporation's board of directors. The board is the only governing body with the power to declare dividends.

Usually, the owner's original investment to start a business is used to purchase stock of the corporation. This stock will provide the owner with voting rights used for, among other things, the election of the board of directors. The purchase of this stock may result in additional paid-in capital, as explained later. The corporation's earnings are kept (retained) by the corporation until they are declared as dividends to the shareholders.

Exhibit 11 illustrates how the equity section of a corporation is affected by the various equity transactions.

Common Stock Issued

The stock issued as shown on the financial statement of a corporation is the original issue of its stock to its initial investors. After this original issue, the investors may sell their stock to other investors. This after-issue sale of stock does not affect the corporation's financial records because the corporation is not a party to these market transactions.

Common stock issued is shown on the financial statement at **par value**. The par value is selected by the corporation when it files its articles of incorporation; par value does not have any relationship whatsoever to its real value.

Usually, the par value selected is very low, generally ranging from 1¢ to $1 per share. Low par values are selected because certain states levy a tax on the corporation for its par value of stock, and par value represents the legal capital that must

Exhibit 12 Common Stock Issued and Additional Paid-In Capital

Stock	Amount Recorded as Common Stock Issued	Amount Recorded as Additional Paid-In Capital
Par value	Par value	Excess over par value
No-par with stated value	Stated value	Excess over stated value
No-par without stated value	Entire proceeds	None

be retained by the corporation for protection of its creditors. Thus, most states mandate that a corporation cannot sell its stock below par value.

Because of the confusion between par value and market value, some corporations issue *no-par value stock.* The entire proceeds received from the sale of no-par value stock becomes the legal capital per share, and this amount is the basis for recording to Common Stock Issued. For example, if $50,000 was received from the original sale of no-par value stock, $50,000 would be recorded to the Cash account and the Common Stock Issued account. One disadvantage of no-par value stock is that some states levy a high tax on this type of common stock.

In many states, a company's board of directors is permitted to assign a stated value to no-par value stock which becomes the legal capital per share. Stated value, like par value, has no relationship to market value. The board of directors may change the stated value at any time.

Additional Paid-In Capital

Because par value or stated value does not reflect the stock's real value, the proceeds received from the original issue of a corporation's stock are usually greater than the par or stated value. The amount in excess of par value or stated value is called **additional paid-in capital**.

Some accountants prefer to use an account called *Paid-In Capital in Excess of Par Value* or *Paid-In Capital in Excess of Stated Value.* Regardless of the account title used, the computations are identical and all are equity accounts.

If no-par value stock without a stated value is issued, the entire proceeds from the original issuance of the corporation's stock are recorded as common stock issued and no entry is made to additional paid-in capital.

Exhibit 12 illustrates the relationship of common stock issued, additional paid-in capital, and the role of par value, stated value, and no-par value.

To better understand how additional paid-in capital arises, study the following illustration. Assume the following information for a corporation:

Authorized stock: 50,000 shares of $1 par value common stock
Stock to be issued: 10,000 shares
Selling price per share: $7

The issuance of this stock will produce the following results in the bookkeeping records:

Cash Received: $70,000 (10,000 shares × $7)
Common Stock Issued: $10,000 (10,000 shares × $1 par value)
Additional Paid-In Capital: $60,000 ($70,000 − $10,000)

The $70,000 cash received is the proceeds from the selling price of $7 per share multiplied by the total number of shares sold (10,000 shares in this case). Note that the corporation is not issuing all of its authorized shares. This is not uncommon; a corporation usually applies for more authorized shares than it intends to originally issue. The strategy for this action is to avoid having to amend its corporate charter should the company desire to issue more stock in the future due to working capital needs, expansion, or other reasons.

The common stock issued is always recorded at its par value, if any. In this example, 10,000 shares of $1 par value stock were issued for a total of $10,000 par value.

The $60,000 additional paid-in capital is the amount received of $70,000 less the total par value issued of $10,000. An alternate method of determining the amount in excess of par value is to compute it on a per-share basis. For example, the selling price of $7 per share represents a premium of $6 over the par value of $1 per share. This premium of $6 per share multiplied by the number of shares issued (10,000) also results in additional paid-in capital of $60,000.

Retained Earnings

Retained earnings is an account that represents the lifetime earnings of the corporation not distributed to shareholders in the form of dividends. The net income of the business is an *increase* to retained earnings.

Cash dividends declared are recorded as a *decrease* to retained earnings. This decrease is recorded at the time the dividends are declared by the board of directors, not when they are paid. The payment of dividends affects cash; the declaration of dividends is an allocation of earnings to the shareholders that is recorded at the time the board declares the dividend and the liability for payment at a future date. The declaration of dividends affects corporate equity accounts by way of a *decrease* in the retained earnings account and an *increase* in the dividends payable account.

The dividends payable account is a liability account and will be decreased when the dividends are paid at a future date.

The following is a history of the retained earnings account for a corporation that has been in existence for seven years:

Business Year	Net Income	Dividends Declared	Retained Earnings
1	$ 9,000		$ 9,000
2	15,000		24,000
3	17,000	$7,000	34,000
4	12,000	7,000	39,000
5	(4,000)		35,000
6	(2,000)		33,000
7	10,000		43,000

Preferred Stock Issued

Preferred stock is a special kind of stock used by corporations to attract a different kind of investor, thus expanding the corporation's ability to raise funds. The accounting procedures for preferred stock are similar to those for common stock and will not be enumerated here. One obvious difference is the terminology; the issuance of preferred stock is recorded as *preferred stock issued* rather than *common stock issued*. This distinction shows the different kinds of capital stock issued by the corporation.

The dividend on preferred stock is usually stated as a percentage of par value. In this case, par values are *not* set at a nominal amount. For example, a $100 par value preferred stock with a dividend stated at eight percent will receive an $8 dividend per year. If the preferred stock has no par value, the dividend would be stated as a dollar amount per share.

Dividends on preferred stock, like common stock, must be declared by the board of directors. However, preferred stockholders receive priority over common stockholders as to the receipt of dividends. Thus, it is possible for dividends to be declared on preferred stock and not on common stock.

The right to vote is ordinarily not permitted for preferred stockholders, but some states do allow corporations to issue voting preferred stock if they desire. Preferred stock does have advantages not found in common stock, such as:

- Dividend privileges.
- Conversion privilege.
- Liquidation preference.
- Ending the preferences.

Dividend privileges. What if a company's board decides not to declare dividends on any of its outstanding stock for a period of time? In order to make preferred stock more attractive, the preferred stock could be issued as *cumulative preferred stock*. Past dividends that have not been paid to cumulative preferred stockholders are called *dividends in arrears*. These dividends in arrears must be paid to the preferred stockholders before any dividends can be declared on the common stock.

Conversion privilege. The market value of common stock usually reacts more favorably than preferred stock when a company is growing or has a favorable profit pattern. Owners of *convertible preferred stock* have a right to exchange their preferred stock for common stock as stipulated on the stock certificate. For example, a preferred stock could be exchanged at the rate of one preferred share for four shares of common stock or some other exchange ratio.

Liquidation preference. Most preferred stock carries a feature that provides a measure of security for its holders. In the case of corporate dissolution, after all priority claims are paid, the preferred stockholders have first claim over the common stockholders on the remaining assets of the business.

Ending the preferences. The special provisions that make preferred stock more attractive may in time become too expensive for a corporation to sustain. Also, the demands of these special features might work against the common stockholders. To guard against these problems, most preferred stock is issued as *callable preferred stock.* This means that a corporation may buy back (call) its preferred stock and retire it. The *call price* is usually higher than the preferred stock's par or stated value. When preferred stock is callable, the call price per share usually acts as a price ceiling on the open market.

Donated Capital

Sometimes, corporations receive assets (such as land) as gifts from states, cities, or benefactors to increase local employment or encourage business activity in a locality. In such cases, the appropriate asset account would be increased and the **donated capital** equity account would be increased accordingly.

Treasury Stock

A corporation may reacquire shares of its previously issued stock to reduce the number of outstanding and issued shares. This is sometimes done to increase the figure computed for earnings per share, which some regard as an investment guideline. Another reason may be simply to reduce outside ownership.

When stock is reacquired, it is called **treasury stock.** Treasury stock is no longer considered *issued and outstanding;* therefore, it does not pay any dividends and is not associated with voting privileges. However, it may later be sold again.

The cost method is generally used to record the purchase of treasury stock. Under this method, the common stock issued account is not affected; rather, a contra-equity account called *Treasury Stock* is used.

For example, assume that a corporation reacquires 5,000 shares of its $1 par value common stock for a cost of $17,000. The business transaction is recorded as an *increase* of $17,000 in the treasury stock account and a $17,000 *decrease* in the cash account.

Stockholders' Equity on the Balance Sheet

A corporation may present an extensive equity section on its balance sheet depending upon the types of equity transactions it carries out. As an example, the equity section of a balance sheet for a particular corporation may appear as in Exhibit 13. The section titled *Stockholders' Equity* includes the sale of both common and preferred stock, contributions of additional paid-in capital and donated capital, and the deduction of treasury stock reacquired by the corporation.

Limited Liability Company Equity Accounts

An LLC (limited liability company) is a business form that has advantages similar to both a partnership and a corporation. This allows the owners to take advantage of the profit sharing attributes of a partnership, yet enjoy the limited liability protection of a corporation. Accounting for an LLC is similar to that for a partnership. Each owner has an individual equity account in which profits and distributions are recorded.

Exhibit 13 Equity Section of a Corporate Balance Sheet

STOCKHOLDERS' EQUITY	
Paid-In Capital	
Preferred Stock, 9% dividends, $100 par, cumulative, callable, 600 shares authorized and issued	$ 60,000
Common Stock, $1 par, 200,000 shares authorized, 50,000 shares issued, treasury stock 5,000 shares which are deducted below	50,000
Additional Paid-In Capital	70,000
Total Paid-In Capital	$ 180,000
Donated Capital	30,000
Retained Earnings	65,000
Total	$ 275,000
Deduct: Common Treasury Stock at Cost	17,000
Total Stockholders' Equity	$ 258,000

Key Terms

accounts receivable—The amounts owed to a firm by its customers.

accrued payables—Unrecorded liabilities for expenses that have been incurred but not yet paid during the financial reporting period.

accumulated depreciation—Contains the sum of depreciation allocations for all prior years to the present. It is a contra asset because it reduces a related asset.

additional paid-in capital—The amount paid by stockholders in excess of the par or stated value of the stock.

advance deposits—A term used for customer deposits for services not yet rendered or goods not yet delivered.

allowance for doubtful accounts—Represents an estimate of potential receivables that may become uncollectible. It is a contra-asset account because it reduces accounts receivable.

balance sheet accounts—Collective term for accounts known collectively as assets, liabilities, and equity.

bearer bond—A bond with no registered owner's name.

bond certificate—Tangible evidence of ownership of a bond, usually a printed form with information about the bond.

bond indenture—Explains the rights and privileges of a bond holder and special features of the bond.

callable bond—A bond that can be redeemed (called in) and paid before the maturity date.

capital account—An equity account showing the financial interest of owners. Used for proprietorships and partnerships.

convertible bond—A bond that can be converted into common stock.

current assets—Cash or assets that are convertible to cash within twelve months of the balance sheet date.

current portion of long-term debt—Portion of long-term liabilities which is due within 12 months of the balance sheet date.

debenture bond—A bond with no collateral behind it.

discount—With regard to bonds, the amount by which the initial selling price is below face value.

donated capital—Assets received by the corporation as a gift.

equity accounts—A section of the balance sheet showing the financial interest of the owners.

face value—The maturity value of a bond.

fixed assets—A pragmatic term for property and equipment.

goodwill—An intangible asset identifying a business's superior products or service. It can be recorded if it is the result of the purchase of a business and the price paid is in excess of the fair market value of the assets of the business.

hybrid liability—A business liability in which part of the liability is current and part is long-term.

intangible assets—Long-lived asset having no physical substance but conveys certain rights to its owner.

inventories—Items held for sale or consumption.

investments—A term not to be confused with short-term investments. Typically, the term investments in accounting refers to a category that shows the cost of corporate stock held of affiliates and subsidiaries. Also securities failing the short-term investment test are included.

long-lived assets—Assets with a useful life exceeding 12 months.

long-term liabilities—Liabilities due after 12 months of the balance sheet date.

marketable securities—Trading securities (stocks, bonds) that are readily marketable and earmarked by management for conversion into cash.

maturity date—The date at which the issuing company of a bond is obligated to pay the face value of a bond to the bondholder.

notes receivable—Promissory notes (promises to pay) made payable to the hospitality company. They are negotiable instruments when endorsed and involve the payment of interest.

organization costs—Costs involved with the legal formation of a business; usually associated with the corporate form.

other assets—A noncurrent asset category that includes long-lived intangible assets.

par value—A value for common stock selected by the corporation when it files its articles of incorporation. Par value of a stock has no relationship with its real value.

premium—With regard to bonds, the amount by which the initial selling price is greater than face value.

prepaid expenses—A current asset for items paid in advance. Prepaid items are unexpired expenses that will benefit future periods.

property and equipment—A noncurrent asset category that includes long-lived tangible assets.

registered bond—A bond issued in the name of the owner or buyer of the bond.

retained earnings—The lifetime earnings of a corporation net of any lifetime dividends declared.

secured bond—A bond backed with collateral of specific assets

serial bond—A bond spreading the payment of its face value over several maturity dates.

short-term investments—Readily marketable securities that management can sell if cash is needed.

sinking fund—With regard to bonds, cash or other assets periodically put aside to retire bonds.

tangible asset—A long-lived asset having physical substance. Examples are land, building, and equipment.

term bond—A bond maturing at a specified date.

treasury stock—The cost of reacquired stock previously issued by the corporation.

withdrawals account—The drawings of cash or other assets by an owner of a proprietorship or partnership.

Review Questions

1. How are the following classifications of bookkeeping accounts defined?
   a. Asset
   b. Liability
   c. Equity
2. How are the following categories defined?
   a. Current Asset
   b. Property and Equipment
   c. Other Assets
   d. Current Liability
   e. Investments

3. What are the definitions of the following current asset accounts?
   a. Cash
   b. Short-term Investments
   c. Accounts Receivable
   d. Inventories
   e. Prepaid Expenses
4. Why is a 20-year mortgage requiring monthly payments allocated as part current liability and part noncurrent liability on the balance sheet?
5. What are the equity accounts for a proprietorship?
6. What are the equity accounts for a corporation?
7. What is the definition of *Allowance for Doubtful Accounts*, and where does it appear on the balance sheet?
8. How are credit card drafts generally treated and recorded?
9. Why are prepaid expenses treated as an asset and not as an expense?
10. When and how is goodwill recorded according to accounting principles?
11. What is the definition of *Accumulated Depreciation*, and where does it appear on the balance sheet?

Problems

Problem 1

Classify each of the following accounts as an asset (A), liability (L), or equity (EQ) account.

_______ Accounts Payable
_______ Short-term Investments
_______ Land
_______ Mortgage Payable
_______ Capital
_______ Common Stock Issued
_______ Prepaid Rent Expense
_______ Repair Parts Inventory
_______ Accounts Receivable
_______ Investments
_______ Building
_______ Sales Tax Payable
_______ Withdrawals
_______ Retained Earnings
_______ Food Inventory
_______ Paid-In Capital

Problem 2

The Vendome Corporation has purchased 100 shares of stock of the Ford Motor Company, which is listed on the New York Stock Exchange. Would this purchase be recorded as an investment or as short-term investment? State the reason for your conclusion.

Problem 3

The Eller Corporation has purchased 100 percent of the outstanding stock of the Jewel Company. Would this purchase be recorded as an investment or as marketable securities? State the reason for your conclusion.

Problem 4

DORO, Inc., has purchased 1,000 shares of Goldfinders, Inc., from its founder. There is no ready market for this stock. Would this purchase be recorded as an investment or as marketable securities? State the reason for your conclusion.

Problem 5

On March 10, the GGD Company borrowed $36,000 from a bank. The company executed a promissory note for a term of three years, with payments to start on April 10. Monthly payments are required, consisting of $1,000 on the principal plus interest to be computed at the rate specified on the note. On March 31, what amount will appear as a long-term liability on the balance sheet?

Problem 6

In this problem, continue to use the information provided in Problem 5. On April 10, the GGD Company made its first payment on the note; the payment consisted of $1,000 on the principal plus accrued interest on the unpaid balance. On May 10, the company made its second payment on the note, consisting of $1,000 on the principal plus accrued interest on the unpaid balance. What amounts will appear as long-term debt on the balance sheets dated April 30 and May 31?

Problem 7

A corporation issues 100,000 shares of an authorized 500,000 shares of $1 par value common stock. The selling price is $15 per share.

a. How much cash is received?

b. What amount is recorded as common stock issued?

c. What amount, if any, is recorded as additional paid-in capital?

Problem 8

Compute the retained earnings at the end of Year 4 from the following income and dividends records of a corporation:

Income History:

Business Year	Net Income or (Loss)
1	$ (7,000)
2	(4,000)
3	25,000
4	35,000

Dividends History:

In Year 4, dividends of $10,000 were declared.
These dividends were paid in Year 5.

Problem 9

Specify whether each of the following statements is true (T) or false (F).

_______ 1. Balance sheet accounts are the revenue and expense accounts.

_______ 2. A 20-year mortgage with monthly payment terms is shown on the balance sheet only under long-term debt.

_______ 3. Land held for future expansion is shown under *Property and Equipment* on the balance sheet.

_______ 4. MasterCard and VISA card drafts are treated as cash received.

_______ 5. An asset can be a future expense.

_______ 6. Assets – Liabilities = Equity.

_______ 7. China and glassware are long-lived assets appearing in the *Property and Equipment* section.

_______ 8. Treasury stock represents bonds of the United States government.

_______ 9. Assets – Equity = Liabilities.

_______ 10. Capital stock can consist of common and preferred stock.

Problem 10

A business is recording its sales activity for the day and has the following in its cash register: cash at $3,000; in-house credit card drafts at $1,500; VISA credit card drafts at $4,500; and personal checks from customers at $500. What amount will be recorded as cash in the accounting records?

Problem 11

William Garnett is purchasing the assets of the Delta Company for $310,000. The appraised value of the assets is land at $60,000; building at $200,000; and equipment at $40,000. Show how this transaction would appear in the *Assets* section of a classified balance sheet.

Problem 12

On March 2, rent of $5,000 is paid, which covers the period of March 1 to March 31. How much of this amount will be recorded to prepaid rent?

Problem 13

Joseph Roland is starting a new business. He has incurred the following expenditures: $1,000 for legal fees for incorporation; $300 for state incorporation fees; $500 to the electric company as security for utility services; and $75,000 to a franchisor for the right to use its name and other support services. Show how this transaction would appear in the *Assets* section of a balance sheet.

Problem 14

On June 30, 20X7, real estate was purchased with a 15-year mortgage of $270,000. The terms of the mortgage were monthly payments of $1,500 on the principal and 12 percent interest on the unpaid balance, with payments beginning July 30 and due on the 30th of the month thereafter.

a. Show how the mortgage would be presented on the balance sheet for June 30, 20X7.

b. Show how the mortgage would be presented on the balance sheet for July 31, 20X7.

c. Show how the mortgage would be presented on the balance sheet for June 30, 20X8.

Problem 15

A corporation has 750,000 shares of authorized common stock at 10¢ par value. On three separate occasions, it has issued the following shares of common stock:

100,000 shares for $700,000
200,000 shares for $1,300,000
150,000 shares for $900,000

The corporation has since repurchased 50,000 shares for a total of $400,000. It had originally issued this stock for $7 per share.

The retained earnings for the year ended June 30, 20X8, were $425,000. The corporation's net income for the year ended June 30, 20X9, was $250,000. Dividends declared during the year 20X9 were $75,000. As of June 30, 20X9, $25,000 of the dividends have not been paid.

Prepare the *Stockholders' Equity* section for the balance sheet as of June 30, 20X9.

Problem 16

1. The __________explains the rights and privileges of the bond holder.
2. An unsecured bond is also called a __________.
3. A bond maturing at a specified date is a __________.
4. A bond originally issued at less than face value is a bond issued at a __________.
5. Bonds not registered in any name are __________.

Ethics Case

The class has just been seated for the final exam in Hospitality Accounting I. Marty, one of the students, notices that certain formulas and procedures have been written on the wall next to his desk. They obviously were placed there by a student from the previous class.

Marty's grades are marginal. He needs to pass the final exam today in order to pass this course. Marty's father has told him that unless Marty passes all his courses, his parents will no longer pay for his education. Also, the college has notified Marty that he is on academic probation and his continued enrollment depends on his overall grade average.

1. Since Marty did not write the material on the wall, why shouldn't he take advantage of the situation? Support your conclusion and comment on any consequences.
2. What should Marty do? Support your decision.

Chapter 5 Outline

Competencies

1. Define the revenue classification and explain when a sale is recognized. (pp. 110–111)
2. Define and describe the accounting treatment for sales taxes and servers' tips, employee meals, cost of sales, food used, and gross profit. (pp. 111–113)
3. Explain the accounting procedures for a perpetual inventory system and a periodic inventory system, and describe the differences in accounting for purchases and cost of sales. (pp. 113–122)
4. List the typical day-to-day operating and fixed expenses. (p. 123)
5. Define depreciation and explain the difference between depreciation expense and accumulated depreciation. (pp. 123–124)

5

Analysis of Income Statement Accounts

THE INCOME STATEMENT is the most popular and most analyzed statement of the three major financial statements, mainly because it is a profit-oriented statement and easy to read. The income statement reports on the operating results of a company—that is, the income statement shows whether the company had a profit or loss from its operations. The income statement is historical; it shows what has happened, not what will happen. However, ratio and performance analyses can be used to determine operating weaknesses or inefficiencies, from which corrective action can be planned.

The income statement is prepared from the accounts in the *revenue* and *expense* classifications; these accounts are referred to as *income statement accounts.* Exhibit 1 is a list of basic income statement accounts.

The income statement affects the balance sheet, because the net income from the income statement accounts increases the Equity account (capital or retained earnings) found in the balance sheet. Therefore, the income statement has an effect on the accounting equation:

Assets = Liabilities + Equity

The income statement is prepared in an orderly arrangement of accounts with meaningful headings. The revenue and expenses are listed in sufficient detail to provide management with the necessary information to properly manage operations. While every company has sales and expenses, the format of the income statement is customized by industry, such as hospitality, travel, retail, and manufacturing.

This chapter examines the income statement accounts and answers such questions as:

1. What accounts are in the revenue classification?
2. When is a sale recognized and recorded in the accounting records?
3. How are sales taxes, credit card transactions, and employee tips treated under sales accounting procedures?
4. What accounts are in the expense classification?
5. What are the perpetual and periodic inventory systems and their effect on cost of sales expense?

Exhibit 1 Listing of Income Statement Accounts

Revenue Classification

Sales Accounts:
- Rooms
- Food
- Beverage

Expense Classification

Cost of Sales Accounts *(If perpetual inventory system is used)*:
- Cost of Food Sales
- Cost of Beverage Sales

Purchases Accounts *(If periodic inventory system is used)*:
- Food Purchases
- Beverage Purchases

Operating Expenses
- Payroll
- Payroll Taxes
- Employee Benefits
- Employee Meals
- China, Glassware, Silver, Linens, Uniforms
- Supplies
- Advertising
- Telephone
- Kitchen Fuel
- Utilities
- Repairs and Maintenance

Fixed Expenses
- Rent
- Property Taxes
- Insurance
- Interest
- Depreciation
- Amortization

Income Taxes Expense

6. How are employee meals, direct purchases, and storeroom purchases treated under accounting procedures?
7. What is the relationship between depreciation expense and accumulated depreciation?

Revenue Classification

The largest account in the **revenue** classification is sales, which represents the amounts billed to guests for the sales of goods and services. A sale is recognized and recorded in the accounting records at the time services are rendered or when the goods are delivered, regardless of whether the customer pays in full or uses an open account privilege. This treatment is in accordance with the *realization principle,* a generally accepted accounting principle.

Some companies may include non-sale items such as interest income and dividends income in the revenue category. Other companies may treat these incidental items in a separate category called *other income*.

Sales Accounting

The recording of a sale is not dependent upon the receipt of cash or the kind of credit card a customer uses; a sale generates a corresponding increase in cash or accounts receivable. When a sale is made, other elements that arise are sales taxes and servers' tips.

Most states apply a sales tax to the retail price of meals and other products or hotel services. Tips are typical in most establishments, with the exception of fast-food operations. Sales accounting requires special treatment of these items because they are not considered part of the revenue classification.

Sales Taxes

The Sales account does not include amounts charged for sales taxes, since these amounts actually represent a liability rather than revenue. A hospitality business must account for taxes collected from customers and remit these collections to the taxing authority.

For example, assume a guest enjoys dinner at a fine dining establishment and pays $25 for the dinner plus a six percent sales tax (imposed by the state). Suppose the guest pays the tab with cash. This business transaction creates the following events:

1. The Food Sales account (a revenue account) is increased by $25.00.
2. The Sales Tax Payable account (a liability account) is increased by $1.50 ($25.00 × 6%).
3. The Cash account (an asset account) is increased by $26.50.

Servers' Tips

Guests may include service gratuities (tips for servers) on the credit card drafts. However, any tips entered on credit card drafts are excluded from revenue since these amounts belong to employees, not the hospitality company. To facilitate accounting for these tips, hospitality firms often pay the tips to employees at the end of each shift, and then wait for collection from the credit card company.

Expense Classification

The **expense** classification includes those accounts that represent day-to-day expenses incurred in operating the business, expired costs of assets charged to expense by depreciation, and costs of assets (such as inventory) that are consumed in operating the business.

For purposes of discussion, expenses have been grouped into the following topical categories:

- Cost of sales expense
- Operating expenses
- Income taxes expense
- Depreciation

Cost of Sales Expense

Cost of sales expense represents the cost of inventory products used in the selling process, and, therefore, applies only to revenue-producing centers.

Separate accounting is performed for cost of beverage sales and cost of food sales. Cost of beverage sales is the cost of liquor and mixes used to generate sales. Cost of food sales is the cost of food used in the preparation process for resale to guests. The *net food cost* (that is, cost of food sales) does not include meals provided to employees.

Unlike the food and beverage department, the rooms department does not have a cost of room sales account. Rooms are not consumed, nor do they involve a sale of inventory; it is room occupancy that is sold. Expenses associated with the upkeep of rooms (for instance, guest supplies, cleaning supplies, and housekeeping labor) are recorded in various operating expense accounts, rather than a cost of sales account.

Food Cost

Cost of sales is a truly representative accounting term: it is the cost of the raw materials used to make a sale to guests. In a restaurant, this raw material is food; therefore, *food cost* means the same as *cost of sales.* Another accounting term used as a substitute for cost of sales is *cost of goods sold.*

What is food cost? If a restaurant has $1,000 of food used, is the cost of sales (food cost) $1,000? Probably not! Remember that cost of sales represents the cost of food *served to guests.* Many restaurants also provide meals to their employees at no charge or at a nominal charge. The food cost (cost of sales) appearing on the financial statements must not include the cost of employee meals.

Continuing with our example of $1,000 of food used, assume that the cost of employee meals is $50 (before employee payments, if any). The cost of food sold is computed as follows:

Food used	$1,000
Less cost of employee meals	50
Cost of sales	$ 950

Where does this food come from? Food comes from the storeroom; all food in the storeroom is called *inventory.* When the inventory is pulled out and used, it then becomes *cost of sales* and *employee meals expense.*

Exhibit 2 shows that there is food worth a total of $5,000 in the storeroom, which is called *food inventory.* The kitchen then requisitions food worth $1,000 and processes it, which is called *food used.* The employees ate food costing $50, which is

Exhibit 2 Food Cycle: From Inventory, to Expense, to Sales

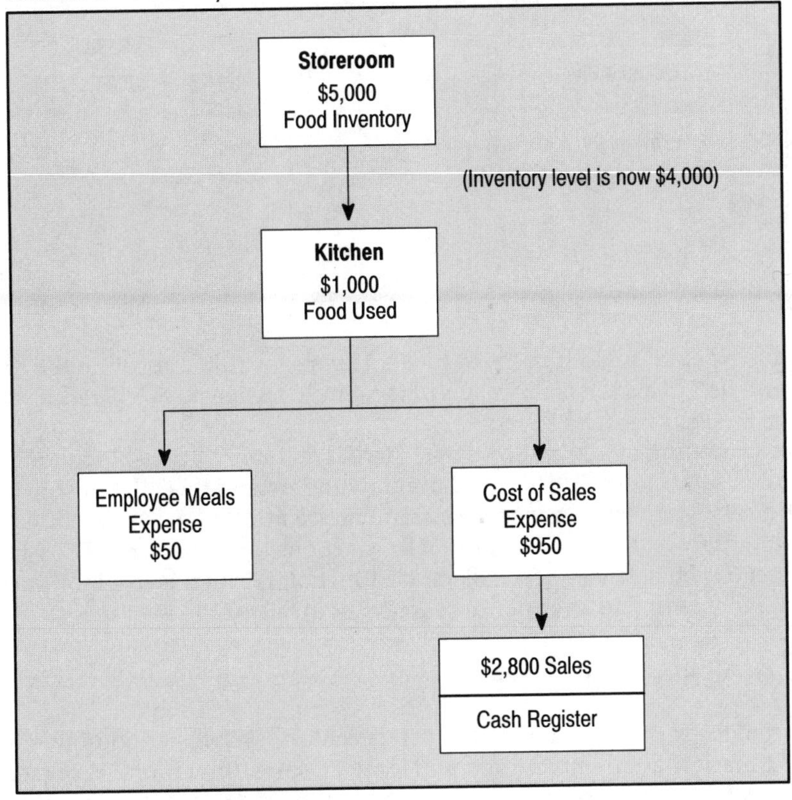

called *Employee Meals Expense;* this expense is an operating expense and not a cost of sales expense. The balance of $950 was used to prepare food for guests and is called *Cost of Sales.*

Gross Profit

The amount of $950 used to serve guests resulted in billings of $2,800; this would be recorded to a *revenue* account called Sales. The profit on the raw materials is called *gross profit* and is calculated as follows:

Sales	$2,800
Cost of sales	$950
Gross profit	$1,850

After the gross profit would appear the deductions for *employee meals, payroll,* and *other operating expenses.* In our example, the employee meals would be a $50 operating expense.

What if the employees were charged for their meals? Continuing with our example, assume employees were charged $30 for their meals. In this case, the

Exhibit 3 Relationship of Inventory, Cost of Sales, and Sales

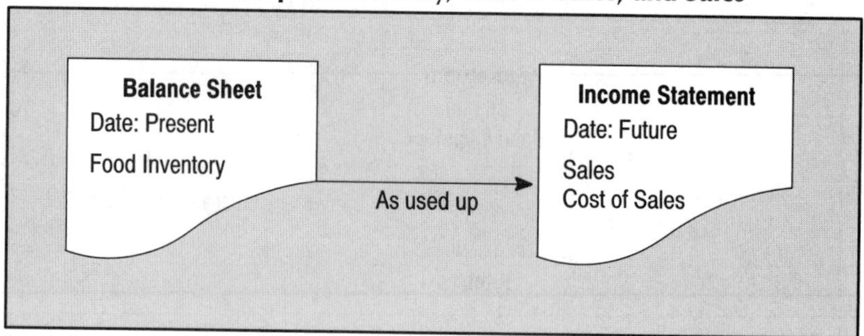

operating expense called Employee Meals Expense would appear on the financial statements as $20, which is the result of the employee meals of $50 reduced by the employee collections of $30.

The preceding material shows that there is an interrelationship among inventory, cost of sales, and sales. It is important to understand this relationship because both the balance sheet and income statement are affected as shown in Exhibit 3. This exhibit shows the flow of financial transactions for these items. Food not used is an asset on the balance sheet called Food Inventory. As it is used for guest purposes, it is converted to an expense called Cost of Sales.

Inventory Systems

In addition to providing internal control, inventory systems are designed to supply information about inventory and cost of sales. Inventory represents the *products not used,* and cost of sales represents the *products used* to produce guest sales.

The specific procedures for recording inventories or cost of sales depend on the type of inventory accounting system used by a hospitality facility. Any facility that sells inventory may use one or a combination of *perpetual* or *periodic* inventory systems.

Perpetual Inventory System

Under a **perpetual inventory system,** the operations area of a hospitality business constantly updates its records on its inventory of food, beverage items, or other inventory products on hand. This means that every time inventory is acquired for the storeroom, the merchandise inventory record is increased; whenever issues are made to the kitchen, inventory is decreased.

Exhibit 4 illustrates how this flow of purchases and issues is processed in the storeroom and shows the subsequent flow of documents to the accounting department. To accomplish the constant updating of information about inventory on hand, the storeroom clerk or other responsible individual must record the receipts and issues on a special document. Exhibit 5 illustrates a perpetual inventory form commonly used for this purpose.

Exhibit 4 Operations Flowchart for a Perpetual Inventory System

Purchases

Goods

Vendor Invoice

Storeroom

Receiving Document

Bookkeeper

Perpetual Inventory Card

Bookkeeping Records

1. Records Receipts
2. Increases Inventory Balance

1. Increases Inventory Account
2. Decreases Cash Account or Increases Accounts Payable

Issues

Kitchen

Storeroom

Summarizes Issues

Bookkeeper

Perpetual Inventory Card

Bookkeeping Records

1. Records Issues
2. Decreases Inventory Balance

1. Increases Cost of Sales
2. Decreases Inventory Account

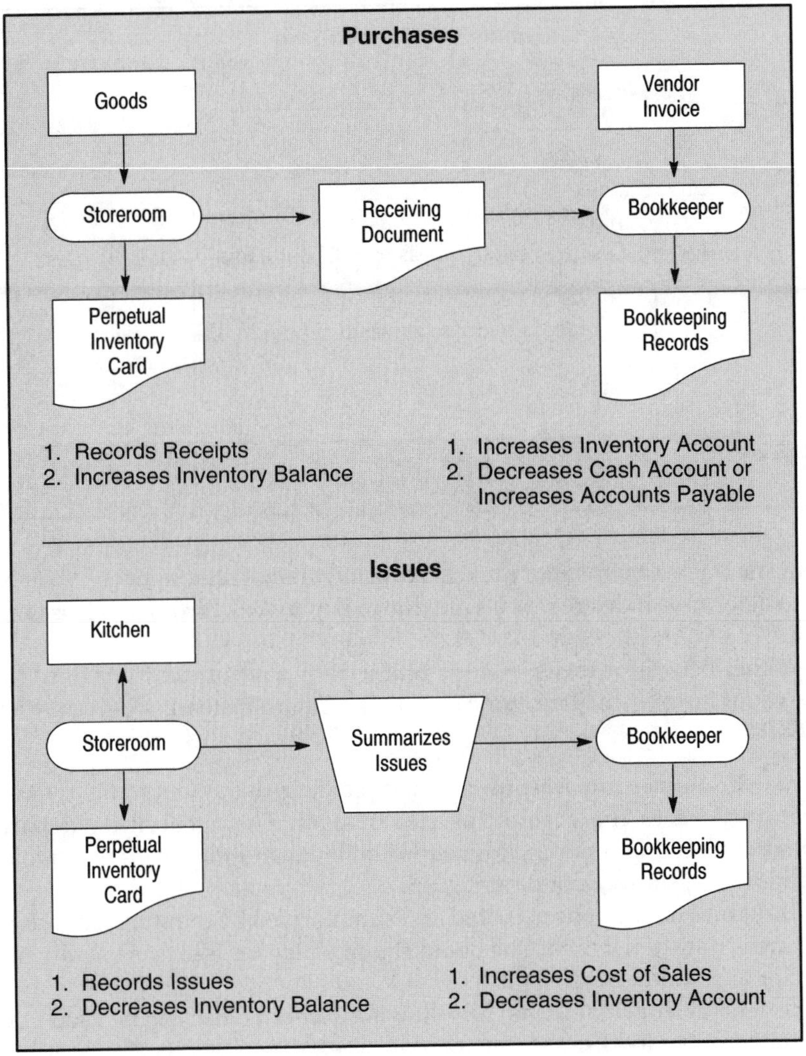

One advantage of the perpetual inventory system is that it provides instant inventory status information from the inventory cards. There is no urgent need to count the inventory in the stockroom to determine if a reorder is needed. In addition, inventory management may be improved by providing reorder points and reorder quantities on the inventory card.

Another advantage of the perpetual inventory system is internal control. The inventory records specify the quantities of each item that *should* be available in the storeroom. During the month, quick spot-checks can be accomplished by physically counting selected items and comparing the quantity counted against the

Exhibit 5 Sample Perpetual Inventory Form

Inventory Ledger Card

No.__________ Description ____________________

Date	Ref.	Purchases			Issues			Balance on Hand		
		Units	Unit Cost	Total	Units	Unit Cost	Total	Units	Unit Cost	Total

amount shown on the inventory cards. Any overages or shortages can then be analyzed to determine if discrepancies are due to paperwork errors or if losses are due to theft.

Another benefit of this system is that it allows a hospitality facility to completely count its inventory any time during the month instead of only at the end of the month.

Perpetual Bookkeeping Accounts. The receiving documents and requisitions (issues) are sent to the accounting department. The accounting department matches the receiving reports with vendor invoices and processes the invoices for journalizing and subsequent payment.

If the issues have not been costed and summarized by the storeroom clerk, this procedure is now performed. The bookkeeping entry for issues is usually made at the end of the month.

The general ledger contains the following accounts that will be used to record the activities of the food storeroom and kitchen:

- Inventory
- Cost of Sales
- Employee Meals Expense

Inventory account. There are separate Inventory accounts for food, beverage items, and merchandise in the gift shop. The Inventory account is a current asset account; its balance at the end of the month should agree with the amount arrived at by totaling all of the perpetual inventory records in the storeroom. This result provides internal control benefits.

Exhibit 6 Recording of Purchases

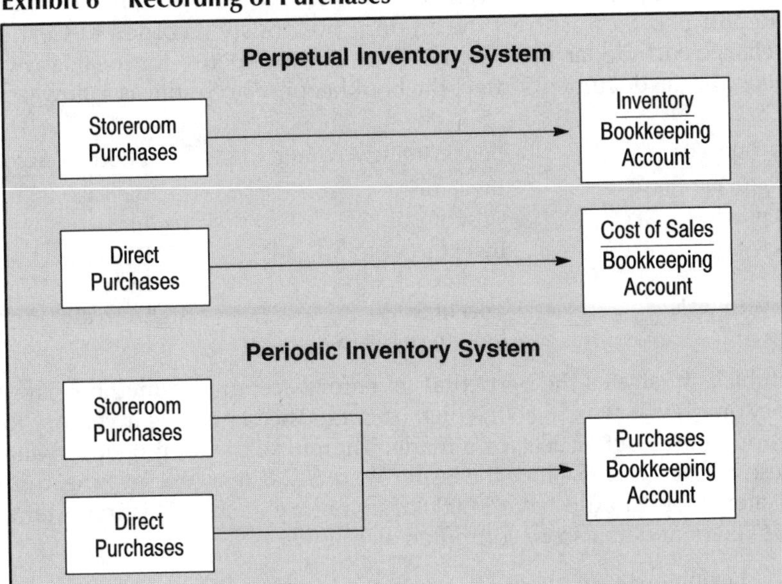

In a perpetual system, the Inventory account is constantly updated for purchases and issues that affect inventory. Exhibit 6 illustrates the recording of purchases. The bookkeeping accounts used to record purchases depend on whether the purchase is a *storeroom purchase* or a *direct purchase.*

A **storeroom purchase** is for goods that will be delivered to the storeroom for later use. Storeroom purchases are recorded as an increase to the Inventory account.

A **direct purchase** is for goods to be delivered by the supplier directly to the kitchen for immediate consumption. Direct purchases are recorded to the Cost of Sales bookkeeping account.

Cost of Sales account. There are separate Cost of Sales accounts to identify the cost of goods sold (food, beverage items, and merchandise from the gift shop). The total issues (at cost) are used to decrease the Inventory account and increase the Cost of Sales account.

Employee Meals Expense account. This account is used to record the cost of employee meals. Each department would have an Employee Meals Expense account, such as Rooms Department—Employee Meals, Food and Beverage Department—Employee Meals, and Administrative and General Department—Employee Meals.

Perpetual Inventory Accounting. The accounting department processes various documents that are recorded to the bookkeeping accounts found in the general ledger. The storeroom requisitions represent issues from the storeroom and usage for sales. Invoices for storeroom purchases are recorded to an Inventory account, and invoices for direct purchases are recorded to a Cost of Sales account. The Employee Meals Report is used to correct the amount previously recorded to Cost of Sales and to charge each department for its share of the expense for meals provided to employees. These documents affect the bookkeeping accounts as follows:

Transaction	Bookkeeping Account	Effect on Account
Storeroom purchase	Inventory	Increase
Direct purchase	Cost of Sales	Increase
Issues	Inventory	Decrease
	Cost of Sales	Increase
Employee meals	Cost of Sales	Decrease
	Employee Meals Expense	Increase

Exhibit 7 illustrates the perpetual inventory accounting method. The ending inventory on May 31 was $3,800, which becomes the beginning inventory for June. In June, purchases of $12,200 were made. Therefore, the total goods available for June were $16,000 *at cost*. Since the issues were $12,000 *at cost* for June, this means that the storeroom should have $4,000 of inventory *at cost*. This important inventory management data can be computed as follows:

Beginning inventory, 6/1	$ 3,800	
Add: Storeroom purchases in June	12,200	
Cost of goods available	16,000	*(food for use)*
Less: Issues for June	12,000	*(food used)*
Ending inventory, 6/30	$ 4,000	*(food not used)*

The purchases would have been recorded as an increase to the Food Inventory account. The issues would have been recorded as an increase to the Cost of Food Sales account, also referred to as Cost of Food Sold.

However, the $12,000 recorded to the Cost of Food Sales account needs refinement. Remember that *food used* might represent not only food prepared for guest consumption; some of it is given to employees. In this case, $180 went for employee meals. Therefore, a bookkeeping entry is made to decrease the Cost of Food Sales account and increase the Employee Meals Expense account. All these activities can now be presented as follows:

Beginning inventory, 6/1	$ 3,800	
Add: Storeroom purchases in June	12,200	
Cost of goods available	16,000	
Less: Employee meals	180	
Less: Cost of sales	11,820	(12,000 − 180)
Ending inventory, 6/30	$ 4,000	

Periodic Inventory System

The use of the word *system* in the name of the **periodic inventory system** can be deceiving because no inventory recordkeeping is performed by operations or accounting within this type of system. Under the periodic inventory system, perpetual inventory cards are not maintained in the storeroom operations.

Exhibit 7 Perpetual Inventory Accounting Method

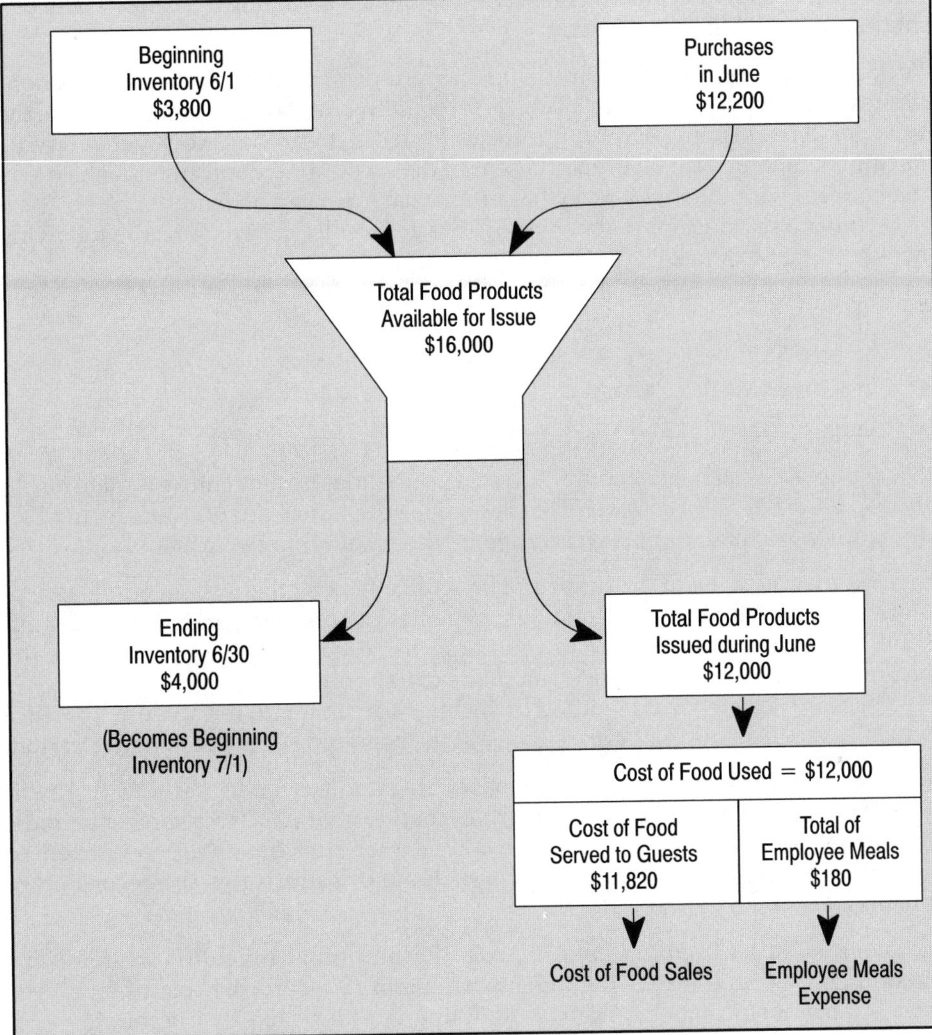

Therefore, inventory ins and outs are basically not monitored with checkpoints because there are no records to compare against.

The major advantage of this inventory system over the perpetual inventory system is that this system does not incur the heavy costs of maintaining perpetual inventory cards.

One obvious disadvantage is that internal control suffers greatly. In addition, inventory management requires constant checking of the actual quantities on hand and usage so that proper reorders are executed.

To accomplish good operational management, timely financial statements must be issued. A hospitality facility that uses a periodic inventory system faces yet another disadvantage: in order to produce meaningful financial statements, the facility must face the inconvenience and expense of taking *a complete physical inventory at the end of each month.*

Periodic Bookkeeping Accounts. Under a periodic inventory system, requisitions (issues) are not prepared. Therefore, the accounting department cannot update the Inventory bookkeeping account for issues from the storeroom. However, receiving documents should still be used and sent to the accounting department, which will match them with the invoices so that proper payment can be made.

Under a periodic inventory system, the general ledger contains the following bookkeeping accounts:

- Inventory
- Purchases
- Employee Meals Expense
- Employee Meals Credit

Notice that the bookkeeping accounts used under this inventory system *do not include a Cost of Sales account.* This is because the issues are not documented by operations and thus cannot be recorded by the accounting department.

Inventory account. As in the perpetual inventory system, this system employs separate Inventory accounts for food, beverage items, and merchandise from the gift shop. Unlike the procedure followed under the perpetual inventory system, the recording of inventory activity is not made to this account.

Because no activity is recorded to the Inventory account, the account's balance will always reflect the inventory balance at the beginning of the accounting period.

Purchases. Storeroom and direct purchases are handled very differently in a periodic inventory system than they are in a perpetual inventory system. In a periodic inventory system, both storeroom and direct purchases are recorded to a bookkeeping account called *Purchases.* Exhibit 6 illustrates the recording of purchases under a periodic system.

Employee Meals Expense account. As in the perpetual inventory system, this account is used in the periodic inventory system to record the cost of employee meals. Each department would have an Employee Meals Expense account.

If an employee pays part or all of his or her meal cost, this account is shown at net of the payment. For example, if the cost of employee meals for the rooms department is $100 and the employees have contributed $40, Rooms Department—Employee Meals is shown at a net cost of $60.

Employee Meals Credit. This account represents employee meals for all departments of the hospitality business. It is used to eliminate the cost of employee meals from food used in order to arrive at food prepared for guests, which is called Cost of Sales.

It is important to fully understand the difference between the Employee Meals Expense account and the Employee Meals Credit account. The expense account is a departmental account that appears on each department's financial statement charging it for the cost of meals consumed by its staff. The effect of the Employee Meals Credit account is to remove the cost of food consumed by all employees from the Food Department.

Periodic Inventory Accounting. Under a periodic inventory accounting method, the general ledger accounts provide very little information that readily shows the inventory balance or cost of sales for the period. To understand how to arrive at these figures, we should first review the month-end status of the bookkeeping accounts:

1. The Inventory account contains only the balance as of the beginning of the period. No purchases or issues are recorded to this account. Therefore, to determine the ending inventory, a physical count and costing of the inventory must be performed.
2. A Cost of Sales account does not exist under a periodic inventory system because issues are not recorded.
3. A Purchases account contains the total purchases for the period.

Exhibit 8 illustrates the limited accounting information provided by a periodic inventory accounting method. However, after the physical inventory has been completed, calculating the cost of sales is simple using the following logic:

- Inventory represents product not used.
- Cost of Sales represents product used for guests.

The accounting records reveal that:

- Beginning inventory is $3,800.
- Purchases for June were $12,200.

The physical inventory shows the following:

- Ending inventory as of June 30 is $4,000 at cost.

The food and beverage manager turns in a monthly report showing the following information:

- Employee meals are $180 at cost.

Accountants have devised a procedure to compute cost of sales from this limited information. The calculations in this procedure are performed as follows:

Beginning inventory, 6/1	$ 3,800	
Add: Purchases for June	12,200	
Cost of goods available	16,000	*(food for use)*
Less: Ending inventory, 6/30	4,000	*(food not used)*
Cost of food used	12,000	*(food used—total)*
Less: Employee meals	180	*(food used—employees)*
Cost of sales	$ 11,820	*(food used—guests)*

Exhibit 8 Periodic Inventory Accounting Method

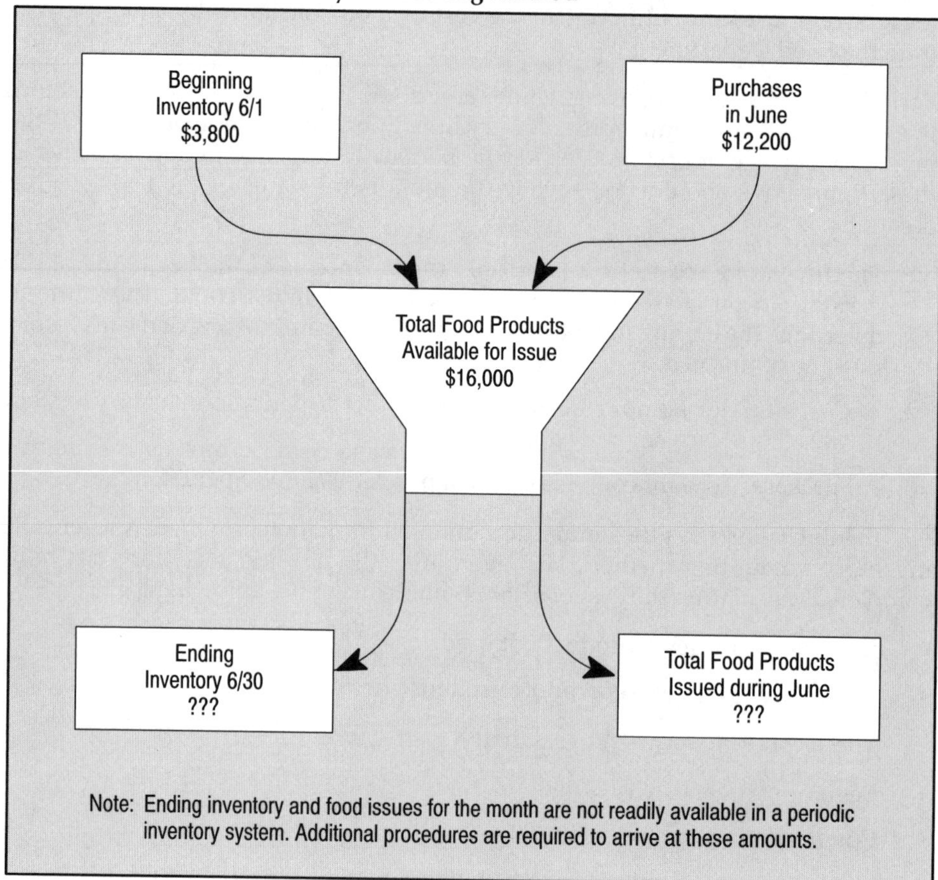

Inventories in Service Areas

The net income shown on the financial statements depends on the accuracy of the ending inventory dollar amount. In the hospitality industry, many items are requisitioned from the storeroom and stored temporarily in the bar or the kitchen in order to provide quality and prompt customer service.

Measuring inventory of bar stock is required in order for records to reflect accurate amounts of items not consumed and sold. Full and open bottles of liquor, wine and beer in kegs, and other beverage inventories on hand must be physically counted since these items are usually of material value.

Measuring inventory of food items in the kitchen area is performed by larger hotels at the end of each month, a required procedure due to its materiality to the financial statements. Small restaurant operations may not perform such procedures for various reasons—for instance, if the effort expended is likely to exceed the intended benefits (cost-benefit rule), or if the results are not expected to have any material effect on the net income.

Other Business Expenses

Cost of sales is only one type of expense found in a hospitality business. The other business expenses can be separated into groups such as operating expenses, fixed expenses, and income taxes. This grouping allows the preparation of a classified income statement which will be more meaningful and easier to read.

Operating Expenses

The day-to-day expenses incurred by a business during its operational activities are referred to as *operating expenses.* The following are typical examples:

Payroll	Supplies
Payroll Taxes	Kitchen Fuel
Employee Meals	Utilities
Advertising	Telephone

Fixed Expenses

Certain kinds of expenses are not an active part of operations, but are incurred regardless of the level of business, even when the business is closed for any reason. These expenses are referred to as *fixed expenses.* The following are examples of fixed expenses:

Rent	Interest
Property Taxes	Depreciation
Property Insurance	Amortization

Income Taxes Expense

These taxes are levied by the federal and state governments on the income of a corporation. Some municipalities may also tax business income. It is possible for a corporation to pay income taxes even if it had a loss for the year, because some states require the "income tax" payment to be the largest amount resulting from the following three computations:

- A specified minimum payment
- A tax computed on corporate equity
- A tax computed on taxable income

Depreciation

Depreciation is a method for allocating the purchase cost of a tangible long-lived asset such as a building or equipment over an estimated useful life. Tangible long-lived assets are also referred to as fixed assets by accountants. Not all fixed assets are depreciated. Land is not a depreciable fixed asset because its life is infinite in the hospitality industry environment.

When an asset is purchased, its cost is recorded to a balance sheet account. Time and usage will decrease the utility of this asset. Remember that anything "used up" is an expense. However, the use of a long-lived asset is fragmented—some this year, some next year, and so on.

How is this fragmented usage measured so that a portion of the cost can be transferred to expense? No scientific methods are available. However, one common method for computing the portion of the cost of a fixed asset that has expired is to allocate the cost over a period of time.

For example, assume that a vehicle was purchased for $12,000. Based on published industry guidelines or planned usage by the particular company, the accountant determines that the vehicle's useful life is expected to be three years. This means that the asset should be decreased by $4,000 and an expense be increased by $4,000 each year over a three-year period.

The income statement will show the allocation of the asset's cost for this period in an account called Depreciation. As with all income statement accounts, Depreciation expense is set to zero at the end of the year to start counting the expense for the next year.

The asset cost on the balance sheet never changes. In this example, it will always remain at $12,000. An account called Accumulated Depreciation is used to record the reduction of the asset's cost basis. This account will contain the sum of all depreciation charges over the life of the asset. Unlike the Depreciation expense account, the Accumulated Depreciation account maintains a cumulative balance; it is not set to zero. Accumulated Depreciation is referred to as a *contra- asset account* because it reduces the basis of another asset.

The **book value** of an asset is not an indication of its market value. Book value is an accounting term that represents the undepreciated cost of an asset. It is arrived at by subtracting the amount for accumulated depreciation from the asset's cost.

The relationship of asset cost, depreciation, and accumulated depreciation is best shown by analyzing the balance sheets and income statements over the three-year period of ownership of the vehicle previously described:

	Balance Sheets		
	End of 1st year	End of 2nd year	End of 3rd year
Property and Equipment Section:			
Vehicle, at cost	$12,000	$12,000	$12,000
Less Accumulated Depreciation	4,000	8,000	12,000
Undepreciated Cost	8,000	4,000	0
	Income Statements		
	End of 1st year	End of 2nd year	End of 3rd year
Depreciation	4,000	4,000	4,000

Key Terms

book value—Asset cost minus accumulated depreciation

direct purchase—Food purchased for immediate use and delivered by the purveyor to the kitchen.

expense—Cost of items used to produce revenue, cost of items consumed, or the expired cost of assets.

periodic inventory system—A system of inventory accounting in which no perpetual inventory records are maintained and cost of sales must be manually computed.

perpetual inventory system—A system of inventory accounting in which inventory records are maintained supplying inventory balances and cost of sales.

revenue—A classification that includes sales and might also include interest income and dividend income.

storeroom purchase—Goods purchased which go to the storeroom for later use.

Review Questions

1. How is the Revenue classification defined?
2. How is the Expense classification defined?
3. At what point is a sale recorded?
4. How does the Sales account differ from the Cost of Sales account?
5. What are the major differences between the perpetual and periodic inventory systems?
6. What are advantages and disadvantages of the two inventory systems discussed in this chapter?
7. How do accounting treatments of storeroom purchases and direct purchases differ under the two types of inventory systems?
8. What is the difference between the expense account Depreciation and the contra-asset account Accumulated Depreciation?

Problems

Problem 1

A restaurant started the month with a food inventory of $3,000 in the storeroom. During the month, food purchases totaling $9,000 were delivered to the storeroom and $8,000 of food was issued from the storeroom. What was the cost of food available for the month?

Problem 2

The accounting records for a restaurant indicate that food sales were $18,000, food used was $5,800, and employee meals at cost were $50. What is the cost of sales?

Problem 3

The accounting records for a restaurant indicate that food sales were $25,000, food used was $8,100, and employee meals at cost were $75. What is the gross profit?

Problem 4

A restaurant started the month with a food inventory of $2,000. Its purchases for the month were $10,000 and its cost of food used was $9,000. What is its ending inventory?

Problem 5

A restaurant ended the month with a food inventory of $4,000. Its purchases for the month were $12,000 and its cost of food used was $11,000. What was its beginning inventory?

Problem 6

An asset was purchased at a cost of $20,000. It is being depreciated at the rate of $4,000 per year. What is its useful life expressed in years?

Problem 7

Specify whether each of the following statements is true (T) or false (F).

_______ 1. Balance sheet accounts are the revenue and expense accounts.

2. Land is a depreciable fixed asset in the hospitality industry.

_______ 3. If a guest tab shows food at $40 and sales tax of $2.40, the amount recorded as a sale will be $42.40.

_______ 4. If a guest orders a $2,000 banquet and pays $2,000 on the banquet to be scheduled next month, a sale of $2,000 is recorded.

_______ 5. Storeroom purchases under a periodic inventory system are recorded to an Inventory account.

_______ 6. Direct purchases under a periodic inventory system are recorded to a Cost of Sales account.

_______ 7. Accumulated Depreciation is an expense account.

_______ 8. A guest tab shows food at $80 and sales tax of $4.80; the guest pays with an in-house credit card. The $80 amount cannot be treated as a sale.

_______ 9. *Food used* is the same as *cost of food sold.*

_______ 10. The income statement accounts do not affect the accounting equation: Assets = Liabilities + Equity.

Problem 8

Calculate the cost of food sales under a periodic inventory system for the period ended October 31 given the following information:

Inventory on October 31 is $7,000.
Sales for the period were $200,000.
Purchases for the period were $69,000.
Inventory on September 30 was $8,000.

Free employee meals for the period were as follows:

Rooms Department	$ 500
Food Department	900
Administrative and General Department	375

Problem 9

Calculate the cost of food sales under a perpetual inventory system for the month ended March 31 given the following information:

Inventory on March 31 was $2,900.
Storeroom purchases for the month were $36,000.
Storeroom issues for the month were $36,500.
Direct purchases for the month were $626.
Free employee meals for the month were $225.

Problem 10

A building is purchased on January 1 for $240,000. The cost of this asset is to be allocated on the basis of $8,000 per year. What is its book value at the end of the first year?

Problem 11

Equipment is purchased on June 1 for $7,500 and its cost is to be allocated at $625 per month.

a. What would be its book value on June 30?
b. What would be its book value on July 31?

Problem 12

A vehicle is purchased for $10,200 and is estimated to have a useful life of three years. At the end of three years, its estimated book value is zero. What should be the annual charge to depreciation expense?

Problem 13

A hospitality company uses the perpetual inventory system. Its food inventory was $2,700 on August 1 and $3,000 on August 31. Total deliveries to the storeroom in August were $15,000. What were the food issues from the storeroom in August?

Problem 14

A hospitality business uses the perpetual inventory system. For October, storeroom issues (food used) totaled $25,875 and the cost of sales equaled $25,615. What was the amount for free employee meals for October?

Problem 15

A hospitality business uses the periodic inventory system. On November 1, the food inventory was $2,000. During November, food purchases totaled $9,000 and free employee meals were $200. The cost of food sales for the month equaled $4,000. What is the ending inventory on November 30?

Problem 16

Specify if the following are an operating expense, a fixed expense, or a cost of sales item.

	Operating Expense	Fixed Expense	Cost Of Sales
Payroll			
Utilities			
Advertising			
Rent			
Insurance			
Property Taxes			
Kitchen Fuel			
Employee Benefits			
China, Glassware			
Repairs			
Cost of Food Sold			
Food Purchases			
Depreciation			
Interest			
Amortization			

Ethics Case

Brady Dumais owns a small proprietorship that operates on a cash-only basis; no credit cards are accepted. Brady has taken a bookkeeping course and a tax preparation course. With the help of his spouse, he is able to perform all the bookkeeping duties and prepare his tax returns.

Brady discovers that federal and state income taxes take away 35 percent of his profits. Because his is a cash business, Brady has started the practice of "skimming" sales. Because these sales will not appear in the business records, they will escape taxation, and Brady will be able to retain 100 percent of these revenue dollars.

1. Identify the stakeholders in this case.
2. Comment on the legal and ethical issues involved in skimming.

Chapter 6 Outline

Competencies

1. Define and describe bookkeeping and double-entry accounting, and identify common bookkeeping accounts and tools. (pp. 131–134)
2. Use three basic questions to analyze business transactions. (pp. 135–142)
3. Define debits and credits and use them to record business transactions. (pp. 142–150)
4. Define contra accounts, identify common contra accounts, and explain how these accounts are used. (pp. 151–152)
5. Identify the normal account balances for each account classification. (pp. 152–153)

6

The Bookkeeping Process

COMPUTERS HAVE SIMPLIFIED AND EXPEDITED the bookkeeping process. However, a computer cannot analyze a business transaction and determine the proper accounts that are involved. The proper application of debits and credits to the correct accounts is vital to the accuracy of any management information system. To process a business transaction, familiarity with the accounts in the five classifications (assets, liabilities, equity, revenue, and expenses) is an emphatic prerequisite. It is impossible to clearly analyze a business transaction and easily understand the debit and credit rules if one does not first fully learn the accounts in these five classifications.

Properly designed input forms and accounting procedures simplify the determination of debits and credits critical to a reliable financial system. Nonetheless, the computer and other modern systems have not eliminated the necessity for having a personal knowledge of debits and credits.

This chapter presents the basic and essential information every well-grounded businessperson is expected to know. First, 21 business transactions representing a preponderance of day-to-day operations are analyzed for their effect on the bookkeeping accounts. Next, these 21 transactions are recorded, using debits and credits.

This chapter provides answers to such questions as:

1. What is double-entry accounting?
2. What is a bookkeeping account?
3. What is the general ledger?
4. How are business transactions analyzed?
5. What are the debit and credit rules?
6. What are contra accounts?
7. What is meant by normal balance in a general ledger account?

21st Century Bookkeeping

Bookkeeping is the first function in the accounting department. Without bookkeeping, there would be no financial information or statements. Business transactions trigger the bookkeeping process. Evidential matter, such as invoices, checks, cash register tapes, bank deposits, and contracts, supports business transactions.

A *business transaction* is an exchange of property, goods, or services for cash or a promise to pay. Purchases and sales transactions are the largest volume of business transactions. A business may purchase goods, property, or services by the payment of cash or a promise to pay. A promise to pay by a business to its purveyors (suppliers) is an *accounts payable* transaction. Customers of a business may purchase its goods, property, or services by the payment of cash or a promise to pay. A promise to pay by the customers of a business is an *accounts receivable* transaction.

Modern bookkeeping now is an *input* function, coding the proper accounts and amounts affected by business transactions. After coding, these transactions are processed by a computerized accounting application called **general ledger** accounting software.

Double-Entry Accounting

Double-entry accounting is a bookkeeping process in which every business transaction affects two or more bookkeeping accounts. This ancient standard has proven itself through time and experience. It has been used since the first bookkeeping system and likely will always be the basis of any accounting system. Double-entry accounting provides built-in checks and balances to determine the accuracy of recording amounts. It would not be possible to generate the multitude of financial information and statements without double-entry accounting.

Bookkeeping Accounts

Financial statements or information reports cannot be produced without an orderly and logical arrangement of headings and account titles. A **bookkeeping account** is an individual record for each account used by a business to record its business transactions. Every hospitality business will use a multitude of accounts from each of the five account classifications. In the initial design phase of a management information system, the accountant, in consultation with executives and managers, determines the bookkeeping accounts necessary to produce the desired financial information and statements. These bookkeeping accounts are listed in an accounting document called the **chart of accounts**. This document is functionally a *table of contents* listing the only authorized bookkeeping accounts in an accounting system. Exhibit 1 shows a typical chart of accounts. This chart will be used to process the 21 universal transactions presented later in this chapter. Review these accounts well before proceeding; a well-grounded understanding of these accounts will greatly simplify the learning of debits and credits.

Account Balance

Each bookkeeping account is headed by its name, followed by entries consisting of a date, source reference, and the amount. At this stage, we do not concern ourselves with this level of detail or whether the amount is a debit or credit. A bookkeeping account is much like a bin containing numerical results that increase or decrease its balance. The bin concept of an account is shown in Exhibit 2. The account balance is computed by taking the beginning balance and increasing or decreasing that balance to arrive at an ending balance. At this level of our learning, we will consider only increases and decreases, and not debits or credits.

Exhibit 1 Sample Chart of Accounts

Asset Accounts

Cash
Marketable Securities
Accounts Receivable
Food Inventory
Beverage Inventory
Supplies Inventory
Prepaid Insurance
Prepaid Rent
Land
Building
Furniture and Equipment
China, Glassware, Silver, Linen, Uniforms
Organization Costs
Security Deposits

Liability Accounts

Accounts Payable
Sales Tax Payable
Income Taxes Payable
Accrued Payroll
Accrued Payroll Taxes
Advance Deposits
Current Maturities of Long-Term Debt
Notes Payable
Mortgage Payable

Equity Accounts

For Corporations:
Common Stock Issued
Additional Paid-In Capital
Retained Earnings

For Proprietorships or Partnerships:
Capital, (owner's name)
Withdrawals, (owner's name)

Revenue Accounts

Room Sales
Food Sales
Beverage Sales

Expense Accounts

Cost of Food Sold (If perpetual inventory system is used)
Cost of Beverage Sold (If perpetual inventory system is used)
Food Purchases (If periodic inventory system is used)
Beverage Purchases (If periodic inventory system is used)
Salaries and Wages
Payroll Taxes
Employee Benefits
Food Department—Employee Meals

(continued)

Exhibit 1 *(continued)*

Rooms Department—Employee Meals
China, Glassware, Silver, Linen, Uniforms
Supplies
Advertising
Telephone
Utilities
Repairs and Maintenance
Rent
Property Taxes
Property Insurance
Interest
Depreciation
Amortization
Income Taxes

Exhibit 2 "Bin" Concept of an Account

Account Title: Cash	
Increase	$1,000
Increase	2,000
Decrease	500
Increase	700
Decrease	1,000
Account Balance	$2,200

Computer Processing of Accounts

In a computerized general ledger system, all accounts have a unique identification number that serves as the basis for computer input. This account number is found in the chart of accounts. A properly designed computerized general ledger program will reject any business transaction that is not recognized by the official chart of accounts.

General Ledger

General ledger is simply a term that refers collectively to all the bookkeeping accounts. It is a part of accounting terminology that all business students and professionals must know. Instead of going to the bookkeeper and asking for "all the bookkeeping accounts," it is more professionally appropriate to ask for "the general ledger." In computer systems, the general ledger is stored on tape, disk, or CD. A printout of the general ledger shows several accounts per page.

Analyzing Business Transactions

Before any business transaction can be processed in the bookkeeping phase, the transaction must be analyzed. This is relatively simple if three basic questions are answered in a specific sequence for every transaction:

1. Which two or more bookkeeping accounts are affected?
2. What are the account classifications (asset, liability, equity, revenue, expense) of these bookkeeping accounts?
3. Is the balance of the bookkeeping account increased or decreased by this business transaction?

The following examples demonstrate the sequence and logic involved in analyzing business transactions.

Example A. Cash food sales for the day total $8,000. (Disregard sales taxes for this example.)

1. Bookkeeping accounts affected?
   Cash
   Food Sales
2. Classification of accounts?
   Assets (Cash)
   Revenue (Food Sales)
3. Increase/Decrease?
   Cash account is increased. (Receipt of cash always increases cash account.)
   Food Sales account is increased.

Example B. The owner of a proprietorship, B. Mercedes, invests personal cash of $50,000.

1. Bookkeeping accounts affected?
   Cash
   Capital, B. Mercedes
2. Classification of accounts?
   Assets (Cash)
   Equity (Capital)
3. Increase/Decrease?
   Cash account is increased.
   Capital account of B. Mercedes is increased.

Example C. On June 1, a restaurant purchases advertising for $1,000 on open account. The newspaper ad will run on June 11 and 12.

1. Bookkeeping accounts affected?
   Advertising
   Accounts Payable

2. Classification of accounts?
   Expense (Advertising)
   Liabilities (Accounts Payable)

3. Increase/Decrease?
   Advertising expense account is increased.
   Accounts Payable account is increased.

Example D. The restaurant in Example C now pays the open account of $1,000.

1. Bookkeeping accounts affected?
   Cash
   Accounts Payable (Advertising cannot be used; if it were, it would create a duplicate entry.)

2. Classification of accounts?
   Assets (Cash)
   Liabilities (Accounts Payable)

3. Increase/Decrease?
   Cash account is decreased. (Payment of cash is always a decrease to cash.)
   Accounts Payable account is decreased.

Analyzing 21 Universal Transactions

You are now ready to test your skills at analyzing transactions. The following 21 transactions represent the bulk of day-to-day business transactions and some month-end adjustments. Read each transaction carefully and answer the three basic questions to analyze the transaction.

Do only one at a time and then compare your answers with the result shown at the bottom of each example. After these 21 transactions are analyzed, we will apply debits and credits.

Example #1. A motel writes a $1,500 check to pay its current monthly rent.

Account	Classification	Effect
Cash	Asset	*Decrease*
Rent Expense	Expense	*Increase*

Reason: An expense (rent) has been incurred, which requires the use of cash. This reduces the balance in the Cash account. The account Rent Expense is incremented (increased) for the period.

Example #2. A lodging operation writes a $1,500 check on April 15, paying its rent for May.

Account	Classification	Effect
Cash	Asset	*Decrease*
Prepaid Rent	Asset	*Increase*

Reason: When rent is paid in advance of the current accounting period, it cannot be charged to Rent Expense. Rather, the prepayment of rent creates an asset (an item that benefits more than one accounting period). This increments the asset account called Prepaid Rent. Issuing a check always reduces cash.

Example #3. A lodging business writes a $1,500 check on August 1, paying its rent for August.

Account	Classification	Effect
Cash	Asset	*Decrease*
Rent Expense	Expense	*Increase*

Reason: While this may appear to be paying the rent in advance, this is not actually the case. Since August is the current accounting period, payment of the August rent on August 1 is an expense incurred *within* that period.

Example #4. A customer's invoice was $50.00 for meals, plus $3.00 for sales tax. The customer pays the $53.00 tab with cash.

Account	Classification	Effect
Cash	Asset	*Increase*
Food Sales	Revenue	*Increase*
Sales Tax Payable	Liability	*Increase*

Reason: All three accounts are incremented by this transaction. Note that a restaurant acts as a collection agent for the state; ultimately, the sales taxes collected for a period must be remitted to the state.

Example #5. A customer's invoice was $50.00 for meals, plus $3.00 for sales tax. The customer uses an open account authorized by the restaurant and charges the total tab of $53.00.

Account	Classification	Effect
Accounts Receivable	Asset	*Increase*
Food Sales	Revenue	*Increase*
Sales Tax Payable	Liability	*Increase*

Reason: The only difference between this transaction and that of Example #4 is that the customer did not pay by cash or cash equivalent. Instead, the restaurant gets the customer's promise to pay in the future.

Example #6. One week after the transaction of Example 5, the restaurant receives a personal check for $53.00 from the customer.

Account	Classification	Effect
Cash	Asset	*Increase*
Accounts Receivable	Asset	*Decrease*

Reason: The receipt of cash is an increase. The customer's payment results in a reduction of the accounts receivable balance.

Example #7. A hotel buys $65.00 worth of food provisions for its storeroom and pays cash on delivery. The perpetual inventory system is used.

Account	Classification	Effect
Cash	Asset	*Decrease*
Food Inventory	Asset	*Increase*

Reason: When the perpetual inventory system is employed, the account called Food Inventory is used to record purchases of food provisions. Food Inventory is incremented by this purchase.

Example #8. A hotel buys $1,200 worth of food provisions for its storeroom and uses an open account previously arranged with the supplier. The perpetual inventory system is used.

Account	Classification	Effect
Food Inventory	Asset	*Increase*
Accounts Payable	Liability	*Increase*

Reason: The hotel has made a promise to pay at some future date; this has increased its liabilities. Purchases on open account are recorded as Accounts Payable.

Example #9. The hotel in Example 8 remits a check for $1,200 to the supplier in payment of inventory purchases that had been made on open account.

Account	Classification	Effect
Cash	Asset	*Decrease*
Accounts Payable	Liability	*Decrease*

Reason: When the purchases were initially made (see Example #8), Accounts Payable was increased to reflect the increase in the hotel's liabilities. The remittance of a check has now reduced this liability.

Example #10. A hotel buys $55.00 worth of food provisions for its storeroom and pays cash on delivery. The periodic inventory system is used.

Account	Classification	Effect
Cash	Asset	*Decrease*
Food Purchases	Expense	*Increase*

Reason: When the periodic inventory system is employed, the account called Food Purchases is used to record purchases of food inventory items. In this transaction, the Food Purchases account is incremented by the purchase of additional food provisions.

Example #11. A hotel buys $900 worth of food provisions for its storeroom and uses an open account previously arranged with the purveyor (supplier). The periodic inventory system is used.

Account	Classification	Effect
Food Purchases	Expense	*Increase*
Accounts Payable	Liability	*Increase*

Reason: The hotel has made a promise to pay at some future date; this promise has increased its liabilities. Purchases on open account are recorded as Accounts Payable.

Example #12. Ken Thomas is starting a new business, a proprietorship called Ken's Restaurant Supply Company. In a single transaction, Ken invests cash of $55,000, plus land and building with a basis, respectively, of $40,000 and $175,000.

Account	Classification	Effect
Cash	Asset	*Increase*
Land	Asset	*Increase*
Building	Asset	*Increase*
Capital, Ken Thomas	Equity	*Increase*

Reason: The assets of the business have been increased by the owner's investment of cash, land, and a building. The Capital account of Ken Thomas is incremented since he has increased his ownership interest in the business. An alternate view is that Ken Thomas has increased his claim to the assets of the business by investing personal assets.

Example #13. Mae Brentwood is starting a new hospitality establishment called Brentwood, Inc. She invests $50,000 into the business for 4,000 shares of $1 par common stock.

Account	Classification	Effect
Cash	Asset	*Increase*
Common Stock Issued	Equity	*Increase*
Additional Paid-In Capital	Equity	*Increase*

Reason: Brentwood, Inc., has received cash, thus incrementing its Cash account. The corporation has also increased its issued and outstanding common stock. Since the corporation has received $50,000 for stock issued at a total par value of $4,000, the stock has been issued at a premium of $46,000. Therefore, the account Additional Paid-In Capital is incremented.

Example #14. Deb Stephens is starting a new lodging operation called Dotco, Inc. She invests $50,000 into the business for 4,000 shares of no-par common stock.

Account	Classification	Effect
Cash	Asset	*Increase*
Common Stock Issued	Equity	*Increase*

Reason: The corporation has received cash and increased its issued and outstanding common stock. There is no premium to record because the corporation issued no-par stock without any "stated" value.

Example #15. Ann Cole is starting a new restaurant called Dorco, Inc. She invests $50,000 into the business for 4,000 shares of no-par common stock that has a stated value of $8 per share.

Account	Classification	Effect
Cash	Asset	*Increase*
Common Stock Issued	Equity	*Increase*
Additional Paid-In Capital	Equity	*Increase*

Reason: The corporation has received cash and increased its issued and outstanding common stock. While the stock issued had no par value, the stock did have a stated value. Since the corporation has received $50,000 for stock issued at a total stated value of $32,000, the stock has been issued at a premium of $18,000. Therefore, the account Additional Paid-In Capital is incremented.

Example #16. A restaurant uses a perpetual inventory system. Issues from the storeroom total $15,000 for the month. This amount represents food used by the kitchen in generating sales and preparing employee meals.

Account	Classification	Effect
Cost of Food Sales	Expense	*Increase*
Food Inventory	Asset	*Decrease*

Reason: Under a perpetual inventory system, the inventory records reflect the cost of food issued from the storeroom. Issues are treated as a reduction to the Food Inventory account and an increase to the expense account called Cost of Food Sales. In the next example, this account is adjusted for the cost of free employee meals.

Example #17. Of the $15,000 total for food issued in Example #16, $300 was used for free employee meals ($200 to Rooms Department employees and $100 to Food Department employees).

Account	Classification	Effect
Rooms Department—Employee Meals Expense	Expense	*Increase*
Food Department—Employee Meals Expense	Expense	*Increase*
Cost of Food Sales	Expense	*Decrease*

Reason: The Cost of Food Sales account should reflect only the cost of food used in the selling process. Therefore, an adjustment must be made for free employee meals, whose total reduces the Cost of Food Sales account. The costs of free employee meals increase departmental expense accounts.

Example #18. A restaurant uses a periodic inventory system. Issues from its storeroom total $15,000 for the month. This amount represents food used by the kitchen in generating sales and preparing employee meals.

Effect

No bookkeeping entries are made for issues under a periodic inventory system.

Reason: Under a periodic inventory system, inventory purchases are recorded as Purchases. Issues from the storeroom are not recorded as they are under a perpetual inventory system.

At the end of each accounting period, the inventory is physically counted and priced at cost, or it is estimated using a procedure such as the gross profit method. After ending inventory has been determined, the following procedure can be used (on either the financial statements or supporting schedules) to compute the cost of food sold:

	Beginning Food Inventory
Plus:	Food Purchases
Result:	Cost of Food Available for Sale
Minus:	Ending Food Inventory
Result:	Cost of Food Used
Minus:	Employee Meals, at cost
Result:	Cost of Food Sold

Example #19. A hospitality operation purchases $875 worth of office supplies from a vendor and charges the purchases to an open account.

To properly analyze this transaction, you must know that there are two methods of accounting for operating supplies and office supplies—the asset method and the expense method. The asset method records the initial purchase to a *Supplies Inventory* account, while the expense method records it to a *Supplies Expense* account. At the end of the accounting period, a physical inventory is taken and the bookkeeping accounts are adjusted to reflect the proper inventory balances and expense (usage); at this time, both methods result in identical amounts. We will use the asset method.

Account	Classification	Effect
Supplies Inventory	Asset	*Increase*
Accounts Payable	Liability	*Increase*

Reason: The asset method is used to record the purchase of office supplies. The supplies were purchased on open account.

Example #20. A check is issued for $1,200 on 3/1/X1 in payment of a property insurance policy with a term of 3/1/X1 to 3/1/X2.

Account	Classification	Effect
Cash	Asset	*Decrease*
Prepaid Insurance	Asset	*Increase*

Reason: This payment is for an insurance policy with a term of one year. Prepaid insurance is an asset. Each month, the passage of time will expire a portion of the

Exhibit 3 Common Debit/Credit Misconceptions

Misconception	Truth
Debits add and credits subtract.	False. Debits add *and* subtract. Credits also add *and* subtract.
Debits are positive and credits are negative.	False. Positive and negative have no relation to debits and credits.
Debits and credits do not make sense.	False. Their use is based on logic.
Learning debits and credits is complex.	False. Only a basic knowledge of the classification of accounts and the increase/decrease effect of a business transaction is required.
I do not really need to know about debits and credits.	False. You do not need to be an expert, but, as a business student and aspiring professional, you should have a working knowledge because the person you will someday compete with for a promotion has that knowledge.

asset. The only entry required at this time is that of recording the purchase of prepaid insurance, which is a temporary asset benefiting future periods.

Example #21. It is now 3/31/X1 for the company in Example #20. The insurance accountant submits the following adjusting entry for the above policy.

Account	Classification	Effect
Prepaid Insurance	Asset	*Decrease*
Insurance Expense	Expense	*Increase*

Reason: The passage of one month has expired 1/12 of the prepaid insurance amount.

The Nature of Debits and Credits

Recording business transactions requires a standard system to produce consistent results. The double-entry accounting system requires that each business transaction affect two or more bookkeeping accounts. Using records that indicate "increase" and "decrease" next to amounts would be difficult to read and process, especially by a computerized system. Instead of stating "increase" or "decrease," debits and credits are used in the double-entry system.

Exhibit 3 presents many commonly believed fallacies regarding what debits and credits really mean and what they do. When **debit** is used in accounting, it means to record an amount in the left side of an account. The term **credit** is used to record an amount in the right side of an account. To illustrate, we use a two-column account format. This two-column format is also called a *T-account* because it resembles the letter *T*.

Name of Account	
Debit	Credit
(Dr)	(Cr)

Notice the placement of debits and credits in this T-account; debits are in the left side and credits are in the right side. The abbreviations **dr** and **cr** can be used to respectively indicate debit or credit. The **account balance** (the difference between the total debits and total credits) can be either a debit balance or credit balance, depending on which side has the largest amount.

Equality of Debits and Credits

A benefit of the double-entry system is that the accuracy of recording dollar amounts can be verified. For example, if cash is debited for $100, any credit entry or entries must also total $100. This is referred to as the **equality of debits and credits**. Therefore, in the recording of any business transaction, the sum of the debit dollars must equal the sum of the credit dollars. Keep in mind, however, that testing the equality of debits and credits does not verify that the amounts were recorded in the *correct* accounts; for example, the recording of equal debit and credit amounts in two incorrect accounts will result in an equality of debits and credits.

Computer Audit Trail

A batch number for control purposes is manually assigned to an assemblage of entries prior to submitting them for computer processing. During computer processing, each entry is given a computer-generated sequence number for identification. Computerized general ledger software applications have a routine in their data entry program that checks the equality of debits and credits. If an out-of-balance condition occurs, the entry with an input error can easily be located and corrected.

A printout listing the computer-processed entries shows the batch number, the processed entries, and dollar totals of debits and credits. Some programs compare these totals and print a message such as "Batch In Balance" or "Batch Out of Balance" (depending on condition) at the bottom of the report.

Debit and Credit Rules

Before attempting to learn the rules of debits and credits, you should have competence in (1) classification of accounts and (2) analyzing a business transaction.

Many methods can be used to learn the rules for applying debits and credits to record business transactions. The easiest and fastest method is to learn one central rule and then apply logic to that central rule.

The basic central rule governing the use of debits and credits is:

Use a debit to *increase* an asset or expense account.

With this central *rule of increase,* we can now use simple logic to determine how to increase the other three classifications. If we use a debit to increase an asset or expense account, then the only remaining option is to use a credit to increase the other three classifications. With logic, we can now visualize the debit and credit rules as follows:

Rule of Increase

	Debit	Credit
Asset	X	
Liability		X
Equity		X
Revenue		X
Expense	X	

The question arises, "How do you decrease an account?" Most of you already have the answer because you continued the process of logic. To *decrease an account,* you do the *opposite of the rule of increase.* Therefore, the debit and credit rules can be concluded as follows:

	Increase	Decrease
Asset	Debit	Credit
Liability	Credit	Debit
Equity	Credit	Debit
Revenue	Credit	Debit
Expense	Debit	Credit

Thus far, we have learned how to analyze a business transaction and the debit and credit rules. The next step is to journalize these transactions. Journalizing can be performed on a two-column amount journal or an in-house custom-designed input form. To simplify learning debits and credits, we dispense with technical format considerations and, for academic purposes, treat each entry as a separate item to allow for discussion.

Recording 21 Universal Transactions

The following are the 21 transactions we analyzed earlier in the chapter. Two standard procedures in journalizing entries state that the debit part of an entry is written before the credit part, and the credit part of an entry is indented for additional sight verification.

Use the chart of accounts in Exhibit 1 to process these 21 transactions. For each business transaction, perform the analysis and apply the debits and credits. Look at the first entry to familiarize yourself with the academic format used to record these business transactions. Thereafter, solve each successive entry, compare your answer with the text result, and resolve any issues before proceeding to the next entry.

Example #1. A motel writes a $1,500 check to pay its current monthly rent.

Date	Description		Debit			Credit		
1.	*Rent Expense*		1	500	00			
	Cash					1	500	00

Account	Classification	Effect	Debit/Credit
Cash	Asset	*Decrease*	Credit
Rent Expense	Expense	*Increase*	Debit

Example #2. A lodging operation writes a $1,500 check on April 15, paying its rent for May.

2.	*Prepaid Rent*		1	500	00			
	Cash					1	500	00

Account	Classification	Effect	Debit/Credit
Cash	Asset	*Decrease*	Credit
Prepaid Rent	Asset	*Increase*	Debit

Example #3. A lodging business writes a $1,500 check on August 1, paying its rent for August.

3.	*Rent Expense*		1	500	00			
	Cash					1	500	00

Account	Classification	Effect	Debit/Credit
Cash	Asset	*Decrease*	Credit
Rent Expense	Expense	*Increase*	Debit

Example #4. A customer's invoice was $50.00 for meals, plus $3.00 for sales tax. The customer pays the $53.00 tab with cash.

4.	*Cash*			53	00			
	Food Sales						50	00
	Sales Tax Payable						3	00

Account	Classification	Effect	Debit/Credit
Cash	Asset	*Increase*	Debit
Food Sales	Revenue	*Increase*	Credit
Sales Tax Payable	Liability	*Increase*	Credit

Example #5. A customer's invoice was $50.00 for meals, plus $3.00 for sales tax. The customer uses an open account authorized by the restaurant and charges the total tab of $53.00.

5.	*Accounts Receivable*			53	00			
	Food						50	00
	Sales Tax Payable						3	00

Account	Classification	Effect	Debit/Credit
Accounts Receivable	Asset	*Increase*	Debit
Food Sales	Revenue	*Increase*	Credit
Sales Tax Payable	Liability	*Increase*	Credit

Example #6. One week following the transaction in Example #5, the restaurant receives a personal check for $53.00 from the customer.

6.	*Cash*			53	00			
	Accounts Receivable						53	00

Account	Classification	Effect	Debit/Credit
Cash	Asset	*Increase*	Debit
Accounts Receivable	Asset	*Decrease*	Credit

Example #7. A hotel buys $65.00 worth of food provisions for its storeroom and pays cash on delivery. The perpetual inventory system is used.

7.	*Food Inventory*			65	00			
	Cash						65	00

Account	Classification	Effect	Debit/Credit
Cash	Asset	*Decrease*	Credit
Food Inventory	Asset	*Increase*	Debit

Example #8. A hotel buys $1,200 worth of food provisions for its storeroom and uses an open account previously arranged with the supplier. The perpetual inventory system is used.

8.	*Food Inventory*		1	200	00			
	Accounts Payable					1	200	00

Account	Classification	Effect	Debit/Credit
Food Inventory	Asset	*Increase*	Debit
Accounts Payable	Liability	*Increase*	Credit

Example #9. The hotel in Example #8 remits a check for $1,200 to the supplier in payment of inventory purchases that had been made on open account.

9.	Accounts Payable		1	200	00			
	Cash					1	200	00

Account	Classification	Effect	Debit/Credit
Cash	Asset	*Decrease*	Credit
Accounts Payable	Liability	*Decrease*	Debit

Example #10. A hotel buys $55.00 worth of food provisions for its storeroom and pays cash on delivery. The periodic inventory system is used.

10.	Food Purchases			55	00			
	Cash						55	00

Account	Classification	Effect	Debit/Credit
Cash	Asset	*Decrease*	Credit
Food Purchases	Expense	*Increase*	Debit

Example #11. A hotel buys $900 worth of food provisions for its storeroom and uses an open account previously arranged with the purveyor (supplier). The periodic inventory system is used.

11.	Food Purchases			900	00			
	Accounts Payable						900	00

Account	Classification	Effect	Debit/Credit
Food Purchases	Expense	*Increase*	Debit
Accounts Payable	Liability	*Increase*	Credit

Example #12. Ken Thomas is starting a new business, a proprietorship called Ken's Restaurant Supply Company. In a single transaction, Ken invests cash of $55,000, plus land and building with a basis, respectively, of $40,000 and $175,000.

12.	Cash		55	000	00			
	Land		40	000	00			
	Building		175	000	00			
	Capital, Ken Thomas					270	000	00

Account	Classification	Effect	Debit/Credit
Cash	Asset	*Increase*	Debit
Land	Asset	*Increase*	Debit
Building	Asset	*Increase*	Debit
Capital, Ken Thomas	Equity	*Increase*	Credit

Example #13. Mae Brentwood is starting a new hospitality establishment called Brentwood, Inc. She invests $50,000 into the business for 4,000 shares of $1 par common stock.

13.	Cash		50	000	00			
	Common Stock Issued					4	000	00
	Additional Paid-In Capital					46	000	00

Account	Classification	Effect	Debit/Credit
Cash	Asset	*Increase*	Debit
Common Stock Issued	Equity	*Increase*	Credit
Additional Paid-In Capital	Equity	*Increase*	Credit

Example #14. Deb Stephens is starting a new lodging operation called Dotco, Inc. She invests $50,000 into the business for 4,000 shares of no-par common stock.

14.	Cash		50	000	00			
	Common Stock Issued					50	000	00

Account	Classification	Effect	Debit/Credit
Cash	Asset	*Increase*	Debit
Common Stock Issued	Equity	*Increase*	Credit

Example #15. Ann Cole is starting a new restaurant called Dorco, Inc. She invests $50,000 into the business for 4,000 shares of no-par common stock that has a stated value of $8 per share.

15.	*Cash*		50	000	00			
	Common Stock Issued					32	000	00
	Additional Paid-In Capital					18	000	00

Account	Classification	Effect	Debit/Credit
Cash	Asset	*Increase*	Debit
Common Stock Issued	Equity	*Increase*	Credit
Additional Paid-In Capital	Equity	*Increase*	Credit

Example #16. A restaurant uses a perpetual inventory system. Issues from the storeroom total $15,000 for the month. This amount represents food used by the kitchen in generating sales and preparing employee meals.

16.	*Cost of Food Sales*		15	000	00			
	Food Inventory					15	000	00

Account	Classification	Effect	Debit/Credit
Cost of Food Sales	Expense	*Increase*	Debit
Food Inventory	Asset	*Decrease*	Credit

Example #17. Of the $15,000 total for food issued in Example #16, $300 was used for free employee meals ($200 to Rooms Department employees and $100 to Food Department employees).

17.	*Rooms Dept.—Employee Meals*			200	00			
	Food Dept.—Employee Meals			100	00			
	Cost of Food Sales						300	00

Account	Classification	Effect	Debit/Credit
Rooms Department—Employee Meals Expense	Expense	*Increase*	Debit

Food Department—Employee Meals Expense	Expense	*Increase*	Debit
Cost of Food Sales	Expense	*Decrease*	Credit

Example #18. A restaurant uses a periodic inventory system. Issues from its storeroom total $15,000 for the month. This amount represents food used by the kitchen in generating sales and preparing employee meals.

Effect

No bookkeeping entries are made for issues under a periodic inventory system.

Example #19. A hospitality operation purchases $875 worth of office supplies from a vendor and charges the purchase to an open account. The asset method is used to record supplies.

19.	*Supplies Inventory*			*875*	*00*			
	Accounts Payable						*875*	*00*

Account	Classification	Effect	Debit/Credit
Supplies Inventory	Asset	*Increase*	Debit
Accounts Payable	Liability	*Increase*	Credit

Example #20. A check is issued for $1,200 on 3/1/X1 in payment of a property insurance policy with a term of 3/1/X1 to 3/1/X2.

20.	*Prepaid Insurance*		*1*	*200*	*00*			
	Cash					*1*	*200*	*00*

Account	Classification	Effect	Debit/Credit
Cash	Asset	*Decrease*	Credit
Prepaid Insurance	Asset	*Increase*	Debit

Example #21. It is now 3/31/X1 for the company in Example #20. The insurance accountant submits the following adjusting entry for the above policy.

21.	*Insurance Expense*			*100*	*00*			
	Prepaid Insurance						*100*	*00*

Account	Classification	Effect	Debit/Credit
Insurance Expense	Expense	*Increase*	Debit
Prepaid Insurance	Asset	*Decrease*	Credit

Contra Accounts

Contra accounts are bookkeeping accounts that have a *contrary* or *reverse* effect in their account classification. For example, accumulated depreciation is a contra-asset account; its function is a minus in the asset section. Contra accounts generally exist only in the following account classifications:

- Assets
- Equity
- Revenue

Learning the debit and credit rule for contra accounts is actually quite simple if we use *reverse logic* regarding the central rule of increase for assets and state the *rule of increase for contra accounts* as:

> Use a credit to *increase* a contra-asset account.

Continuing with contra-account logic, it follows that a *debit* is used to increase *contra-equity* or *contra-revenue* accounts. The following is a listing of the common contraaccounts and how to increase them:

Contra Account	Classification	Rule of Increase
Allowance for Doubtful Accounts	Asset	Credit
Accumulated Depreciation	Asset	Credit
Withdrawals	Equity	Debit
Treasury Stock	Equity	Debit
Sales Allowances	Revenue	Debit

Following are three sample entries involving contra accounts.

Withdrawals. Ken Thomas owns a proprietorship called Ken's Restaurant Supply Company. Because a proprietorship cannot pay salaries or wages to its owner, Ken Thomas must draw funds from the business as necessary. A business check is issued for $1,000, payable to Ken Thomas.

Account	Classification	Effect	Debit/Credit
Cash	Asset	*Decrease*	Credit
Withdrawals, Ken Thomas	Equity (Contra)	*Increase*	Debit

The journal entry to record the $1,000 withdrawal of funds is as follows:

	Withdrawals, Ken Thomas		*1*	*000*	*00*			
	Cash					*1*	*000*	*00*

Allowance for Doubtful Accounts. The contra-asset account called *Allowance for Doubtful Accounts* contains an estimated amount of accounts receivable that might become a bad debt. When the estimate is updated, an expense account called *Bad Debts Expense* (or *Provision for Doubtful Accounts*) is charged.

An aging of accounts receivable indicates that the Allowance for Doubtful Accounts should be increased by $1,000. An analysis of this transaction shows:

Account	Classification	Effect	Debit/Credit
Bad Debts Expense	Expense	*Increase*	Debit
Allowance for Doubtful Accounts	Asset (Contra)	*Increase*	Credit

The journal entry to record this estimate is as follows:

	Bad Debts Expense		1	000	00			
	Allowance for Doubtful Accounts					1	000	00

Accumulated Depreciation. The contra-asset called *Accumulated Deprecation* contains the depreciation for all prior periods up to the current period. When accumulated depreciation is updated, an expense account called Depreciation Expense is charged.

An asset depreciation study shows that depreciation for the current month is $2,000. An analysis of this transaction shows:

Account	Classification	Effect	Debit/Credit
Depreciation Expense	Expense	*Increase*	Debit
Accumulated Depreciation	Asset (Contra)	*Increase*	Credit

The entry to record the $2,000 depreciation for the current period is as follows:

	Depreciation Expense		2	000	00			
	Accumulated Depreciation					2	000	00

Normal Account Balance

The balance of an account is determined by the difference of its debit and credit amounts. The account has a debit balance if the debit total is greater, or a credit balance if the credit total is greater. Exhibit 4 illustrates one method to determine an account balance. The type of account balance (debit or credit) is another important audit tool. If debits are used to increase an asset account, it follows that an asset account should have a debit balance; otherwise the account might need analysis.

Exhibit 4 Entries and Account Balance

	Cash	
	1000	500
	2000	1000
	700	
Total	3700	1500
Balance	2200	

(Translation: Account has a debit balance of $2200.)

Exhibit 5 Summary of Normal Balances by Classification

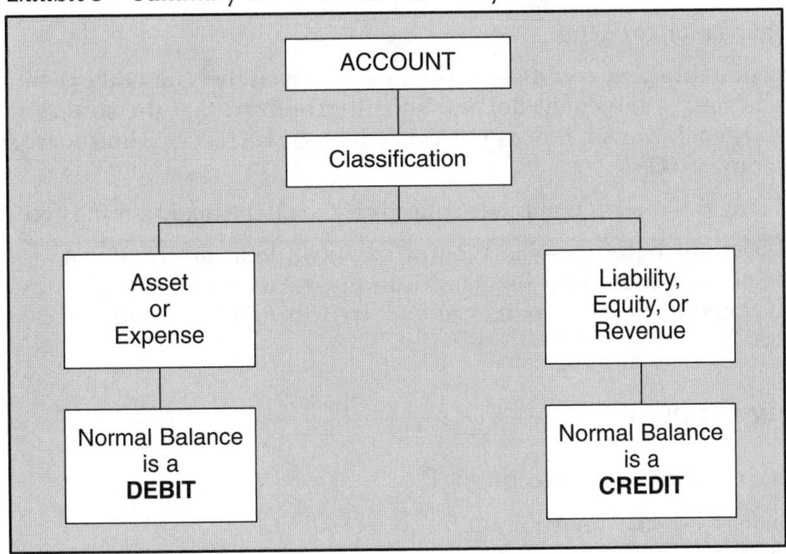

For example, cash should have a debit balance of not less than zero. A credit balance would indicate either an error in recording an entry or an overdrawn condition. In either case, investigation is necessary.

The **normal account balance** rule is that the account should have a balance in conformity with the rules of increase. Exhibit 5 illustrates the normal balances of accounts. This exhibit is also useful in learning the rules of increase for the account classifications.

Key Terms

account balance—The difference between the total debits and credits in an account. The larger amount determines if the balance is debit or credit.

bookkeeping account—An individual record for each account a business uses to record its business transactions.

chart of accounts—A table of contents listing every authorized bookkeeping account in the accounting system.

contra accounts—Bookkeeping accounts that have a contrary or reverse effect in their account classification.

cr—Abbreviation for credit.

credit—Indicates that amounts are to be recorded in the right side of an account. A credit increases a liability, equity, or revenue account.

debit—Indicates that amounts are to be recorded in the left side of an account. A debit increases an asset or expense account.

double-entry accounting—A bookkeeping process in which every business transaction affects two or more bookkeeping accounts.

dr—Abbreviation for debit.

equality of debits and credits—A condition in which the sum of the debit dollars equals the sum of the credit dollars. Equality confirms that the correct amounts were recorded; however, it does not verify that the correct accounts were used in the recording process.

general ledger—A term that refers collectively to all the bookkeeping accounts.

normal account balance—The type of balance (debit or credit) an account is expected to have based on its classification. Debits are expected in asset and expense accounts, while credits are expected in liability, equity, and revenue accounts.

Review Questions

1. What is double-entry accounting?
2. What is a bookkeeping account?
3. What is a chart of accounts?
4. What is a general ledger?
5. What are the three basic questions applied in analyzing a business transaction?
6. What is meant by the equality of debits and credits?
7. With the exception of contra accounts, a debit will increase which of the five classifications of accounts?
8. With the exception of contra accounts, a credit will increase which of the five classifications of accounts?
9. What is a contra account?
10. What is meant by normal account balance?

Problems

Problem 1

Classify the following accounts as Asset (A), Liability (L), Equity (EQ), Revenue (R), or Expense (EX).

a. Accrued Payroll
b. Payroll
c. Prepaid Rent
d. Rent
e. Cash
f. Accounts Payable
g. Supplies Inventory
h. Supplies
i. Food Sales
j. Food Inventory
k. Retained Earnings
l. Building
m. Common Stock Issued
n. Owner's Capital
o. Owner's Withdrawals
p. Payroll Taxes
q. Accounts Receivable
r. Additional Paid-In Capital

Problem 2

Indicate whether cash is increased or decreased by the following business transactions:

1. The owner invests cash in the business.
2. Cash sales for the day are $2,000.
3. The business issues a check.
4. The business receives payment from a customer who had made a previous purchase on open account.
5. The business pays its outstanding balance on an account payable.

Problem 3

Complete the following statements by specifying whether the stated accounts are increased or decreased by the business transaction:

1. A business incurs a repair expense of $200. The account Repairs Expense is ___________.
2. A customer buys services on open account. The account called Accounts Receivable is ___________.
3. A customer pays his/her open account balance. The account called Accounts Receivable is ___________.
4. On March 10, a business writes a check for the April rent. The account Prepaid Rent is ___________.
5. In April, the account Prepaid Rent referred to in the previous transaction (Number 4) is ___________ and the account Rent Expense is ___________.

Problem 4

For the following business transactions, identify the bookkeeping accounts affected; classify the bookkeeping accounts as Asset (A), Liability (L), Equity (EQ), Revenue (R), or Expense (EX); and determine whether the effect is an increase or decrease on the bookkeeping accounts.

1. On July 5, a lodging business issues a check paying the July rent.
2. The asset method of accounting for supplies is used by a hospitality operation. Supplies of $600 are purchased on open account.
3. A hospitality facility uses the perpetual inventory system. Storeroom purchases of $1,000 are made on open account.
4. A hospitality business uses the perpetual inventory system. The Storeroom Requisitions Report shows that food provisions of $3,000 were issued for the month.
5. Continue using the information from the previous transaction (Number 4). The food and beverage manager's report shows that total employee meals for the month were $60.
6. A guest tab shows the following information: food at $60; beverage at $20; and sales tax at $4.80. The guest paid with a VISA credit card.
7. A business issues a check paying the currently due mortgage. The principal is $800 and the interest is $900.

Problem 5

Specify whether each of the following statements is true (T) or false (F).

_______ 1. A business transaction is initially recorded in the general ledger.

_______ 2. Posting is the process of entering a transaction in a journal.

_______ 3. In a periodic inventory system, purchases of storeroom food inventory are recorded in an account called Food Inventory.

_______ 4. The account Cost of Food Sales is found in the periodic inventory system.

_______ 5. Inventory is an expense account.

_______ 6. The equity accounts for a proprietorship are Capital and Withdrawals.

_______ 7. Sales is a revenue account.

_______ 8. Cost of Sales is an expense account under the perpetual inventory accounting method.

_______ 9. Purchases is an expense account under the periodic inventory accounting method.

_______ 10. Prepaid Expense is an asset account.

Problem 6

Assume that a hospitality operation uses a perpetual inventory system. Name the accounts affected by the following transactions and specify whether the effect is an increase or a decrease.

a. Liquor sales for the day total $525, $400 of which was paid in cash with the balance charged to customers' open accounts.

b. A storeroom purchase of liquor totaling $725 is charged by the operation to an open account.

c. A direct purchase of liquor totaling $67 is made. Check number 978 is issued upon purchase.

d. Issues from the liquor storeroom for the month total $1,525.

Problem 7

Assume the hospitality operation instead uses a periodic inventory system. Name the accounts affected by the following transactions and specify whether the effect is an increase or a decrease.

a. Liquor sales for the day total $525, $400 of which was paid in cash with the balance charged to customers' open accounts.

b. A storeroom purchase of liquor totaling $725 is charged by the operation to an open account.

c. A direct purchase of liquor totaling $67 is made. Check number 978 is issued upon purchase.

Problem 8

Specify which of the following account classifications are increased by the use of a debit. (Write the word *debit* in the blank next to the appropriate account classifications.)

Account Classification	To Increase
Asset	________
Liability	________
Equity	________
Revenue	________
Expense	________

Problem 9

Specify which of the following account classifications are increased by the use of a credit. (Write the word *credit* in the blank next to the appropriate account classifications.)

Account Classification	To Increase
Asset	________
Liability	________
Equity	________
Revenue	________
Expense	________

Problem 10

Classify the following contra accounts.

Allowance for Doubtful Accounts	Contra	______
Accumulated Depreciation	Contra	______
Withdrawals	Contra	______
Treasury Stock	Contra	______
Allowances	Contra	______

Problem 11

Indicate whether a debit or a credit will increase the balance of the following contra accounts.

Allowance for Doubtful Accounts	______
Accumulated Depreciation	______
Withdrawals	______
Treasury Stock	______
Allowances	______

Problem 12

Identify which account will be debited in each of the following circumstances if the transaction shown is a credit to Accounts Payable.

Transaction	Inventory System	Account Debited
a. Purchase of food for storeroom	Perpetual	______
b. Purchase of food for kitchen	Perpetual	______
c. Purchase of food for storeroom	Periodic	______
d. Purchase of food for kitchen	Periodic	______
e. Purchase of liquor for storeroom	Perpetual	______
f. Purchase of liquor for storeroom	Periodic	______
g. Purchase of supplies	Asset	______

Problem 13

Assume that a hospitality operation uses a perpetual inventory system. Journalize the following transactions on a two-column journal.

a. Liquor sales for the day total $525, $400 of which was paid in cash with the balance charged to customers' open accounts.

b. A storeroom purchase of liquor totaling $725 is charged by the operation to an open account.

c. A direct purchase of liquor totaling $67 is made. Check number 978 is issued upon purchase.

d. Issues from the liquor storeroom for the month total $1,525.

Problem 14

Assume the hospitality operation instead uses a periodic inventory system. Journalize the following transactions on a two-column journal.

a. Liquor sales for the day total $525, $400 of which was paid in cash with the balance charged to customers' open accounts.

b. A storeroom purchase of liquor totaling $725 is charged by the operation to an open account.

c. A direct purchase of liquor totaling $67 is made. Check number 978 is issued upon purchase.

Problem 15

The Blue Ribbon Steakhouse uses a perpetual inventory system for food and beverages. Supplies inventory and expense accounts are separately maintained for the following types of supplies: Guest, Cleaning, Office, and Kitchen. Purchases of supplies are charged to either an inventory (asset) account or an expense account based on the destination of the supplies (storeroom or direct use).

Journalize the following transactions on a two-column journal for the Blue Ribbon Steakhouse.

20X1

March 1: The sales report for the day presented the following information:

Food	$1,985.75
Beverage	425.00
Sales Tax	144.65
Cash received and bank credit cards	1,550.65
In-house credit cards	1,003.68
Cash shortage	1.07

(Cash shortages or overages are recorded to one account called Cash Short or Over.)

March 1: Issued check number 645 for $1,600 to Baker Realty in payment of the March rent.

March 1: Purchased $900 of food provisions for the storeroom on open account from Daxell Supply.

March 1: Purchased $250 of liquor on open account for the storeroom from Tri-State Distributors.

March 1: Paid for newspaper advertising to run on March 15. Issued check number 646 for $350 to *City News*.

March 2: The sales report for the day presented the following information:

Food	$1,856.50
Beverage	395.00
Sales Tax	135.09
Cash received and bank credit cards	1,495.84

In-house credit cards	891.13
Cash overage	.38

March 2: Issued check number 647 for $1,500 to Capital Insurance for a one-year policy on contents of building. Term of the policy is March 8, 20X1, to March 8, 20X2.

March 2: Paid for newspaper advertising to run on April 8. Issued check number 648 for $850 to *City News.*

March 2: Issued check number 649 for $225 to Eastern Telephone for the period March 1 to March 31.

March 2: Purchased (on open account) the following items from Kimble Supply, intended for the storerooms:

Kitchen utensils, paper, twine, pots, and pans	$980.00
Pens, pencils, cash register rolls, staplers, and pads	200.00
Matchbooks provided free to guests	150.00
Cleaning solvents and polish	175.00

March 2: Recorded the following issues reports from the storerooms:

Issues from the storeroom to the kitchen	$1,225
Issues from the storeroom to the bar	200

March 2: The cost of free employee meals is recorded in a Food Department Employee Meals Expense account and a Beverage Department Employee Meals Expense account for management information purposes. Recorded the food manager's report of free meals provided to employees for March 1 and 2, which provided the following information:

Free meals to bar employees, at cost	$15
Free meals to food department employees, at cost	40

Problem 16

The Sunshine Motel uses a perpetual inventory system for food and beverages. Inventory and expense accounts are separately maintained for the following types of supplies: Rooms, Restaurant, and Administrative Supplies. Purchases of supplies are charged to either an inventory (asset) account or an expense account based on the destination of the supplies (storeroom or direct use).

Journalize the following transactions involving the Sunshine Motel on a two-column journal.

<u>20X8</u>

May 1: The sales report for the day presented the following information:

Room Sales	$5,210.00
Food	1,863.25
Beverage	375.00
Sales Tax	372.41
Cash received and bank credit cards	2,125.83
In-house credit cards	5,695.68
Cash overage	.85

May 2: Purchased $875 of food provisions for the storeroom on open account from Prince Supply.

May 2: Purchased $315 of liquor for the storeroom on open account from Hodges Distributors.

May 2: Paid for newspaper advertising which ran on March 9. Issued check number 864 for $350 to *State Tribune.*

May 2: The sales report for the day presented the following information:

Room Sales	$4,968.50
Food	2,265.95
Beverage	575.00
Sales Tax	390.47
Cash received and bank credit cards	5,365.38
In-house credit cards	2,834.09
Cash shortage	.45

May 2: Issued check number 865 for $4,200 to Zenith Insurance for a one-year workers' compensation policy. Term of the policy is May 1, 20X8, to May 1, 20X9.

May 2: Issued check number 866 for $625 to Central Telephone for the period May 1 to May 31.

May 2: Purchased (on open account) the following items from Kimble Supply, intended for the storerooms:

Amenities for room guests	$750.00
Pens, pencils, and other office supplies	500.00
Kitchen utensils, paper, twine, pots, and pans	600.00

May 3: Recorded the following issues reports from the storerooms:

Issues from the storeroom to the kitchen	$1,500
Issues from the storeroom to the bar	300

May 3: The cost of free employee meals is recorded to separate departmental expense accounts. Recorded the food manager's report of free meals furnished to employees for May 1 and 2, which provided the following information:

Free meals to rooms department employees, at cost	$75
Free meals to food and bar department employees, at cost	50
Free meals to administrative and general department employees, at cost	25

Problem 17

Judy Barnes starts a new proprietorship called the Rialto Bistro on April 5, 20X5. The operation does not serve liquor; it uses a periodic inventory system for food items. Inventory and expense accounts are set up for Operating Supplies and Office Supplies (four separate accounts). Purchases of storeroom supplies are recorded to an inventory account; direct purchases are recorded to an expense account.

Journalize the following transactions on a two-column journal.

20X5

April 5: Judy invested $75,000 into the business. This amount was used to open a business checking account.

April 5: Purchased the following property:

Land	$ 45,000
Building	165,000
	$ 210,000

Issued check number 101 for $40,000 to State Bank, and financed the balance by a mortgage with State Bank.

April 5: Issued check number 102 for $5,000 to National Supply and executed a $35,000 promissory note payable to National Supply in order to purchase the following items:

Operating Supplies	$ 1,200
Office Supplies	800
Furniture	18,000
Equipment	14,000
China, Glassware, Silver	6,000

April 5: Issued check number 103 for $1,400 to Fidelity Insurance for a one-year fire insurance policy.

April 5: Issued check number 104 for $200 to City Utilities as a deposit for utility services.

April 5: Purchased $2,500 of food provisions on open account from Statewide Purveyors.

April 8: Issued check number 105 for $500 to Judy Barnes for personal use.

Problem 18

Joshua Kim starts a new corporation called Jokim, Inc., on May 12, 20X7. The operation uses a periodic inventory system for food items. The inventory and expense accounts set up for supplies are Operating Supplies and Office Supplies. Purchases of storeroom supplies are recorded to an inventory account, and direct purchases are recorded to a supplies expense account.

Journalize the following transactions on a two-column journal.

20X7

May 12: Jokim, Inc., issues 200,000 authorized shares of $1 par common stock. Of this total, 10,000 shares are issued to the owner, Joshua Kim, for $80,000. The owner issues a personal check payable to Jokim, Inc., which is used to open a company checking account.

May 12: Purchased the following property:

Land	$ 35,000
Building	155,000
	$ 190,000

Issued check number 101 for $50,000 to County Bank, and financed the balance by a mortgage with County Bank.

May 12: Issued check number 102 for $7,000 to Provident Supply, and executed a $40,000 promissory note with Provident Supply in order to purchase the following items:

Operating Supplies	$ 900
Office Supplies	600
Furniture	19,500
Equipment	18,000
China, Glassware, Silver	8,000

May 12: Issued check number 103 for $400 to City Utilities as a deposit for utility services.

May 15: Issued check number 104 for $2,100 to Fidelity Insurance for a one-year fire insurance policy.

May 16: Purchased $6,700 of food provisions on open account from Star Purveyors.

Ethics Case

The accounting department of Dandon Corporation is preparing the company's monthly financial statements. After reviewing the data, the company's controller, Sue Roberts, discovers that Dandon's current liabilities exceed its current assets. This latest information brings the company's poor liquidity position to light.

The company has an outstanding bank loan that requires that monthly financial statements be provided to the bank's commercial loan department. The terms of the loan provide protection for the bank should the security of repayment become doubtful: the bank may call for full payment, demand more collateral, or increase the rate of interest.

Dandon Corporation's profits have been satisfactory, and it has made timely payments to the bank during the course of the loan. The corporation foresees no difficulty in the future in continuing to make the loan payments.

However, to avoid any potential problems with the bank, the president of Dandon instructs Sue to treat all of a loan with another bank as a long-term liability. If Sue makes this change, the current portion of this other bank loan would be eliminated from current liabilities and instead show up as long-term debt. This change in accounting would make the company's current assets larger than its current liabilities.

1. Should the controller follow the president's instructions?
2. Comment on the change in accounting treatment.
3. What real harm is caused by temporarily changing the current versus the long-term portion of a loan? Doesn't all debt require payment anyway?

Chapter 7 Outline

Advantages of Computerized Systems
- Potential Disadvantages

Input Forms
- General Journal
- Special Journals

Output Forms
- Three-Column Account Format
- Subsidiary Ledgers
- Guest and City Ledgers

On-Line Accounting System
- Point-of-Sale Terminals
- Electronic Cash Registers
- Bar Codes

Features of Accounting Packages

Standard General Ledger Modules
- Chart of Accounts Module
- Starting Balances Module
- Comparative Data Module
- Journal and Posting Module
- Trial Balance Module
- Financial Statements Module
- General Ledger Printout Module
- Year-End Module

Selecting General Ledger Accounting Software

Competencies

1. Describe the advantages and potential disadvantages of using a computerized accounting system. (pp. 166–167)
2. Describe the general journal and the various special journals. (pp. 167–170)
3. Describe the three-column account format and the various ledgers that can be used. (pp. 170–172)
4. Describe an on-line accounting system and its hardware components. (pp. 172–173)
5. Identify the standard modules in a general ledger software package and describe the function of each module. (pp. 173–181)
6. List factors to consider when selecting a general ledger software package. (pp. 181–183)

7

General Ledger Software

UNTIL RELATIVELY RECENTLY, only mainframe computers were available and only larger companies could afford them. In addition to their high cost, those mainframes also needed programmers and other technicians. Now, with the microcomputer, or personal computer (PC), small businesses can computerize their accounting systems and other operations. Directly related is the variety of ready-to-use business application software now available at modest cost.

Numerous inexpensive accounting software packages are available that offer "turnkey" installations. The features provided by these packages range from fundamental to sophisticated, although all of them can:

- Record transactions.
- Post transactions.
- Print a trial balance.
- Print a general ledger.
- Print financial statements.

Computers make the accounting and bookkeeping process easier, faster, and more accurate. Little computer expertise is necessary, and the *initial* bookkeeping procedures are similar whether they are performed manually or on a computer. A meaningful advantage of computerized accounting is that the tedious and repetitive clerical procedures have been eliminated or significantly reduced.

This chapter describes computerized general ledger accounting software. The terms and content apply to most commercially available packages. In addition to contributing to an understanding of accounting software, the text answers such questions as:

1. What are the advantages of a computerized accounting system?
2. What are the typical input and output forms in a computerized accounting system?
3. What is an on-line accounting system?
4. What are the features and modules of a general ledger software application?
5. What are the functions of the various modules in general ledger software?
6. What are some considerations in selecting a general ledger software package?

Advantages of Computerized Systems

The computer has become an integral tool in managing a hospitality business because it can process data quickly, accurately, and efficiently. Computerized accounting systems offer the following advantages over a manual system:

- Speed
- Error safeguards
- Automatic posting
- Automatic account balance calculation
- Automatic report generation

Speed. A computer can process a vast amount of data at speeds that human effort cannot approach. Once the data is entered, it can be processed in any sequence and retrieved with minimal clerical effort.

Error Safeguards. A computer does not make errors in math or posting in an account. Furthermore, good computer programs scrutinize the incoming data and will not allow faulty transactions such as invalid account numbers and out-of balance journals. Computerized general ledgers may have other features that safeguard the validity of financial data as well.

Automatic Posting. In a manual system, the first bookkeeping procedures are journalizing and then transferring the information from a journal to the bookkeeping accounts. In a computerized system, the journals still require manual input, but the posting is automatic. Once the computer receives the journal input, it readily transfers this data to the specified bookkeeping accounts. This feature is a fantastic time-saver and provides significant error-reduction over a manual system. Typically, the manual posting process is slow, tedious, and prone to math errors, and posting is routinely performed to the wrong accounts.

Automatic Account Balance Calculation. In a manual system, after the month-end posting process is completed, the bookkeeper has to go through each bookkeeping account and bring the account balances up to date. This procedure also contributes to computational errors and an out-of-balance general ledger that compound problems with a trial balance and worksheet. A computerized accounting system is designed to update the account balances immediately after posting, and these up-to-date records are available at any time for management's analysis.

Automatic Report Generation. Because the data is stored in a computer file, it can be sorted in any sequence, and a user can quickly provide monitor displays or printouts of the general ledger, financial statements, and management reports.

Potential Disadvantages

The biggest potential disadvantage of any computerized system is power failure or computer breakdown. Unless contingent manual procedures are developed, computerized tasks come to a halt. Other emergency alternatives include the use of a battery backup or use of another computer system.

Exhibit 1 General Journal

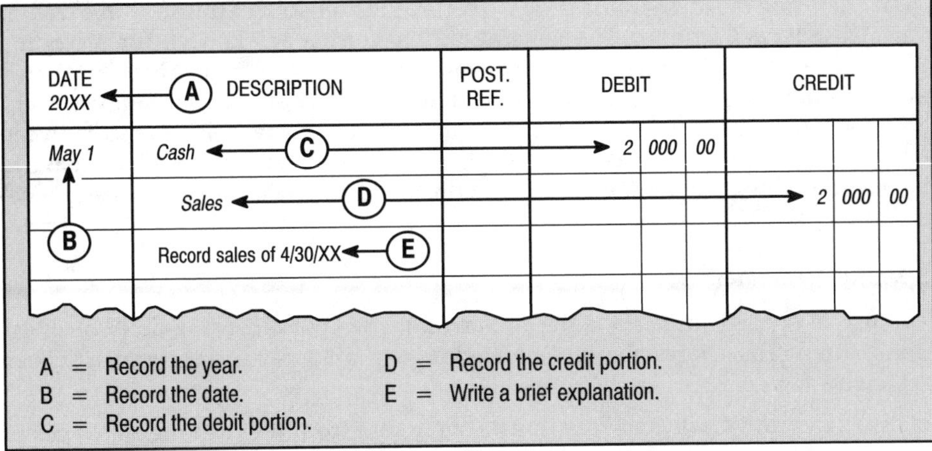

Computerized operations usually require painstaking adherence to procedures. Any departure from procedures might disrupt the entire operation, especially if the operation uses an integrated accounting package (described later). Both the efficiency and quality of customer service may be affected.

Another consideration in computer automation is that the technical nature and detailed requirements of a computerized application may require personnel with higher skill levels than those the business has. It may be necessary to invest in special training and/or recruiting efforts.

Input Forms

Any computer system must be given the transactions that are to be processed. An **input form** is any document or form that contains information to be entered into the computer system. In addition to business transactions, an accounting system must also process other non-daily transactions, such as end-of-month prepaid insurance, accumulated depreciation, and any of a number of other accounts needing adjustment.

A skilled accountant can select or design input forms that are easy to use and whose training requirement is negligible. Properly designed input forms reduce errors and provide internal control. Using a manual entry system, these transactions are written on an input form and entered by keyboard.

General Journal

Entering transaction data (journal entries) on a form is called **journalizing**. The **general journal** is a two-column form used to enter transaction data (see Exhibit 1). This simple and traditional general journal is used in all accounting systems. Notice that the debit amount is on the left side and the credit amount is on the right side. While the debited account name is to the left and the credited account name is indented to the right, this procedure is optional in a computerized system.

As the name implies, it is a general form. It can be used for many purposes, from recording business transactions to recording adjustment transactions. Its universal use is well known. The general journal format works well for recording adjustments or summaries of business transactions, such as monthly totals. However, it is not designed to record daily business transactions. This is because every account must be identified on a line-by-line basis; for example, if cash is in ten transactions, cash must be identified ten times and the amounts would also have to be recorded the same number of times in the bookkeeping account. The use of special journals solves this problem.

Special Journals

The use of **special journals** is the preferred method of recording daily business transactions. These journals are custom-designed for a particular company. They typically include:

- A **Sales and Cash Receipts Journal** prepared from the cash register tapes or cashier's report.
- An **Accounts Payable Journal** prepared from invoices received from suppliers and service providers.
- A **Cash Payments Journal** prepared from the checks issued to suppliers and service providers; this is sometimes called a *check register.*
- A **Payroll Journal** prepared from the checks issued to employees for salaries and wages.

Examples of these special journals are shown in Exhibit 2. Notice that the column headings contain the account name and code and whether the account is debited and credited. The **sundry column** is for those accounts for which a specific column is not provided. Items that appear in the sundry column are those that do not have frequent and repetitive entries. Special journals do not necessarily follow the debits on left side and credits on right side format. One design approach is to place the most active columns nearest the description column; another is to place the accounts to be debited first (left side), followed by all accounts to be credited. The arrangement is immaterial, because in the end, only the total of each column is posted.

Note that the columns in Exhibit 2 have been totaled. Totaling the amounts in a column (a vertical process) is called **footing**. When you calculate the sum of each column total by adding the debits and subtracting the credits, the result should be zero, indicating equality of debits and credits. Totaling amounts in a row (a horizontal process) is called **crossfooting**.

The special journal can be used as an input form, or the summary totals of each column and the individual sundry entries could be entered on a general journal.

Output Forms

An **output form** is any document, report, or form produced by a computer system. Computerized financial statements and other outputs are similar between a

Exhibit 2 Special Journals

Sales and Cash Receipts Journal

Date	Food Sales cr 401	Sales Tax Payable cr 211	Customer Collections cr 112	Cash to Bank dr 102	Customer Charges dr 112	Cash Short (Over) dr (cr) 754	Sundry Items: Account Title	Sundry Items: Acct. No.	Sundry Items: Amount dr
Dec. 8	*1 350 67*	*81 04*	*185 00*	*1 407 06*	*200 00*	*90*	*Cost of Food Sales*	*501*	*8 75*
15	*1 268 52*	*76 11*	*—*	*1 286 93*	*48 65*	*(40)*	*Operating Supplies*	*727*	*9 45*
Total	*2 619 19*	*157 15*	*185 00*	*2 693 99*	*248 65*	*50*			*18 20*

Accounts Payable Journal

Date	Vendor	Accounts Payable cr 201	Food Inventory dr 121	Supplies Inventory dr 131	Utilities dr 712	Sundry Items: Account Title	Sundry Items: Acct. No.	Sundry Items: Amount dr
Dec. 7	*Star Purveyors*	*300 00*	*300 00*					
14	*Pompano Purveyors*	*500 00*	*500 00*					
	TOTAL	*800 00*	*800 00*	*—*	*—*			*—*

Cash Payments Journal

Date	Paid To:	Check Number	Cash—Checking cr 102	Food Inventory dr 121	Accounts Payable dr 201	Sundry Items: Account Title	Sundry Items: Acct. No.	Sundry Items: Amount dr
Dec. 2	*DSK Realty*	*348*	*800 00*			*Rent Expense*	*801*	*800 00*
2	*Associated Insurance Co.*	*349*	*2 400 00*			*Prepaid Insurance*	*132*	*2 400 00*
31	*Regional Telephone*	*358*	*65 16*			*Telephone*	*751*	*65 16*
	TOTAL		*10 262 92*	*200 00*	*4 600 00*			*5 462 92*

Payroll Journal

	Paid To:	Check No.	Gross Wages dr 601	FICA cr 215	FIT cr 215	Net Pay cr 103
	Christine Robert	*621*	*32 16*	*7 85*	*2 00*	*22 31*
	Elizabeth David	*622*	*30 15*	*7 36*	*6 00*	*16 79*
	TOTAL		*868 71*	*79 36*	*59 00*	*730 35*

Exhibit 3 Three-Column Account Format

Title: Accounts Receivable					**Account No.:** 112
	Explanation	**Ref.**	**Dr**	**Cr**	**Balance**
Nov. 30					*185 00*
Dec. 31		*S*	*248 65*	*185 00*	*248 65*

Title: Accounts Payable					**Account No.:** 201
	Explanation	**Ref.**	**Dr**	**Cr**	**Balance**
Nov. 30					*(4 600 00)*
Dec. 31		*CP*	*4 600 00*		
31		*AP*		*800 00*	*(800 00)*

manual system and a computer system. Financial statements have been previously discussed and illustrated. Within an accounting system are various types of ledgers such as the general ledger and subsidiary ledgers.

Three-Column Account Format

Business transactions, adjustments, and other entries must be recorded in the bookkeeping accounts. The three-column account format shown in Exhibit 3 is very popular and easy to read and use. Included in the three columns are debits, credits, and balances. The debit column is placed to the left of the credit column. Note that the first amount in the balance column does not have a debit or credit amount; this indicates that it is a beginning balance. Some systems use "bf" (balance forward) notation or another indicator to highlight a beginning balance.

The posting reference column shows a cross-reference of the source for the entry. In our case, the debit and credit entries come from:

- Sales Journal (S).
- Accounts Payable Journal (AP).
- Cash Payments Journal (CP).
- Payroll Journal (PR).

If a transaction source document is a general journal, a common practice is to use the letter *J* followed by a number; typically the list begins with the number *1* each month and is incremented for each general journal entry prepared during that month. The codes for source documents are determined at installation design.

In the balance column, a means to identify a debit or credit balance is needed. A credit balance is "signed" by enclosing the amount with parentheses, or by the use of a negative sign or "cr" after the amount. An unsigned amount represents a debit balance.

A simple way to compute an account balance is to treat debits as positive and credits as negative. The Accounts Receivable account in Exhibit 3 is one example.

Exhibit 4 Accounts Receivable Subsidiary Ledger

NAME *DEBCO, Inc.*
ADDRESS

DATE 20X2	ITEM	POST. REF.	DEBIT	CREDIT	BALANCE
Dec. 8	Tab 1812	S	200 00		200 00

NAME *J.R. Rickles*
ADDRESS

DATE 20X2	ITEM	POST. REF.	DEBIT	CREDIT	BALANCE
Nov. 18	Tab 1511	S	185 00		185 00
Dec. 8	Payment	S		185 00	-0-
15	Tab 1849	S	48 65		48 65

The beginning debit balance of $185 and the debit entry of $248.65 are added; the credit entry of $185 is subtracted to arrive at its ending *debit balance* of $248.65.

The Accounts Payable account in Exhibit 3 is an example of an account that starts with a credit balance. Compute the balance by starting with a negative amount of $4,600, add the debit entry of $4,600, and subtract the credit entry of $800; you should have a resulting *credit balance* of $800.

Subsidiary Ledgers

A **subsidiary ledger** is separate from the general ledger. Its purpose is to provide supporting detail for certain accounts in the general ledger. These accounts are sometimes referred to as *controlling accounts*. For example, the Accounts Receivable account in the general ledger shows only a balance due from all customers; it does not indicate who the customers are. The most common subsidiary ledgers are the accounts receivable subsidiary ledger and the accounts payable subsidiary ledger.

The **accounts receivable subsidiary ledger** shows each customer receivable and supporting detail. A separate record is maintained for each customer. A sample accounts receivable ledger is shown in Exhibit 4. Each record shows the dates of activity, the source of the charge, and any payments.

The **accounts payable subsidiary ledger** shows detailed information about amounts owed by the business to its suppliers and the account activity (dates, purchases, payments). It is a separate subsidiary ledger but its format is identical to the accounts receivable ledger format.

Guest and City Ledgers

Guest ledgers and city ledgers are types of accounts receivable subsidiary ledgers used in a lodging operation. The **guest ledger** is used to record transactions involving registered guests. The **city ledger** is used to record transactions for all customers other than registered guests. Once a registered guest checks out, that person is no longer a registered guest. A city ledger could contain the following:

- Sales transactions for rental of conference rooms
- Unregistered guests charging food purchases
- The unpaid balance for previously registered guests who checked out

On-Line Accounting System

In an on-line accounting system, business transactions are recorded as they occur. This type of computerized data entry system is sometimes called a *real-time* system or an *integrated* accounting system. On-line systems are popular in areas such as:

- Reservations.
- Food order entry.
- Sales.
- Inventory control.
- Accounting.

Point-of-Sale Terminals

A point-of-sale (POS) terminal contains its own input/output units and possibly a small storage memory. A POS terminal must be connected to a remote central processing unit (CPU), an expensive component that can handle multiple POS terminals. POS terminals can have peripherals such as magnetic stripe readers, check readers, scales, and bar code scanners. Sales POS terminals record the sale and post it in the general ledger almost simultaneously.

Electronic Cash Registers

An electronic cash register (ECR) is a cash register with programmable features that can be customized for specific needs of the user. It is a standalone hardware computer system. All the required hardware components are in the ECR, and its keyboard (customized for its particular operation) is the input device. The display unit, storage memory, and CPU are contained within the ECR housing. Its flexibility offers management timely revenue and cash information resulting in better management and internal control.

Bar Codes

Most of us are familiar with the bar code systems used in the retail industry. The product is passed over a scanner that reads the bar code. In these systems, the following events occur concurrently:

- The selling price is displayed to the customer.
- The selling price is recorded in a sales journal.
- The sale is recorded in the general ledger.
- Inventory records are updated.

Bar codes can be used to track products from receiving through sale, making possible an automated perpetual inventory system.

Features of Accounting Packages

Sophisticated accounting packages can provide the following automated accounting capabilities:

- Billing
- Accounts receivable
- Accounts payable
- Inventory control
- Depreciation
- Payroll

Basic accounting packages merely perform the bookkeeping function, while the more sophisticated packages automate much of the clerical function. Regardless of its sophistication, each package has:

- Modules.
- Menus/windows.
- Audit trails.
- Computer fraud considerations.

Modules. Accounting software packages are designed to perform designated tasks by a series of callable programs usually referred to as *modules*. Pull-down menus or windows are used to select these modules.

Pull-Down Menus. Menu-driven programs use the monitor display to array a list of menus. By positioning the on-screen arrow over a menu title with the mouse, pushing the mouse button, and moving the arrow down, a user can "pull down" a module chosen for execution.

Windows. A window is an area on the screen that is used by the program to furnish the same capability as a menu but offers other features, such as the following:

- Menu items are replaced with pictures ("icons") and "buttons." A button is "pushed" by positioning the on-screen arrow over it and pushing the mouse button. Menu items represented by icons are activated in the same way, except that the user is often required to push the mouse button twice.

- A windows environment often lets the user run several applications at the same time. The *taskbar* (usually shown at the bottom of the screen) indicates which applications are running.
- A windows environment also allows the user to access more than one document at the same time.

Audit Trails. An **audit trail** allows a user to trace transactions that were processed in the computerized accounting system. Any sophisticated computerized accounting system (1) permits the user to trace entries back to a source document and (2) furnishes a record of any data entered into the accounting system

Computer Fraud. As in any manual system, the safeguarding of business assets and confidential information is a major challenge. The vigilance against fraud requires an effective system of *internal control* characterized by authoritative management policies and assurance that the safeguards are being followed by personnel.

Standard General Ledger Modules

The purpose of a *manual* general ledger system is to update the general ledger, print a trial balance, and, finally, assemble the financial statements. A *computerized* general ledger can also perform these functions because it likewise has a separate record for each bookkeeping account showing the account's identification number and title and changes to its balance.

A typical computerized accounting package consists of the following **modules**:

- Chart of accounts
- Starting balances
- Comparative data
- Journal and posting
- Trial balance
- Financial statements
- General ledger printout
- Year-end

Chart of Accounts Module

The chart of accounts module allows the user to set up the bookkeeping accounts and perform routine file maintenance on these accounts. This module permits the user to:

- Set up the bookkeeping account titles and account identification numbers.
- Enter the current account balances.
- Add or change account titles and account identification numbers.

Entering the Bookkeeping Accounts. The requirements for entering the bookkeeping accounts depend on the accounting package; each has its own procedures. A versatile package permits the user to select account titles and account identification numbers. The account identification numbers that can be assigned must be within the range allowed by the general ledger package. Some packages allow only three-digit account numbers, while others may allow account numbers with four digits or more. Many accounting packages do not allow the user to select an account number composed of all nines, such as 999 or 9999. The reason is that the computer software reserves these numbers for either suspense accounts (described later) or its internal function of determining profit or loss.

A user must exercise caution when setting up the account numbers. The computer will sort or group accounts based on selected parameters within the report program modules. Therefore, the numbering system should have the capacity for new accounts as needed.

Many general ledger modules do not require an Income Summary account in the general ledger, because the determination of income or loss is built into the program.

Classification of Account Numbers. The method for classifying accounts as assets, liabilities, equity, revenue, or expenses varies by general ledger package. All packages contain specific instructions for account number classifications. The accounting package might stipulate that asset accounts be numbered between 1000–1999 and liability accounts between 2000–2999 and that the equity, revenue, and expense accounts also be within given number ranges.

Level of Account. In addition to the type of account, some packages require that each account be described in terms of its *level*. The term "level" refers to how the account will appear on the financial statements. The level describes if the account is to be printed individually on a single line or combined with other accounts and printed as one caption (line item) on the financial statements. In some packages, the level is defined in the report format module instead of the chart of accounts module.

Exhibit 5 illustrates one method of setting up a chart of accounts. The level of the account is not required in this particular chart of accounts module. In the exhibit, assets are in the 1000–1999 range with current assets (CA) in the 1000 series and property and equipment in the 1500 series. Current liabilities (CL) are in the 2000 series, equity (EQ) in the 3000 series, sales (REV) in the 4000 series, and expenses (EX) in the 5000 series.

Starting Balances Module

It is unlikely that a computerized general ledger will be started on the first day of a business year for an existing business. Therefore, programmers have provided ways for existing businesses to enter the starting balances when converting from a manual system to a computerized system.

Some packages let the user set up a chart of accounts with the starting balances. Other packages require that a chart of accounts be set up first, and afterward the current account balances are entered by a general journal. The general ledger

Exhibit 5 Computerized Chart of Accounts

101	Cash on Hand	ACC
102	Cash-Regular Checking	ACC
103	Cash-Payroll Checking	ACC
112	Accounts Receivable	ACR
121	Food Inventory	ACI
131	Supplies Inventory	ACI
132	Prepaid Insurance	ACP
147	Furniture & Equipment	AFF
149	China, Glassware & Silver	AFF
157	Accumulated Depreciation	AFD
201	Accounts Payable	LCA
211	Sales Tax Payable	LCE
215	Employee Taxes Withheld	LCE
231	Accrued Payroll	LCE
232	Accrued Payroll Taxes	LCE
301	Capital, Ann Dancer	CSC

package has built-in safeguards against alterations of the balance without an authorized transaction that provides an audit trail.

Comparative Data Module

More sophisticated general ledger packages have features that allow the entry of last year's balances, budgets, or other comparative data that can be used to produce comparative financial statements or other comparative reports for management. Generally, only the income statement accounts contain budgeted data because operating budgets are revenue- and expense-oriented.

Many computerized systems allow the retention of data from the previous year *(year-1 past)* and the year prior to the previous year *(year-2 past)*. After a system is computerized and has gone through a year-end closing, there is no need to enter the previous year's balances, because each year at year-end the computer software automatically moves the current closing balances to year-1 past data and the old year-1 balances to year-2 past data.

Journal and Posting Module

This module records the journal entries in the bookkeeping accounts and prints the journals or a journal summary. The recording of journal entries in bookkeeping accounts is called **posting**. Some general ledger packages might call this module a *journal module* or a *posting module;* regardless of its name, they all perform the same function. Even though a system may be on line, there are transactions that must be entered using input forms. There are many methods to prepare computer input; cost, hardware, software, and skilled personnel all play a role in determining how input is prepared.

Smaller companies with single-page journals might use the original journals as the input documents. Larger companies (not on an integrated system) have journals consisting of numerous entries and pages; therefore, they may prefer to use a separate input form for the convenience of the keyboard operator and for internal control reasons.

The data on the input document is entered by keyboard. The journal and posting module then prints a summary journal and posts the data to the bookkeeping accounts. The journal printout serves as an audit trail to substantiate the changes to the general ledger (bookkeeping accounts). In some packages, the printout shows an *entry sequence number* that serves as an identification number should analysis be necessary due to an input error. Some packages also allow the entry of a *batch control number* to provide more controls and audit trails.

Suspense Account. A **suspense account** is an account in which the computer software posts an amount if the computer cannot find the account number in its chart of accounts. This prevents the general ledger from being out of balance, but the suspense account may contain several transactions that will require analysis. The suspense account should be cleared before any further processing is performed.

Some packages do not have a suspense account, because they will not process input data that is out of balance. Instead, the software either rejects the batch or prints an error message during processing and lets the user instantly make the correction.

Most software packages print an "in balance" statement at the bottom of the journal printout to indicate that the debit and credit totals are in balance. Conversely, an "out of balance" message will print if a balance error occurs.

Exhibit 6 shows a sales and cash receipts journal that was prepared manually. This journal was used as a source document to prepare the computer input form that is illustrated in Exhibit 7. The input form is given to a keyboard operator who enters the information into the computer software's journal and posting module. Exhibit 8 shows the computerized audit trail that indicates the journal was processed (posted) and account balances (the general ledger) updated.

Trial Balance Module

This module prints a trial balance that is a primary tool the accountant uses to prepare analyses, reconciliations, and adjusting entries. A **trial balance** is a listing of all the general ledger accounts with their balances. The accountant uses a trial balance to examine the accounts, prepare adjustments, and verify the equality of debits and credits. A typical procedure an accountant might use is:

1. Analyze the trial balance to determine adjustments.
2. Prepare the adjusting entries and forward them to the keyboard operator.
3. Have the journal and posting module process the adjusting entries.
4. Request a new trial balance.

Exhibit 6 Sales and Cash Receipts Journal

SALES & CASH RECEIPTS JOURNAL (S)
December 20X2

Date	Food Sales cr 401	Sales Tax Payable cr 211	Customer Collections cr 112	Cash to Bank dr 102	Customer Charges dr 112	Cash Short (Over) dr (cr) 754	Sundry Items		
							Account Title	Acct. No.	Amount dr
Dec. 8	*1 350 67*	*81 04*	*185 00*	*1 407 06*	*200 00*	*90*	*Cost of Food Sales*	*501✓*	*8 75*
15	*1 268 52*	*76 11*	—	*1 286 93*	*48 65*	*(40)*	*Operating Supplies*	*727✓*	*9 45*
Total	*2 619 19*	*157 15*	*185 00*	*2 693 99*	*248 65*	*50*			*18 20*
	✓	✓	✓	✓	✓	✓			

Exhibit 7 Input Form for Keyboard Operator

Journal Input Form
Posting Date: 12/30/X2 Batch No: 1
Journal Code: S

Account	Debit	Credit
401		2 619 19
211		157 15
112		185 00
102	2 693 99	
112	248 65	
754	50	
501	8 75	
727	9 45	
Batch Total	2 961 34	2 961 34

Exhibit 8 Journal Printed by Computer

Journal: S
Posting Date: 12/31/X2 Batch Number: 1
Run Date: 1/10/X3

Sequence	Account		Debit	Credit
001	102	Cash—Regular Checking	2,693.99	
002	112	Accounts Receivable	248.65	185.00
003	211	Sales Tax Payable		157.15
004	401	Food Sales		2,619.19
005	501	Cost of Food Sales	8.75	
006	727	Operating Supplies	9.45	
007	754	Cash Short or Over	.50	
Batch Total			2,961.34	2,961.34
			IN BALANCE	

Exhibit 9 Trial Balance

		Trial Balance	
		Dr	Cr
101	Cash on Hand	1 000 00	
102	Cash—Regular Checking	18 223 23	
103	Cash—Payroll Checking	200 00	
112	Accounts Receivable	248 65	
121	Food Inventory	5 875 00	
131	Supplies Inventory	1 100 00	
132	Prepaid Insurance	2 400 00	
147	Furniture & Equipment	45 000 00	
149	China, Glassware & Silver	9 000 00	
157	Acc. Depreciation—F&E		27 000 00
201	Accounts Payable		800 00
211	Sales Tax Payable		157 15
215	Employee Taxes Withheld		138 36
231	Accrued Payroll		
232	Accrued Payroll Taxes		
301	Capital, Ann Dancer		74 324 73
302	Withdrawals, Ann Dancer	38 000 00	
401	Food Sales		165 209 94
501	Cost of Food Sales	57 158 75	
601	Payroll	49 774 87	
602	Payroll Taxes	4 788 75	
605	Employee Benefits	2 164 18	
607	Employee Meals	2 875 00	
712	Utilities	3 345 31	
721	China, Glassware & Silver	1 650 00	
727	Operating Supplies	2 908 11	
751	Telephone	915 44	
752	Office Supplies	923 14	
753	Credit Card Fees	1 868 75	
754	Cash Short or Over	137 66	
761	Repairs & Maintenance	2 489 34	
801	Rent	9 600 00	
821	Insurance	1 859 00	
891	Depreciation	4 125 00	
	TOTAL	267 630 18	267 630 18

Exhibit 9shows one format used for trial balances. Some computerized systems print the balances in only a single column; credit balances are identified by parentheses.

Financial Statements Module

All general ledger packages print the income statement, balance sheet, statement of retained earnings, and statement of owners' equity. Not all packages have the ability to print the statement of cash flows and not all packages offer the same flexibility in formatting the financial statements.

Some general ledger packages allow the user to customize the financial statements in any format desired with customized headings and totals. Other packages

Exhibit 10 Computer General Ledger Account Format

102	Cash—Regular Checking			25,792.16
	12/31/09	CP	(10,262.92)	
	12/31/09	S	2,693.99	
				18,223.23

Comments:

- The account number is 102. The name of the account follows its number code.
- The beginning balance of 25,792.16 is shown at the rightmost position.
- This general ledger software shows credit amounts in parenthesis.
- The posting references are the journals CP and S shown next to the transaction date of 12/31/09.
- This general ledger software highlights the ending balance with a "star."

do not allow any flexibility; the user must adopt the headings, line totals, and format provided by the software. Most packages offer reasonable capability to format a user's financial statements according to the user's requirements.

General Ledger Printout Module

This module prints the general ledger, usually in a three-column account format. Most packages permit the following options:

- Print the entire general ledger.
- Print a series of accounts.
- Print one account.

At first, reading an account printed by a general ledger might be puzzling. Depending on the software, the account format might be different from what is customary with a manual system. Exhibit 10 shows an account printed by a computerized general ledger. Notice that there is a balance column showing the beginning balance and ending balance. However, there are no separate debit and credit columns. Instead, the debits are shown as positive numbers and the credits are shown as negative numbers (using parentheses). To better grasp the general ledger concept, rework the amounts in the account shown in Exhibit 10 and check your result with the ending balance.

Year-End Module

This module clears the balances in the revenue and expense accounts (and the withdrawals account, if applicable) and updates the retained earnings account or capital account without any need for closing entries. The accountant merely activates the year-end module from among the menu options and the year-end closing process is executed. Some packages automatically print a post-closing trial balance, while others require that it be requested via a menu print option.

Exhibit 11 Post-Closing Trial Balance

101	Cash on Hand	1	000	00			
102	Cash—Regular Checking	18	223	23			
103	Cash—Payroll Checking		200	00			
112	Accounts Receivable		248	65			
121	Food Inventory	5	157	00			
131	Supplies Inventory	1	000	00			
132	Prepaid Insurance	2	200	00			
147	Furniture & Equipment	45	000	00			
149	China, Glassware & Silver	8	850	00			
157	Accumulated Depreciation—F&E				27	375	00
201	Accounts Payable					800	00
211	Sales Tax Payable					157	15
215	Employee Taxes Withheld					138	36
231	Accrued Payroll					385	00
232	Accrued Payroll Taxes					366	00
301	Capital, Ann Dancer				52	657	37
	Total	81	878	88	81	878	88

A **post-closing trial balance** is a listing of the balance sheet accounts. It lists only the balance sheet accounts because after the year-end closing entries are performed, the income statement accounts contain only zero balances. Exhibit 11 shows a post-closing trial balance. The purpose of the post-closing trial balance is to show the equality of debits and credits after the closing process and to serve as an audit trial when the ending balances are carried over as beginning balances for the next accounting year.

In addition to performing the closing process, this module may automatically move the revenue and expense closing balances to year-1 past data, and the old year-1 past data to year-2 past data.

Selecting General Ledger Accounting Software

Naturally, the most preferable software selection method is to have the opportunity to see the software in action, especially when it is operating at a real company instead of a seminar or trade show. Even this visual experience requires investigating certain features because not every company has identical staff, resources, and needs. No checklist can be considered complete, but the following are some features to explore:

Basic Considerations

- Audit trails of input
- Flexible chart of accounts for customization of account names and codes
- Inquiry capability to examine balances and transactions
- Audit trails
  - –Unauthorized account numbers
  - –Out-of-balance entries or batches
  - –Reference to source documents or input identification
  - –Accounting period date
  - –Processed date
- Special journal formats appropriate for your requirements
- Customization of financial statements
- Physical limitations of software:
  - –Number of accounts
  - –Maximum entry amount
  - –Maximum account balance
  - –Maximum characters in account description
  - –Maximum number of journal entries
- Rounding of dollar amounts in financial reporting

Advanced Considerations

- Departmentalized accounting
- Consolidation of multiple locations or companies
- Comparative reports (budgets, history)
- On-line capability
- Other built-in applications:
  - –Accounts receivable
  - –Accounts payable
  - –Payroll
  - –Fixed assets
  - –Inventory
  - –Order entry
  - –Purchase order

- Flash reports
- Graphical reports

Finally, of course, are the cost of the software and level of customer support provided by the supplier after you purchase the software.

Key Terms

accounts payable journal—A special journal prepared from invoices received from suppliers and service providers.

accounts payable subsidiary ledger—A ledger showing the activity and detail of amounts owed to suppliers and service providers.

accounts receivable subsidiary ledger—A ledger showing the activity and detail for each customer receivable.

audit trail—Any reference or document that allows the tracing of transactions back to a source document.

cash payments journal—A special journal prepared from checks issued to suppliers and service providers.

city ledger—An accounts receivable subsidiary ledger used by lodging operations for transactions by any unregistered guest.

crossfooting—Totaling amounts in a row (a horizontal process).

footing—Totaling the amounts in a column (a vertical process).

general journal—A two-column form used to journalize transactions.

guest ledger—An accounts receivable subsidiary ledger used by lodging operations for transactions by registered guests.

input form—Any document or form containing information to be entered into a computer system.

journalizing—The entering of transaction data in the form of journal entries on a journal form.

modules—Programs performing specific tasks.

output form—A document, report, or form produced by a computer system.

payroll journal—A special journal prepared from checks issued to employees for salaries and wages.

post-closing trial balance—A trial balance (after the closing entries are processed) listing the balance sheet accounts with their balances.

posting—Transferring amounts from a journal by entering them in the bookkeeping accounts of the general ledger.

sales and cash receipts journal—A special journal prepared from cash register tapes or cashier's reports.

special journal—A journal that is custom designed for a particular use.

subsidiary ledger—A separate ledger providing supporting detail for a specific account in the general ledger.

sundry column—A column for those accounts not having a specific column.

suspense account—An account in which computer software posts an amount if the account number being processed is not authorized by the chart of accounts.

trial balance—A trial balance is a listing of all the general ledger accounts with their balances.

Review Questions

1. What are the advantages and disadvantages of a computerized system?
2. What is the definition of the following?

   General journal

   Special journal

   Sundry column
3. From which source are the following special journals prepared?

   Sales and Cash Receipts Journal

   Accounts Payable Journal

   Cash Payments Journal

   Payroll Journal
4. What is footing and crossfooting?
5. What is the definition of the each following terms?

   Subsidiary Ledger

   Accounts Receivable Subsidiary Ledger

   Accounts Payable Subsidiary Ledger

   Guest Ledger

   City Ledger
6. What are a point-of-sale terminal and an electronic cash register?
7. How are each of the following modules found in a general ledger software package used?

   Chart of Accounts Module

   Starting Balances Module

   Comparative Data Module

   Journal and Posting Module

   Trial Balance Module

   Financial Statements Module

General Ledger Printout Module

Year-end Module

8. What is a suspense account?
9. What is an audit trail?
10. What is a three-column account form?
11. How are the following defined?

    Journalizing

    Posting

    Trial Balance

    Post-closing Trial Balance

Problems

Problem 1

Indicate the journal in which the following transactions will be recorded by making a checkmark under the appropriate heading.

	Sales	Accounts Payable	Payroll	Cash Payments
a. Payroll checks	____	____	____	____
b. Checks to suppliers	____	____	____	____
c. Sales for the day	____	____	____	____
d. Invoice to be paid next week	____	____	____	____
e. Issued check for rent payment	____	____	____	____

Problem 2

Specify whether the columns on the following special journals are a debit or a credit. Wherever a column is not applicable to a particular journal, an "x" has been inserted.

Journal Column	Sales & Cash Receipts	Accounts Payable	Cash Payments
Cash	____	x	____
Sales Tax Payable	____	x	____
Customer Collections	____	x	x
Customer Charges	____	x	x

Accounts Payable	x		
Food Sales		x	x
Food Inventory	x		
Allowances		x	x
Cash Shortage		x	x
Sundry Items			

Problem 3

Prepare a general journal entry in proper format using the following totals as shown on a payroll journal:

Gross wages	$5,000
FICA withheld	400
FIT withheld	800

Problem 4

Compute the ending balance in the following accounts.

Title: Food Inventory										**Account No.:** 121	
	Explanation	**Ref.**	**Dr**			**Cr**			**Balance**		
Nov. 30									*4*	*875*	*00*
Dec. 31		*CP*		*200*	*00*						
31		*AP*		*800*	*00*				*5*	*875*	*00*
31		*J6*					*718*	*00*			

Title: Sales Tax Payable										**Account No.:** 211	
	Explanation	**Ref.**	**Dr**			**Cr**			**Balance**		
Nov. 30									*(1*	*216*	*75)*
Dec. 31		*S*					*157*	*15*			
31		*CP*	*1*	*216*	*75*						

Problem 5

A hotel has the following subsidiary ledgers:

Guest Ledger	$250,000
City Ledger	120,000
Accounts payable	60,000

What amount will appear as accounts receivable on the balance sheet?

Problem 6

The following is an abstract of an accounts payable journal with footings. Analyze and comment.

	Accounts Payable cr	Inventory dr	Utilities dr	Advertising dr
3/4	1,000	1,000		
3/8	125		125	
3/15	69			96
3/31	416	416		
3/31	87		87	
Totals	1,697	1,416	212	96

Problem 7

Specify whether each of the following statements is true (T) or false (F).

________ 1. Journalizing is the process of transferring an amount to an account.

________ 2. The total of the sundry column in a special journal is posted in the general ledger.

________ 3. Special journals have a special design that is suitable for any company.

________ 4. A post-closing trial balance shows the balance sheet and income statement accounts with their balances.

________ 5. A suspense account contains a reserve amount for casualties such as fire or theft.

________ 6. Computer software packages cannot print financial statements.

________ 7. The most popular account format in a general ledger software package is the "T" account.

________ 8. A city ledger is a custom designed ledger for municipalities.

________ 9. Conversion from a manual system to a computerized system must start at the beginning of a year because account balances during a year cannot be brought forward.

________ 10. A trial balance shows only suspense accounts in the general ledger.

Ethics Case

Al Bender is the controller of the Diabco Company. Sara Labont is the assistant controller. Al is a close friend of the company president, and Sara is a relatively new employee. Sara is a recent college graduate with high honors from a prestigious university.

(continued)

Prior to Sara's employment, the company's accounting system did not produce the timely, useful information which management required. After Sara was hired, Al assigned her the task of designing a new accounting system. He also told Sara to devote all of her effort to this assignment. After several months of Sara's hard work and long hours, the new system was completed, installed, and highly successful.

The company's executive managers have been greatly impressed with the new system's results and the significant improvement in accuracy and turnaround time. Recently, Diabco's president asked Al who designed the system. Al, seeking an opportunity to promote his image, told the president that the system was his original idea and design. Further, he told the president that, while the development of the system required a tremendous amount of his personal time, the company's needs have priority.

Later, Al tells Sara about his conversation with the president. Al suggests to Sara that her silence would be her best course of action in this matter.

1. What are the relevant facts in this case?
2. What are the ethical issues?
3. What are Sara's possible alternatives for her next course of action?

Chapter 8 Outline

Competencies

1. Describe the accounting cycle and the difference between accrual and cash basis accounting. (pp. 191–193)
2. Explain the steps necessary to convert from a manual accounting system to a computerized accounting system. (pp. 193–196)
3. Describe how special journals can be used as the source document for input to the computerized accounting system. (pp. 196–200)
4. Describe a working trial balance and identify adjusting entries. (pp. 200–206)
5. Explain how net income or loss is manually calculated to verify the accuracy of the computerized financial statements. (pp. 206–214)

8

Computerized Accounting Cycle

THE EXACT METHOD OF PROCESSING TRANSACTIONS in a computerized accounting system depends on the type of computer (mainframe or personal) and general ledger software used. Nevertheless, all computerized systems require similar input and produce similar output.

Despite all its advantages, the computer has not eliminated the need for human professional judgment. An accountant still must analyze data for correctness and up-to-date status. Errors can occur during the journalizing process because even though a computer system may reject unauthorized account numbers, it cannot determine if a valid account might actually be an incorrect account for a particular transaction. Most companies need monthly financial statements for successful management. Reliable financial statements require the expertise of an accountant to analyze such items as expired insurance, depreciation, doubtful accounts, and other entries that must be updated by the use of *adjusting entries.*

The *accounting cycle* begins with business transactions, continues with month-end adjusting entries and printing of financial statements, and terminates with the year-end process. This chapter covers a computerized accounting cycle from start to finish, using Tower Restaurant as a demonstration case. To make the chapter more pragmatic, Tower Restaurant, currently on a manual accounting system, will be converted to a computerized accounting system. The chapter provides comprehensive coverage of the operation of a computerized accounting system and answers such questions as:

1. How is a manual system converted to a computerized accounting system?
2. How are business transactions processed in a computerized accounting system?
3. What are adjusting entries and how are they determined and processed?
4. How can net income (or loss) be manually verified?
5. Which financial statements are produced in a computerized accounting system?
6. What is the computerized year-end process?

Accounting Cycle

The **accounting cycle** is the sequence of accounting procedures performed during an accounting period; it is a continuing process of recording and reporting financial information. An *accounting system* is a database of financial information about

Exhibit 1 Accounting Cycle

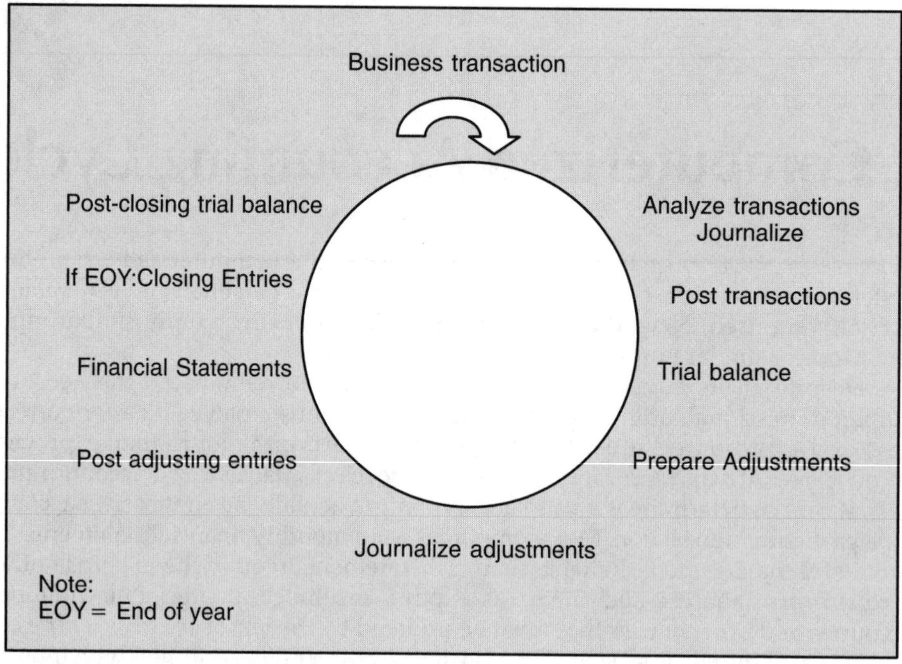

a company. No two companies have exactly the same database because each company has different information requirements that vary with size, industry, and customer market. However, *the accounting cycle* illustrated in Exhibit 1 is the one attribute of an accounting system that *is a constant*. The following summarizes the functions of the accounting cycle:

- Analyze and journalize transactions.
- Post transactions to the general ledger.
- Print a trial balance.
- Analyze the trial balance; prepare, journalize, and post adjusting entries.
- Issue the financial statements.
- At end of year, close income statement accounts; print post-closing trial balance.

Cash Basis Accounting

Under **cash basis accounting**, revenue is recorded only when cash is received, and an expense is recorded only when cash is paid. This basis of accounting produces misleading information because it fails to record revenue when earned (realization principle) and does not enter expenses incurred in the production of this revenue (matching principle). Therefore, the cash basis of accounting *is not in compliance with generally accepted accounting principles (GAAP).*

A small business is justified in keeping its books on the cash basis of accounting; however, an accountant will prepare a worksheet and convert these records to accrual basis if financial statements are to be issued to external users.

Accrual Basis Accounting

Under **accrual basis accounting,** all revenue and expense transactions are recorded in the period in which they occur. The accrual basis of accounting is in compliance with GAAP and must be used by accountants in the preparation of financial statements. The accrual basis of accounting also requires adjustments prior to preparation of financial statements for particulars such as invoices not yet received, expired assets (prepaid items, depreciation), potential bad debts, and other items to comply with the matching principle.

Computerized vs. Manual Accounting Cycle

The elements of the accounting cycle are identical for both manual and computerized accounting systems. Each phase of the cycle is required. The only difference is the method of processing—manual vs. computer. In this chapter, we cover the computer process; for those interested in the manual elements of accounting, such as the formidable worksheet and reversing entries, an example is provided in Appendix A to this chapter.

Tower Restaurant: A Computerized Demonstration

Tower Restaurant is a family-operated small business formed as a proprietorship and owned by Ann Dancer, who is a full-time hospitality teacher. It is a relatively new business and its market is local residents in a rural town. Tower's accounting year is a calendar year. The restaurant has been on a manual system and is planning to convert to a computerized accounting system. The management of Tower has elected to end its manual system as of the November 30 accounting period, which is the end of its busy season. In December, the restaurant is closed for most of the month except for two small banquets on December 8 and December 15. Therefore, this cutoff of the manual system is an ideal time for a conversion to an automated system.

Tower's Input Procedures

Because Tower is a small business, its management has decided not to invest in an on-line system or enter daily transactions in the computer system. After consultation with its accountant, Tower decided on the following procedure for processing its business transactions:

- Continue to use the existing special journals.
  - Sales and Cash Receipts Journal
  - Cash Payments Journal
  - Accounts Payable Journal
  - Payroll Journal

- Enter the data manually on these journals.
- At the end of the month, use the journal footings and individual sundry items as input to the computer system.

Tower's Computer Software

Tower purchased a low-cost computer and an inexpensive, commercially available general ledger software package. The software 's specific features include capabilities that:

- Show credit amounts in parentheses and debit amounts unsigned.
- Display equality of debits and credits as "Net DR/CR $0.00."
- Customize a chart of accounts.
- Customize financial statements.

Since December is the last month of Tower's business year, its management has decided not to enter any comparative or historical data in the *Comparative Data Module*. Tower has decided to use the following modules of this computer package:

- Chart of Accounts
- Starting Balances
- Posting
- Trial Balance
- Financial Statements
- General Ledger
- Year-end

For the conversion to a computerized accounting system, Tower's accountant has the following assignment:

- Set up a computerized chart of accounts.
- Enter the starting balances in the computer system.
- Manually enter the December transactions on special journals.
- Post the special journals in the computer system.
- Print a trial balance.
- Analyze the trial balance.
- Determine adjustments.
- Journalize and post the adjusting entries in the computer system.
- Print financial statements.
- Print general ledger.
- Perform the year-end process (December 31 is end of the accounting year).

– Closing entries
– Post-closing trial balance

Conversion from Manual to Computerized System

All software packages allow the user to set up account balances so that a conversion from a manual system to a computerized system can take place at any time of the year. Some software packages allow the use of existing account numbers or provide flexibility in designing an account number coding system. Setting up a chart of accounts for a computerized system requires that each bookkeeping account be assigned an account number and an account type.

An account number is required in computer systems to simplify the input process and avoid writing the account name in journal entries to the computer, which can lead to rejections or errors.

Setting Up the Computer Chart of Accounts

The general ledger package permits Tower Restaurant to use its existing chart of accounts. Fortunately, the manual account coding system was logically designed by Tower's accountant and can be used by the software. Tower uses a three-digit numbering code as follows:

1xx Assets
2xx Liabilities
3xx Equity
4xx Revenue
5xx Cost of sales expense
6xx Payroll and related expenses
7xx Operating expenses
8xx Fixed expenses

The second digit of the number code also has a special meaning. For example, assets were further subdivided as follows:

10x Cash items
11x Receivables
12x Food and other merchandise inventories
13x Supplies inventory
14x Fixed assets
15x Accumulated depreciation

For the other classifications of accounts, a similar indexing approach was used for the second digit of the account number. The third digit of the number code is a sequential number, leaving open numbers for expansion. Use of 9xx numbers was avoided to avoid conflict with any built-in suspense account or automatic functions of the package.

The *type* of account must be specified because these letter codes are used to customize the printing of financial statements. This particular computer package uses a three-letter code to specify the type of account. Easy-to-follow instructions to code the accounts are provided. A sample of the type of account coding follows:

A = Asset
  C = Current
    C = Cash
    R = Receivable
    I = Inventory
    P = Prepaid
  F = Fixed asset
    F = Furniture and equipment
    D = Depreciation
L = Liability
  C = Current
    A = Accounts payable

The software package allows the accountant to set up the chart of accounts and enter the beginning balances during the same computer processing operation. Therefore, the accountant decided to use this feature and enter the account balances before submitting any input to the computer.

Computer Input of Account Balances

After the codes are determined, the next step is to enter the beginning balances of each account. The ending balances as of November 30 are entered because they also represent the beginning balances for December 1. The codes and balances have been manually entered on a form, which could be either a two-column journal or other useful format. This form is input to the computer software's Chart of Accounts Module, and the data is entered via a keyboard. The computer processing result is shown in Exhibit 2, which indicates that the chart of accounts is now computerized, the balances are entered, and there was equality of debits and credits.

Journalizing the Monthly Business Transactions

The business transactions during the month of December have been manually recorded in the special journals. The entries in these journals are illustrated in Exhibits 3 through 6.

Notice that these journals are footed. The accountant has proven the equality of debits and credits by crossfooting the columnar totals. These journals will be input documents for the computer system.

The columnar headings on each journal indicate the account number and identify the column as either a debit or credit entry. To the right of the journal name is the posting reference; in our case, the posting references are S, CP, AP, and PR, as assigned to the specific journal.

Computerized Posting of the Special Journals

Special journals become input to the computer software's Posting Module; the data is entered via a keyboard. The footing of each column for a specific account is entered, but each item in the sundry column must be individually entered, because

Exhibit 2 Chart of Accounts with Starting Balances

CHART OF ACCOUNTS
Tower Restaurant

Account	Description	Type	11/30/08
101	Cash on Hand	ACC	1,000.00
102	Cash-Regular Checking	ACC	25,792.16
103	Cash-Payroll Checking	ACC	200.00
112	Accounts Receivable	ACR	185.00
121	Food Inventory	ACI	4,875.00
131	Supplies Inventory	ACI	1,100.00
132	Prepaid Insurance	ACP	0.00
147	Furniture & Equipment	AFF	45,000.00
149	China, Glassware & Silver	AFF	9,000.00
157	Accumulated Depreciation	AFD	(27,000.00)
201	Accounts Payable	LCA	(4,600.00)
211	Sales Tax Payable	LCE	(1,216.75)
215	Employee Taxes Withheld	LCE	0.00
231	Accrued Payroll	LCE	0.00
232	Accrued Payroll Taxes	LCE	0.00
301	Capital, Ann Dancer	CSC	(74,324.73)
302	Withdrawals, Ann Dancer	CST	38,000.00
401	Food Sales	ISS	(162,590.75)
501	Cost of Food Sales	ECP	57,150.00
601	Payroll	EOA	48,906.16
602	Payroll Taxes	EOA	4,788.75
605	Employee Benefits	EOA	2,164.18
607	Employee Meals	EOA	2,875.00
712	Utilities	EOO	3,094.65
721	China, Glassware & Silver	EOO	1,650.00
727	Operating Supplies	EOO	2,898.66
751	Telephone	EOO	850.28
752	Office Supplies	EOO	923.14
753	Credit Card Fees	EOO	1,868.75
754	Cash Short or Over	EOO	137.16
761	Repairs & Maintenance	EOO	2,489.34
801	Rent	EOF	8,800.00
821	Insurance	EOF	1,859.00
891	Depreciation	EOF	4,125.00
	NET DR/CR		0.00

the total of a sundry column is not representative of any one particular account. The computer processing result is shown in Exhibits 7 through 10. Notice that the computer report is in two sections for each journal. The top section shows:

- A posting reference called Journal Number, in this case S, CP, AP, PR.
- A replication of the sequence of the items as they were on the source document (special journal).
- The account number.
- The debit or credit amount posted to the account number.
- Equality of debits and credits.

The bottom section of the report is a Journal Summary, which shows the same information, but by account number sequence.

End-of-Month Accounting

The business transactions that have been posted were for the month of December. If financial statements were printed at this time, they would be incomplete because

Exhibit 3 Manual Sales & Cash Receipts Journal

Tower Restaurant
SALES & CASH RECEIPTS JOURNAL (S)
December 2008

Date	Food Sales cr 401	Sales Tax Payable cr 211	Customer Collections cr 112	Cash to Bank dr 102	Customer Charges dr 112	Cash Short (Over) dr (cr) 754	Sundry Items		
							Account Title	Acct. No.	Amount dr
Dec. 8	*1 350 67*	*81 04*	*185 00*	*1 407 06*	*200 00*	*90*	*Cost of Food Sales*	*501*	*8 75*
15	*1 268 52*	*76 11*	*—*	*1 286 93*	*48 65*	*(40)*	*Operating Supplies*	*727*	*9 45*
Total	*2 619 19*	*157 15*	*185 00*	*2 693 99*	*248 65*	*50*			*18 20*

Exhibit 4 Manual Cash Payments Journal

Tower Restaurant
CASH PAYMENTS JOURNAL (CP)
December 2008

Date	Paid To:	Check Number	Cash—Checking cr 102	Food Inventory dr 121	Accounts Payable dr 201	Sundry Items		
						Account Title	Acct. No.	Amount dr
Dec.2	*DSK Realty*	*348*	*800 00*			*Rent Expense*	*801*	*800 00*
2	*Associated Insurance Co.*	*349*	*2 400 00*			*Prepaid Insurance*	*132*	*2 400 00*
6	*Star Purveyors*	*350*	*2 150 00*		*2 150 00*			
6	*VOID*	*351*	*—*					
7	*Tom's Seafood*	*352*	*75 00*	*75 00*				
7	*State Dept. of Taxation*	*353*	*1 216 75*			*Sales Tax Payable*	*211*	*1 216 75*
9	*Pompano Purveyors*	*354*	*2 450 00*		*2 450 00*			
14	*Tom's Seafood*	*355*	*125 00*	*125 00*				
16	*Tower Payroll Account*	*356*	*730 35*			*Cash—Payroll Checking*	*103*	*730 35*
31	*City Utilities*	*357*	*250 66*			*Utilities*	*712*	*250 66*
31	*Regional Telephone*	*358*	*65 16*			*Telephone*	*751*	*65 16*
	TOTAL		*10 262 92*	*200 00*	*4 600 00*			*5 462 92*

Exhibit 5 Manual Accounts Payable Journal

Tower Restaurant
ACCOUNTS PAYABLE JOURNAL (AP)
December 2008

Date	Vendor	Accounts Payable cr 201	Food Inventory dr 121	Supplies Inventory dr 131	Utilities dr 712	Sundry Items		
						Account Title	Acct. No.	Amount dr
Dec. 7	*Star Purveyors*	*300 00*	*300 00*					
14	*Pompano Purveyors*	*500 00*	*500 00*					
	TOTAL	*800 00*	*800 00*	—	—			—

Exhibit 6 Manual Payroll Journal

Tower Restaurant
PAYROLL REGISTER (PR)
December 16, 2008

		1	2	3	4	5
	Paid To:	Check No.	Gross Wages dr 601	FICA cr 215	FIT cr 215	Net Pay cr 103
	Christine Robert	*621*	*32 16*	*7 85*	*2 00*	*22 31*
	Elizabeth David	*622*	*30 15*	*7 36*	*6 00*	*16 79*
	Ann Tasha	*623*	*42 00*	*9 94*	*10 00*	*22 06*
	Mary Alcrep	*624*	*24 40*	*2 41*	—	*21 99*
	Tom Paul	*625*	*140 00*	*9 80*	*6 00*	*124 20*
	Steve Towe	*626*	*600 00*	*42 00*	*35 00*	*523 00*
	TOTAL		*868 71*	*79 36*	*59 00*	*730 35*

Exhibit 7 Computerized Sales & Cash Receipts Journal

Tower Restaurant
Sales & Cash Recipts Journal
Current P/E Date: 12/31/08

PAGE 1

Journal Number: S

Date	Ref #	Description	Account	Amount
12/31		Food Sales	401	(2,619.19)
12/31		Sales Tax Payable	211	(157.15)
12/31		Customer Collections	112	(185.00)
12/31		Cash to Bank	102	2,693.99
12/31		Customer Charges	112	248.65
12/31		Cash Short	754	0.50
12/31		Cost of Food Sales	501	8.75
12/31		Operating Supplies	727	9.45
			Net DR/CR	$0.00

Journal Summary

Account	Description	Net Posting
102	Cash-Regular Checking	2,693.99
112	Accounts Receivable	63.65
211	Sales Tax Payable	(157.15)
401	Food Sales	(2,619.19)
501	Cost of Food Sales	8.75
727	Operating Supplies	9.45
754	Cash Short or Over	0.50
	Net DR/CR	$0.00

there are adjustments that must be determined and posted. This is probably the most complex phase of the accounting process and usually requires the experience of an accountant.

In a manual system, a multi-section worksheet is required, its sections consisting of Trial Balance, Adjustments, Adjusted Trial Balance, Income Statement, and Balance Sheet. Each section is separated into a debit and credit column. First, the accounts and their balances are entered in the trial balance section. Then the accountant computes and enters the adjustments in the adjustment column. The remainder of the worksheet can then be completed. This is a tedious, time-consuming process subject to mathematical errors that require even more time to correct. The complete worksheet procedure and associated exhibits appear in Appendix A to this chapter.

Working Trial Balance

Since Tower is using a computerized system, a worksheet is not necessary. Nevertheless, an accountant must manually determine the adjustments. The first step is to use the Trial Balance Module and print a preliminary trial balance called a **working trial balance** or an unadjusted trial balance. The working trial balance is shown in Exhibit 11, indicating a net income before adjustments of $18,626.64.

The next step is the most difficult. Adjustments must be determined and computed, requiring the skill and knowledge of an experienced accountant. The

Exhibit 8 Computerized Cash Payments Journal

Tower Restaurant
Cash Payments Journal
Current P/E Date: 12/31/08

PAGE 1

Journal Number: CP

Date	Ref #	Description	Account	Amount
12/31		Cash-Checking	102	(10,262.92)
12/31		Food Inventory	121	200.00
12/31		Accounts Payable	201	4,600.00
12/31		Rent Expense	801	800.00
12/31		Prepaid Insurance	132	2,400.00
12/31		Sales Tax Payable	211	1,216.75
12/31		Cash-Payroll Checking	103	730.35
12/31		Utilities	712	250.66
12/31		Telephone	751	65.16
			Net DR/CR	$0.00

Journal Summary

Account Description		Net Posting
102	Cash-Regular Checking	(10,262.92)
103	Cash-Payroll Checking	730.35
121	Food Inventory	200.00
132	Prepaid Insurance	2,400.00
201	Accounts Payable	4,600.00
211	Sales Tax Payable	1,216.75
712	Utilities	250.66
751	Telephone	65.16
801	Rent	800.00
	Net DR/CR	$0.00

Exhibit 9 Computerized Accounts Payable Journal

Tower Restaurant
Accounts Payable Journal
Current P/E Date: 12/31/08

PAGE 1

Journal Number: AP

Date	Ref #	Description	Account	Amount
12/31		Accounts Payable	201	(800.00)
12/31		Food Inventory	121	800.00
			Net DR/CR	$0.00

Journal Summary

Account Description		Net Posting
121	Food Inventory	800.00
201	Accounts Payable	(800.00)
	Net DR/CR	$0.00

Exhibit 10 Computerized Payroll Journal

Tower Restaurant
Payroll Journal
Current P/E Date: 12/31/08

PAGE 1

Journal Number: PR

Date	Ref #	Description	Account	Amount
12/31		Gross Wages	601	868.71
12/31		FICA	215	(79.36)
12/31		FIT	215	(59.00)
12/31		Net Pay	103	(730.35)
			Net DR/CR	$0.00

Journal Summary

Account Description	Net Posting
103 Cash-Payroll Checking	(730.35)
215 Employee Taxes Withheld	(138.36)
601 Payroll	868.71
Net DR/CR	$0.00

adjustments for Tower are not highly complex because it is a small business. Typically, a hospitality business will adjust for the following items at month end:

- Cost of food used in the revenue process
- Cost of employee meals
- Supplies consumed during the month
- Prepaid insurance expired by the passage of one month
- Depreciation increase by the passage of one month
- Depreciation of china, glassware, and silver
- Unpaid payroll days at the end of the month
- Unpaid payroll taxes at the end of the month

Adjusting Entries

The purpose of **adjusting entries** is to bring the general ledger up to date to comply with the revenue recognition principle and the matching principle. The day-to-day transactions do not take into account items such as consumption of inventories and estimates of depreciation, or unpaid payrolls. As the accountant determines the adjustments, each adjusting entry is entered in a general journal. Exhibit 12 shows the adjusting entries manually entered on this journal. Note that the journal is numbered J1 (first general journal in December) and each entry is separated by a

Exhibit 11 Computerized Working Trial Balance

Tower Restaurant
Working Trial Balance
Current P/E Date: 12/31/08

Account	Unadjusted Balance		Adjustments	
	Debit	Credit	Debit	Credit
101 Cash on Hand	1,000.00			
102 Cash—Regular Checking	18,223.23			
103 Cash—Payroll Checking	200.00			
112 Accounts Receivable	248.65			
121 Food Inventory	5,875.00			
131 Supplies Inventory	1,100.00			
132 Prepaid Insurance	2,400.00			
147 Furniture & Equipment	45,000.00			
149 China, Glassware & Silver	9,000.00			
157 Accumulated Depreciation		27,000.00		
201 Accounts Payable		800.00		
211 Sales Tax Payable		157.15		
215 Employee Taxes Withheld		138.36		
231 Accrued Payroll		0.00		
232 Accrued Payroll Taxes		0.00		
301 Capital, Ann Dancer		74,324.73		
302 Withdrawals	38,000.00			
401 Food Sales		165,209.94		
501 Cost of Food Sales	57,158.75			
601 Payroll	49,774.87			
602 Payroll Taxes	4,788.75			
605 Employee Benefits	2,164.18			
607 Employee Meals	2,875.00			
712 Utilities	3,345.31			
721 China, Glassware & Silver	1,650.00			
727 Operating Supplies	2,908.11			
751 Telephone	915.44			
752 Office Supplies	923.14			
753 Credit Card Fees	1,868.75			
754 Cash Short or Over	137.66			
764 Repairs & Maintenance	2,489.34			
801 Rent	9,600.00			
821 Insurance	1,859.00			
891 Depreciation	4,125.00			
Total	267,630.18	267,630.18		

Net income before adjustments 18,626.64

Exhibit 12 Manual Adjusting Entries

JOURNAL				Page J1
Date 2008	Description	Post. Ref.	Debit	Credit
	(a)			
Dec. 31	Cost of Food Sales	501	718 00	
	Food Inventory	121		718 00
	Record storeroom issues to kitchen			
	(b)			
31	Employee Meals	607	35 00	
	Cost of Food Sales	501		35 00
	Record food used for free employee meals			
	(c)			
31	Operating Supplies	727	100 00	
	Supplies Inventory	131		100 00
	Adjust inventory account to physical			
	(d)			
31	Insurance	821	200 00	
	Prepaid Insurance	132		200 00
	Charge expired premium to expense			
	(e)			
31	Depreciation	891	375 00	
	Accumulated Depreciation—F & E	157		375 00
	Record 1/12 annual depreciation			
	(f)			
31	China, Glassware & Silver (Expense)	721	150 00	
	China, Glassware & Silver (Asset)	149		150 00
	Record 1/12 annual depreciation			
	(g)			
31	Payroll	601	385 00	
	Accrued Payroll	231		385 00
	Record unpaid wages as of 12/31/X2			
	(h)			
31	Payroll Taxes	602	366 00	
	Accrued Payroll Taxes	232		366 00
	Record unpaid employer's taxes as of 12/31			

letter code of a, b, c, etc. This letter code is not required, but it does provide additional reference for audit trail purposes.

Correcting Entries. The term "adjusting entries" is not used for any entries whose purpose is to fix errors in the general ledger; error-fixing entries are called **correcting entries**.

Cost of Sales. Tower uses the perpetual system for inventory. The issues from the storeroom total $718. See entry (a) in Exhibit 12, which *increases* cost of food sales expense and *reduces* the food inventory.

Employee Meals. The storeroom issues in entry (a) include food served to both guests and employees, which is a problem because the cost of food sales account must show only the cost of food served to customers. Therefore, an adjustment is necessary to remove that portion applicable to food served to employees. The food manager's listing showing a $35 cost for employee meals is used to prepare this adjustment. See entry (b) in Exhibit 12, which *increases* the employee meals expense and *reduces* the cost of food sales expense.

Supplies Used. Tower uses the asset method to record purchases of supplies. The asset method records all purchases to supplies inventory. A listing of supplies drawn from the inventory is used to process this transaction; the supplies used this month total $100. See entry (c) in Exhibit 12, which *increases* the supplies expense and *reduces* the supplies inventory.

Prepaid Insurance. On December 2, Tower Restaurant purchased a $2,400 property and liability insurance policy and set up an asset called Prepaid Insurance (see Cash Payments Journal). The $2,400 premium was for twelve months, starting December 2 of this year and ending on December 2 of next year. Therefore $200 of the policy's cost basis expires each month (1/12 of $2,400). See entry (d) in Exhibit 12, which *increases* the insurance expense and *reduces* the prepaid insurance.

Depreciation. The purchase of all long-lived assets is recorded to a type of property and equipment asset account. Depreciation is a method in which the cost of a long-lived tangible asset is allocated over its useful life. Depreciation has been calculated at $375 for December. See entry (e) in Exhibit 12, which *increases* depreciation expense and *increases* the accumulated depreciation contra-asset account.

China, Glassware, Silver. Replacements of china, glassware, and silver are charged to expense; however, the initial purchase had been charged to an asset account. This group of assets is depreciated over its useful life, but the entry is slightly different from that for buildings, furniture, and equipment. An accumulated depreciation account is not used; instead, the depreciation computation is used to reduce the cost basis of the asset. Depreciation has been calculated at $150 for December. See entry (f) in Exhibit 12, which *increases* the china, glassware, and silver expense and *reduces* the cost basis of these assets.

Payroll. A business will always have unpaid payroll at the end of any week or month. The reason is that the workweek and payday are different. For example, a workweek of Sunday to Saturday might be paid on Wednesday (payday) of the following week. This can be seen in the following partial calendar:

End of March/Beginning of April

S	M	T	W	T	F	S
27	28	29	30	31	1	2
3	4	5	6	7	8	9

The workweek ended April 2 was paid on April 6. The result is that the workdays from March 27 to March 31 are unpaid as of March 31, and a payroll adjusting entry is required to properly reflect the payroll expense for the month of March.

In Tower's case, the unpaid workdays total $385. See entry (g) in Exhibit 12, which *increases* the payroll expense and *increases* the accrued payroll liability account.

Payroll Taxes. Federal and state governments levy payroll taxes on the employer, with payment due the following month or at some later date. The unpaid payroll taxes for Tower amount to $366. See entry (h) in Exhibit 12, which *increases* the payroll tax expense and *increases* the accrued payroll taxes liability account.

Computer Input of Adjusting Entries

The adjusting entries that have been manually entered on a general journal are input to the computer system. The Posting Module is again used to input the journal entries. Exhibit 13 shows the computer printout after the computer has posted the journal entries. Notice that the change to net income is a reduction of $2,294.

At this point, the accountant could have the financial statements printed. However, it is more prudent to review another trial balance to ensure that all accounts requiring adjustment have indeed been adjusted. This additional trial balance also ensures that there are no problems involving posting to incorrect accounts during the adjustment phase and that all account balances are normal. Therefore, the accountant again uses the Trial Balance Module. This trial balance can also be called an *Adjusted Trial Balance* because the account balances shown are those reflecting the posting of adjusting entries. Exhibit 14 shows the resulting computerized adjusted trial balance and a net income of $16,332.64. Using audit trails, we can verify the mathematical accuracy of this amount as follows:

- The unadjusted trial balance (Exhibit 11) shows net income of $18,626.64.
- The adjustments entered in the computer system (Exhibit 13) show a net reduction to income of $2,294.
- Net income of $18,626.64 minus a net reduction to income of $2,294.00 does in fact equal 16,332.64, as shown on the adjusted trial balance (Exhibit 14).

Computation of Net Income or Loss

Though the computer is capable of computing net income or net loss without human intervention, all accomplished business students or professionals should be familiar with this easy procedure. Only the revenue and expense accounts are used to compute net income or loss. One procedure is as follows:

Exhibit 13 Computerized Adjusting Entries

Tower Restaurant
Adjusting Entries
Current P/E Date: 12/31/08

Journal Number: J1

		Debit	Credit
501	Cost of Food Sales	718.00	
121	Food Inventory		718.00
607	Employee Meals	35.00	
501	Cost of Food Sales		35.00
727	Operating Supplies	100.00	
131	Supplies Inventory		100.00
821	Insurance	200.00	
132	Prepaid Insurance		200.00
891	Depreciation	375.00	
157	Accumulated Depreciation		375.00
721	China, Glassware & Silver	150.00	
149	China, Glassware & Silver		150.00
601	Payroll	385.00	
231	Accrued Payroll		385.00
602	Payroll Taxes	366.00	
232	Accrued Payroll Taxes		366.00
	TOTALS	2,329.00	2,329.00
Effect on Net Income	(2,294.00)		

- Add sales and other credit accounts in the revenue classification.
- Add expenses.
- Subtract expenses from revenue.
- If the revenue is larger, the difference is income.

To apply this procedure to Exhibit 14, total the revenue accounts (account 401) and then calculate the total of the expense accounts (accounts 501–891). The results are as follows:

Revenue total	$ 165,209.94
Expenses total	148,877.30
Net income	$ 16,332.64

Here is another method. The normal balance of sales is a credit, and expenses have a normal debit balance. The *excess of credits indicates net income.* In Exhibit 14, use accounts 401–891, subtract credits and add debits, and you arrive at a credit of $16,332.64, indicating net income.

Exhibit 14 Computerized Adjusted Trial Balance

Tower Restaurant
Adjusted Trial Balance
Current P/E Date: 12/31/08

Account		Debit	Credit
101	Cash on Hand	1,000.00	
102	Cash—Regular Checking	18,223.23	
103	Cash—Payroll Checking	200.00	
112	Accounts Receivable	248.65	
121	Food Inventory	5,157.00	
131	Supplies Inventory	1,000.00	
132	Prepaid Insurance	2,200.00	
147	Furniture & Equipment	45,000.00	
149	China, Glassware & Silver	8,850.00	
157	Accumulated Depreciation		27,375.00
201	Accounts Payable		800.00
211	Sales Tax Payable		157.15
215	Employee Taxes Withheld		138.36
231	Accrued Payroll	385.00	
232	Accrued Payroll Taxes		366.00
301	Capital, Ann Dancer		74,324.73
302	Withdrawals	38,000.00	
401	Food Sales		165,209.94
501	Cost of Food Sales	57,841.75	
601	Payroll	50,159.87	
602	Payroll Taxes	5,154.75	
605	Employee Benefits	2,164.18	
607	Employee Meals	2,910.00	
712	Utilities	3,345.31	
721	China, Glassware & Silver	1,800.00	
727	Operating Supplies	3,008.11	
751	Telephone	915.44	
752	Office Supplies	923.14	
753	Credit Card Fees	1,868.75	
754	Cash Short or Over	137.66	
764	Repairs & Maintenance	2,489.34	
801	Rent	9,600.00	
821	Insurance	2,059.00	
891	Depreciation	4,500.00	
	Total	268,756.18	268,756.18
		Net income	16,332.64

Proprietorship Net Income

The equity accounts of a proprietorship are capital and withdrawals. The net income from operations of the business increases owner's capital and a net loss decreases owner's capital. The owner's withdrawals are not necessarily related to net income. Generally, withdrawals—a reduction of owner's capital—are limited to cash or other assets on hand.

Corporation Net Income

The net income of a corporation belongs to the corporation and cannot be withdrawn unless the board of directors declares a dividend. The equity accounts of a corporation are related to stock issued, paid-in capital, and retained earnings. A Dividends Declared account is not necessary because the declaration of dividends can be treated as a direct reduction of retained earnings. The net income from operations is an increase to retained earnings.

Computerized Financial Statements

After reviewing the adjusted trial balance, the accountant concludes that all adjustments have been entered and the general ledger contains reliable and up-to-date financial information. Without further clerical effort, the Financial Statements Module is used to print the financial statements. Tower has elected to show only rounded dollar amounts in the financial statements. The three major financial statements are shown in Exhibits 15 through 17.

The statement of owner's equity is not required because the changes to equity are shown in the equity section of the balance sheet.

Computerized General Ledger

Printing the general ledger is time-consuming because of its volume. In a computerized system, the general ledger does not have to be printed until after the financial statements are completed, owing to the inquiry capabilities of the software. If an account requires analysis, the General Ledger Module can be used to display one account or a series of accounts on the computer screen (monitor) or as printer output.

All computer software packages demand some compromise. In this case, the popular three-column account format is not available. Instead, the beginning and ending balances are shown in the right-most column; to the left of this column are the posting entries. Credits are shown in parentheses and debits are unsigned. The General Ledger Module is used to print the entire general ledger. Exhibit 18 shows a sampling of general ledger accounts; the complete general ledger for Tower Restaurant is not illustrated due to space limitations. Note that an ending account balance is indicated by a star (*). Each general ledger account ending balance is identical to the balance shown in the adjusted trial balance and in the financial statements.

Exhibit 15 Computerized Income Statement

Tower Restaurant
Income Statement
For the Period Ended December 31, 2008

REVENUE	
Sales	$ 165,210
COST OF SALES	
Cost of Food Sales	57,842
GROSS PROFIT (LOSS)	107,368
OPERATING EXPENSES	
Payroll & Related	
Payroll	50,160
Payroll Taxes	5,155
Employee Benefits	2,164
Employee Meals	2,910
Total Payroll & Related	60,389
Other Operating Expenses	
Utilities	3,345
China, Glassware & Silver	1,800
Operating Supplies	3,008
Telephone	915
Office Supplies	923
Credit Card Fees	1,869
Cash Short or Over	138
Repairs & Maintenance	2,489
Total Operating Expenses	14,487
Fixed Expenses	
Rent	9,600
Insurance	2,059
Depreciation	4,500
Total Fixed Expenses	16,159
Total Expenses	91,035
Net Income (Loss)	$ 16,333

Reversing Entries

After the financial statements and general ledger have been printed, it is often helpful to prepare reversing entries (an optional bookkeeping procedure) before the start of the next accounting period. A reversing entry is the exact opposite of an adjusting entry. The accountant must determine which adjusting entries posted in the period just ended should be reversed. Reversing entries are usually dated as of the first day of the next accounting period. Appendix B of this chapter presents an in-depth description and demonstration of reversing entries.

Exhibit 16 Computerized Balance Sheet

Tower Restaurant Balance Sheet December 31, 2008	
ASSETS	
CURRENT ASSETS	
Cash	$ 19,423
Accounts Receivable	249
Food Inventory	5,157
Supplies Inventory	1,000
Prepaid Insurance	2,200
TOTAL CURRENT ASSETS	28,029
PROPERTY and EQUIPMENT	
Furniture and Fixtures	45,000
Accumulated Depreciation	(27,375)
China, Glassware & Silver	8,850
TOTAL PROPERTY and EQUIPMENT	26,475
TOTAL ASSETS	$ 54,504
LIABILITIES & OWNER'S EQUITY	
CURRENT LIABILITIES	
Accounts Payable	$ 800
Sales Tax Payable	157
Employee Taxes Withheld	138
Accrued Payroll	385
Accrued Payroll Taxes	366
TOTAL CURRENT LIABILITIES	1,846
TOTAL LIABILITIES	1,846
OWNER'S EQUITY	
Capital, Ann Dancer	74,325
Withdrawals, Ann Dancer	(38,000)
Net Income	16,333
TOTAL OWNER'S EQUITY	52,658
TOTAL LIABILITIES & OWNER'S EQUITY	$ 54,504

Computerized Year-End Processing

In former manual systems, the year-just-ended accounting activities generally required considerable time and effort. **Closing entries** were manually prepared and posted, a post-closing trial balance was manually prepared, and the ending balances for all balance sheet accounts had to be transferred to the new general ledger for the next business year. These manual procedures also were prone to errors.

Exhibit 17 Computerized Statement of Cash Flows

Tower Restaurant
Statement of Cash Flows
For the Period Ended December 31, 2008

Cash Flows from Operating Activities:	
Cash provided from operations	$ 22,933
Cash Flows from Investing Activities:	
Cash purchase of equipment	(10,000)
Cash used by investing activities	(10,000)
Cash Flows from Financing Activities	0
Increase (decrease) in cash for the year	12,933
Cash at the beginning of the year	6,490
Cash at the end of the year	$ 19,423

While these errors were detected, even more clerical effort was required to correct them and review the data again.

Automatic Closing Entries

At the end of a business year, all the income statement accounts and withdrawals (and dividends declared, if any) must be set to zero by closing entries to avoid bringing these balances forward to the next year. The balance sheet account balances are brought forward because they represent beginning balances for the new business year. The technicalities of closing entries are no longer a task in a computerized system. The Year-End Module automatically performs these tasks without a need for manual closing entries.

In addition to performing the closing process, the Year-End Module automatically moves the account balances to year-1 past data, making it possible for comparative reports in the following year. At the option of the user, the previous year-1 past data can be shifted to year-2 past data.

Post-Closing Trial Balance

A post-closing trial balance shows only the balance sheet accounts since the income statement accounts have been set to zero. The Trial Balance Module is used to print a post-closing trial balance. The post-closing trial balance is an audit trail verifying that the year-end process was properly performed.

Exhibit 19 shows a computerized post-closing trial balance. Notice that the capital account has been updated for the withdrawals and net income of the business and is now $52,657.37. This amount reconciles with the equity total of $52,658 shown on the balance sheet (except for a $1 variance due to rounding in the financial statements).

The post-closing trial balance signifies the end of the accounting cycle for the business year just ended; the transfer of balance sheet amounts to the new ledger initiates the accounting cycle for the new business year.

Exhibit 18 Computerized General Ledger

Tower Restaurant
General Ledger
December 31, 2008

101	Cash on Hand			1,000.00 *
102	Cash – Regular Checking			25,792.16
	12/31/08	CP	(10,262.92)	
	12/31/08	S	2,693.99	
				18,223.23 *
103	Cash – Payroll Checking			200.00
	12/31/08	CP	730.35	
	12/31/08	PR	(730.35)	
				200.00 *
112	Accounts Receivable			185.00
	12/31/08	S	(185.00)	
	12/31/08	S	248.65	
				248.65 *
121	Food Inventory			4,875.00
	12/31/08	CP	800.00	
	12/31/08	AP	200.00	
	12/31/08	J1	(718.00)	5,157.00 *
131	Supplies Inventory			1,100.00
	12/31/08	J1	(100.00)	
				1,000.00 *
201	Accounts Payable			(4,600.00)
	12/31/08	CP	4,600.00	
	12/31/08	AP	800.00	(800.00)*
401	Food Sales			(162,590.75)
	12/31/08	S	(2,619.19)	
				(165,209.94)*

Key Terms

accounting cycle—The sequence of accounting procedures during an accounting period. It is a continuing process of recording and reporting financial information.

accrual basis accounting—An accounting system in which all revenue and expenses are recorded in the period incurred regardless of the presence of cash in the transaction.

adjusting entries—Entries that bring the general ledger up to date to comply with the revenue recognition and matching principles.

Exhibit 19 Computerized Post-closing Trial Balance

Tower Restaurant
Post-closing Trial Balance
December 31, 2008

Account		Debit	Credit
101	Cash on Hand	1,000.00	
102	Cash – Regular Checking	18,223.23	
103	Cash – Payroll Checking	200.00	
112	Accounts Receivable	248.65	
121	Food Inventory	5,157.00	
131	Supplies Inventory	1,000.00	
132	Prepaid Insurance	2,200.00	
147	Furniture & Equipment	45,000.00	
149	China, Glassware & Silver	8,850.00	
157	Accumulated Depreciation		27,375.00
201	Accounts Payable		800.00
211	Sales Tax Payable		157.15
215	Employee Taxes Withheld		138.36
231	Accrued Payroll		385.00
232	Accrued Payroll Taxes		366.00
301	Capital, Ann Dancer		52,657.37
302	Withdrawals		0.00
Total		81,878.88	81,878.88

cash basis accounting—An accounting system in which revenue is recorded only when cash is received and expenses are recorded only when paid.

closing entries—Entries that set the revenue, expense, withdrawals, and dividends declared accounts to zero.

correcting entries—Entries that fix errors. Correcting entries are not adjusting entries.

working trial balance—A preliminary trial balance listing the accounts with their unadjusted balances. The accountant uses this trial balance to determine adjustments.

Review Questions

1. What is an accounting cycle?
2. What are cash basis accounting and accrual basis accounting?
3. What is the posting procedure for special journals?

4. What is a working trial balance and its purpose?
5. What is the purpose of adjusting entries and correcting entries?
6. What are some typical adjustment areas any hospitality business might have at month end?
7. Why does the cost of food sales account need adjustment after recording the issues from a perpetual inventory system?
8. Why does any business have an unpaid payroll on the same day that payroll checks are given to its employees?
9. What does the computerized year-end process accomplish?
10. What does the post-closing trial balance signify?

Problems

Problem 1

1. A small hotel is designing its chart of accounts for conversion to a computerized software package. The package allows the use of a three-digit identification system as follows:

Assets 1xx		
	Current	11x
	Property & Equipment	15x
Liabilities 2xx		
	Current	22x
	Long-term	25x
Equity 3xx		
	Capital	31x
	Withdrawals	39x
Revenue 4xx		
	Room Sales	41x
Expense 5xx		
	Payroll	51x
	Payroll Taxes	51x
	Advertising	52x
	Commissions	53x
	Telephone	54x

Specify the first two digits of the three-digit account number for the following:

_____ Cash	_____ Wages Expense
_____ Owner's Capital	_____ Building
_____ Accounts Receivable	_____ Accumulated Depreciation
_____ Accounts Payable	_____ Room Sales
_____ Land	_____ Mortgage Payable
_____ Sales Tax Payable	_____ Supplies Inventory

Problem 2

Rearrange the steps below into the proper sequence for converting from a manual accounting system to a computerized accounting system.

a. Print financial statements.
b. Post the current month's activity.
c. Set up a chart of accounts.
d. Enter starting balances.
e. Request a trial balance.

Problem 3

Computer Assignment: The following problem for Roman II Restaurant can be performed on any computerized general ledger.

Requirements:

1. Convert the manual general ledger to a computerized general ledger.
2. Process the current month's journals.
3. Print a trial balance.
4. Process the adjusting entries.
5. Print a trial balance.
6. Print the financial statements.
7. Print the general ledger.

Chart of Accounts and Balances as of August 31, 2007.

No.	Dr	Cr
101 Cash on Hand	1,500.00	
102 Cash—Regular Checking	20,201.16	
103 Cash—Payroll Checking	400.00	
112 Accounts Receivable	250.00	
121 Food Inventory	5,100.00	
131 Supplies Inventory	1,200.00	
132 Prepaid Insurance	1,000.00	
147 Furniture & Equipment	39,000.00	
149 China, Glassware, & Silver	7,500.00	
157 Accumulated Depreciation		22,000.00
201 Accounts Payable		5,100.00
211 Sales Tax Payable		1,418.29
215 Employee Taxes Withheld		419.20
231 Accrued Payroll		1,200.00
232 Accrued Payroll Taxes		700.00
301 Capital, Ann Dancer		56,134.27
302 Withdrawals	20,000.00	
401 Food Sales		108,393.84
501 Cost of Food Sales	38,296.50	
601 Payroll	32,767.43	
602 Payroll Taxes	3,208.63	
605 Employee Benefits	1,450.00	

607 Employee Meals	1,926.00	
712 Utilities	2,073.65	
721 China, Glassware, & Silver	1,105.00	
727 Operating Supplies	1,942.33	
751 Telephone	570.17	
752 Office Supplies	618.41	
753 Credit Card Fees	1,252.56	
754 Cash Short or Over	91.79	
764 Repairs & Maintenance	1,666.97	
801 Rent	8,000.00	
821 Insurance	1,245.00	
891 Depreciation	3,000.00	
Total	195,365.60	195,365.60

The journals for the month of September 2007 are as follows:

Roman II Restaurant
SALES & CASH RECEIPTS JOURNAL (S)
September 1998

Date	Food Sales cr 401	Sales Tax Payable cr 211	Customer Collections cr 112	Cash to Bank dr 102	Customer Charges dr 112	Cash Short (Over) dr (cr) 754	Sundry Items: Account Title	Acct. No.	Amount dr
TOTAL	14 780 00	886 80	500 00	15 228 82	700 00	2 98			235 00
							Recap of Sundry Items:		
							Cost of Food Sales	501	120 00
							Repairs & Maintenance	761	75 00
							Operating Supplies	727	40 00
							Total Sundry Items		235 00

Roman II Restaurant
CASH PAYMENTS JOURNAL (CP)
September 1998

Date	Paid To	Check Number	Cash—Checking cr 102	Food Inventory dr 121	Accounts Payable dr 201	Sundry Items: Account Title	Acct. No.	Amount dr
	TOTAL		11 057 62	75 00	4 850 25			6 132 37
						Recap of Sundry Items:		
						Cash-Payroll Checking	103	3 630 33
						Sales Tax Payable	211	1 418 29
						Telephone	751	83 75
						Rent	801	1 000 00
						Total Sundry Items		6 132 37

Roman II Restaurant
ACCOUNTS PAYABLE JOURNAL (AP)
September 2007

Date	Vendor	Accounts Payable cr 201	Food Inventory dr 121	Supplies Inventory dr 131	Utilities dr 712	Sundry Items: Account Title	Acct. No.	Amount dr
	TOTAL	5 687 10	4 950 86	415 12	321 12			-

Roman II Restaurant
PAYROLL REGISTER (PR)
September 2007

	Paid To	1 Check No.	2 Gross Wages dr 601	3 FICA cr 215	4 FIT cr 215	5 Net Pay cr 103
	TOTAL		4 446 01	395 68	420 00	3 630 33

The adjusting journal entries for September 30, 2007, are:

Cost of Food Sold	4,200.00	
Food Inventory		4,200.00
Employee Meals	200.00	
Cost of Food Sold		200.00
Operating Supplies	230.00	
Supplies Inventory		230.00
Insurance	250.00	
Prepaid Insurance		250.00
Depreciation	400.00	
Accumulated Depreciation		400.00
China, Glassware, & Silver (expense)	120.00	
China, Glassware, & Silver		120.00

Problem 4

A company's financial statements show the following sales:

Month of January	$ 100,000
Two months ended February	180,000
Three months ended March	320,000

What is the sales amount for the month of February?

Problem 5

On July 1, a one-year fire insurance policy was purchased at a cost of $6,000. What is the insurance expense for the month of July?

Problem 6

On July 31, the bookkeeping account Supplies Inventory shows a debit balance of $1,000. A physical inventory taken on that date indicates that $800 of supplies are on hand. What amount of supplies were used in July?

Problem 7

The income statement section of a worksheet shows the following results:

Total debits:	$ 65,000
Total credits:	$ 72,000

Specify whether the company has a net income or loss for the period, and determine the amount.

Problem 8

The income statement section of a worksheet shows the following results:

Total debits:	$ 84,000
Total credits:	$ 78,000

Specify whether the company has a net income or loss for the period, and determine the amount.

Problem 9

A proprietorship shows the following results on its worksheet:

Capital, beginning of year	$50,000
Withdrawals for the year	30,000
Net income for the year	20,000

What will be the new balance in the Capital account after the closing entries have been posted?

Problem 10

Supplement to Manual Worksheet in Chapter Appendix A.

Prepare a complete worksheet from the following information:

	General Ledger		Adjustments	
	Dr	Cr	Dr	Cr
Cash	10,000			
Accounts Receivable	2,000			
Supplies Inventory	1,500			(a) 600
Prepaid Insurance	3,200			(b) 1,500
Equipment	4,000			
Accumulated Depreciation		1,600		(c) 800
Accounts Payable		3,200		
Capital		11,500		
Withdrawals	40,000			
Sales		63,000		
Rent	12,000			
Telephone	2,200			
Advertising	4,400			
Supplies			(a) 600	
Insurance			(b) 1,500	
Depreciation			(c) 800	
Total	79,300	79,300	2,900	2,900

Ethics Case

Jessica Taylor is the director of computer services for the Wallace Corporation. The Wallace Corporation needs to purchase a new computer, so Jessica has been researching the prices and capabilities of various computer models.

After Jessica finishes comparing the different models and prices, her research shows that her final choice is between two different computers; one is offered for sale by the Sterling Computer Company and the other by the Ultra Computer Company. The capabilities of both of these computers are identical. The Sterling Company's computer is more expensive than the Ultra Company's computer. However, the Ultra computer is not as mechanically reliable as the Sterling model.

After considering both models, Jessica orders the Sterling computer. The management of the Wallace Corporation is not aware that the salesperson for the Sterling Computer Company is Jessica's brother-in-law.

1. Is Jessica's decision or behavior unethical?
2. What should Jessica do under these circumstances?

Chapter Appendix A: Preparing the Manual Worksheet

A *Worksheet* is a multi-column form used as an accounting tool to centralize the trial balance, adjustments, and other data necessary to produce financial statements. Exhibit A-1 illustrates the following five sections of the worksheet:

- Trial Balance
- Adjustments
- Adjusted Trial Balance
- Income Statement
- Balance Sheet

Exhibit A-1 Worksheet Sections and Sources of Data

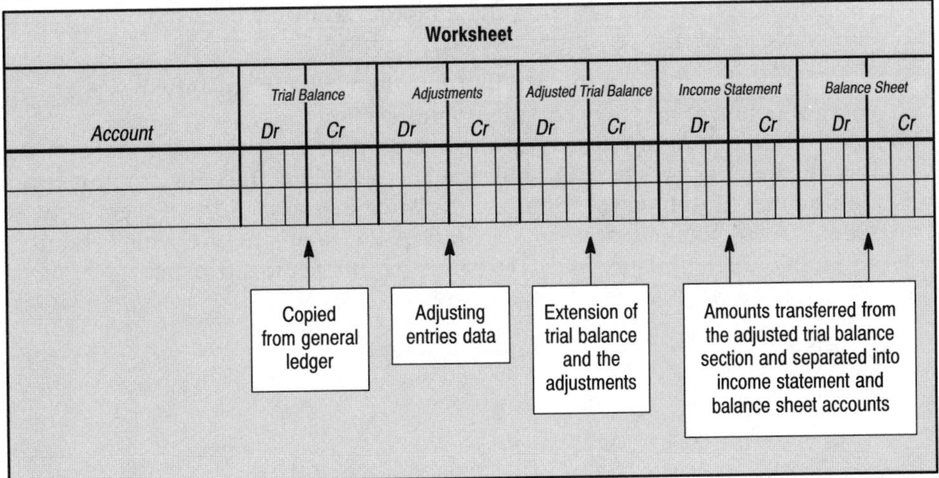

Each section is divided into debit and credit columns. The progression of a worksheet from start to completion for the Tower Restaurant is used as a demonstration. Following are the steps in completing this worksheet.

- The *Trial Balance* section is merely a copy function, copying the accounts and balances from the general ledger. This copy job is shown in Exhibit A-2. Notice the equality of debits and credits of the footings for this section.
- The *Adjustments* section requires a study of the accounts, the entries are those determined by the accountant. These are provided for you and shown in Exhibit A-3. Notice the equality of debits and credits of the footings for this section.
- The *Adjusted Trial Balance* section is the result of a simple math function—adding the debits and subtracting the credits from the Trial Balance section and the Adjustments section. The result is shown in Exhibit A-4. Notice the equality of debits and credits of the footings for this section.

- The *Income Statement* section is the result of examining the Adjusted Trial Balance section and plainly transferring the amounts from the revenue and expense accounts. The result is shown in Exhibit A-5.

  Note that there is no equality of debits and credits in the usual footings. The reason is that only the revenue and expense accounts have been transferred. It is in this section that the net income (or loss) is computed. Notice also that the difference between the footings is a credit of $16,332.64 (indicating net income). A debit is entered in the Income Statement section and a credit is entered in the Balance Sheet section. This is because net income increases the capital account, and a credit is necessary to perform an increase to capital. After the computation of net income, notice that there now is equality of debits and credits of the footings for this section.

- The *Balance Sheet* section is the result of examining the Adjusted Trial Balance section and plainly transferring the amounts from the assets, liabilities, and equity accounts. The result is shown in Exhibit A-5.

  Notice that the preliminary footings do not have equality; however, the entry of net income brings equality to this section.

  The financial statements can now be prepared from the data in the Income Statement section and Balance Sheet section. Trace the amounts from the Income Statement section and Balance Sheet section, respectively, to Exhibit A-6 (Income Statement), Exhibit A-7 (Statement of Owner's Equity), and Exhibit A-8 (Balance Sheet) to complete this demonstration.

Exhibit A-2 Tower Restaurant—Trial Balance on a Worksheet

Tower Restaurant
Worksheet
December 31, 2008

		1 Trial Balance	2	3 Adjustments	4	5 Adjusted Trial Balance	6	7 Income Statement	8	9 Balance Sheet	10
		Dr	Cr	Dr	Cr	Dr	Cr	Dr	Cr	Dr	Cr
101	Cash on Hand	1 000 00									
102	Cash—Regular Checking	18 223 23									
103	Cash—Payroll Checking	200 00									
112	Accounts Receivable	248 65									
121	Food Inventory	5 875 00									
131	Supplies Inventory	1 100 00									
132	Prepaid Insurance	2 400 00									
147	Furniture & Equipment	45 000 00									
149	China, Glassware & Silver	9 000 00									
157	Acc. Depreciation—F&E		27 000 00								
201	Accounts Payable		800 00								
211	Sales Tax Payable		157 15								
215	Employee Taxes Withheld		138 36								
231	Accrued Payroll										
232	Accrued Payroll Taxes										
301	Capital, Ann Dancer		74 324 73								
302	Withdrawals, Ann Dancer	38 000 00									
401	Food Sales		165 209 94								
501	Cost of Food Sales	57 158 75									
601	Payroll	49 774 87									
602	Payroll Taxes	4 788 75									
605	Employee Benefits	2 164 18									
607	Employee Meals	2 875 00									
712	Utilities	3 345 31									
721	China, Glassware & Silver	1 650 00									
727	Operating Supplies	2 908 11									
751	Telephone	915 44									
752	Office Supplies	923 14									
753	Credit Card Fees	1 868 75									
754	Cash Short or Over	137 66									
761	Repairs & Maintenance	2 489 34									
801	Rent	9 600 00									
821	Insurance	1 859 00									
891	Depreciation	4 125 00									
	TOTAL	267 630 18	267 630 18								

Exhibit A-3 Tower Restaurant—Worksheet with Adjustments

Tower Restaurant
Worksheet
December 31, 2008

		1 Trial Balance Dr	2 Trial Balance Cr	3 Adjustments Dr	4 Adjustments Cr	5 Adjusted Trial Balance Dr	6 Adjusted Trial Balance Cr	7 Income Statement Dr	8 Income Statement Cr	9 Balance Sheet Dr	10 Balance Sheet Cr
101	Cash on Hand	1 000 00									
102	Cash—Regular Checking	18 223 23									
103	Cash—Payroll Checking	200 00									
112	Accounts Receivable	248 65									
121	Food Inventory	5 875 00			(a) 718 00						
131	Supplies Inventory	1 100 00			(c) 100 00						
132	Prepaid Insurance	2 400 00			(d) 200 00						
147	Furniture & Equipment	45 000 00									
149	China, Glassware & Silver	9 000 00			(f) 150 00						
157	Acc. Depreciation—F&E		27 000 00		(e) 375 00						
201	Accounts Payable		800 00								
211	Sales Tax Payable		157 15								
215	Employee Taxes Withheld		138 36								
231	Accrued Payroll				(g) 385 00						
232	Accrued Payroll Taxes				(h) 366 00						
301	Capital, Ann Dancer		74 324 73								
302	Withdrawals, Ann Dancer	38 000 00									
401	Food Sales		165 209 94								
501	Cost of Food Sales	57 158 75		(a) 718 00	(b) 35 00						
601	Payroll	49 774 87		(g) 385 00							
602	Payroll Taxes	4 788 75		(h) 366 00							
605	Employee Benefits	2 164 18									
607	Employee Meals	2 875 00		(b) 35 00							
712	Utilities	3 345 31									
721	China, Glassware & Silver	1 650 00		(f) 150 00							
727	Operating Supplies	2 908 11		(c) 100 00							
751	Telephone	915 44									
752	Office Supplies	923 14									
753	Credit Card Fees	1 868 75									
754	Cash Short or Over	137 66									
761	Repairs & Maintenance	2 489 34									
801	Rent	9 600 00									
821	Insurance	1 859 00		(d) 200 00							
891	Depreciation	4 125 00		(e) 375 00							
	TOTAL	267 630 18	267 630 18	2 329 00	2 329 00						

Exhibit A-4 Tower Restaurant—Worksheet to the Adjusted Trial Balance Sheet

Tower Restaurant
Worksheet
December 31, 2008

		1 Trial Balance Dr	2 Trial Balance Cr	3 Adjustments Dr	4 Adjustments Cr	5 Adjusted Trial Balance Dr	6 Adjusted Trial Balance Cr	7 Income Statement Dr	8 Income Statement Cr	9 Balance Sheet Dr	10 Balance Sheet Cr
101	Cash on Hand	1 000 00				1 000 00					
102	Cash—Regular Checking	18 223 23				18 223 23					
103	Cash—Payroll Checking	200 00				200 00					
112	Accounts Receivable	248 65				248 65					
121	Food Inventory	5 875 00			(a) 718 00	5 157 00					
131	Supplies Inventory	1 100 00			(c) 100 00	1 000 00					
132	Prepaid Insurance	2 400 00			(d) 200 00	2 200 00					
147	Furniture & Equipment	45 000 00				45 000 00					
149	China, Glassware & Silver	9 000 00			(f) 150 00	8 850 00					
157	Acc. Depreciation—F&E		27 000 00		(e) 375 00		27 375 00				
201	Accounts Payable		800 00				800 00				
211	Sales Tax Payable		157 15				157 15				
215	Employee Taxes Withheld		138 36				138 36				
231	Accrued Payroll				(g) 385 00		385 00				
232	Accrued Payroll Taxes				(h) 366 00		366 00				
301	Capital, Ann Dancer		74 324 73				74 324 73				
302	Withdrawals, Ann Dancer	38 000 00				38 000 00					
401	Food Sales		165 209 94				165 209 94				
501	Cost of Food Sales	57 158 75		(a) 718 00	(b) 35 00	57 841 75					
601	Payroll	49 774 87		(g) 385 00		50 159 87					
602	Payroll Taxes	4 788 75		(h) 366 00		5 154 75					
605	Employee Benefits	2 164 18				2 164 18					
607	Employee Meals	2 875 00		(b) 35 00		2 910 00					
712	Utilities	3 345 31				3 345 31					
721	China, Glassware & Silver	1 650 00		(f) 150 00		1 800 00					
727	Operating Supplies	2 908 11		(c) 100 00		3 008 11					
751	Telephone	915 44				915 44					
752	Office Supplies	923 14				923 14					
753	Credit Card Fees	1 868 75				1 868 75					
754	Cash Short or Over	137 66				137 66					
761	Repairs & Maintenance	2 489 34				2 489 34					
801	Rent	9 600 00				9 600 00					
821	Insurance	1 859 00		(d) 200 00		2 059 00					
891	Depreciation	4 125 00		(e) 375 00		4 500 00					
	TOTAL	267 630 18	267 630 18	2 329 00	2 329 00	268 756 18	268 756 18				

Exhibit A-5 Tower Restaurant—Completed Worksheet

Tower Restaurant
Worksheet
December 31, 2008

		1 Trial Balance Dr	2 Trial Balance Cr	3 Adjustments Dr	4 Adjustments Cr	5 Adjusted Trial Balance Dr	6 Adjusted Trial Balance Cr	7 Income Statement Dr	8 Income Statement Cr	9 Balance Sheet Dr	10 Balance Sheet Cr
101	Cash on Hand	1 000 00				1 000 00				1 000 00	
102	Cash—Regular Checking	18 223 23				18 223 23				18 223 23	
103	Cash—Payroll Checking	200 00				200 00				200 00	
112	Accounts Receivable	248 65				248 65				248 65	
121	Food Inventory	5 875 00			(a) 718 00	5 157 00				5 157 00	
131	Supplies Inventory	1 100 00			(c) 100 00	1 000 00				1 000 00	
132	Prepaid Insurance	2 400 00			(d) 200 00	2 200 00				2 200 00	
147	Furniture & Equipment	45 000 00				45 000 00				45 000 00	
149	China, Glassware & Silver	9 000 00			(f) 150 00	8 850 00				8 850 00	
157	Acc. Depreciation—F&E		27 000 00		(e) 375 00		27 375 00				27 375 00
201	Accounts Payable		800 00				800 00				800 00
211	Sales Tax Payable		157 15				157 15				157 15
215	Employee Taxes Withheld		138 36				138 36				138 36
231	Accrued Payroll				(g) 385 00		385 00				385 00
232	Accrued Payroll Taxes				(h) 366 00		366 00				366 00
301	Capital, Ann Dancer		74 324 73				74 324 73				74 324 73
302	Withdrawals, Ann Dancer	38 000 00				38 000 00				38 000 00	
401	Food Sales		165 209 94				165 209 94		165 209 94		
501	Cost of Food Sales	57 158 75		(a) 718 00	(b) 35 00	57 841 75		57 841 75			
601	Payroll	49 774 87		(g) 385 00		50 159 87		50 159 87			
602	Payroll Taxes	4 788 75		(h) 366 00		5 154 75		5 154 75			
605	Employee Benefits	2 164 18				2 164 18		2 164 18			
607	Employee Meals	2 875 00		(b) 35 00		2 910 00		2 910 00			
712	Utilities	3 345 31				3 345 31		3 345 31			
721	China, Glassware & Silver	1 650 00		(f) 150 00		1 800 00		1 800 00			
727	Operating Supplies	2 908 11		(c) 100 00		3 008 11		3 008 11			
751	Telephone	915 44				915 44		915 44			
752	Office Supplies	923 14				923 14		923 14			
753	Credit Card Fees	1 868 75				1 868 75		1 868 75			
754	Cash Short or Over	137 66				137 66		137 66			
761	Repairs & Maintenance	2 489 34				2 489 34		2 489 34			
801	Rent	9 600 00				9 600 00		9 600 00			
821	Insurance	1 859 00		(d) 200 00		2 059 00		2 059 00			
891	Depreciation	4 125 00		(e) 375 00		4 500 00		4 500 00			
	TOTAL	267 630 18	267 630 18	2 329 00	2 329 00	268 756 18	268 756 18	148 877 30	165 209 94	119 878 88	103 546 24
	Net Income							16 332 64			16 332 64
	TOTAL							165 209 94	165 209 94	119 878 88	119 878 88

Exhibit A-6 Tower Restaurant—Income Statement

Tower Restaurant
Income Statement
For the Year Ended December 31, 2008

Food Sales	$165,209.94
Cost of Food Sales	57,841.75
Gross Profit	107,368.19
OPERATING EXPENSES:	
Payroll	50,159.87
Payroll Taxes	5,154.75
Employee Meals and Other Benefits	5,074.18
Utilities	3,345.31
China, Glassware & Silver	1,800.00
Operating Supplies	3,008.11
Telephone	915.44
Office Supplies	923.14
Credit Card Fees	1,868.75
Cash Short or Over	137.66
Repairs & Maintenance	2,489.34
Total Operating Expenses	74,876.55
INCOME BEFORE FIXED CHARGES	32,491.64
FIXED CHARGES:	
Rent	9,600.00
Insurance	2,059.00
Depreciation	4,500.00
Total Fixed Charges	16,159.00
NET INCOME	$ 16,332.64

Exhibit A-7 Tower Restaurant—Statement of Owner's Equity

Tower Restaurant
Statement Owner's Equity
For the Year Ended December 31, 2008

Ann Dancer, Capital, January 1, 2008	$74,324.73
Net income for the year	16,332.64
Total	$90,657.37
Less: Withdrawals during the year	38,000.00
Ann Dancer, Capital, December 31, 2008	$52,657.37

Exhibit A-8 Tower Restaurant—Balance Sheet

Tower Restaurant
Balance Sheet
December 31, 2008

ASSETS

CURRENT ASSETS				
Cash			$ 19,423.23	
Accounts Receivable			248.65	
Food Inventory			5,157.00	
Supplies Inventory			1,000.00	
Prepaid Insurance			2,200.00	
Total Current Assets				$ 28,028.88
PROPERTY & EQUIPMENT				
	Cost	Accumulated Depreciation		
Furniture & Equipment	45,000.00	27,375.00		
China, Glassware, Silver	8,850.00			
Total	53,850.00	27,375.00		26,475.00
TOTAL ASSETS				$ 54,503.88

LIABILITIES AND OWNER'S EQUITY

CURRENT LIABILITIES		
Accounts Payable	$ 800.00	
Sales Tax Payable	157.15	
Employee Taxes Withheld	138.36	
Accrued Expenses	751.00	
Total Current Liabilities		$ 1,846.51
OWNER'S EQUITY		
Capital, Ann Dancer		52,657.37
TOTAL LIABILITIES AND OWNER'S EQUITY		$ 54,503.88

Chapter Appendix B: Reversing Entries

The use of reversing entries is an optional bookkeeping procedure. The purpose of reversing entries is to simplify the recording of routine transactions such as cash receipts and cash payments in the next period. Without reversing entries, it would be necessary to refer to prior adjusting entries to properly record routine transactions in the next accounting period.

A good case supporting the use of reversing entries is the need to make an adjusting entry to accrue unpaid salaries and wages. For example, earlier in this chapter an adjusting entry was made for a particular business for unpaid payroll as of August 31. Recall that the calendar for August was as follows:

S	M	T	W	T	F	S
	1	2	3	4	5	6
7	8	9	10	11	12	13
14	15	16	17	18	19	20
21	22	23	24	25	26	27
28	29	30	31			

On August 31, employees were paid for the workweek of August 21 to 27. The payroll days of August 28 to 31 will be included in the paycheck for the first Wednesday in September. Therefore, on August 31, there are four days of payroll expenses not recorded in the accounting month of August.

The adjusting entry on August 31 provided for $4/7$ of an average $7,000 payroll week, debiting Payroll Expense for $4,000 and crediting Accrued Payroll for $4,000.

After the journal entry was posted, the general ledger accounts appeared as follows:

Payroll Expense			Accrued Payroll	
8/31 AJE	4,000	(Wages 8/2–8/31)		8/31 AJE 4,000

Scenario When Not Using a Reversing Entry. The wages for the workweek of August 28 to September 3 will be paid on September 7.

	S	M	T	W	T	F	S
August	28	29	30	31			
September					1	2	3
	4	5	6	7			

↑ (at 7) Payday for previous week of Sunday to Saturday (8/28–9/3)

Assume the payroll for the workweek of 8/28 to 9/3 is $7,000. On September 7, this routine transaction is entered in the payroll journal; the gross wages (payroll expense) will be recorded as $7,000 for the first week of September, and the ledger will appear as follows:

Payroll Expense

8/31 AJE	4,000	(Wages 8/28–8/31)	
9/7 PR	7,000	(Wages 8/28–9/3)	

Accrued Payroll

		8/31 AJE	4,000

Not all of the $7,000 payroll expense applies to September; this payroll contains $4,000 applicable to August. A reversing entry provides a convenient method to avoid these accounting complications.

Scenario When Using a Reversing Entry. In review, the ledger accounts initially appeared on August 31 as follows:

Payroll Expense

8/31 AJE	4,000	(Wages 8/28–8/31)	

Accrued Payroll

		8/31 AJE	4,000

Reversing entries are prepared at the beginning of the new accounting month. As the name implies, a reversing entry is the exact reverse of an adjusting entry. It contains the same account titles and amounts as the adjusting entry, except that the debits and credits are the reverse of those in the adjusting entry.

The reversing entry on September 1 is as follows:

Sep. 1	*Accrued Payroll*		*4*	*000*	*00*			
	Payroll Expense					*4*	*000*	*00*

After posting the reversing entry on September 1, the ledger accounts are as follows:

Payroll Expense

8/31 AJE	4,000	9/1 RJE	4,000

Accrued Payroll

9/1 RJE	4,000	8/31 AJE	4,000
		Balance	0

After the payroll journal is posted on September 7, the general ledger account Payroll Expense will appear as follows:

Payroll Expense

8/31 AJE	4,000	9/1 RJE	4,000
9/7 PR	7,000		

The postings of 9/1 and 9/7 now accurately reflect the $3,000 wages expense for September.

Which Adjusting Entries May Require Reversing Entries? Not all adjusting entries require reversing entries. Generally, any adjusting entry that will affect future cash receipts or cash payments should have a reversing entry in the next period. Adjusting entries that affect inventories, supplies on hand, and other items that require adjustment at each month's end may not require a reversing entry because the next month's adjusting entry will rectify the account balance.

The use of reversing entries depends on the accounting system and conventions of a particular business. Because of the unique nature of reversing entries and the fact that accounting policies vary from business to business, a universal rule is difficult to state. Generally, the following set of guidelines may be followed:

1. Search the prior month's adjusting entries and locate any entries that credit a liability account or debit an asset account. These are the entries that either increased a liability or asset account.
2. When such entries are located, it may be possible to determine whether a reversing entry is required.

Reversing Entries for the Tower Restaurant

The Tower Restaurant uses a simple method to determine those adjusting entries that will require reversing entries. Its policy is to use an "accrued" account to flag those adjustments that are to be reversed on the first day of the next accounting month.

Refer to Exhibit B-1 and search for each adjusting entry that used some type of "accrued" account in its entry. The two entries that meet this parameter are the Accrued Payroll and Accrued Payroll Taxes entries. Note that these adjusting entries also increased liability accounts. The reversing entries are dated January 1, 2009 and are as follows:

Jan. 1	*Accrued Payroll*				*385*	*00*		
	Payroll Expense						*385*	*00*
Jan. 1	*Accrued Payroll Taxes*				*366*	*00*		
	Payroll Taxes Expense						*366*	*00*

Exhibit B-1 Tower Restaurant—Journalized Adjusting Entries

JOURNAL				Page *J6*
Date *2008*	Description	Post. Ref.	Debit	Credit
	(a)			
Dec. 31	*Cost of Food Sales*	*501*	*718 00*	
	Food Inventory	*121*		*718 00*
	Record storeroom issues to kitchen			
	(b)			
31	*Employee Meals*	*607*	*35 00*	
	Cost of Food Sales	*501*		*35 00*
	Record food used for free employee meals			
	(c)			
31	*Operating Supplies*	*727*	*100 00*	
	Supplies Inventory	*131*		*100 00*
	Adjust inventory account to physical			
	(d)			
31	*Insurance*	*821*	*200 00*	
	Prepaid Insurance	*132*		*200 00*
	Charge expired premium to expense			
	(e)			
31	*Depreciation*	*891*	*375 00*	
	Accumulated Depreciation—F & E	*157*		*375 00*
	Record 1/12 annual depreciation			
	(f)			
31	*China, Glassware & Silver (Expense)*	*721*	*150 00*	
	China, Glassware & Silver (Asset)	*149*		*150 00*
	Record 1/12 annual depreciation			
	(g)			
31	*Payroll*	*601*	*385 00*	
	Accrued Payroll	*231*		*385 00*
	Record unpaid wages as of 12/31/X2			
	(h)			
31	*Payroll Taxes*	*602*	*366 00*	
	Accrued Payroll Taxes	*232*		*366 00*
	Record unpaid employer's taxes as of 12/31			

Chapter 9 Outline

Competencies

1. Describe the income statements and the accounting procedures for full-service and fast-food restaurants in accordance with the *Uniform System of Accounts for Restaurants.* (pp. 235–236)
2. Describe basic elements for food and beverage sales accounting. (pp. 236–239)
3. Describe the measurement of food and beverage costs and the various operating expenses. (pp. 239–245)
4. Define the terms and describe the accounting procedures for service charges and other income. (pp. 245–249)
5. Describe how a restaurant's balance sheet and chart of accounts may differ from those of other industries. (pp. 249–250)
6. Identify and explain the various food sales and beverage sales analysis statistics. (pp. 250–256)

9

Restaurant Accounting

RESTAURANT ACCOUNTING IS AN AMBIGUOUS TERM in that it covers a multitude of different restaurant operations—stand-alone restaurants, chain operations, in-plant operations, department store restaurants, and restaurants in hotels, clubs, hospitals, and other institutions.

Stand-alone commercial restaurants must absorb all expenses, including occupancy costs, depreciation, and interest. Restaurants in department stores, hotels, clubs, and hospitals have the benefit of other income-producing departments contributing to the support of their overhead and fixed expenses. Hospitals and other institutions often have accounting systems to comply with governmental regulations, while in-plant operations are often under contract and in many instances subsidized by their contractor.

These different facilities make it impossible to generalize about restaurant accounting. Therefore, this chapter concentrates on the commercial restaurant, which is an operation unto itself and not an ancillary department such as in a hotel, hospital, or subsidized operation.

The accounting procedures and statements appearing in this chapter are those endorsed in the *Uniform System of Accounts for Restaurants (USAR),*[1] the accounting standard adopted and recommended by the National Restaurant Association. This chapter addresses such questions as:

1. Which financial statement formats for full-service restaurants and fast-food restaurants are recommended by the *USAR*?
2. What sales and expense accounting procedures for full-service restaurants and fast-food restaurants are recommended by the *USAR*?
3. How are service charges and other income treated?
4. What are occupancy expenses?
5. What ratios and statistical analyses are useful to measure the efficiency of food and beverage operations?

Restaurant Income Statement

The *USAR* provides financial statement formats for various restaurant operations. The major components of an income statement common to any restaurant are:

	Sales
−	Cost of Sales
=	Gross Profit

− Operating Expenses
= Operating Income
− Interest
= Income Before Income Taxes
− Income Taxes
= Net Income

An income statement is usually accompanied by numerous supporting schedules that itemize the various components of a single line item on the statement. For example, the line item *food sales* will have supporting schedules such as food sales by facility (outlet) and food sales by meal period. Similar supporting schedules are prepared for beverage sales. Other supporting schedules detail salaries and wages, employee benefits, and each expense appearing as a line item on the income statement. Several of these schedules are explained and exhibited in the following paragraphs.

The distinction between full-service and limited-service restaurants is sometimes vague because today's limited-service restaurants can have extensive menus. Instead, we will distinguish between full-service and fast-food operations.

Full-service restaurants sell food and beverages in an elegant or casual setting characterized by distinctive customer attention and table service that distinguishes them from fast-food operations. The income statement in Exhibit 1 depicts an income statement from the *USAR* for a full-service restaurant with food and beverage sales. Such statements can be adapted for a small restaurant, large restaurant, or chain operation.

Fast-food restaurants offer convenience, predictable quality, and expeditious food delivery. Fast food has become a part of the American lifestyle. A fast-food operation serves food quickly but with little or no customer service. Typically, the menu is on a display board and customers order from a cashier, pay at time of order, progress in line, and receive their meals. The customer may order the meal to take out or elect to sit at a table. Exhibit 2 shows an income statement from the *USAR* for a fast-food restaurant serving food only. Notice the addition of the paper goods part of cost of sales for a fast-food restaurant. Paper goods are described in detail in the cost of sales section later in this chapter.

Food Sales Accounting

Food sales include the sales of food, coffee, tea, milk, and fruit juices. Sales of soft drinks are included in food sales if there is no service of liquor, beer, and wine. Sales taxes are not part of food sales because the collection of these taxes is a liability until they are paid to the government.

If pastry or baked goods are sold at a counter, it might be advantageous to account for these sales separately. The same might be true of take-out sales of prepared foods which, if sufficiently large, may require a separate departmental statement. The separation of sales among food, beverage, and other noteworthy categories is important for the calculation of meaningful operating ratios and cost measurement.

Exhibit 1 Income Statement: Full-Service Restaurant with Food and Beverage Sales

Sales:	
Food	$
Beverage	
Total Sales	
Cost of Sales:	
Food	
Beverage	
Total Cost of Sales	
Gross Profit	
Operating Expenses:	
Salaries and Wages	
Employee Benefits	
Direct Operating Expenses	
Music and Entertainment	
Marketing	
Utility Services	
Repairs and Maintenance	
Occupancy	
Depreciation	
Administrative and General Expenses	
Other Income	
Total Operating Expenses	
Operating Income	
Interest Expense	
Income Before Income Taxes	
Income Taxes	
Net Income	**$**

Coupons

Coupons and other discount programs are used as promotions to increase business. The treatment of coupon sales must comply with any sales tax regulations in effect. One method is to register the sale at normal retail and enter the coupon amount as a reduction. This procedure keeps track of coupon usage and its promotional effectiveness. Coupon usage can be recorded to a contra-sales account such as Sales Discounts—Coupons.

Service Charges

Some hospitality operations are adopting a policy of adding a **service charge** to customers' checks in lieu of tips. Advantages of this policy include a standard gratuity for employees and elimination of the governmental requirement of tip

Exhibit 2 Income Statement: Limited-Service, Fast-Food Restaurant Selling Food Only

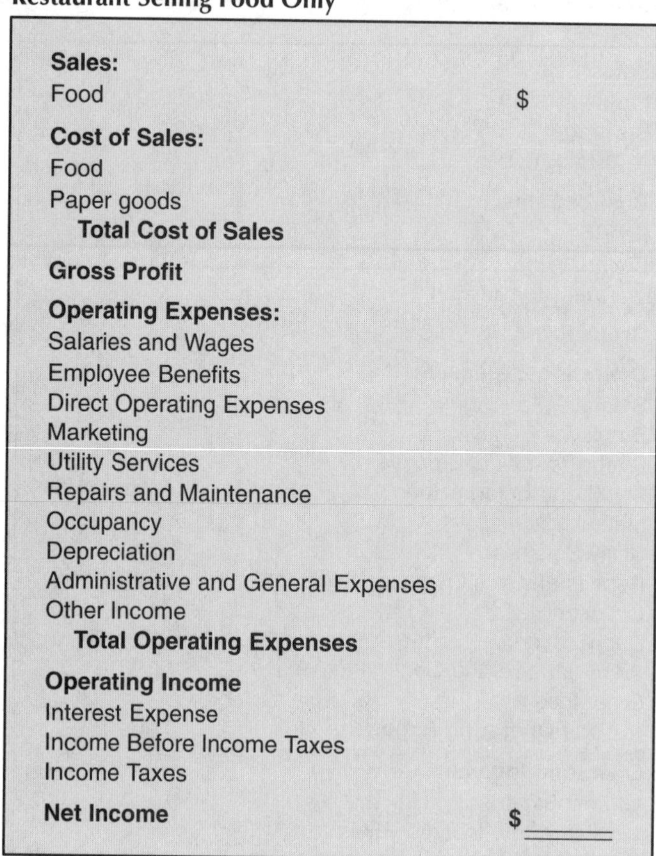

Sales:	
Food	$
Cost of Sales:	
Food	
Paper goods	
Total Cost of Sales	
Gross Profit	
Operating Expenses:	
Salaries and Wages	
Employee Benefits	
Direct Operating Expenses	
Marketing	
Utility Services	
Repairs and Maintenance	
Occupancy	
Depreciation	
Administrative and General Expenses	
Other Income	
Total Operating Expenses	
Operating Income	
Interest Expense	
Income Before Income Taxes	
Income Taxes	
Net Income	$

recordkeeping. However, public acceptance of this policy is mixed. Management must consider the possibility that some waitstaff feel there no longer is a need to earn a tip, resulting in an impairment of customer service.

Service charges are not recorded to food sales; they are recorded as *Other Income.* Some operations distribute the entire amount of service charges collected to their employees, while others retain a small portion to cover such items as administrative costs or payment of bonuses. Regardless of the method of distributing service charges to employees, 100 percent of the amount collected is recorded to Other Income. When the service charge is distributed, Other Income is reduced.

Beverage Sales Accounting

Beverage sales include all alcoholic beverages and soft drinks. (Coffee, tea, milk, and fruit juices are food items.) Sales taxes are not part of beverage sales. Food sales and beverage sales must be recorded in separate bookkeeping accounts to provide management with meaningful sales and cost analyses. Some of the reasons for this separation are:

- The markup on liquor is considerably different from that on food.
- Inventory life is longer for liquor than for food.
- Selling liquor is not as labor-intensive as selling food.

Cashiering Single Price, Sales Tax Included

Some establishments quote a single price for alcoholic beverages with the tax included. For example, a price of $5.30 includes the sales tax, and the amount is cashiered as $5.30. This practice requires special attention because the sale amount includes the sales tax. A simple method to restate the cashiered beverage amounts into sales and sales tax is:

$$\frac{\text{Amount Cashiered}}{100\% + \text{Sales Tax}\%} = \text{Amount of Sale Excluding Sales Tax}$$

For example, assume the $5.30 includes a six percent sales tax:

$$\frac{\text{Amount Cashiered}}{100\% + \text{Sales Tax}\%} = \frac{\$5.30}{106\%} = \$5.00 \text{ Amount of Sale}$$

Applying the six percent sales tax to the $5.00 sale yields a $.30 sales tax. The sale of $5.00 plus the sales tax of $.30 reconciles to the original $5.30 cashiered amount. This calculation is performed daily or at the end of the month.

Liquor laws vary by state and can be troublesome to interpret. While a state might allow cashiering drinks at a single price that includes the sales tax, a rate of higher than the stated tax rate (in this case six percent) might be imposed on the facility unless its drink prices are posted and show the selling price and sales tax amount separately.

Cost of Sales

The costs of sales for food and beverages are accounted for independently and represent the cost of food or beverage used to generate a customer sale. *Cost of food sales* can also be called cost of food sold or **net food cost**. *Cost of beverage sales* is also called cost of beverage sold or **net beverage cost**.

The cost of employee meals and officers' checks should not be included in the cost of sales amount. The computation of cost of sales depends on the type of inventory system used in the storeroom. Some restaurants use the periodic system for food and the perpetual system for beverages, especially when expensive wines are involved.

Fast-Food Restaurants

The procedure for computing food cost is identical for a full-service restaurant, limited-service restaurant, or fast-food restaurant. However, the food cost of sales for a fast-food restaurant has an additional cost. Unlike table service restaurants, fast-food restaurants package the meal and supply disposable meal utensils. These packaging materials are called paper goods (see Exhibit 2) and include items such as:

- Paper wrappers and napkins.
- Paper and foam cups.
- Take-out containers.
- Plastic utensils and straws.

Employee Meals and Officers' Checks

Various methods are used to calculate cost of employee meals. The most convenient is to use an estimated or standard cost based on the type of meal—breakfast, lunch, or dinner. Multiplying this standard cost by the number of meals served to employees renders the total cost of employee meals.

Certain employees, such as executives and department heads, may have dining room privileges, with their meals recorded *at menu prices* on **officer's checks.** These checks are not cashiered as a customer sale. An easy method to arrive at the cost of officers' meals is to use a standard food cost percentage. For example, if officers' checks total $2,000 at menu price for a month and the usual food cost is 30 percent, then the cost of officers' meals is $600 ($2,000 × 30%).

Perpetual Inventory System

A perpetual inventory system has many advantages, such as inventory control and daily balances. In addition, its recordkeeping function automatically gives the cost of sales information. However, the recordkeeping can be expensive, even if a computerized system is used, because every receipt and issue requires clerical effort in the manual recordkeeping or the computer input process. Smaller operations may find the perpetual system too expensive, time-consuming, and inefficient for its production process.

The following example shows how cost of food sales is computed under a perpetual system:

Storeroom issues	$350,000
Add transfers from bar	400
Less transfers to bar	(100)
Cost of food used	$350,300
Less officers' checks	
($2,000 menu prices × 30% food cost)	(600)
Less employee meals	(200)
Cost of food sold to customers	$349,500

The procedure to compute cost of beverage sold is similar.

Periodic Inventory System

Storeroom inventory records are not maintained in a periodic inventory system; therefore, inventory control is inadequate. Its only advantage is simplicity and low cost. Because inventory records are absent, it is necessary to take a month-end physical inventory to arrive at an accurate cost of sales. The month-end inventory for the current month becomes the beginning inventory for the next month. Information from the accounting department, such as purchases, is required to compute cost of sales.

The following is an example of how to compute cost of food sales under a periodic system:

Beginning inventory	$ 55,000
Add purchases	375,000
Add transfers from bar	400
Less transfers to bar	(100)
Less ending inventory	(80,000)
Cost of food used	$350,300
Less officers' checks ($2,000 menu prices × 30% food cost)	(600)
Less employee meals	(200)
Cost of food sold to customers	$349,500

The procedure to compute cost of beverage sold is similar.

Operating Expenses

Operating expenses represent expenses directly related to the day-to-day operations of the business and reflect operating policies and management efficiency. Operating expenses do not include cost of sales, interest expense, and income taxes. Other income is included in the operating expenses section as a contra item; it is subtracted to arrive at total operating expenses.

Operating expenses according to the *USAR* are:

- Salaries and wages.
- Employee benefits.
- Direct operating expenses.
- Music and entertainment.
- Marketing expenses.
- Utility services.
- Repairs and maintenance.
- Occupancy expenses.
- Depreciation.
- Administrative and general expenses.
- Other income.

Salaries and Wages

The largest controllable expense is salaries and wages for management and staff. A proprietorship would not have a payroll expense for its owner because the Internal

Revenue Service does not allow such a deduction. However, if the restaurant is a one-owner corporation, a payroll expense is allowed for its owner. The payroll line item on the income statement is supported by a supplementary schedule. Exhibit 3 shows an example of a salaries and wages schedule for a full-service restaurant; Exhibit 4 shows this schedule for a fast-food restaurant.

Employee Benefits

Employee benefits are payroll-related and represent another significant expense. Many employees are not aware that the employer pays significant payroll taxes that will provide future benefits for them. The taxes withheld by the employer from the employees are not included in expense; the withholding of payroll taxes is treated as a liability and the funds are forwarded to the taxing agency. The payroll taxes imposed on the employer that provide future employee benefits are:

- Social Security taxes that will someday provide a retirement benefit and Medicare.
- State and federal unemployment taxes that provide state benefits in the event of involuntary loss of employment.
- State disability taxes that provide benefits for work absences due to sickness.

The employer also pays workers' compensation insurance, which provides benefits due to job-related injuries. The Employee Benefits line item on the income statement is supported by a supplementary schedule. Exhibit 5 shows an example of an employee benefits schedule. The expense for employee meals could be included in the employee benefits schedule or shown as a single line item on the income statement, depending on its materiality.

Direct Operating Expenses

A **direct operating expense** is an expense directly involved in servicing customers (other than payroll and payroll-related). The Direct Operating Expense line item on the income statement is supported by a supplementary schedule. The extent of the detail of this schedule is determined by management's need for such information. Exhibit 6 shows an example of a direct operating expenses schedule for a full-service restaurant; Exhibit 7 is an example of this schedule for a fast-food restaurant.

Many of the items listed under direct operating expenses are self-explanatory. However, a few need commentary. Part of the expense for *China, glassware, and silver* is the cost of their replacement and part is from depreciating the original asset purchase. *Paper supplies* for a full- or limited-service restaurant include items such as liners, napkins, plates, wrapping paper, soufflé cups, pastry bags, other kitchen papers, and twine. Paper supplies for a fast-food restaurant include similar items, except for those materials used to package the meal. As previously explained, these packaging items are a cost of food sold expense. *Guest supplies* are items furnished free to guests such as matches, toothpicks, and other favors. *Contract cleaning* is for services such as janitorial, window washing, and extermination.

Exhibit 3 Salaries and Wages Schedule: Full-Service Restaurant

	Number of Employees	Regular Wages	Other Wages*
SERVICE			
Captains, hostesses		$	$
Waitstaff			
Buspersons			
Cashiers and checkers			
Total Service			
BEVERAGES			
Bartenders			
Bar cashiers			
Wine steward and wine room attendants			
Total Beverage			
PREPARATION			
Chef, head dietitian, kitchen manager			
Cooks and short order cooks			
Pantry, salads, vegetable cleaners			
Potwashers			
Steward and assistants			
Total Preparation			
SANITATION			
Dishwashers			
Cleaners			
Total Sanitation			
PURCHASING AND STORING			
Purchasing steward			
Receiving clerk			
Storeroom personnel			
Food controller			
Total Purchasing and Storing			
ADMINISTRATIVE			
Officers			
Manager			
Manager's staff			
Sales			
Accounting			
Personnel			
Data processing			
Security			
Total Administrative			
OTHER			
Engineers			
Maintenance			
Door attendants			
Parking lot attendants			
Total Other			
TOTAL SALARIES AND WAGES			

* Other wages include overtime, vacation, commissions, and bonuses

Exhibit 4 Salaries and Wages Schedule: Fast-Food Restaurant

	Number of Employees	Regular Wages	Other Wages*
Service		$	$
Preparation			
Administrative and general			
Other			
Total Salaries and Wages			

* Other wages include overtime, vacation, commissions, and bonuses

Exhibit 5 Employee Benefits Schedule

FEDERAL AND STATE PAYROLL TAXES	
Social Security	$ ______
Medicare	
Federal unemployment	
State unemployment	
Total Federal and State Payroll Taxes	
SOCIAL INSURANCE	
Workers' compensation	
Pensions	
Health and hospitalization	
Group life	
Total Social Insurance	
OTHER EMPLOYEE BENEFITS	
Tuition reimbursement	
Parties	
Sports	
Credit union	
Awards and prizes	
Total Other	
TOTAL EMPLOYEE BENEFITS	**$ ______**

Music and Entertainment

Music and entertainment expenses are costs associated with guest entertainment and include items such as:

- Fees for booking agents.
- Fees for musicians and entertainers.
- Meals served to musicians and entertainers.
- Mechanical music.

Exhibit 6 Direct Operating Expenses Schedule: Full-Service Restaurant

Uniforms	$ _____
Laundry	
Linen rental	
Replacement of china, glassware, silver	
Kitchen utensils	
Paper supplies	
Guest supplies	
Bar supplies	
Cleaning supplies	
Menus	
Dry cleaning	
Contract cleaning	
Flowers and decorations	
Employee transportation	
Parking lot rental	
Licenses and permits	
Other	
Total Direct Operating Expenses	$ =====

Exhibit 7 Direct Operating Expenses Schedule: Fast-Food Restaurant

Uniforms	$ _____
Utensils	
Supplies	
Contract cleaning	
Licenses and permits	
Miscellaneous	
Total Direct Operating Expenses	$ =====

- Contracted wire service.
- Records, sheet music, programs, and films.

Marketing Expenses

Marketing's prime objective is to promote the restaurant's name, location, service, and ambiance through such activities as public relations, advertising, promotional programs, product research, and market research. Because a franchised name is readily noticeable by the public, franchise fees or royalties are charged to marketing. Exhibit 8 shows an example of a marketing expense schedule for a full-service restaurant; Exhibit 9 is an example of this schedule for a fast-food restaurant.

Utility Services

Expenses associated with utility services—fuel, water, and removal of waste—are included in this line item. *USAR* recommends that electric bulbs and ice for

Exhibit 8 Marketing Expense Schedule: Full-Service Restaurant

SELLING AND PROMOTION	
Solicitation travel	$
Direct mail	
Promotional entertainment	
Postage	
ADVERTISING	
Newspapers	
Magazines and trade journals	
Radio and TV	
Circulars and brochures	
Directories and guides	
Outdoor signs	
PUBLIC RELATIONS AND PUBLICITY	
Civic and community projects	
Donations	
Sports team sponsorship	
FEES AND COMMISSIONS	
Franchise fees/royalties	
Advertising agency fees	
RESEARCH	
Research travel	
Research agency	
Product testing	
Total Marketing Expense	$

Exhibit 9 Marketing Expense Schedule: Fast-Food Restaurant

SELLING AND PROMOTION	
Advertising	$
Public relations and publicity	
Franchise fees/royalties	
Research	
Total Marketing Expense	$

consumption should also be charged to utility services. However, some restaurant operators do not agree with this treatment of ice and prefer to treat ice expense as a direct operating expense.

Kitchen fuel is the fuel (gas, electric, charcoal, and other) used for cooking. Unless there is a separate meter in the kitchen, accounting for kitchen fuel might be impractical; furthermore, management might not wish to estimate this expense. Under these conditions, kitchen fuel is included in the Utility Services expense line item on the income statement.

Repairs and Maintenance

The repairs and maintenance expenses include any cost of material, service, or contracts associated with normal maintenance of equipment, buildings, and grounds. These expenses include items such as:

- Painting and decorating.
- Repairs to furniture, equipment, buildings, and grounds.
- Gardening.
- Maintenance contracts.

Occupancy Expense

USAR includes the following as occupancy expenses:

- Rent
- Property insurance
- Property taxes

These expenses have fixed characteristics. Regardless of volume, or whether the restaurant is open or closed, these expenses are incurred and cannot be directly managed.

Rent is any payment for rentals of building, grounds, and equipment. Property insurance is property damage insurance on buildings and contents (liability insurance is an administrative and general expense). Property taxes include items such as real estate taxes, personal property taxes, sewer tax, and corporation renewal fees.

Depreciation

Depreciation and amortization are often lumped together and simply called depreciation because both involve allocating the cost of long-lived assets over their useful lives. *Depreciation* is the allocation of the cost of tangible long-lived assets over their useful lives; *amortization* is a similar expense except that it deals with intangible long-lived assets. Unlike other expenses, depreciation and amortization are expenses that never require a cash payment.

Administrative and General

The *Administrative and General* expenses (often referred to as A&G) represent office and management expenses, an overhead expense category not affiliated with directly servicing the customer. A&G contains some items one would perhaps not expect to find under this heading, such as *bad debts, cash shortages,* and *credit card fees.* The rationale in charging A&G for these operational costs are:

- A&G is accountable for the timely collection of accounts receivable and the prevention of bad debts.

Exhibit 10 Administrative and General Expenses: Full-Service Restaurant

Office stationery	$
Postage (except chargeable to advertising department)	
Dues and subscriptions	
Travel (except chargeable to advertising department)	
Insurance—general	
Credit card fees	
Bad debts expense	
Cash shortages	
Legal and professional fees	
Telephone (except chargeable to advertising department)	
Data processing costs	
Management fees from central office	
Outside management fees	
Total Administrative and General Expenses	**$**

Exhibit 11 Administrative and General Expenses: Fast-Food Restaurant

Insurance—general	$
Cash shortages	
Legal and professional fees	
Help wanted ads	
Telephone (except chargeable to advertising department)	
Data processing costs	
Miscellaneous	
Total Administrative and General Expenses	**$**

- It is the responsibility of A&G to provide internal control and equipment and procedures to eliminate cash shortages.
- Credit card fees are an administrative policy and cannot be considered as advertising or marketing.

The Administrative and General line item on the income statement is supported by a supplementary schedule. Exhibit 10 shows an A&G expenses schedule for a full-service restaurant. Exhibit 11 shows this schedule for a fast-food restaurant.

Other Income

The type of activities falling under *Other Income* (also called Other Revenue), depends on the nature of ancillary sales in a restaurant operation. Today's restaurants are increasingly creative in their efforts to expand their operations to supplement revenue from food and beverage operations. All items of other income should be separately listed in a supplementary schedule attached to the financial statements. The total of this schedule appears as a single line item on the income statement. Other Income includes such items as:

- Service charges (net of paid-outs to waitstaff).
- Cover and minimum charges.
- Banquet room rentals.
- Rental of display cases.
- Concession rentals (coat room, parking).
- Vending machine commissions.
- Telephone commissions.
- Salvage and waste sales.
- Menu advertising.
- Cash discounts.

Cash discounts may be treated as a reduction of the cost of an item and not as other income. This net cost method is more practical for the small restaurant because only one entry is made—the net amount invoiced for the item.

In large operations, grease sales could be credited to cost of food sales instead of salvage and waste sales; however, the removal of what was once salable waste has now changed to an expense in many communities.

Restaurant Balance Sheet

An income statement varies by type of industry because of the differences in sales (products and services) and the kinds of expenses incurred. However, the balance sheet is fairly standard regardless of the industry. Every business has assets, liabilities, and equity. The accounts in these three classifications are also common to any industry. A balance sheet for a restaurant differs from other industries in the following areas:

- China, glassware, silver, linen, and uniforms
- Preopening expenses
- Cost of bar license
- Franchise contract

China, Glassware, Silver, Linen, and Uniforms. The initial cost of purchasing sets of china, glassware, silver, linen, and uniforms is charged to an asset and depreciated. The net asset portion appears in the property and equipment section of the balance sheet. Replacements are charged directly to expense.

Preopening Expenses. Costs incurred before opening a restaurant, such as employee training and grand opening advertising, can be charged directly to expense or set up as a temporary asset and amortized over a 12-month period. A preopening expense asset appears in the Other Assets section of the balance sheet.

Cost of Bar License. In some states, the quantity or type of liquor licenses is restricted and their availability is only by purchase on the open market, usually at considerable cost. A purchased liquor license is an asset appearing in the Other Assets section of the balance sheet.

Franchise Contract. This line item represents a deposit on a franchise contract or purchase of a franchise right. The major franchise contract or right appears in the Other Assets section of the balance sheet.

Chart of Accounts for Restaurants

USAR provides a numbering system for the income and expense classifications. It specifies that the codes presented are not the only method for classifying the accounts. However, it is an acceptable standard used by many restaurants. The manual further states that its coding system is flexible and accounts can be added or deleted to suit an individual restaurant. The Appendix to this chapter is a reproduction of a chart of accounts from *USAR*.

Food and Beverage Ratio Analysis

Ratio analysis involves examining the mathematical relationship between two amounts, with the relationship expressed in percentage or decimal format. This mathematical format is compared to a budget, standard, historical data, or industry average. If it is compared to industry averages, it is important that *USAR* be adopted or that the user be aware of any deviations.

Ratios are only indicators. Decisions should not be based solely on a mathematical result. A ratio that differs significantly from its base of comparison indicates the need for further investigation to determine the cause of variance.

Ratios are used to analyze balance sheet items and income statement items. The most popular ratios used by a food and beverage manager are the food cost percentage and the beverage cost percentage.

Food Cost Percentage

The *food cost percentage* measures cost efficiency in generating customer sales. The formula is:

$$\frac{\text{Cost of Food Sold}}{\text{Food Sales}} = \text{Food Cost Percentage}$$

This ratio expresses the food cost as a percentage of (net) food sales. For example, if actual food sales are \$100,000 and the actual food cost is \$33,000, the food cost percentage is 33 percent, calculated as follows:

$$\frac{\text{Cost of Food Sold}}{\text{Food Sales}} = \frac{\$33{,}000}{\$100{,}000} = 33\%$$

If the budgeted food cost was 30 percent, this means that food costs are running three percent higher than expected. This could be due to standard recipes not being followed, increased costs from suppliers, or lower menu prices. The sales mix can have an effect on the departmental food cost percentage because not all meals share the same food cost percentage. Generally, chicken has a lower food cost percentage than steaks. If the sales mix shows a trend toward more steak sales than planned, the food cost percentage will increase.

Beverage Cost Percentage

The utility of this ratio is similar to that of the food cost percentage. The formula is:

$$\frac{\text{Cost of Beverage Sold}}{\text{Beverage Sales}} = \text{Beverage Cost Percentage}$$

The beverage cost percentage is more useful if it is maintained by type of drink. The sales mix also has an effect on a restaurant's overall beverage cost percentage because of the differences in costs and pricing for beer, wine, and liquor.

Food Sales Statistics and Analysis

Food sales statistics provide management with a basis for analyzing selling prices, sales mix, efficiency, and profitability. For example, statistics can be used to determine if:

- Menu prices are reasonable.
- Customer volume is satisfactory.
- Average check is adequate.
- Seat turnover is sufficient.

The amount of sales reporting depends on management's desire for detailed information and the operation's sales mix. **Sales mix** is the relationship of an element of sales to the total. The formula to compute sales mix is:

$$\frac{\text{Item Sales \$}}{\text{Total Sales \$}} = \text{Sales Mix \%}$$

For example, if food sales are $80,000 and beverage sales are $20,000, then the sales mix is 80 percent food and 20 percent beverage, computed as follows:

		Food			Beverage		
Item Sales $ / Total Sales $	=	$80,000 / $100,000	=	80%	$20,000 / $100,000	=	20%

The sales mix can also be used to analyze the relationship of specific food sales such as steak, chicken, and pasta to total food sales.

Food sales statistics are calculated on a daily basis and summarized for the month. Useful statistics are as follows:

- Food sales analysis by meal period
- Food sales analysis by dining facility
- Average food check
- Average food sales per seat
- Customer turnover

Food Sales Analysis by Meal Period

This analysis is helpful in determining whether a particular meal period warrants being open for business or if sales are sufficient for satisfactory profitability. The following is a daily report analyzing sales by meal period:

Schedule of Food Sales by Meal Period
For Tuesday, June 26, 20XX

	Meals Served	Sales	Percent
Breakfast	120	$ 480	14.6%
Lunch	150	1,200	36.6%
Dinner	80	1,600	48.8%
Total	350	$3,280	100.0%

The percentages are computed by dividing each individual sale amount by the total. For example, the breakfast sales percent is calculated as follows:

$$\frac{\text{Item Sales \$}}{\text{Total Sales \$}} = \frac{\$480}{\$3{,}280} = 14.6\%$$

Food Sales Analysis by Dining Facility

Another useful report is one showing the same data arranged by dining facility instead of by meal period. This analysis is helpful in determining whether a given food service facility (outlet) is customer justified. A large food operation may have outlets such as a main dining room, coffee shop, lunch counter, cafeteria, patio, drive-in, and banquet facilities all in one physical location.

The following is a daily report analyzing sales by dining facility:

Schedule of Food Sales by Dining Facility
For Tuesday, June 26, 20XX

	Meals Served	Sales	Percent
Counter	30	$ 400	12.2%
Dining Room	320	2,880	87.8%
Total	350	$3,280	100.0%

The percentages are computed by dividing each individual sale amount by the total. For example, the counter sales percent is calculated as follows:

$$\frac{\text{Item Sales \$}}{\text{Total Sales \$}} = \frac{\$400}{\$3{,}280} = 12.2\%$$

Average Food Check

The average check statistic reveals how much, on average, a guest is spending. If the average check is lower than projected, the profit target might not be realized, especially if any increase in volume is not sufficient to offset the deficiency. If the average check is higher but guest volume is declining, it is possible that the menu prices are having an adverse effect and will reduce sales in the long run.

The formula to calculate average food check is:

$$\frac{\text{Meal Period Sales \$}}{\text{Number of Customers}} = \text{Average Food Check}$$

The average check must be computed for each type of meal for the information to be useful. Often, the number of customers is referred to as **covers**. The following is an average check computation:

Average Food Check
For Tuesday, June 26, 20XX

	Sales	Guests	Average Check
Breakfast	$ 480	120	$ 4.00
Lunch	1,200	150	8.00
Dinner	1,600	80	20.00
Total	$3,280	350	

The sales amount for each meal period is divided by the number of guests for that meal period. For example, the breakfast average check is computed as follows:

$$\frac{\text{Meal Period Sales \$}}{\text{Number of Guests Served}} = \frac{\$480}{120} = \$4$$

Generally, the average check differs by meal period, with breakfast the lowest and dinner the highest.

Average Food Sale per Seat

The average sale per seat is computed using the total number of available seats in the facility, regardless of whether they were occupied during the meal period. If the average check is satisfactory, but the average sale per seat is too low, an analysis should be made to determine if the size of the facility is much larger than needed to satisfy customer demand.

The formula is as follows:

$$\frac{\text{Food Sales \$}}{\text{Available Seats}} = \text{Average Food Sale per Seat}$$

The average food sale per seat is more meaningful if it is computed by meal period. The following is a food sale per seat analysis:

Average Food Sale per Seat
For Tuesday, June 26, 20XX

	Sales	Seats	Average per Seat
Breakfast	$ 480	25	$19.20
Lunch	1,200	80	15.00
Dinner	1,600	70	22.86
Total	$3,280		

The average sale per seat is an average of all seats available during a meal period. As shown above, this restaurant has different numbers of available seats per meal period based on seating arrangements; the counter seats are available only for breakfast and lunch.

Seat Turnover

Seat turnover defines the number of times that a seat is occupied during a meal period. The more times a seat can be occupied by a different customer, the greater the sales generation during a meal period. The meal period, type of menu items, customer market, and staff efficiency affect the seat turnover statistic.

The formula to calculate seat turnover is:

$$\frac{\text{Guests Served}}{\text{Available Seats}} = \text{Seat Turnover}$$

Generally, the turnover is lowest during the dinner period because of the type of meal and dining experience expected by the guest. Following is a seat turnover analysis:

Average Seat Turnover
For Tuesday, June 26, 20XX

	Guests	Seats	Seat Turnover
Breakfast	120	25	4.8
Lunch	150	80	1.9
Dinner	80	70	1.1

The number of guests for each period is divided by the number of seats for that meal period to arrive at seat turnover.

Beverage Sales Statistics

The percentage of cost and gross profit varies considerably among the different kinds of beverage sales (liquor, wine, beer, and soft drinks). Therefore, any point-of-sale system should record the type of beverage sale in addition to the price.

Gathering statistics on the number of customers served and sales per customer can be difficult, if not impossible, because the consumption of beverages is not coincidental with the consumption of food. For example, at a table of five guests, maybe only one purchases a drink. On the other hand, a table of five guests may generate orders for ten drinks.

Some useful beverage sales statistics are:

- Sales by meal period.
- Food/beverage sales ratio.
- Sales by type of drink.
- Sales by facility.

Beverage Sales by Meal Period

Each state has regulations governing the hours for the legal sale of alcoholic beverages. Additionally, management might decide to limit the sale of beverages to the lunch and dinner periods. The following is a daily report analyzing sales by meal period:

Schedule of Beverage Sales by Meal Period
For Tuesday, June 26, 20XX

	Sales	Percent
Breakfast	$ 0	n/a
Lunch	240	27.3%
Dinner	640	72.7%
Total	$880	100.0%

Beverage/Food Sales Ratio

While the sales by meal period is important information, supplementing this data with the relationship of beverage sales to food sales improves the usefulness in analyzing beverage sales. This relationship is computed as follows:

$$\frac{\text{Beverage Sales \$}}{\text{Food Sales \$}} = \text{Beverage/Food Ratio}$$

The following is an analysis of the beverage and food sales relationship.

Analysis of Beverage Sales to Food Sales Ratio
For Tuesday, June 26, 20XX

	Food Sales	Beverage Sales	Beverage/Food Ratio
Breakfast	$ 480	$ 0	n/a
Lunch	1,200	240	20%
Dinner	1,600	640	40%
Total	$3,280	880	

The amount of beverage sales for each meal period is divided by the amount of food sales for that meal period. For example, the beverage/food ratio for the lunch period is calculated as follows:

$$\frac{\text{Beverage Sales \$}}{\text{Food Sales \$}} = \frac{\$240}{\$1{,}200} = 20\%$$

This analysis shows that during the lunch period, beverage sales equal 20 percent of food sales, and during the dinner period, beverage sales equal 40 percent of food sales. As expected, the beverage/food ratio is higher during the dinner period. These ratios are more meaningful if prior periods, forecasts, or industry statistics are compared against the actual results. Disappointing ratios might indicate the need for training the staff to improve the marketing effort at the customer-service level, table promotions, or other marketing efforts.

Beverage Sales by Type

An analysis by type of drink is helpful for inventory forecasting and profit management. Different drinks produce different profit margins and the higher margin drinks might enjoy a sales increase through menu design, table promotions, and waitstaff training. Following is an analysis by type of drink.

Schedule of Beverage Sales by Type of Drink
For Tuesday, June 26, 20XX

Mixed drinks and cocktails	$450	51.2% *
Beer and ale	120	13.6%
Wines	200	22.7%
Soft drinks	$ 110	12.5%
	$880	100.0%

* The actual computation for mixed drinks and cocktails is 51.1 percent. However, when working with percentages, sometimes the sum of the items does not equal 100 percent due to rounding differences. An arbitrary procedure is to adjust the largest number to arrive at a sum of 100 percent.

Beverage Sales by Facility

Following is an analysis format for beverage sales by facility that might be used by an operation with multi-outlet beverage sales.

Schedule of Beverage Sales by Facility
For Tuesday, June 26, 20XX

	Amount	Percent
Main bar	$	%
Service bar		
Dining room		
Grill		
Banquets and parties		
Total	$	%

An analysis by facility is not necessary if a restaurant sells beverages in only one outlet.

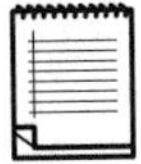

Endnotes

1. For a comprehensive description of recognized accounting procedures and statements for the food and beverage industry, refer to the *Uniform System of Accounts for Restaurants*, 7th revised ed. (Washington, D.C.: National Restaurant Association, 1996), prepared by Deloitte & Touche LLP.

Key Terms

covers—The number of guests served.

direct operating expense—An expense directly involved in servicing a customer (other than payroll and related).

net beverage cost—A term similar to cost of beverage sold or cost of beverage sales.

net food cost—A term similar to cost of food sold or cost of food sales.

officers' check—A tab showing meals and beverages provided to management at menu prices but not treated as a customer sale.

sales mix—The relationship of an element of sales to total sales.

seat turnover—The number of times a seat is occupied during a meal period.

service charge—A separate charge on a customer's tab in lieu of tips.

Review Questions

1. What items are included in food sales?
2. What is the definition of sales mix?
3. What is the formula for the following?
   a. Sales mix
   b. Average food check
   c. Average food sales per seat
   d. Seat turnover
   e. Beverage/food sales ratio
4. What items are included in beverage sales?
5. What are the major differences between the perpetual and periodic inventory systems for a storeroom?
6. What is the procedure for calculating cost of food sold if a perpetual inventory system is used in the storeroom for a full-service restaurant?
7. What is the procedure for calculating cost of food sold if a periodic inventory system is used in the storeroom for a full-service restaurant?

8. What is a service charge and what should management consider before instituting this policy?
9. What items are considered other income?
10. What are the components of occupancy expense?
11. What is the major difference in accounting for cost of food sold between a full-service restaurant and fast-food restaurant?

Problems

Problem 1

Food sales are $300,000, cost of food sales $120,000, direct operating expenses $60,000, and occupancy costs $80,000. What is the gross profit?

Problem 2

Meals served are $10,000, coffee $300, milk $200, soft drinks $400, beer $1,000, wine $1,500, mixed drinks $800. What is the amount of food sales?

Problem 3

Complete the following schedule of food sales by meal period. If necessary, show the percentages with one decimal position, properly rounded.

	Meals Served	Sales	Percent
Breakfast	100	$ 375	____%
Lunch	200	1,000	____%
Dinner	150	$1,200	____%
Total	___	___	___

Problem 4

Use the data supplied in Problem 3 to compute the average check for each meal period.

Problem 5

The available seats are 35 for breakfast, 75 for lunch, and 75 for dinner. Use the data supplied in Problem 3 to calculate average seat turnover. If necessary, show the percentages with one decimal position, properly rounded.

Problem 6

Beverage sales are $60 breakfast, $268 lunch, and $475 dinner. Use the data supplied in Problem 3 to calculate the beverage/food ratio. If necessary, show the percentages with one decimal position, properly rounded.

Problem 7

The restaurant's cost of sales percentage averages 32 percent for any month. Following are transactions for the month of April:

Transfers from bar	$ 220	
Transfers to bar	75	
Officers' checks	500	at menu price
Employee meals	130	at standard cost
Storeroom issues	$40,000	

Compute the cost of food sold for the month of April if the perpetual inventory system is used in the storeroom.

Problem 8

A restaurant has a food cost average of 30 percent. The inventory on June 30 is $10,000 and the inventory on July 31 is $10,888. Following are transactions for the month of July:

Purchases	$30,000	
Officers' checks were	800	at menu price
Employee meals	150	at standard cost
Transfer to bar	70	
Transfer from bar	90	

Compute the cost of food sold for the month of July if the periodic inventory system is used in the storeroom.

Problem 9

The accounting results for a month show food sales of $500,000 and cost of food sold at $175,000. Compute the food cost percentage for the month.

Problem 10

Beverage sales are cashiered with the sales tax included. Compute the separate amounts for beverage sales and sales tax if the total cashiered sales of $114,490 included a seven percent sales tax.

Ethics Case

Hubert Gundan is the senior accountant for Funtime Amusement Parks Company. The company's sales are $30 million, and the company plans to open more amusement parks in the United States.

Funtime's board of directors has scheduled a meeting with bankers to discuss financing the expansion. The company's current financial statements will

(continued)

be an important part of the discussions. Hubert has a deadline for preparing the statements which must be met without failure. A courier will pick up the financial statements and deliver them to the board's chairperson at 8 A.M. on the day of the meeting.

The day before the deadline, Hubert discovers that the trial balance does not balance. The credits exceed the debits by $1,202.16. Hubert realizes that even if there is no error, he and his staff will be working until at least midnight to prepare the financial statements and supporting schedules. Hubert is forced to make a decision. Because the discrepancy is small, he decides to enter the $1,202.16 as a debit to the Repairs Expense account. He supports this decision with the following reasoning:

- The Repairs Expense account is very active and significant. Entering the small amount of $1,202.16 will not affect anyone's decision-making.
- No one can accuse the company of trying to inflate its profits because the difference has been charged to an expense account.
- High-level executives are waiting for the financial information. It would be embarrassing for the company to cancel its meeting.

1. Who are the stakeholders in this case?
2. What are the ethical issues involved?
3. What, if any, are the alternative courses of action available to Hubert?

Chapter Appendix

Sample Chart of Accounts Based on *Uniform System Accounts for Restaurants*

The chart of accounts is a numbering system for the income and expense classifications conforming to the *Uniform System of Accounts for Restaurants.* The codes used here are not the only method for classifying the accounts; however, this is an acceptable standard grouping used by many restaurants. The illustrated code-numbering system is designed to be flexible and to be added to or reduced to fit the requirements of the individual restaurant owner. Some type of account code-numbering system must be used.

The listing that follows is intended to be quite comprehensive. Most restaurants will not require all of the account categories listed. If an account is used very rarely (or never), it should not be included in the chart of accounts. Use of fewer accounts definitely results in less complication.

Source: *Uniform System of Accounts for Restaurants,* 7th revised edition, (Washington, D.C.: National Restaurant Association, 1996), pp. 141–147. Reprinted by permission.

CHART OF ACCOUNTS

ASSETS (1000)

Account Number	Account Name
1100	Cash
1110	Change funds
1120	Cash on deposit
1200	Accounts receivable
1210	Customers
1220	Allowances and complimentaries
1230	Other
1240	Employees' loans and advances
1250	Provision for doubtful accounts
1300	Inventories
1310	Food
1320	Beverages
1330	Supplies
1340	Other
1400	Prepaid expenses
1410	Insurance
1420	Deposits
1430	Taxes
1440	Licenses
1500	Fixed assets
1510	Land
1520	Building
1530	Accumulated depreciation–building
1540	Leasehold improvements
1550	Accumulated amortization of improvements
1560	Furniture, fixtures and equipment (including POS equipment)
1570	Accumulated depreciation–furniture and equipment
1580	Automobiles/trucks
1590	Accumulated depreciation–automobiles/trucks
1600	Deferred charges
1610	Marketing program prepaid
1620	Pre-opening expenses

LIABILITIES (2000)

Account Number	Account Name
2100	Payables
2110	Notes payable
2120	Accounts payable
2200	Taxes withheld and accrued
2210	Income Tax
2220	FICA

2230	Federal unemployment tax
2240	State unemployment tax
2250	Sales tax
2260	Employer's share of payroll taxes
2270	City taxes
2300	Accrued expenses
2310	Rent
2320	Payroll
2330	Interest
2340	Water
2350	Gas
2360	Electricity
2370	Personal property taxes
2380	Vacation
2390	Other
2400	Long-term debt
2410	Mortgage debt
2420	Capital leases
2430	Other debt

SHAREHOLDERS' EQUITY (3000)

3100	Common stock
3200	Capital in excess of par
3300	Retained earnings

SALES (4000)

4100	Food
4200	Beverages

COST OF SALES (5000)
(Detailed sub-accounts, if desired, will vary by type of restaurant)

5100	Cost of sales–food
5200	Cost of sales–beverages

OTHER INCOME (6000)

6100	Cover charges and minimums
6200	Commissions
6210	Gift shop operation–net
6220	Telephone commissions
6230	Concessions
6240	Vending machine/game revenue
6300	Salvage and waste sales
6400	Cash discounts
6500	Meeting/banquet room rental
6900	Miscellaneous

OPERATING EXPENSES (7000)

7100	Salaries and wages
7105	Service
7110	Preparation
7115	Sanitation
7120	Beverages
7125	Administrative
7130	Purchasing and storing
7135	Other
7200	Employee benefits
7205	FICA
7210	Federal unemployment tax
7215	State unemployment tax
7220	Workmen's compensation
7225	Group insurance
7230	State health insurance tax
7235	Welfare plan payments
7240	Pension plan payments
7245	Accident and health insurance premiums
7250	Hospitalization, Blue Cross, Blue Shield
7255	Employee meals
7260	Employee instruction and education expenses
7265	Employee Christmas and other parties
7270	Employee sports activities
7275	Medical expenses
7280	Credit union
7285	Awards and prizes
7290	Transportation and housing
7300	Occupancy costs
7305	Rent—minimum or fixed
7310	Percentage rent
7315	Ground rental
7320	Equipment rental
7325	Real estate taxes
7330	Personal property taxes
7335	Other municipal taxes
7340	Franchise tax
7345	Capital stock tax
7350	Partnership or corporation license fees
7360	Insurance on building and contents
7370	Depreciation
7371	Buildings
7372	Amortization of leasehold
7373	Amortization of leasehold improvements
7374	Furniture, fixtures and equipment
7400	Direct operating expenses
7402	Uniforms
7404	Laundry and dry cleaning
7406	Linen rental
7408	Linen
7410	China and glassware

7412	Silverware
7414	Kitchen utensils
7416	Auto and truck expense
7418	Cleaning supplies
7420	Paper supplies
7422	Guest supplies
7424	Bar supplies
7426	Menus and wine lists
7428	Contract cleaning
7430	Exterminating
7432	Flowers and decorations
7436	Parking lot expenses
7438	Licenses and permits
7440	Banquet expenses
7498	Other operating expenses
7500	Music and entertainment
7505	Musicians
7510	Professional entertainers
7520	Mechanical music
7525	Contracted wire services
7530	Piano rental and tuning
7535	Films, records, tapes and sheet music
7540	Programs
7550	Royalties to ASCAP, BMI
7555	Booking agents fees
7560	Meals served to musicians
7600	Marketing
7601	Selling and promotion
7602	Sales representative service
7603	Travel expense on solicitation
7604	Direct mail
7605	Telephone used for advertising and promotion
7606	Complimentary food and beverage (including gratis meals to customers)
7607	Postage
7610	Advertising
7611	Newspaper
7612	Magazines and trade journals
7613	Circulars, brochures, postal cards and other mailing pieces
7614	Outdoor signs
7615	Radio and television
7616	Programs, directories and guides
7617	Preparation of copy, photographs, etc.
7620	Public relations and publicity
7621	Civic and community projects
7622	Donations
7623	Souvenirs, favors, treasure chest items
7630	Fees and commissions
7631	Advertising or promotional agency fees
7640	Research
7641	Travel in connection with research
7642	Outside research agency

7643	Product testing
7700	Utilities
7705	Electric current
7710	Electric bulbs
7715	Water
7720	Removal of waste
7725	Other fuel
7800	Administrative and general expenses
7805	Office stationery, printing and supplies
7810	Data processing costs
7815	Postage
7820	Telegrams and telephone
7825	Dues and subscriptions
7830	Traveling expenses
7835	Insurance—general
7840	Commissions on credit card charges
7845	Provision for doubtful accounts
7850	Cash over or (short)
7855	Professional fees
7860	Protective and bank pick-up services
7865	Bank charges
7870	Miscellaneous
7900	Repairs and maintenance
7902	Furniture and fixtures
7904	Kitchen equipment
7906	Office equipment
7908	Refrigeration
7910	Air conditioning
7912	Plumbing and heating
7914	Electrical and mechanical
7916	Floors and carpets
7918	Buildings
7920	Parking lot
7922	Gardening and grounds maintenance
7924	Building alterations
7928	Painting, plastering and decorating
7990	Maintenance contracts
7996	Autos and trucks
7998	Other equipment and supplies

INTEREST AND CORPORATE OVERHEAD (8000)

8100	Interest
8105	Notes payable
8110	Long-term debt
8115	Other
8200	Corporate or Executive Office overhead
8205	Officers' salaries
8210	Directors' salaries
8215	Corporate office payroll
8220	Corporate office employee benefits
8225	Corporate office rent

8230	Corporate travel and entertainment
8235	Corporate office automobile expense
8240	Corporate office insurance
8245	Corporate office utilities
8250	Corporate office data processing
8255	Legal and accounting expense
8260	Corporate miscellaneous expense

INCOME TAX (9000)

9000	Income Taxes
9010	Federal
9020	State

Chapter 10 Outline

- Hotel Income Statement
  - Operated Departments Section
  - Undistributed Operating Expenses Section
  - Fixed Expenses Section
- Departmental Statements
- Revenue Accounting
  - Rooms Department
  - Package Plans
  - Food and Beverage Departments
  - Rentals and Other Income
- Expense Accounting
  - Payroll and Related—All Departments
  - Rooms Department
  - Food and Beverage Departments
  - Administrative and General Department
  - Marketing Department
  - Property Operation and Maintenance Department
  - Utility Costs
  - Fixed Expenses
- Hotels with Casino Departments
  - Statement of Gaming Operations
  - Revenue Accounting
  - Expense Accounting
- Hotel Balance Sheet
  - Preopening Expenses
  - China, Glassware, Silver
  - Linen and Uniforms
- Chart of Accounts for Hotels
- Operating Ratios
  - Average Room Rate
  - Occupancy Percentage
  - Average Food Check
  - Food Cost Percentage
  - Beverage Cost Percentage
  - Labor Cost Percentage

Competencies

1. Describe the internal hotel income statement and departmental statement formats recommended by the *Uniform System of Accounts for the Lodging Industry.* (pp. 269–272)
2. Explain the revenue and expense accounting procedures for a lodging property recommended by the *Uniform System of Accounts for the Lodging Industry.* (pp. 273–283)
3. Identify and explain the special accounting considerations for a hotel with a casino department. (pp. 284–286)
4. Identify and explain the unique balance sheet accounting considerations for a lodging property. (p. 286)
5. Describe the composition of a chart of accounts for a lodging property. (pp. 286–295)
6. Identify and describe the operating ratios useful to management of a lodging property. (pp. 295–297)

10

Hotel Accounting

THE *UNIFORM SYSTEM OF ACCOUNTS FOR THE LODGING INDUSTRY (USALI)* is a publication resulting from cooperation between the Hotel Association of New York City, which owns the copyright, and the American Hotel & Lodging Association, which publishes the work. While any lodging operation can use the publication's guidelines, its departmental statements are most applicable to hotel and motel properties.

USALI provides a standardized chart of accounts and standardized financial statement formats from which a property may select and customize to its particular needs. Such standardization makes it possible to produce industry statistics that form a basis for meaningful comparisons. For new properties, *USALI* serves as a turnkey accounting system.

USALI is based on responsibility accounting, which follows the reasoning that managers should be judged on the basis of revenues and expenses directly under their control. Under responsibility accounting, only direct expenses are charged to a department; any cost not associated with a specific department is charged to the hotel as a whole.

The accounting procedures and statements presented in this chapter are those of *USALI*. This chapter will answer such questions as:

1. What is the income statement format recommended by *USALI*?
2. What is the format and kinds of departmental statements?
3. What are the revenue and expense accounting procedures?
4. Which exceptional accounting considerations are necessary for a casino department?
5. What vital accounting policies affect the balance sheet?
6. What is a suitable chart of accounts for hotel accounting?
7. Which operating ratios are helpful to hotel management?

Hotel Income Statement

USALI suggests different income statement formats for internal and external users. The internal format is especially useful to management because it presents on one central report every hotel department and its related revenues and expenses. Exhibit 1 shows this internal hotel income statement. Notice the listing of departments with references to a schedule number. The schedule number references a supporting schedule that provides detailed information about that department.

Exhibit 1 Hotel Statement of Income

SUMMARY STATEMENT OF INCOME

	Schedule	Net Revenues	Cost of Sales	Payroll and Related Expenses	Other Expenses	Income (Loss)
Operated Departments						
Rooms	1	$	$	$	$	$
Food	2					
Beverage	3					
Telecommunications	4					
Garage and Parking	5					
Golf Course	6					
Golf Pro Shop	7					
Guest Laundry	8					
Health Center	9					
Swimming Pool	10					
Tennis	11					
Tennis Pro Shop	12					
Other Operated Departments	13					
Rentals and Other Income	14					
Total Operated Departments						
Undistributed Operating Expenses[1]						
Administrative and General	15					
Human Resources	16					
Information Systems	17					
Security	18					
Marketing	19					
Franchise Fees	19a					
Transportation	20					
Property Operation and Maintenance	21					
Utility Costs	22					
Total Undistributed Operating Expenses						
Totals		$	$	$	$	
Income After Undistributed Operating Expenses						
Management Fees	23					
Rent, Property Taxes, and Insurance	24					
Income Before Interest, Depreciation and Amortization, and Income Taxes[2]						
Interest Expense	25					
Income Before Depreciation, Amortization and Income Taxes						
Depreciation and Amortization	26					
Gain or Loss on Sale of Property						
Income Before Income Taxes						
Income Taxes	27					
Net Income						$

(1)A separate line for preopening expenses can be included if such costs are captured separately.
(2)Also referred to as EBITDA—Earnings before Interest, Taxes, Depreciation and Amortization

Source: *Uniform System of Accounts for the Lodging Industry,* 9th rev. ed. (Lansing, Mich.: Educational Institute of the American Hotel & Lodging Association, 1996), p. 33.

The hotel income statement is separated into three major sections:

- Operated departments
- Undistributed operating expenses
- Fixed expenses

Operated Departments Section

The section labeled **operated departments** contains the revenue centers. A revenue center is any department that sells goods or services to guests. The criterion to classify an outlet as a revenue center is strictly its sales generation and not its profit generation. Only those centers that are owned and operated by the hotel are revenue centers. Concessionaire outlets are not a separate operated department; any rents, commissions, or fees from these outlets are shown on the schedule of rentals and other income.

Undistributed Operating Expenses Section

The **undistributed operating expenses** section reports expenses that are not easily identified with any specific operated department (revenue center). This section contains all the support centers and any franchise fees.

Support Center. A **support center** is a department that has minimal guest contact and does not produce revenue. Support centers provide services to all the revenue centers. Housekeeping is not a support center in this section of the financial statement because it serves only one specific revenue center; the housekeeping expenses are included in the Rooms Department schedule. With the exception of franchise fees and utility costs, the departments shown in the undistributed operating expense section are support centers.

Franchise Fees. Under the former uniform system, franchise fees were included in the marketing department. The revised uniform system now lists this as a separate line item following the marketing department because of its cost significance.

Fixed Expenses Section

Fixed expenses include a group of expenses that are incurred regardless of volume. They include what is termed "occupational costs" (described later) and any outside management company charges. They are incurred even when the operation is closed.

Notice the several line breaks in Exhibit 1. Management fees, rent, property taxes, and insurance are subtracted from *Income After Undistributed Operating Expenses* to arrive at *Income Before Interest, Depreciation, Amortization, and Income Taxes*. Next, the interest expense is subtracted to arrive at *Income Before Depreciation, Amortization, and Income Taxes*. Then the depreciation, amortization, and any gain or loss on sale of property is entered to arrive at *Income Before Income Taxes*. Finally, the income taxes are subtracted to arrive at *Net Income*.

The bottom section of the income statement might appear overly detailed to the casual reader. However, the information is included because of the differing needs of managers; the choice of how much detail is included is up to an individual property's management, based on whether it needs these subtotals of income for proper income measurement. While it is a recommended format, management can decide to tailor the bottom section to its particular needs and convenience. For example, listing all the fixed expenses with one total would be acceptable to avoid the many subtotals of income.

Departmental Statements

The departmental statements are supporting schedules to the hotel income statement that provide detailed information about revenues and expenses. They all share a basic format, which is:

- Revenue.
- Cost of Sales.
- Expenses:
  - – Payroll & Related.
  - – Other.

Naturally, only the operated departments will have revenue and only those outlets selling merchandise will have cost of sales.

It would be redundant to show an illustration of each departmental schedule. Instead, we show only those departments that have significant differences among the various departments of a hotel. Throughout the rest of this chapter, we refer to the following exhibits:

- Hotel Statement of Income — Exhibit 1
- Rooms — Exhibit 2
- Food — Exhibit 3
- Beverage — Exhibit 4
- Rentals and Other Income — Exhibit 5
- Administrative and General — Exhibit 6
- Marketing — Exhibit 7
- Property Operation and Maintenance — Exhibit 8
- Utility Costs — Exhibit 9

Analyzing every revenue and expense account for each outlet would be impractical in the space of one chapter. Such comprehensive coverage and more is available in the text *Accounting for Hospitality Managers* by Raymond Cote and published by the Educational Institute of the American Hotel & Lodging Association. This text also provides a complete set of departmental statements with dollar amounts, which are then analyzed using ratio analysis and other techniques.

Revenue Accounting

A hotel consists of several revenue centers, or **outlets**, and the chart of accounts (explained later) must accommodate recording transactions by department and type of revenue. The types of revenue accounts a hotel uses depend on its business activities and sales/service outlets. Another consideration is the amount of detailed information reporting desired. Management must evaluate the cost to produce the information and its value as a management tool. This is known as a cost/benefit analysis.

Sales taxes are not part of revenue because the collection of these taxes is a liability until they are paid to the government.

In most cases, the name of an operating department indicates the type of revenue accounts that are necessary. The few that need further explanation are discussed in the following paragraphs.

Rooms Department

The Rooms revenue account (see Exhibit 2) includes rentals of guestrooms and apartments. Any separate charges for linen or housekeeping are included. Revenue collected from no shows (guests who guaranteed their reservations but did not show up to use them) is included as a room sale.

Package Plans

To increase the marketing effort, some hotels offer **package plans** in which guests are sold accommodations and other services or products at a single price. This single price might include the room, food, beverages, and a recreational provision. Since the price includes revenue affecting several departments, a procedure is necessary to allocate revenue to the proper departments.

When a package of services is sold, a procedure using market value ratios should allocate each sales item to the appropriate department. The following is an allocation example for a package that was sold for $800:

Package	Market Value	Ratio	Sales Allocation
Rooms	$ 500	50%	$ 400
Food	300	30%	240
Golf	200	20%	160
Total	$1,000	100%	$ 800

The marketing department provides the market value. The ratio is calculated by dividing each market value by the total market value. For example, $500 divided by $1,000 equals 50 percent. The sales allocation is computed by multiplying each ratio by the $800 actual selling price. For example, 50 percent times $800 equals $400.

Exhibit 2 Rooms

Rooms—Schedule 1

	Current Period
REVENUE	$ ______
ALLOWANCES	
NET REVENUE	
EXPENSES	
Salaries and Wages	
Employee Benefits	______
Total Payroll and Related Expenses	______
Other Expenses	
Cable/Satellite Television	
Commissions	
Complimentary Guest Services	
Contract Services	
Guest Relocation	
Guest Transportation	
Laundry and Dry Cleaning	
Linen	
Operating Supplies	
Reservations	
Telecommunications	
Training	
Uniforms	
Other	______
Total Other Expenses	______
TOTAL EXPENSES	______
DEPARTMENTAL INCOME (LOSS)	$ ______

Source: *Uniform System of Accounts for the Lodging Industry*, 9th rev. ed. (Lansing, Mich.: Educational Institute of the American Hotel & Lodging Association, 1996), p. 34.

Food and Beverage Departments

The food and beverage (F&B) operations can be two separate outlets (see Exhibits 3 and 4) or combined as one department. Some properties may decide not to separate the food and beverage departments because of shared space, labor, and other expenses. In any case, food sales and beverage sales are recorded in separate revenue accounts to facilitate inventory control and measurement of cost ratios. Sales of food and nonalcoholic beverages served with meals are considered food sales. Beverage sales include the sale of alcoholic beverages and soft drinks sold by the beverage department.

Other Income—Food and Beverage Department. This account includes revenue from meeting room rentals, cover charges, service charges, and any other miscellaneous sales in the food and beverage departments.

Exhibit 3 Food

Food—Schedule 2

	Current Period
TOTAL REVENUE	$ ______
REVENUE	$
ALLOWANCES	______
NET REVENUE	
COST OF SALES	
Cost of Food	
Less Cost of Employee Meals	
Less Food Transfers to Beverage	
Plus Beverage Transfers to Food	
Net Cost of Food	______
Other Cost of Sales	______
Total Cost of Sales	______
GROSS PROFIT (LOSS) ON FOOD SALES	
OTHER INCOME	
Meeting Room Rentals	
Miscellaneous Banquet Income	
Service Charges	______
Total Other Income	______
GROSS PROFIT (LOSS) AND OTHER INCOME	
EXPENSES	
Salaries and Wages	______
Employee Benefits	______
Total Payroll and Related Expenses	
Other Expenses	
China, Glassware, Silver, and Linen	
Contract Services	
Laundry and Dry Cleaning	
Licenses	
Miscellaneous Banquet Expense	
Music and Entertainment	
Operating Supplies	
Telecommunications	
Training	
Uniforms	
Other	______
Total Other Expenses	______
TOTAL EXPENSES	______
DEPARTMENTAL INCOME (LOSS)	$ ______

Source: *Uniform System of Accounts for the Lodging Industry,* 9th rev. ed. (Lansing, Mich.: Educational Institute of the American Hotel & Lodging Association, 1996), p. 41.

Exhibit 4 Beverage

Beverage—Schedule 3

	Current Period
TOTAL REVENUE	$
REVENUE	$
ALLOWANCES	
NET REVENUE	
COST OF SALES	
Cost of Beverage	
Less Beverage Transfers to Food	
Plus Food Transfers to Beverage	
Net Cost of Beverage	
Other Cost of Sales	
Total Cost of Sales	
GROSS PROFIT (LOSS) ON BEVERAGE SALES	
OTHER INCOME	
Cover Charges	
Service Charges	
Total Other Income	
GROSS PROFIT (LOSS) AND OTHER INCOME	
EXPENSES	
Salaries and Wages	
Employee Benefits	
Total Payroll and Related Expenses	
Other Expenses	
China, Glassware, Silver, and Linen	
Contract Services	
Gratis Food	
Laundry and Dry Cleaning	
Licenses	
Music and Entertainment	
Operating Supplies	
Telecommunications	
Training	
Uniforms	
Other	
Total Other Expenses	
TOTAL EXPENSES	
DEPARTMENTAL INCOME (LOSS)	$

Source: *Uniform System of Accounts for the Lodging Industry,* 9th rev. ed. (Lansing, Mich.: Educational Institute of the American Hotel & Lodging Association, 1996), p. 48.

Exhibit 5 Rentals and Other Income

Rentals and Other Income—Schedule 14	Current Period
Space Rentals and Concessions	$ _______
Commissions	
Cash Discounts Earned	
Cancellation Penalty	
Foreign Currency Transactions Gains (Losses)	
Interest Income	
Other	_______
TOTAL RENTALS AND OTHER INCOME	$ _______

Source: *Uniform System of Accounts for the Lodging Industry,* 9th rev. ed. (Lansing, Mich.: Educational Institute of the American Hotel & Lodging Association, 1996), p. 93.

Rentals and Other Income

Revenue from concessionaires and other revenue not attributable to a specific operated department are in a schedule called Rentals and Other Income shown in Exhibit 5. Some of the revenue items that are considered rentals and other income are:

- Interest and dividend income.
- Income from rental of stores, offices, and clubs.
- Concessions income.
- Commissions income.
- Vending machine profits (if owned).
- Cash discounts earned (purchase discounts).
- Salvage income.

Noteworthy is the accounting for *purchase discounts*. These discounts go to the hotel as a whole on the Rentals and Other Income schedule. For example, cash discounts on food purchases do not go to the food department. Cash discounts are earned only if an invoice with discount provisions is paid within a specified date. A revenue center is not responsible for paying invoices; this is the function of a support center.

Expense Accounting

A hotel consists of many revenue outlets and support centers, and the chart of accounts (described later) must accommodate recording transactions by department and type of expense. A department is charged for only those expenses that are directly associated with that department and only if the department's manager has control over that expense under the rationale of responsibility accounting.

Direct expenses are charged to each department. Support centers incur direct and indirect expenses because of their nature of service to the operating outlets. The following is a presentation of various expenses that have notable accounting procedures or practice.

Payroll and Related—All Departments

The Payroll and Related section is identical for all departments, showing salaries, wages, and employee benefits. Salaries and wages include regular pay and amounts paid for overtime, commissions, bonuses, vacations, holidays, and sick leave. If leased labor is significant, it should be shown as a separate line item.

Employee benefits include expenses related to payroll and employees such as:

- Payroll taxes.
- Employee meals.
- Workers' compensation insurance.
- Employee group plans (health, life, retirement).

Rooms Department

The rooms department does not have a cost of sales expense because it does not sell any merchandise. Sales of food items or beverages in the rooms are credited to the food and beverage departments. The expenses on the rooms department schedule shown in Exhibit 2 are for the most part self-explanatory. Those needing further elaboration follow.

Commissions. The Commissions expense account includes commissions paid to travel agents and rental agents. Volume discounts given to travel agencies are not treated as commissions, they are a reduction of rooms sales.

Complimentary Guest Services. This expense includes the cost of providing food and beverages to guests on a complimentary basis, such as continental breakfast service.

Guest Relocation. This expense includes renting of rooms elsewhere to accommodate guests when no space is available and any incidental costs such as gratuities or compensation in connection with this circumstance.

Operating Supplies. This expense includes gratis guest items, cleaning supplies, forms, and other operating supplies.

Food and Beverage Departments

Even though food and beverage (F&B) outlets might be two separate departments, they have similar expenses. Therefore, this discussion of expenses for the two outlets will be presented as a single topic. The expenses shown on the F&B

schedules are for the most part self-explanatory. Those needing further discussion follow.

Cost of Sales. The cost of food sales and cost of beverage sales are recorded separately to improve inventory control and measurement of cost ratios. The cost of employee meals and officers' checks is excluded from cost of food or cost of beverage sales. The accounting for cost of food and cost of beverage sales differs, depending on whether the perpetual or periodic inventory method is used. The computation is identical to that for a standalone restaurant.

China, Glassware, and Silver Expense. This expense represents the ordinary replacement of china, glassware, and silver, plus the periodic depreciation write-off of the initial purchase cost of the ensemble.

Administrative and General Department

Exhibit 6 shows the administrative and general (A&G) department schedule. This department includes executives, such as the general manager, the general manager's staff, accounting and payroll departments, and other administrative staff. In smaller properties, it may also include the human resources and information systems departments, although these support centers may also be broken out as separate departments. Most of the expenses on the A&G schedule are self-defining; those benefiting from elaboration are discussed in the following paragraphs.

Cash Overages and Shortages. The account for cashiers' overages and shortages is charged to the A&G department.

Communication Systems. This expense includes costs related to telex, beepers, pagers, and cellular phones used by hotel employees.

Credit Card Commissions. The expense and any rebates on credit cards accrue to in the A&G department, regardless of the department benefiting from guest usage of credit cards.

Head Office. This expense includes allocation of head office charges from corporate headquarters and any food or accommodations provided to head office staff while on business on the property.

Provision for Doubtful Accounts. This account is an expense resulting from estimates of accounts or notes receivable that might become a bad debt. The estimate is based on an aging of customer accounts and using a loss estimate.

Marketing Department

Exhibit 7 shows the marketing department schedule. As the department responsible for the hotel's sales and public relations, it conducts research aimed at developing sources of potential sales and designs package plans to attract more customers.

Property Operation and Maintenance Department

Exhibit 8 shows the property operation and maintenance (POM) department schedule. This department is charged for all repairs, regardless of the department

Exhibit 6 Administrative and General

Administrative and General—Schedule 15

	Current Period
PAYROLL AND RELATED EXPENSES	
Salaries and Wages	$
Employee Benefits	
Total Payroll and Related Expenses	
OTHER EXPENSES	
Bank Charges	
Cash Overages and Shortages	
Communication Systems	
Contract Services	
Credit and Collection	
Credit Card Commissions	
Donations	
Dues and Subscriptions	
Head Office	
Human Resources	
Information Systems	
Internal Audit	
Internal Communications	
Loss and Damage	
Meals and Entertainment	
Operating Supplies and Equipment	
Postage	
Printing and Stationery	
Professional Fees	
Provision for Doubtful Accounts	
Security	
Telecommunications	
Training	
Transportation	
Travel	
Other	
Total Other Expenses	
TOTAL ADMINISTRATIVE AND GENERAL EXPENSES	$

Source: *Uniform System of Accounts for the Lodging Association*, 9th rev. ed. (Lansing, Mich.: Educational Institute of the American Hotel & Lodging Association, 1996), p. 95.

benefiting from the repair. These charges include in-house repairs and contracted repair services. For example, the POM department is charged for repairs to kitchen equipment or rooms department furniture. However, housekeeping is a rooms department expense and contract cleaning by outside service firms is charged to the specific department getting such service.

The POM schedule shows the payroll and related costs, supplies, maintenance or repairs to the specific types of furniture, equipment, buildings, and grounds.

Exhibit 7 Marketing

Marketing—Schedule 19	Current Period
SELLING	
PAYROLL AND RELATED EXPENSES	
Salaries and Wages	$_______
Employee Benefits	_______
Total Payroll and Related Expenses	
OTHER EXPENSES	
Complimentary Guests	
Contract Services	
Dues and Subscriptions	
Meals and Entertainment	
Printing and Stationery	
Postage	
Trade Shows	
Telecommunications	
Training	
Travel	
Other	_______
Total Other Expenses	_______
TOTAL SELLING EXPENSES	
ADVERTISING AND MERCHANDISING	
PAYROLL AND RELATED EXPENSES	
Salaries and Wages	
Employee Benefits	_______
Total Payroll and Related Expenses	_______
OTHER EXPENSES	
Collateral Material	
Contract Services	
Direct Mail	
Frequent Stay Programs	
In-House Graphics	
Media	
Outdoor	
Point-of-Sale Material	
Special Promotional Vouchers	
Telecommunications	_______
Other	_______
Total Other Expenses	
TOTAL ADVERTISING AND MERCHANDISING EXPENSES	
FEES AND COMMISSIONS	
Agency Fees	
Other	_______
Total Fees and Commissions	
OTHER MARKETING EXPENSES	_______
TOTAL MARKETING EXPENSES	$_______

Source: *Uniform System of Accounts for the Lodging Industry,* 9th rev. ed. (Lansing, Mich.: Educational Institute of the American Hotel & Lodging Association, 1996), p. 109.

Exhibit 8 Property Operation and Maintenance

Property Operation and Maintenance—Schedule 21

	Current Period
PAYROLL AND RELATED EXPENSES	
Salaries and Wages	$
Employee Benefits	
Total Payroll and Related Expenses	
OTHER EXPENSES	
Building Supplies	
Contract Services	
Curtains and Draperies	
Electrical and Mechanical Equipment	
Elevators	
Engineering Supplies	
Floor Covering	
Furniture	
Grounds and Landscaping	
Heating, Ventilating, and Air Conditioning Equipment	
Kitchen Equipment	
Laundry Equipment	
Life/Safety	
Light Bulbs	
Locks and Keys	
Operating Supplies	
Painting and Decorating	
Removal of Waste Matter	
Swimming Pool	
Telecommunications	
Training	
Uniforms	
Vehicle Maintenance	
Other	
Total Other Expenses	
TOTAL PROPERTY OPERATION AND MAINTENANCE EXPENSES	$

Source: *Uniform System of Accounts for the Lodging Industry,* 9th rev. ed. (Lansing, Mich.: Educational Institute of the American Hotel & Lodging Association, 1996), p. 118.

Utility Costs

Exhibit 9 shows the schedule of utility costs. The financial reporting center called Utility Costs has no physical existence; it is simply a schedule that captures all energy expenses in one reporting area. However, energy used for cooking in the kitchen is charged to the food department as kitchen fuel. Reimbursements from separate entities such as managed condominiums or tenants are called recoveries and reduce the gross utility expense.

Exhibit 9 Utility Costs

Utility Costs—Schedule 22

	Current Period
UTILITY COSTS	
Electricity	$
Gas	
Oil	
Steam	
Water	
Other Fuels	
Total Utility Costs	
RECOVERIES	
Recoveries from other entities	
Charges to other departments	
Total Recoveries	
NET UTILITY COSTS	$

Source: *Uniform System of Accounts for the Lodging Industry*, 9th rev. ed. (Lansing, Mich.: Educational Institute of the American Hotel & Lodging Association, 1996), p. 122.

Fixed Expenses

The fixed expenses, also called *fixed costs*, consist of **management fees** and **occupation costs**. A management fee is an expense that represents the cost of having an independent management company operating the property. Occupation costs are:

- Rent.
- Interest.
- Insurance.
- Property taxes.
- Depreciation.
- Amortization.

Rent is any payment for rentals of building, grounds, and equipment. Interest includes interest on mortgages, bonds, and other indebtedness. Insurance expense includes property and general insurance. Property taxes include items such as real estate taxes, personal property taxes, sewer tax, and corporation renewal fees. Depreciation is the allocation of the cost of tangible long-lived assets over their useful lives; amortization is a similar expense except it refers to intangible long-lived assets.

Depreciation does not include the depreciation of china, glassware, silverware, linen, and uniforms, because such depreciation is recorded as a reduction of the cost basis of these assets.

Hotels with Casino Departments

Gaming is becoming increasingly popular in the global hospitality environment. A segment of the public enjoys it as a form of recreation, hospitality operations enjoy its income potential, and government views it as another source of revenue.

A hotel-owned-and-operated casino department is a separate revenue center with its own departmental statement that appears on the hotel's Summary Statement of Income.

Statement of Gaming Operations

The statement for gaming operations is prepared for the casino department, as shown in Exhibit 10. Because the format and line items on the statement are general in nature, they may not apply to all lodging properties with gaming operations as an ancillary revenue source. Individual properties should make modifications accordingly to fit their particular requirements.

Revenue Accounting

Gaming revenue is defined as the difference between gaming wins and losses; it is not the total amount wagered. The two methods of accounting for gaming revenue are to treat:

1. Casino revenue as gaming revenue only.
2. Casino revenue as gaming revenue *and* the retail value of complimentary items (free amenities to guests).

Complimentary Allowances. The account called Complimentary Allowances is used only if total casino revenue is composed of both gaming revenue *and* complimentary items (at retail).

Expense Accounting

Giving free goods and services to guests as complimentary items (also called *promotional*) is a prevalent gaming industry practice. These allowances might include rooms, food, beverage, travel, and other amenities free of charge as an incentive to gamble at the casino. The approximate retail value is used to account for these items.

Payroll, employee benefits, and other expenses for the casino department are accounted for in similar manner to that of other operating departments. Of special interest are the following:

- Credit and collection expense
- Gaming taxes, licenses, and fees expense
- Postage expense
- **Complimentaries** expense

Exhibit 10 Casino Department

Casino Department

	Current Period
REVENUE	$
LESS COMPLIMENTARY ALLOWANCES (used only if above revenue includes complimentaries)	______
NET REVENUE	
PAYROLL AND RELATED EXPENSES	
Salaries and Wages	
Employee Benefits	______
Total Payroll and Related Expenses	______
OTHER EXPENSES	
Complimentaries:	
Rooms	
Food	
Beverage	
Travel	
Special Events	
Other Amenities	
Contract Services	
Credit and Collection	
Gaming Taxes, License Fees, and Regulatory Costs	
Operating Supplies	
Postage	
Provision for Doubtful Accounts	
Telecommunications	
Training	
Uniforms	
Other	______
Total Other Expenses	______
TOTAL EXPENSES	______
DEPARTMENTAL INCOME (LOSS)	$ ______

Source: *Uniform System of Accounts for the Lodging Industry,* 9th rev. ed. (Lansing, Mich.: Educational Institute of the American Hotel & Lodging Association, 1996), p. 145.

The credit and collection expenses associated with collecting casino charge account customers are assessed to the casino, unlike other operating departments, where credit and collect expenses are charged to the A&G department.

The specialized casino licensing fees are charged to the casino department, similar in logic to charging the beverage department for its special beverage license fee.

Postage expense related to casino promotions or direct mail programs is charged directly to the casino instead of A&G or the marketing department.

The free guest amenities given to casino customers appear as separate line items under Other Expenses listed by type of complimentary. This procedure is used *regardless* of the revenue method of accounting for the casino department.

Hotel Balance Sheet

As with any balance sheet, the hotel format is fairly standard because every business has assets, liabilities, and equity. The accounts in these three classifications are also common to any industry.

The following paragraphs focus on significant accounting policies recommended by *USALI* that require special accounting treatment due to the particular requirements of the lodging industry.

Preopening Expenses

The common U.S. lodging industry practice is to charge preopening expenses to expense as incurred or charge them to an asset and amortize that asset over a period not to exceed one year. However, international practice continues to amortize this expense over several years. Hotels that have previously used the asset approach may continue to amortize preopening expenses over the initial projected period.

China, Glassware, Silver

The initial cost of purchasing sets of china, glassware, and silver is charged to an asset and depreciated, thus reducing the asset's cost basis, instead of using an accumulated depreciation account. *USALI* recommends that a relatively short amortization period be established and that all replacements be expensed. (The relatively short period is not defined.)

Linen and Uniforms

The initial cost of purchasing linen and uniforms is charged to an asset and depreciated, thus reducing the asset's cost basis, instead of using an accumulated depreciation account. *USALI* recommends that a relatively short amortization period be established and that all replacements be expensed. (Again, the relatively short period is not defined.)

Chart of Accounts for Hotels

A chart of accounts is a listing of the authorized bookkeeping accounts in an accounting system. Only these accounts can be used to record transactions. Computerized accounting systems require an account number to facilitate the processing of transactions. Since there is no universal accounting numbering system, a property may create any numbering system that best fits its needs.

USALI provides a turnkey chart of accounts as a convenience for a new lodging property.

The first step is to determine the departmental numbers that will form the basis of departmental statements. *USALI* recommends the following department numbers:

000 The whole lodging property; no specific department
100 Rooms Department
200 Food Department
300 Beverage Department
400 Telecommunications Department
500 Gift Shop
550 Garage and Parking
570 Other Operated Departments
590 Rentals and Other income
600 Administrative and General
700 Marketing
800 Property Operation and Maintenance
850 Utility Costs
900 Management Fees
950 Fixed Charges

Larger operations may decide to employ a more detailed departmental accounting system. For example, the Food Department might be subdivided as 210 Coffee Shop, 220 Fine Dining Room, and 230 Banquet. Any department can be subdivided into its various outlets or support services; the final composition is determined by the accounting department and management's need for that information.

The next step in designing an account numbering system is to develop a broad range of numbers for the account classifications. The expenses usually are further systematized. *USALI* recommends the following broad classifications:

100–199	Assets
200–279	Liabilities
280–299	Equity
300–399	Revenue
400–499	Cost of Sales
500–599	Payroll and Related
600–699	Other Expenses
700–799	Fixed Charges

This six-digit account numbering system is constructed as follows:

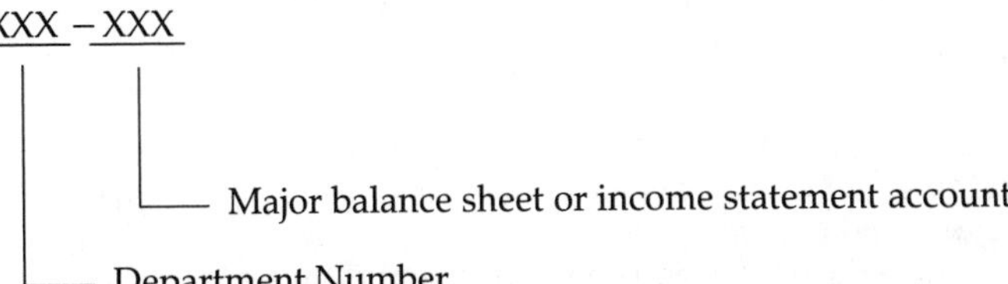

Exhibit 11, from *USALI*, shows the major balance sheet and income statement accounts. This system is uncomplicated and logical. For example, account number

Exhibit 11 Sample Chart of Accounts

ASSETS

- 100 Cash
  - 101 House Funds
  - 103 Checking Account
  - 105 Payroll Account
  - 107 Savings Account
  - 109 Petty Cash
- 110 Short-Term Investments
- 120 Accounts Receivable
  - 121 Guest Ledger
  - 122 Credit Card Accounts
  - 123 Direct Bill
  - 124 Notes Receivable (Current)
  - 125 Due from Employees
  - 126 Receivable from Owner
  - 127 Other Accounts Receivable
  - 128 Intercompany Receivables
  - 129 Allowance for Doubtful Accounts
- 130 Inventory
  - 131 Food
  - 132 Liquor
  - 133 Wine
  - 135 Operating Supplies
  - 136 Paper Supplies
  - 137 Cleaning Supplies
  - 138 China, Glassware, Silver, Linen, and Uniforms (Unopened Stock)
  - 139 Other
- 140 Prepaids
  - 141 Prepaid Insurance
  - 142 Prepaid Taxes
  - 143 Prepaid Workers' Compensation
  - 144 Prepaid Supplies
  - 145 Prepaid Contracts
  - 146 Current Deferred Tax Asset
  - 147 Barter Contracts Asset
  - 149 Other Prepaids
- 150 Noncurrent Receivables
- 155 Investments (not short-term)
- 160 Property and Equipment
  - 161 Land
  - 162 Buildings
  - 163 Accumulated Depreciation—Buildings
  - 164 Leaseholds and Leasehold Improvements
  - 165 Accumulated Depreciation—Leaseholds
  - 166 Furniture and Fixtures
  - 167 Accumulated Depreciation—Furniture and Fixtures
  - 168 Machinery and Equipment
  - 169 Accumulated Depreciation—Machinery and Equipment

Exhibit 11 *(continued)*

170 Information Systems Equipment
171 Accumulated Depreciation—Information Systems Equipment
172 Automobiles and Trucks
173 Accumulated Depreciation—Automobiles and Trucks
174 Construction in Progress
175 China
176 Glassware
177 Silver
178 Linen
179 Uniforms
180 Accumulated Depreciation—China, Glassware, Silver, Linen, and Uniforms

190 Other Assets
191 Security Deposits
192 Deferred Charges
193 Long-Term Deferred Tax Asset
196 Cash Surrender Value—Life Insurance
197 Goodwill
199 Miscellaneous

LIABILITIES

200 Payables
201 Accounts Payable
205 Dividends Payable
207 Notes Payable
209 Intercompany Payables

210 Employee Withholdings
211 FICA—Employee
212 State Disability—Employee
213 SUTA—Employee
214 Medical Insurance—Employee
215 Life Insurance—Employee
216 Dental Insurance—Employee
217 Credit Union
218 United Way
219 Miscellaneous Deductions

220 Employer Payroll Taxes
221 FICA—Employer
222 FUTA—Employer
223 SUTA—Employer
224 Medical Insurance—Employer
225 Life Insurance—Employer
226 Dental Insurance—Employer
227 Disability—Employer
228 Workers' Compensation—Employer
229 Miscellaneous Contributions

230 Taxes

(continued)

Exhibit 11 *(continued)*

231 Federal Withholding Tax
232 State Withholding Tax
233 County Withholding Tax
234 City Withholding Tax
236 Sales Tax
238 Property Tax
241 Federal Income Tax
242 State Income Tax
244 City Income Tax
255 Advance Deposits
260 Accruals
261 Accrued Payables
262 Accrued Utilities
263 Accrued Vacation
264 Accrued Taxes
267 Barter Contracts Liability
269 Accrued Expenses—Other
270 Current Portion—Long-Term Debt
272 Other Current Liabilities
273 Current Deferred Tax Liability
275 Long-Term Debt
276 Capital Leases
277 Other Long-Term Debt
278 Long-Term Deferred Tax Liability

EQUITY

For Proprietorships and Partnerships:
280–287 Owner's or Partners' Capital Accounts
290–297 Owner's or Partners' Withdrawal Accounts
299 Income Summary
For Corporations:
280–285 Capital Stock
286 Paid-in Capital
289 Retained Earnings
290 Treasury Stock
291 Unrealized Gain (Loss) on Marketable Equity Securities
292 Cumulative Foreign Currency Translation Adjustments
299 Income Summary

REVENUE

300 Rooms Revenue
301 Transient—Regular
302 Transient—Corporate
303 Transient—Package
304 Transient—Preferred Customer
309 Day Use
311 Group—Convention
312 Group—Tour

Exhibit 11 *(continued)*

317 Permanent
318 Meeting Room Rental
319 Other Room Revenue
320 Food Revenue
321 Food Sales
322 Banquet Food
326 Service Charges
328 Meeting Room Rental
329 Other Food Revenue
330 Beverage Revenue
331 Liquor Sales
332 Wine Sales
335 Cover Charges
336 Service Charges
339 Other Beverage Revenue
340 Telephone Revenue
341 Local Call Revenue
342 Long-Distance Call Revenue
343 Service Charges
345 Commissions
346 Pay Station Revenue
349 Other Telephone Revenue
350 Gift Shop Revenue
360 Garage and Parking Revenue
361 Parking and Storage
362 Merchandise Sales
369 Other Garage and Parking Revenue
370 Space Rentals
371 Clubs
372 Offices
373 Stores
379 Other Rental Income
380 Other Income
381 Concessions
382 Laundry/Valet Commissions
383 Games and Vending Machines
384 In-house Movies
385 Cash Discounts
386 Interest Income
387 Foreign Currency Exchange Gains
388 Salvage
389 Other
390 Allowances
391 Rooms Allowance
392 Food Allowance
393 Beverage Allowance
394 Telephone Allowance

(continued)

Exhibit 11 *(continued)*

395 Gift Shop Allowance
396 Garage and Parking Allowance
399 Other Allowance

COST OF SALES

420 Cost of Food Sales
421 Food Purchases
427 Trade Discounts
428 Transportation Charges
429 Other Cost of Food Sales
430 Cost of Beverage Sales
431 Liquor Purchases
432 Wine Purchases
433 Beer Purchases
434 Other Beverage Purchases
437 Trade Discounts
438 Transportation Charges
439 Other Cost of Beverage Sales
440 Cost of Telephone Calls
441 Local Calls
442 Long-Distance Calls
450 Cost of Gift Shop Sales
451 Gift Shop Purchases
457 Trade Discounts
458 Transportation Charges
460 Cost of Garage and Parking Sales
461 Garage and Parking Purchases
467 Trade Discounts
468 Transportation Charges
490 Cost of Employee Meals
492 Bottle Deposit Refunds
495 Grease and Bone Sales Revenue
496 Empty Bottle/Barrel Sales Revenue

PAYROLL

510 Salaries and Wages
511–519 Departmental Management and Supervisory Staff
521–539 Departmental Line Employees
550 Payroll Taxes
551 Payroll Taxes—FICA
552 Payroll Taxes—FUTA
553 Payroll Taxes—SUTA
558 Workers' Compensation
560 Employee Benefits
564 Medical Insurance
565 Life Insurance
566 Dental Insurance
567 Disability

Exhibit 11 *(continued)*

568 Pension and Profit Sharing Contributions
569 Employee Meals
599 Payroll Tax and Benefit Allocation

OTHER EXPENSES

600 Operating Supplies
601 Cleaning Supplies
602 Guest Supplies
603 Paper Supplies
604 Postage and Telegrams
605 Printing and Stationery
606 Menus
607 Utensils
610 Linen, China, Glassware, etc.
611 China
612 Glassware
613 Silver
614 Linen
618 Uniforms
621 Contract Cleaning Expenses
623 Laundry and Dry Cleaning Expenses
624 Laundry Supplies
625 Licenses
627 Kitchen Fuel
628 Music and Entertainment Expenses
629 Reservations Expenses
630 Information Systems Expenses
631 Hardware Maintenance
632 Software Maintenance
635 Service Bureau Fees
639 Other Information Systems Expenses
640 Human Resources Expenses
641 Dues and Subscriptions
642 Employee Housing
643 Employee Relations
644 Medical Expenses
645 Recruitment
646 Relocation
647 Training
648 Transportation
650 Administrative Expenses
651 Credit Card Commissions
652 Donations
653 Insurance—General
654 Credit and Collections Expenses
655 Professional Fees
656 Losses and Damages

(continued)

Exhibit 11 *(continued)*

657 Provision for Doubtful Accounts
658 Cash Over/Short
659 Travel and Entertainment

660 Marketing Expenses
661 Commissions
662 Direct Mail Expenses
663 In-house Graphics
664 Outdoor Advertising
665 Point-of-Sale Materials
666 Print Materials
667 Radio and Television Expenses
668 Selling Aids
669 Franchise Fees

670 Property Operation Expenses
671 Building Supplies
672 Electrical and Mechanical Equipment
673 Elevators
674 Engineering Supplies
675 Furniture, Fixtures, Equipment, and Decor
676 Grounds and Landscaping
677 Painting and Decorating
678 Removal of Waste Matter
679 Swimming Pool Expenses

680 Utility Costs
681 Electrical Cost
682 Fuel Cost
686 Steam Cost
687 Water Cost
689 Other Utility Costs

690 Guest Transportation
691 Fuel and Oil
693 Insurance
695 Repairs and Maintenance
699 Other Expenses

FIXED CHARGES

700 Management Fees

710 Rent or Lease Expenses
711 Land
712 Buildings
713 Equipment
714 Telecommunications Equipment
715 Information Systems Equipment
716 Software (includes any license fees)
717 Vehicles

720 Tax Expense
721 Real Estate Taxes
722 Personal Property Taxes

Exhibit 11 *(continued)*

	723 Utility Taxes
	724 Business and Occupation Taxes
730	Building and Content Insurance
740	Interest Expense
	741 Mortgage Interest
	742 Notes Payable Interest
	743 Interest on Capital Leases
	744 Amortization of Deferred Financing Costs
750	Depreciation and Amortization
	751 Building and Improvements
	752 Leaseholds and Leasehold Improvements
	753 Furniture and Fixtures
	754 Machinery and Equipment
	755 Information Systems Equipment
	756 Automobiles and Trucks
	757 Capital Leases
	758 Preopening Expenses
770	Gain or Loss on Sale of Property
790	Income Taxes
	791 Current Federal Income Tax
	792 Deferred Federal Income Tax
	795 Current State Income Tax
	796 Deferred State Income Tax

Source: *Uniform System of Accounts for the Lodging Industry,* 9th rev. ed. (Lansing, Mich.: Educational Institute of the American Hotel & Lodging Association, 1996), p. 190–198.

200-602 tells us that the department is *Food* (see previous department listing) and the transaction is for *Guest Supplies*. Balance sheet accounts do not have a department; therefore, the house funds would have an account number of 000-101.

Operating Ratios

Financial statements with dollar amounts are not sufficient for management to analyze the efficiency of operations and sales statistics. The use of ratio analysis compared to budgeted ratios or goals helps management determine if there is need for more analysis or corrective action. Some of the more common ratios used by hotel management are:

- Average room rate.
- Occupancy percentage.
- Average food check.
- Food cost percentage.
- Beverage cost percentage.
- Labor cost percentage.

Average Room Rate

Even though room rates vary by room type or class, the calculation of an average room rate provides helpful information. The average room rate (ARR—also called the average daily rate or ADR) is actually an average selling price of all the paid rooms occupied. The formula is:

$$\text{Average Room Rate} = \frac{\text{Rooms Revenue}}{\text{Paid Rooms Occupied}}$$

Occupancy Percentage

The occupancy percentage is important because it measures actual sales revenue in relationship to the hotel's sales potential. The formula is:

$$\text{Occupancy Percentage} = \frac{\text{Paid Rooms Occupied}}{\text{Rooms Available}} \times 100$$

This ratio can be computed only if a hotel maintains statistics on rooms available for sale, complimentary rooms, and actual rooms sold (paid rooms occupied).

Average Food Check

The average food check reveals how much, on average, any guest is spending. It is a measure of food sales related to the number of customers (covers). If the average check is lower than projected, the profit target may not be realized. The formula is:

$$\text{Average Food Check} = \frac{\text{Food Revenue}}{\text{Number of Covers}}$$

For average check to be useful as management information, it should be computed for each type of meal (breakfast, lunch, and dinner) and each dining facility (coffee shop, fine dining room).

Food Cost Percentage

The food cost percentage shows the relationship of food cost to food sales. This is a popular ratio used to measure the profitability and efficiency of a food outlet. The ratio shows the cost of food per one dollar of sales. The formula is:

$$\text{Food Cost Percentage} = \frac{\text{Cost of Food Sales}}{\text{Food Revenue}} \times 100$$

This ratio is more meaningful if it is computed for each dining facility.

Beverage Cost Percentage

The beverage cost percentage ratio is computed similar to the food cost percentage except that beverage statistics are used in the numerator and denominator. The formula is:

$$\text{Beverage Cost Percentage} = \frac{\text{Cost of Beverage Sales}}{\text{Beverage Revenue}} \times 100$$

Brand variation and type of drink affect the beverage cost percentage. This ratio is more meaningful if it can be computed separately for beer, wine, and liquor.

Labor Cost Percentage

Labor can be the largest operating expense for a lodging property. Labor includes payroll and payroll related expenses. The formula is:

$$\text{Labor Cost Percentage} = \frac{\text{Payroll \& Related}}{\text{Revenue}} \times 100$$

This ratio can be computed for each revenue center or for the hotel as a whole.

Key Terms

complimentaries—In casino hotels, free goods and services given to casino customers.

direct expense—An expense identifiable and associated with one specific department.

gaming revenue—The difference between gaming wins and losses.

management fee—An expense that represents the cost of having an independent management company operate the property.

occupation costs—Expenses for such items as rent, interest, property taxes, depreciation, and amortization.

operated department—Revenue center owned and operated by a hotel.

outlet—A general term for any revenue center.

package plans—Promotional package including accommodations, food, recreation, or other incentives at a single price.

support center—A department providing services to all operated departments.

undistributed operating expenses—Expenses not easily identified with any specific operated department.

Review Questions

1. What is the definition of each of the following?
   a. Operated department
   b. Undistributed operating expense
   c. Support center
   d. Fixed expense

2. How are revenues from separately stated linen charges and from no shows accounted for in the rooms department?
3. What is a package plan and what special accounting procedure is required to record it?
4. What items are included in the following?
    a. Other income—F&B Department
    b. Rentals and other income—Hotel
    c. Employee benefits
5. What personnel are generally included in the Administrative and General Department?
6. What items are considered fixed expenses?
7. What is the definition of gaming revenue?
8. What are the two methods of accounting for casino revenue?
9. What does *USALI* recommend for the following:
    a. Preopening expenses
    b. China, glassware, silver
    c. Linen and uniforms
10. What is the definition of a chart of accounts?

Problems

Problem 1

A hotel's daily cashiers report shows the following:

Room sales	$100,000
Sales tax on rooms	5,000
Food sales	20,000
Sales tax on food	1,000
Beverage sales	4,000
Sales tax on beverages	200

What are the rooms sales, food sales, and beverage sales?

Problem 2

The rooms department has the following expenses:

Salaries	$ 7,000
Wages	10,000
Employee meals	200
Health insurance premiums	2,000

Workers compensation insurance	800
Payroll taxes—federal	1,600
Payroll taxes—state	1,000

Prepare the payroll and related section for the rooms department schedule.

Problem 3

A hotel offers a couples weekend package plan for $300. This plan includes accommodations for two nights, two breakfasts, two dinners, a welcome bottle of champagne, and a cocktail with each dinner. The market value of these items is $350 rooms, $100 food, and $50 beverages. Allocate the revenue to the proper departments for each plan sold.

Problem 4

Identify the following as revenue center or support center:

Administrative and general
Marketing department
Rooms department
Information services
Food department
Telecommunications department
Property operation and maintenance

Problem 5

In which section (Operated Departments, Undistributed Operating Expense, or Fixed Expense) of the internal hotel income statement will the following appear?

Rentals and other income
Depreciation
Rooms department
Administrative and general
Franchise fees
Food and beverage department
Marketing department
Utility costs
Interest expense
Insurance expense
Property taxes
Property operation and maintenance department

Problem 6

Identify the department or schedule that will be charged for the following items:

Cash shortage in the restaurant
Relocation costs for a new employee
Credit card fees—rooms sales

Water used in rooms department
Repair of kitchen dishwasher
Postage for casino mailing
Direct mail costs
Travel agent commissions
Free continental breakfast
Meals for Head Office personnel
Gas used for cooking
Electricity for A&G

Problem 7

A motel has the following annual information. (Net indicates revenue after allowances.)

Rooms revenue (net)	$ 897,500	
Food revenue (net)	358,300	
Beverage revenue (net)	159,870	
Cost of food sales	135,200	
Paid rooms occupied	17,950	
Rooms available (75 daily)	27,375	(75 × 365)
Food covers	37,716	

Compute the following ratios:

Average room rate
Occupancy percentage
Average food check
Food cost percentage

Ethics Case

Great Fast Foods, Inc., is a highly successful company. The business's sales and profits have increased significantly during each of the past five years. The company's management is confident that the trend will continue.

The stock of the company is publicly held. The members of the management team are substantial shareholders in the corporation. The stock is traded on a major stock exchange and has enjoyed a steady rise in its price per share. The management team believes that a year of record earnings would bring the company national attention, increased investor demand, and a considerable increase in the market price per share of the stock.

The stock market has already valued Great Fast Foods' stock based on the company's history of steady growth and previous earnings picture. Thus, its expected good performance will not provide additional stimulus in the market. The management team, after careful analysis of customer demand, has determined that the company can increase sales prices by 10 percent and produce that special record year. The company's costs will not change from last year.

1. Identify the stakeholders in this case.
2. Comment on the ethical issues.
3. Comment on the business issues.

Chapter 11 Outline

- Definition and Objectives of Internal Control
  - Limitations of Internal Control
- Internal Control of Cash Receipts
  - Daily Cashiers Report
- Internal Control of Cash Disbursements
- Bank Reconciliation
  - Bank Statement
  - Reconciling Items
  - Bank Reconciliation Procedure
  - Example of a Bank Reconciliation
  - Journal Entries

Competencies

1. Define internal control and explain its objectives and limitations. (pp. 303–304)
2. Describe the principles of internal control for cash receipts and prepare a daily cashiers report. (pp. 304–308)
3. Describe the principles of internal control for cash disbursements. (p. 308)
4. Explain the purpose of a bank reconciliation, describe reconciling items, and prepare a bank reconciliation. (pp. 308–314)

11

Internal Control of Cash

THE HOSPITALITY INDUSTRY IS A RETAIL PROVIDER of goods and services. While many customers use credit cards, numerous cash sales will still require special attention. The term *cash* includes cash, personal checks, money orders, and travelers checks. While cash is more vulnerable to theft, credit card transactions can also be an embezzlement problem.

Cash receipts are only one side of the internal control problem. The payment of cash (cash disbursements) requires specific internal control procedures to prevent misuse of house funds and wrongful issuance of checks. The cash transactions from the cash receipts journal and cash disbursements journal are posted in the cash general ledger account. The balance in the cash general ledger accounts should equal the cash balance in the checkbook.

Under the Foreign Corrupt Practices Act of 1977, all major U.S. corporations are required to have an internal control system. This act applies to all corporations falling under jurisdiction of the Securities and Exchange Commission, whether or not they have any foreign operations. A company that fails to comply with this act is subject to fines, and its officers could face imprisonment.

Definition and Objectives of Internal Control

Internal control is a system designed to accomplish four major objectives:

1. *Safeguard assets.* Assets include cash, investments, inventory, furniture, equipment, vehicles, and property. The protection of these assets focuses on theft prevention as well as proper maintenance. Inventories also require systems to reduce waste and spoilage.
2. *Ensure compliance with company policies.* Many companies have written policies covering personnel and operational matters. Management expects adherence to these rules. Authorization is required for deviation from any standard policy.
3. *Facilitate operational efficiency.* A hospitality business requires suitable equipment and properly trained personnel to serve its guests at a satisfactory level. All businesses need profits to survive, and services should be achieved without incurring unnecessary costs.
4. *Ensure accurate financial information.* Management requires accurate financial information to properly manage profitable operations. Accurate and timely reporting to governmental agencies is necessary to avoid legal action.

Limitations of Internal Control

There is no perfect or universally applicable system of internal control. Any system can be defeated by acts of **collusion**. By definition, collusion occurs when two or more employees operate together to defraud the company.

The design of an internal control system should not be so complex that customer service or productivity is impaired. The design of a good internal system must weigh that system's effect on operations and customers and evaluate the costs relative to the intended benefits.

Internal Control of Cash Receipts

Designing an effective and all-inclusive internal control system for cash receipts requires an extremely experienced accountant. The most we can do here without being overly detailed is explain the academic theory. Therefore, only basic issues are presented here, emphasizing the critical points of a cash receipts internal control system.

A policy for the protection of cash receipts, at a minimum, should include these fundamentals:

- *Bonding of employees.* An insurance company should bond employees who handle large amounts of cash. The insurance company screens employees before bonding them and will prosecute offenders. This insurance bond reimburses the hotel or restaurant if dishonest employees misappropriate assets.
- *Daily deposit of cash in a bank account.*
- *Proper accounting procedures for checks received.* Checks received by mail should not be forwarded directly to the accounts receivable department. The designated department or individual authorized to receive checks by mail should remove the remittance advices, prepare a list of all checks received (in duplicate), and stamp the reverse of the checks with a restrictive endorsement ("For Deposit Only"). A copy of the list and all checks should then be sent to the general cashier for deposit. The second copy of the list and the remittance advices should be forwarded to the accounts receivable department for posting to customer accounts.
- *Checks and balances in the food department.* In food service operations, controls should be implemented such as duplicate checks or electronic systems that coordinate the production of meals and beverages with the service, collection, and recording of funds.
- *A control system for house banks and petty cash funds,* such as an **imprest system**. An imprest system is one in which a fund is kept at a predetermined fixed amount. This imprest balance is maintained by reimbursing the fund for any paid-outs. At unannounced intervals, surprise audits of these funds should be conducted. The cash and paid-out documents should total the imprest amount. Any shortages or IOUs should be investigated.

Exhibit 1 Cashier Reconciliation—Electronic Cash Register

Date: 12/15/X2 Saturday Weather: Rainy & cold
Cashier: Jim

Z

Food sales	$ 1,350.67	+
Sales tax	81.04	+
Tips due servers	50.00	+
Customer collections	185.00	+
Food purchases	8.75	–
Tips paid out	50.00	–
Customer charges	200.00	–
Cash to account for	$ 1,407.96	=
Cash drop	1,407.06	–
Cash shortage	.90	=

Quantity of checks: 10
Quantity of credit cards: 15

Accounts Receivable Tenders

Account	Amount		
212	200.00	+	Charge
855	185.00	–	Collection

- *A cash registering system.* All sales should be recorded using a cash register or other electronic equipment. The cash register should have a display clearly visible to the customer or waitstaff.
- *Shared preparation of the cashiers report.* At the end of work shifts, supervisory personnel and cashiers should participate in preparation or analysis of the daily cashiers report.

Daily Cashiers Report

A **daily cashiers report** is an internal control document that reconciles the sales from the register readings with the cash drawer. Today's electronic sales equipment generates the daily cashiers report. Exhibit 1 illustrates a reconciliation generated by an electronic cash register. In this facility, the cashier counts the drawer and makes what is known as a "blind drop" because the cashier does not have knowledge of the register readings. Managers use a special key to get the register readings. Selecting the symbol "Z" prints the readings and indicates that the register counters are reset to zero. A symbol "X" indicates that a reading has been taken during a shift but register counters are not reset to zero.

All hospitality students and professionals should have an understanding of the mechanics of how this tally is performed. There is no better way to do this than by doing it manually.

Our example will look at a restaurant that uses a cash register, but manually prepares the final daily cashiers report. Before processing this report, it is important to be familiar with the following restaurant policies:

- The restaurant does not accept credit cards that do not offer cash treatment as provided by bank credit cards.
- Tips on charges and credit cards are paid out to waitstaff at the end of each shift.
- The shift supervisor is the only authorized individual with access to the cash register readings.
- An authorized individual must approve any voids.

Exhibit 2 illustrates a completed manual daily cashiers report for this restaurant. It is divided into two major sections: *To Be Accounted For* and *Accounted For.*

Contents of the *To Be Accounted For* Section. This section represents the *target;* its total is the *control* total. If everything was as intended, this control total would be the actual deposit. However, this is not always the case because shortages and overages do occur for various reasons. The *To Be Accounted For* section includes:

- Sales calculated from register readings.
- Sales taxes calculated from register readings.
- Tips charged (entered on credit cards or charge accounts).
- Customer collections (payment of prior charge accounts).
- Amount of change fund at start of shift.

Contents of the *Accounted For* Section. This section represents the *offer.* It consists of:

- Cash (including credit cards that are treated as cash).
- Purchases paid out (small COD deliveries or incidental purchases).
- Tips paid out (should be equal to the tips charged).
- Customer charges (new house charges by customers).
- Return of change fund.
- Resulting cash shortage or overage.

Preparing the Daily Cashiers Report. Preparing this report requires an orderly processing of the cash drawer and its contents. The shift supervisor (or other authorized individual) and cashier should be in attendance for this important tally. The basic steps are:

- Enter the readings of the previous shift and this shift. The differences—less any voids—are the results for this shift.
- Count the cash drawer and replenish the change fund.

Exhibit 2 Daily Cashiers Report

Daily Cashiers Report

DATE *12/8/X2* Day: *Sat.* Weather: *Rainy + Cold*

	Key A (Sales)	Key B (Sales Tax)
Z Readings	*1 350 67*	*81 04*
TOTAL TO BE ACCOUNTED FOR:		
Food Sales	*1 350 67*	
Sales Tax	*81 04*	
Tips Charged	*50 00*	
Customer Collections	*185 00*	
Change Fund (Start)	*150 00*	
CONTROL TOTAL	*1 816 71*	
TOTAL ACCOUNTED FOR:		
Cash for Deposit	*1 407 06*	
Purchases Paid Out	*8 75*	
Tips Paid Out	*50 00*	
Customer Charges	*200 00*	
Change Fund (Return)	*150 00*	
Total Receipts and Paid Outs	*1 815 81*	
Cash Short (+)	*90*	
Cash Over (−)		
TOTAL ACCOUNTED FOR	*1 816 71*	

EXPLANATION OF CUSTOMER COLLECTIONS & CHARGES:

CUSTOMER	TAB	COLLECTION	CHARGE
DEBCO, Inc.	*1812*		*200 00*
J.R. Rickles		*185 00*	
TOTAL		*185 00*	*200 00*

EXPLANATION OF PURCHASES PAID OUT:

PAID TO	PURPOSE	AMOUNT
Ted's Market	*Food items for kitchen*	*8 75*
TOTAL		*8 75*

- Calculate the *cash to be deposited.* This is the sum of cash, personal checks, travelers checks, money orders, and credit cards treated as cash by the bank.
- Tally charges and paid-outs.
- Enter all information in the applicable sections of the report.
- Total each section as follows:

To be accounted for = Control total (the target)
Accounted for = Total receipts and paid-outs (the offer)

Cash Shortage or Cash Overage. A **cash shortage** occurs if the control total is *larger* than the total receipts and paid-outs. It results when the *target* is not reached by the *offer.* A **cash overage** occurs when the control total is *smaller* than the total receipts and paid-outs. It results when the *offer* exceeds the *target*.

Many managers concentrate only on shortages. However, cash overages are also important; they could be due to an embezzler's processing errors. Another danger signal is when the tally is, for example, $20 short one day and $20 over on another. These swings might indicate an employee is "borrowing" and "paying back," which, of course, is an unacceptable cash management practice.

Internal Control of Cash Disbursements

Cash disbursements include payments from checking accounts and house banks or petty cash funds. As with cash receipts, designing an effective and all-inclusive internal control system for cash disbursements requires a highly experienced accountant. The internal control of cash payments should, at a minimum, include the following fundamental principles:

- Payments from house or petty cash funds should be supported by documentary evidence such as an invoice. A stipulated maximum single payment amount should be part of the internal control policy.
- Unless the operation is very small, it is preferable to have two checking accounts, one for payroll and the other for all other types of payments.
- Checks should be prenumbered and signature policies established and enforced.
- Paid invoices should be canceled by stamping them "Paid" or perforating them with devices made for that purpose, to indicate that they have been paid.
- Voided checks should be defaced or their signature portion removed.
- A check protection device that imprints the check amount should be used to prevent alteration.

Bank Reconciliation

A **bank reconciliation** is an internal control document that reconciles the cash balance on the bank statement with the cash balance per the accounting records (books). This reconciling process detects any bookkeeping or bank errors. Individuals who do *not* have a role in cash receipts or disbursement should prepare the

Exhibit 3 Bank Statement

Hartman Savings and Trust

Harrisburg, PA 17112

Period Ending
May 31, 20XX

James Company
HACC Way
Harrisburg, PA 17112

Account Number 4092

Beginning balance	Checks/Debits	Number	Deposits/Credits	Number	NEW BALANCE
30402.90	13850.30	9	14760.00	4	30312.60

CHECKING ACCOUNT DETAIL OF TRANSACTIONS

Date	Check Number	CHECKS AND DEBITS Amount	Check Number	Amount	Deposits/Credits Amount	Daily Balance
4/30						29402.90
5/1					2860.00	32262.90
5/8	919	1500.00	910	1800.00	4900.00	33862.90
5/12	911	150.00				33712.91
5/14	912	1100.00			3000.00	35612.90
5/22	913	1200.00				34412.90
5/23					4000.00	38412.90
5/26	916	3300.00				35112.90
5/27	917	4700.00				30412.90
5/31	NSF	80.00	SC	20.30		30312.60

bank reconciliation. This follows the internal control principle of *separation of duties*. Cash embezzlement can be concealed if the principle of separation of duties is ignored.

Bank Statement

A bank sends monthly bank statements to its checking account customers. This **bank statement** shows the customer's beginning and ending cash balances, deposits, checks cashed, and other transactions. Exhibit 3 shows a typical bank statement. Some banks return the **canceled checks** (checks cashed by the bank), others send a list of the canceled checks, and still others send nothing extra because all canceled check transactions appear on the bank statement.

The ending cash balance in the accounting records generally does not match the amount shown on the bank statement, even though both may be correct. To verify the accuracy of the accounting records, a bank reconciliation is prepared that explains the reasons for the difference between the bank statement and accounting records.

Bank's Use of Debits and Credits. Confusion can result from attempting to interpret the bank's use of the terms *debit* and *credit*. A customer account represents a liability to the bank because the customer owns the cash in the account. Therefore, when a bank uses a debit, it is reducing that liability. The term credit is used for deposits because they increase the bank's liability to the customer.

Reconciling Items

The disparity between the ending cash balance per the bank statement and the ending cash balance per the accounting records is generally caused by timing differences in processing transactions and other events. These require special procedures called *reconciling items,* some of which are:

- Deposits in transit.
- Outstanding checks.
- Interest earned.
- Bank service charges.
- ATM withdrawals.
- NSF checks.
- Bookkeeping errors.
- Bank errors.

Deposits in Transit. A deposit entered in the cash receipts journal (or checkbook) at the end of a month but not appearing on the bank statement is a **deposit in transit**. Deposits in transit are detected by comparing the deposits in the accounting records with those on the bank statement; any deposit not on the bank statement is a deposit in transit (assuming an end-of-month situation).

Deposits in transit occur because a bank may not date a deposit with the date shown on the deposit slip. For example, a bank's bookkeeping day may end at 2 p.m. Any deposit made on March 31 after 2 p.m. will be dated by the bank as April 1 and will appear on the April bank statement.

Credit cards can also be deposits in transit. The electronic credit card process involves the retailer, credit card company, and the retailer's bank. The retailer transmits the credit card sales and is dependent upon the credit card service provider to deposit funds into the retailer's bank account. If the service provider is slow in depositing the funds, it is possible that three days' worth of credit card sales have not yet been deposited at the end of the month.

Interestingly, retailers using manual credit card vouchers under a direct bank deposit arrangement might receive funds for credit card deposits faster than if they were on an electronic system. The retailer manually deposits the bank credit card vouchers along with cash at the retailer's bank, and the bank provides instant credit for that deposit; there is no waiting for a third party to transmit the credit card sales. The disadvantage of using credit card vouchers for manual direct deposit is that the credit card fee is generally higher.

Outstanding Checks. Issued checks not appearing on the bank statement are called **outstanding checks.** Outstanding checks are detected by comparing entries on this month's cash payments journal (or checkbook) and last month's listing of outstanding checks against the canceled checks, or a listing of bank processed checks, or bank statement.

It sometimes occurs that a check outstanding in May, for example, is still outstanding in June (and even in subsequent months). An *outstanding checks listing* accompanies the internal bank reconciliation and, with the current month's cash payments journal, forms the basis for determining outstanding checks.

Interest Earned. Commercial checking accounts cannot earn interest because current bank regulations prohibit it. Some banks do offer interest on personal checking accounts; in such cases, the interest becomes a reconciling item and is not known until the bank statement is received.

Bank Service Charges. Bank service charges include the monthly checking account fee, printing of checks, and credit card fees. If these items are not entered in the current month charged by the bank, they are a reconciling item.

Credit Card Fees. The gross amount of credit card sales deposited or transmitted is not the true cash deposit, because the credit card company deducts a fee for its services. Merchant credit card providers generally deduct this fee on each credit card batch electronically processed. The fee can be read at the end of the batch process, therefore enabling the bookkeeper to journalize the fee on a current basis. A hospitality business that deposits its cards directly into its checking account might not know the fee until receipt of its monthly bank statement. In any case, if these credit card fees are not entered in the current month, they become a reconciling item.

ATM Withdrawals. ATM transactions are associated with personal checking accounts. Withdrawals should be entered as they are made, though it is not unusual for account holders to neglect recording a withdrawal in their checkbooks. These unrecorded ATM withdrawals are detected upon examination of the bank statement.

NSF Check. This check is commonly called a *rubber check*. NSF means nonsufficient funds. An **NSF check** is an unsuspected check included as part of a deposit, recorded, and subsequently rejected and returned by the bank. A journal entry is required to correct the original deposit; if such an entry is not made, the amount of the NSF check is a reconciling item.

Bookkeeping Errors. Transposition (the reversing of digits) is often a cause of bookkeeping errors. For example, a check for $196 could have been entered in the checkbook erroneously as $169, or a deposit for $578 could have been erroneously entered as $587. The differences between the entry and actual amount are reconciling items. (A telltale transposition error is that the difference is divisible by nine).

Bookkeeping errors have been eliminated or significantly reduced by the use of computerized systems that, for example, print checks and update the cash payments journal in the same process.

Bank Errors. Bank errors should be a rare occurrence, but they do happen. One common error is the processing of checks. These checks are manually encoded by the bank's processing center and then processed in the bank statement. It is possible that the person encoding the amount misread the check's written amount.

Exhibit 4 Working Format Bank Reconciliation

Bank Reconciliation Date: ____________

	Ending balance per bank statement	
+	Deposits in transit	
−	Outstanding checks	
=	**Adjusted Bank Balance**	xxx
	Ending balance per books	
+	Unrecorded interest earned	
−	Unrecorded bank service charges	
−	Unrecorded ATM withdrawals	
−	Unrecorded NSF checks	
+/−	Bookkeeping error (see explanation below)	
=	**Adjusted Book Balance**	xxx

Listing of Outstanding Checks:

Date Issued	Check Number	Amount
XXX	XXX	XXX
↓	↓	↓
Total		XXX

Explanation of +/− Bookkeeping error:
− If check actually issued is more than amount recorded in checkbook
+ If check actually issued is less than amount recorded in checkbook
− If deposit entered in checkbook is more than amount on bank statement
+ If deposit entered in checkbook is less than amount on bank statement

Encoding errors can be detected by comparing the check amount magnetic coding at the bottom of the check with the original written check amount.

Bank Reconciliation Procedure

Exhibit 4 shows a working format for a bank reconciliation. Notice that it is in two parts. Since the likelihood of a bank error is remote, the bank statement portion is the top part and is prepared first. The steps for completing this part are:

- Enter the ending balance from the bank statement amount.
- Enter the applicable reconciling items.
- Conclude with a total called *Adjusted Bank Balance.*

The bottom portion pertains to the accounting records and is completed by:

- Entering the ending balance per books.

- Entering the applicable reconciling items.
- Concluding with a total called *Adjusted Book Balance.*

The bank reconciliation is successful when the adjusted bank balance is equal to the adjusted book balance. The top of the form (bank portion) is given credibility if the bank reconciliation is at first not successful. If, after rechecking all steps, the bookkeeper is still unsuccessful in detecting an error, the possibility of a bank error can be investigated by comparing each transaction amount on the bank statement with corresponding accounting records and canceled checks (or list).

Example of a Bank Reconciliation

The Edal Company has received its bank statement for the month ending May 31, which shows the following:

- Ending balance $30,312.60
- Service charge 20.30
- NSF Check 80.00

After checking the accounting records, the accountant determines that:

- The May 31 checking account book balance is $29,112.90.
- The bank service charge and NSF check were not entered by the bookkeeper.
- A $2,100 deposit made on May 31 is not on the bank statement.
- Outstanding checks total $3,400.

The outstanding checks are listed showing date, check number, and amount to supplement the bank reconciliation. Exhibit 5 shows the completed bank reconciliation prepared by the accountant. Notice that the adjusted bank balance is equal to the adjusted book balance.

Journal Entries

A completed bank reconciliation also serves as the source document that could prompt entries in the checkbook to correct the cash balance and a journal entry to correct the general ledger cash account.

Any reconciling item in the "books" section of the reconciliation form requires corrective action in the checkbook and general ledger. For example, using the reconciliation in Exhibit 5, the following journal entry is required:

Bank Service Charge	20.30	
Accounts Receivable	80.00	
Cash—Checking Account		100.30

To record adjustments from the May 20XX bank reconciliation for the following:
Monthly bank service charge $20.30
Return of NSF check issued by Horton, Inc. $80.00

Exhibit 5 Completed Bank Reconciliation

Bank Reconciliation – May 31, 20XX

Ending balance per bank statement	$	30,312.60
Deposits in transit (5/31)		2,100.00
Outstanding checks		(3,400.00)
Adjusted Bank Balance	$	29,012.60
Ending balance per books	$	29,112.90
Unrecorded bank service charge		(20.30)
Unrecorded NSF check		(80.00)
Adjusted Book Balance	$	29,012.60

Listing of Outstanding Checks:

Date Issued	Check Number	Amount
5/26	914	$ 1,200.00
5/26	915	800.00
5/27	918	1,400.00
Total		$ 3,400.00

Key Terms

bank reconciliation—An internal control document reconciling the cash balance per the bank statement with the cash balance per the books (accounting records).

bank statement—A document generated by a bank that shows the customer's monthly beginning and ending cash balances.

canceled checks—Checks that have been "cashed" by the bank.

cash overage—A situation in which the control total is smaller than the total receipts and paid-outs.

cash shortage—A situation in which the control total is larger than the total receipts and paid-outs.

collusion—Two or more employees operate together to defraud the company.

daily cashiers report—An internal control document reconciling the register readings with the cash drawer.

deposit in transit—An end-of-month deposit that does not appear on the bank statement.

imprest system—A system in which a house bank, petty cash fund, or other account is kept at a predetermined fixed amount.

internal control—A system with four major objectives: 1) safeguarding of assets, 2) ensuring compliance with company policies, 3) bringing about operational efficiency, 4) ensuring accurate financial information.

NSF check—A check deposited in good faith but returned by the bank because the issuer has "non-sufficient funds."

outstanding checks—Checks that have been issued but not yet "cashed" by the bank.

Review Questions

1. What items are included in the term *cash*?
2. What is the definition of internal control, and what are its objectives?
3. What assets are intended to be safeguarded?
4. What is collusion?
5. What is the advantage of bonding employees?
6. What is an internal control procedure for house banks?
7. What is the purpose of the daily cashiers report?
8. What is the purpose of a bank reconciliation?
9. What is the definition of the following terms?
   a. Canceled checks
   b. Deposit in transit
   c. Outstanding checks
   d. NSF check
10. Why does the balance shown on the bank statement generally not equal the balance shown in the checkbook (accounting records)?

Problems

Problem 1

Indicate the correct section of the daily cashiers report in which the following activities will be entered.

	"Accounted For" Section	"To Be Accounted For" Section
Customer charges	______	______
Cash to be deposited	______	______
Sales	______	______
Customer collections	______	______
Initial change fund	______	______
Sales tax	______	______
Return of change fund	______	______
Control total	______	______

Problem 2

The daily cashiers report is being prepared. The total of the *To Be Accounted For* section is $2,080.20 and the total of the *Accounted For* section is $2,080.30. Is there an overage or a shortage for this shift?

Problem 3

The Ranger Inn has a $400 change fund for each shift. The following is the summary of today's daily cashiers report.

To Be Accounted For		Accounted For	
Sales	$812.36	Cash for deposit	$1,300.90
Sales tax	40.60	Paid outs	10.56
Collections	100.50	Customer charges	42.00
Control total	$953.46	Accounted for	$1,353.46

What appears to be the reason why the control total and the "Accounted For" amount do not agree?

Problem 4

Tom's Diner has a $100 change fund for each shift. The following is the summary of today's register activity.

The cash drawer contains $685.25 cash, paid-out slips totaling $8.23, and a customer charge of $9.45. The register readings show sales of $607.58 and sales tax of $28.93. Determine the cash overage or shortage for the day.

Problem 5

As the food and beverage supervisor, your responsibility is to reconcile the transactions for the day with the cash register readings. Following are the results of your check-out procedures for the bar.

Register Readings:

	Sales	Sales Tax
This shift's close	$126,875.95	$6,343.80
Prior shift's close	126,195.45	6,309.77

There are no voids to consider for this shift. The change fund is on a $200 imprest system. Following are the contents of the cash drawer:

Return of change fund	$200.00
Cash for deposit	620.00
Bank credit cards	29.36
Traveler's checks	50.00

In addition to register funds, there is a paid-out voucher of $12.76 for supplies.

What is the cash shortage or overage for this shift?

Problem 6

The Dorco Company has received its bank statement for the month ending May 31, which showed the following:

Ending balance	$10,650.05
NSF check	63.40
Service charge	10.70

After checking the bank statement and accounting records, the accountant has determined that:

- The May 31 cash balance per books is $10,781.76.
- The bank's service charge and an NSF check were not entered by the bookkeeper.
- A $354.60 deposit made on May 31 is not on the bank statement.
- Outstanding checks total $296.99.

Prepare a bank reconciliation in proper format.

Problem 7

Jim has received his bank statement for the month ending July 31 showing:

Ending balance	$328.25
NSF check	55.00
Service charge	15.00
Interest earned	0.25

After reviewing the checkbook and bank statement, he determines that:

- The July 31 checkbook balance is $808.00.
- Bank service charges, an NSF check, and interest have not been recorded.
- A $642.00 deposit made on July 31 is not on the bank statement.
- Outstanding checks total $232.00.

Prepare a bank reconciliation in proper format.

Problem 8

Sara has received her bank statement for the month ending November 30, which showed the following:

Ending balance	$641.50
Service charge	15.00
ATM withdrawal	70.00
Interest earned	0.50

After reviewing the checkbook and bank statement, she determines that:

- The November 30 checkbook balance is $1,136.00.
- Bank service charges, an ATM withdrawal, and interest had not been recorded.
- A $954.00 deposit made on November 30 is not on the bank statement.
- Outstanding checks total $544.00.

Prepare a bank reconciliation in proper format.

Problem 9

On July 31, Don's checkbook balance was $1,667.90, and the bank statement as of that date showed a balance of $1,828.80. A comparison of the bank statement and accounting records showed the following:

- Outstanding checks were:

Number	Amount
114	$79.50
117	96.42
118	17.48

- Check number 112 for $19.00 had been issued, processed by the bank, and charged on the bank statement, but was not recorded in the checkbook.
- A bank service charge of $4.50 was not recorded in the checkbook.
- Check number 116 was written for $121.00 and processed by the bank for $121.00. It was entered and deducted in the checkbook as $112.00.

Prepare a bank reconciliation in proper format. List and total the outstanding checks at the bottom of the bank reconciliation.

Problem 10

On March 31, Sigment Company had a $44,547.60 checkbook balance. The bank statement showed a balance on that date of $46,574.10, and the following information on the bank statement had not been entered in the checkbook:

$24.75 Service charge
$68.85 NSF check

A review of the bank statement and checkbook showed a deposit in transit of $3,919.44 and outstanding checks as follows:

- Number 234 for $281.34
- Number 236 for $445.12
- Number 237 for $2,901.60
- Number 238 for $2,411.48.

Prepare a bank reconciliation in proper format. List and total the outstanding checks at the bottom of the bank reconciliation.

Problem 11

The following is a completed bank reconciliation for June 20XX. Prepare the necessary journal entry from the information provided.

Ending balance per bank statement	$44,002.00
Deposits in transit (5/31)	3,500.00
Outstanding checks	(6,850.00)
Adjusted Bank Balance	$40,652.00
Ending balance per books	$40,897.00
Unrecorded bank service charge	(45.00)
Unrecorded NSF check (Photo, Inc.)	(200.00)
Adjusted Book Balance	$40,652.00

Ethics Case

The Siesta Hotel is owned by several individuals who also manage its operations. These management team members are individuals of high integrity with a strong commitment to guest service. They realize that making a profit is necessary, but they also recognize the importance of product quality and customer satisfaction.

In the hospitality industry, ethics is a critical issue for top management, as are operational, financial, and promotional considerations. Any hotel's business is to sell the occupancy of its rooms. Any room occupancy that is not sold for the night represents revenue that is lost forever. Overbooking occurs when a hotel sells more room occupancy than is actually available. This practice is very common among hotels because of no-shows and cancellations.

The managers of the Siesta Hotel do allow the hotel's front office staff to overbook. Overbooking does not necessarily result in the hotel's inability to honor reservations. However, when overbooking does result in the inability to honor a reservation, the procedure for "walking a guest" is most gracious and generous; the hotel will arrange and pay for accommodations at another hotel, arrange and pay for travel to that hotel, and pay for dinner for the party.

1. Ethics is composed of two attitudes: ideological and operational. (*Ideological* refers to beliefs and convictions. *Operational* refers to actual actions or practices.) Discuss the difference between these attitudes as related to this case.
2. Hospitality managers are affected by ethical ignorance and professional cynicism. (*Ethical ignorance* refers to being unknowing or unaware. *Professional cynicism* refers to having a pessimistic or distrustful attitude.) Discuss these factors as related to this case.
3. Discuss why hospitality managers may find that dealing with ethical issues on the job can be stressful.

Chapter 12 Outline

Financial Statement Package
- Notes to the Financial Statements
- Accountant's Letter

The Money Illusion
- Revenue, Expenses, and Net Income
- Assets, Liabilities, and Equity

Overview of Analytical Methods

The Income Statement
- Reading the Income Statement
- Common Size Analysis
- Comparative Analysis
- Ratio Analysis

The Balance Sheet
- Reading the Balance Sheet
- Common Size Analysis
- Comparative Analysis
- Ratio Analysis

Statement of Cash Flows
- Reading the SCF
- Cash Flows from Operating Activities
- Cash Flows from Investing Activities
- Cash Flows from Financing Activities

Competencies

1. Explain the composition of a financial statement package including the footnotes and the accountant's letter accompanying services such as audit, review, and compilation. (pp. 321–323)
2. Explain why the monetary amounts on financial statements can give a false illusion and describe the effect of accrual accounting on revenue, expenses, net income, assets, liabilities, and equity. (pp. 323–324)
3. Describe the composition of and how to read and analyze the income statement, balance sheet, and statement of cash flows using analytical methods. (pp. 324–338)

12

How to Read and Analyze Financial Statements

FINANCIAL STATEMENTS SERVE as a means of communication between the issuing company and the statements' readers. These readers may be internal, such as executives and managers, or external, such as stockholders and creditors. The internal and external forms of financial statements differ in their amount of detail. Internal statements are management tools and thus are quite detailed and include departmental statements. External statements are condensed for reader convenience and exclude departmental statements. The term *financial statement package* is often used to describe the complete set of either external or internal financial statements.

While these statements are tools of communication, the reader must know both how to read them and how to interpret them. Many readers do not properly interpret important finanacial statement information because of certain misconceptions.

This chapter is a "capstone" chapter. It is a review of accounting principles and financial statements designed to take the reader to a new level of competence in understanding, interpreting, and analyzing monetary information in the form of financial statements. Each component of the income statement, balance sheet, and statement of cash flows is examined in detail.

This chapter answers such questions as:

1. What is the content of a financial statement package?
2. What different levels of financial statement services are available from a certified public accountant?
3. What are some common money illusions and other misconceptions about financial statements?
4. What are some common analytical methods used to interpret financial statements and how are they applied?

Financial Statement Package

The three basic financial statements in a financial statement package are the income statement, the balance sheet, and the statement of cash flows.

As stated above, the level of detail of a financial statement package depends on whether it is prepared for internal readers, such as executives and managers, or external readers, such as stockholders and creditors. Beyond this difference, a financial statement package intended for external readers consists of more than just financial statements; included as well are notes to the financial statement and an accountant's letter.

Notes to the Financial Statements

The notes to the financial statements, also called **footnotes**, supplement the dollar amounts shown on the statements. These notes provide information that explains important non-monetary items or events. The notes serve as disclosures to reveal facts or news that the reader should know to be properly informed about the company. These include such items as:

- Accounting policies.
- Depreciation methods.
- Inventory accounting methods.
- Leases (terms and conditions).
- Pending lawsuit (contingent liability).
- Procedures for computing income taxes.

Accountant's Letter

An accountant (CPA or non-CPA) employed by a hospitality company may prepare statements for internal readers, but since he or she is an employee (therefore not independent), the employee-accountant cannot prepare financial statements intended for stockholders. Independence means being free of influence from the party for whom the statements are prepared. It is also possible that creditors such as banks or suppliers might demand that the company seeking a loan or credit privileges engage the services of an independent public accountant.

The public accountant will provide an **accountant's letter** to accompany the statements that explains the level of service performed by the accountant. A public accountant may perform an audit, a review, or a compilation.

An **audit** of financial statements is the highest level of service a public accountant can perform. Because it is highly detailed, it is also extremely expensive. An audit is a comprehensive examination of a company's accounting records. It includes observation of physical inventories and confirmation of accounts receivable and accounts payable. The physical inventories include verifying the existence of food, liquor, supplies, investments, autos, equipment, and other assets recorded in the accounting records. The purpose of an audit is to ensure that the information in the financial statements is presented fairly and in conformity with generally accepted accounting principles. The term "present fairly" covers many issues; perhaps the most important is that the information does not deceive the reader. An audit is not intended to detect fraud, comment on the competence of management, or evaluate the company as a quality investment for stockholders or investors.

Because audits are extremely expensive, the Securities and Exchange Commission allows businesses to report their financial positions to stockholders via quarterly reviewed financial statements. Banks and creditors also may agree to accept statements prepared under a review scope of service. A **review** of the financial statements is substantially smaller in scope than an audit. The observation of physical inventories is not part of a review service and the confirmation of accounts receivable and accounts payable is not required. A review service provides limited assurance that no material changes are necessary to the financial statements for conformity with generally accepted accounting principles.

Though a review service is less expensive than an audit, the review services performed by a CPA are still costly. Therefore, banks and creditors may accept statements prepared under a compilation service. Compiled financial statements, also called **compilations**, are the lowest level of service performed by a public accountant. The statements are a representation of management, and the accountant provides assurance only to the extent that the statements were prepared in accordance with standards for unaudited financial statements.

The Money Illusion

Because the financial statements are stated in absolute values (dollars), it is easy to assume that the amounts represent money transactions. This is not a valid assumption, however, in part because the balance sheet and income statement are prepared using the accrual system of accounting. The accrual system ignores whether cash is present in a business transaction; accrual accounting instead looks for the exchange of goods or services for a promise to pay. A customer's promise to pay is called an account receivable; a business's promise to pay is called an account payable. Strict cash basis accounting is not used to prepare balance sheets or income statements because it ignores accounts receivable and accounts payable transactions. The only statement based on cash transactions is the statement of cash flows.

This "money illusion"—the notion that financial statement figures stated in dollars are somehow equivalent to money or cash—is a misconception that can play out in different ways in different financial statements. Sometimes, the accrual accounting system is behind the illusion (as is the case with revenue, expenses, and net income). Sometimes, the dollar amounts are not really money or cash amounts for other reasons (as is the case with some balance sheet accounts). Let's look at some specific examples.

Revenue, Expenses, and Net Income

The accrual basis of accounting is used to report revenue and expenses on the income statement. The principle of any accrual system is that revenue is recorded when earned, and expenses are recorded when incurred. The largest revenue item for any hospitality business is sales. Sales can be made instantly for cash or billed to a customer, creating an account receivable. Significant credit card volume can also affect cash if the deposit "float" is more than two or three days. A sales amount of $310,000 shown on an income statement represents total *billings*, regardless of whether they have been paid by the customer or are still in accounts receivable. The income statement does not reveal the cash sales.

Operating expenses such as payroll, inventories, advertising, utility services, and other items are recorded under the accrual basis of accounting, even though many of these expenses that appear on an income statement have yet to be paid. Part or all of the prior week's payroll for the month ended is recorded in the current month, but paid in the following month. A business has open credit with its suppliers to purchase inventories and services, but payment is usually due in the following month upon receipt of a statement.

Depreciation and amortization are peculiar expenses because they do not and never will require a cash payment. Both of these expenses are the allocation of a long-lived asset's cost over an estimated useful life. Depreciation relates to tangible assets and amortization relates to intangible assets. Because of their similarity, sometimes only the term depreciation appears on the financial statements to represent both depreciation and amortization.

Net income does not represent money income because:

- Sales are a combination of cash sales and billings not yet collected (accounts receivable).
- Many expenses are a combination of payments and invoices or charges not yet paid (accounts payable).
- Depreciation and amortization are never a cash expense.

Assets, Liabilities, and Equity

The money illusion may affect balance sheet accounts as well. The accounts receivable shown on a balance sheet may not be 100 percent collectible. The allowance for doubtful accounts (potential bad debts) is an estimate. Also, the amount shown for land, buildings, and other assets may not represent the true cash value of these items.

Even the *cash* account may not represent the potential cash position. Cash might be inflated because the payment of accounts payable and other liabilities has been deferred. Cash might be understated because short-term investments can always be sold to bolster the cash position. Another consideration is that the cash position of a company does not reflect its borrowing power.

The equity section of a balance sheet is composed of cumulative net income of the present and the past, which does not relate to cash. The stock issued amounts relate to the original issue date and amount; those funds have long been spent.

Overview of Analytical Methods

The income statement, balance sheet, and statement of cash flows are mathematically related. Despite the differences in format, the tools for analyzing these statements are quite similar. The most common of these analytical tools or methods are:

- Common-size analysis.
- Comparative analysis.
- Ratio analysis.

Common-size analysis, also called **vertical analysis,** provides a means of evaluating relative values as opposed to absolute values. **Relative values** are stated in percentages. In the case of a common-size analysis, each line item on the financial statement is divided by a common divisor. The common divisor represents 100 percent and each line item represents a part of that 100 percent. The results of a common-size analysis are often used to construct pie charts or other graphic representations.

Comparative analysis, also called **horizontal analysis,** provides a means of evaluating the changes in **absolute** (dollar) **values.** A comparative analysis compares the dollar amount of the current period with that of another period, or a standard, or a budget. Each line item is independently compared and the dollar change becomes the basis of examination.

Ratios are a means of expressing the relationship between two numbers, arrived at by dividing one by the other. The two numbers may come from different financial statements, and unlike common-size analysis, with **ratio analysis,** there is no common divisor. These ratios serve as a benchmark for comparison against industry standards, budgets, or historical data. Ratios are useful in pointing to possible problem areas that might require investigation or study. A number of ratios are used to analyze the many items on the financial statements.

The Income Statement

The income statement, also called the profit and loss statement, shows revenue, expenses, and the resulting net income. The reporting period usually shows the current month and the year-to-date results, generally not exceeding one year for the current reporting period. The date of an income statement is specified as:

For the (period) ended (date)

Exhibit 1 shows that the income statement period for Southern Fast Food is one year ending on December 31, 20X2. This means that the monetary amounts are from January 1, 20X2, through December 31, 20X2.

Reading the Income Statement

Income statement formats will vary from industry to industry and company to company, though all follow this general format:

Sales
– Allowances, Discounts, Rebates
= Net Sales
– Cost of Sales
= Gross Profit
– Operating Expenses
= Operating Income
+ Gains on Sale of Assets
– Losses on Sale of Assets

Exhibit 1 Southern Fast Food—Income Statement

Southern Fast Food, Inc.
Income Statement
For the period ended 12/31/X2

Sales	$ 310,000	100.0%
Cost of food and paper goods	122,450	39.5%
Gross profit	187,550	60.5%
OPERATING EXPENSES		
Salaries and wages	64,480	20.8%
Employee benefits	9,300	3.0%
Direct operating expenses	5,580	1.8%
Marketing	28,520	9.2%
Utility services	8,680	2.8%
Occupancy costs	22,630	7.3%
Depreciation	18,000	5.8%
Amortization	500	.2%
General and administrative	6,830	2.2%
Other expenses	8,830	2.8%
Total operating expenses	173,350	55.9%
Operating income	14,200	4.6%
Gain on sale of equipment	1,000	.3%
Loss on sale of marketable securities	(1,200)	(.4%)
Income before income taxes (IBIT)	14,000	4.5%
Income taxes	5,000	1.6%
Net income	$ 9,000	2.9%

= IBIT (Income Before Income Taxes)
− Income Taxes
= Net Income

The amount for *Net Sales* is the result of total billings less allowances, discounts, and rebates. Some income statements show the total billings, the deductions, then net sales as follows:

Sales	$ 311,000
Allowances and rebates	1,000
Net Sales	$ 310,000

Other income statements may simply start with net sales because the allowances, discounts, and rebates are not material to reading the statement. Most income statements that start with only the net sales amount label that line item simply as *Sales* for purposes of brevity; it is implied that the amount is really net sales. Using Exhibit 1 as an example, the line item labeled *Sales* is actually net sales of $310,000.

The income statement is a series of steps and subtotals. It is relatively easy to read. Again using Exhibit 1 as an example:

- Net sales less cost of sales produces a subtotal called *gross profit*; it represents the profit after deducting the cost of materials used in producing sales to customers.
- Deducting the operating expenses produces another subtotal called *operating income*; it represents the profit made by the business in its day-to-day operations.
- Non-operating gains are added and non-operating losses are subtracted to produce another subtotal called *income before income taxes* (IBIT).
- *Net income* (the final total) is the result of IBIT less income taxes.

Common-Size Analysis

Common-size percentages are computed by dividing every amount on the income statement by *net sales* and may be illustrated by the following formula:

$$\frac{\text{Dollar amount of line item on income statement}}{\text{(Net) Sales}}$$

Using Exhibit 1, the common-size percentage for *depreciation* is computed as follows:

$$\frac{\$18{,}000}{\$310{,}000} = 5.8\%$$

The common-size percentage of 5.8 percent means that depreciation amounted to 5.8 percent of net sales, or almost six cents of the sales dollar.

Reading a common-size analysis of an income statement is relatively simple:

- Each percentage represents a relationship to net sales.
- Each percentage can be restated as a unit of the sales dollar. For example, the line item *Marketing* shows that the marketing expense takes up about nine cents of the sales dollar ($28,520 ÷ $310,000).
- The common-size percentages are mathematically related because a common divisor (net sales) was used. Using Exhibit 1, for example:

  –Sales of 100 percent less cost of sales of 39.5 percent = 60.5 percent gross profit.

  –Adding all the operating expenses = 55.9 percent.

  –Gross profit of 60.5 percent less operating expenses of 55.9 percent = 4.6 percent operating income.

  –Operating income of 4.6 percent plus gains of 0.3 percent less losses of 0.4 percent = 4.5 percent IBIT.

  –4.5 percent IBIT less income taxes of 1.6 percent = 2.9 percent.

Comparative Analysis

The data for prior periods and budgets can be used to perform a comparative analysis on the income statement. Because budgets are extensively used with income statements and managers often receive bonuses for favorable performance, a budget example is used. Using Exhibit 1, if the budget for the line item *Sales* is $315,000 and the budget for the line item *Salaries and wages* is $66,480, a budgetary comparative analysis would look like the following:

	Budget	Actual	Over (Under) Budget
Sales	$ 315,000	$ 310,000	$ (5,000)
Salaries and wages	66,480	64,480	(2000)

The sales variance result of $5,000 under the budget is *not favorable*. The salaries and wages variance of $2,000 under the budget is *favorable*. In simplistic terms, budgetary variances are favorable when actual sales exceed the budget or when actual expenses are under the budget.

Computing the variance as a percentage of the budget can expand a comparative analysis. Using this same example, a full comparative analysis would look like this:

	Budget	Actual	Over (Under) Budget	% Variance
Sales	$ 315,000	$ 310,000	$ (5,000)	(1.6%)
Salaries and wages	66,480	64,480	(2000)	(3.0%)

The sales variance percentage of 1.6 percent is computed by dividing its variance of $5,000 by the sales budget of $315,000; the salaries and wages variance is computed by dividing its variance of $2,000 by the salaries and wages budget of $66,480. Notice that the mathematical "sign" of the variance is the same as that of the dollar variance. In this case, sales were under the budget by 1.6 percent and other expenses were under the budget by 3.0 percent.

Unlike a common-size analysis, the percentages of one line item are not related to the percentages of any other line item because a common divisor is not used to compute these percentages.

Ratio Analysis

A multitude of ratios are used to analyze the income statement. Ratio analysis of the income statement is used to measure the following:

- Profitability—measuring profit margins and income to sales or equity
- Asset management—measuring income generated by use of assets
- Operating—measuring effectiveness and efficiency of operations
- Occupancy—measuring the success of rooms management at hotels

This chapter focuses on the following most popular of the operating and profitability ratios:

- Food cost percentage
- Beverage cost percentage
- Labor cost percentage
- Prime cost percentage
- Profit margin ratio

Food Cost Percentage. This ratio expresses the food cost as a percentage of (net) food sales. Using Exhibit 1, actual food sales are $310,000 and the actual food cost is $122,450; the food cost percentage is 39.5 percent, calculated as follows:

$$\frac{\text{Cost of Food Sold}}{\text{Food Sales}} = \frac{\$122{,}450}{\$310{,}000} = 39.5\%$$

If the budgeted food cost had been 36.5 percent, then food costs would be running three percent higher than planned. Such results could be due to not following standard recipes, increased costs from suppliers, or lower menu price changes. The sales mix can have an effect on the departmental food cost percentage because not all meals share the same food cost percentage.

Southern Fast Food's cost of food consists of food items plus "paper goods," which is standard accounting procedure for fast-food operations. The term *paper goods* includes items that accompany the meal, such as:

- Paper wrappers and napkins.
- Paper and foam cups.
- Takeout containers.
- Plastic utensils and straws.

In Southern Fast Food's case, the cost of food sold takes up almost 40 cents of the sales dollar, an amount that would be considered high for a full-service restaurant but normal for a fast-food operation. Lower labor costs in a fast-food operation offset higher food costs.

Beverage Cost Percentage. Southern Fast Food does not serve liquor. The utility of the beverage cost percentage is similar to that of the food cost percentage. The formula is:

$$\frac{\text{Cost of Beverage Sold}}{\text{Beverage Sales}} = \text{Beverage Cost Percentage}$$

Labor Cost Percentage. Labor cost includes not just salaries and wages, but employee benefits as well because of their direct relationship to salaries and wages. Employee benefits include such items as payroll taxes, health and life insurance, employee meals, vacations and holidays, and worker's compensation insurance.

The labor cost ratio expresses the total labor cost (payroll and related) as a percentage of (net) food sales. Using Exhibit 1, the labor cost percentage is 23.8 percent, calculated as follows:

$$\frac{\text{Salaries and Wages + Employee Benefits}}{\text{Food Sales}} = \frac{\$64{,}480 + \$9{,}300}{\$310{,}000} = 23.8\%$$

This ratio tells us that total payroll costs are taking up almost 24 cents of the sales dollar at Southern Fast Food.

Prime Cost Percentage. Prime cost includes cost of sales plus total labor cost (salaries, wages, and employee benefits). It can be computed by adding the dollar amounts for these items and dividing by net sales. Another method is to take the previously computed ratios or common-size percentages and add them as follows:

Cost of food sold	39.5%
Total labor cost ratio	23.8%
Prime Cost Ratio	63.3%

In the case of Southern Fast Food, the prime cost is 63.3 cents of the sales dollar, leaving 36.7 cents of the sales dollar to cover expenses such as direct operating, marketing, occupancy, and other costs. It also leaves something for the profit.

Profit Margin Ratio. The profit margin ratio measures the amount of net income (income after income taxes) produced by each sales dollar.

Actual food sales in Exhibit 1 are $310,000, net income is $9,000, and the profit margin ratio is 2.9 percent, calculated as follows:

$$\frac{\text{Net Income}}{\text{Food Sales}} = \frac{\$9{,}000}{\$310{,}000} = 2.9\%$$

For each sales dollar (100 cents), Southern Fast Food realized a net income of almost three cents. Depending on the economy, competition, and geographic location, this profit margin might be acceptable. Southern Fast Food is a corporation and the owner's salary is included in labor; thus, the owner benefits from the salary and benefits paid by the business plus its net income. Another benefit is that the customers are indirectly paying for the assets of the business, ultimately producing owner's wealth when the business is sold.

The $9,000 net income might seem small, but remember that looking only at a money amount can be an illusion. Depreciation and amortization are always noncash expenses. In the case of Southern Fast Food, these expenses total $18,500 and have been deducted to arrive at the $9,000 net income. The statement of cash flows will reveal the true *cash* net income from operations.

The Balance Sheet

The balance sheet shows assets, liabilities, and equity. The reporting period of a balance sheet is a discrete point in time, not a cumulative period of time. The

Exhibit 2 Southern Fast Food Balance Sheet

Balance Sheet
Southern Fast Food, Inc.
12/31/X2 and 12/31/X1

	20X2	20X1	Increase (Decrease)
Cash	$ 39,000	$ 45,000	$ (6,000)
Short-term investments	0	5,000	(5,000)
Accounts receivable (net)	28,000	18,500	9,500
Inventories	10,000	12,000	(2,000)
Prepaid expenses	3,000	2,000	1,000
Total current assets	$ 80,000	$ 82,500	$ (2,500)
Property and equipment (net)	190,000	130,000	60,000
Other assets (net)	5,000	5,500	(500)
Total assets	$ 275,000	$ 218,000	$ 57,000
Accounts payable	$ 88,000	$ 89,500	$ (1,500)
Sales tax payable	2,000	1,200	800
Accrued expenses	6,000	7,300	(1,300)
Dividends payable	3,000	0	3,000
Current portion of mortgage	5,000	0	5,000
Total current liabilities	$ 104,000	$ 98,000	$ 6,000
Mortgage payable (net)	27,000	0	27,000
Note payable due 2/1/X4	30,000	0	30,000
Capital stock issued (no-par)	117,000	108,000	9,000
Treasury stock	(20,000)	0	(20,000)
Retained earnings	17,000	12,000	5,000
Total liabilities and equity	$ 275,000	$ 218,000	$ 57,000

amounts are those as of the close of a business day, typically the last day of the month. The date for a balance sheet is expressed as:

Month, Day, Year

The date on the balance sheet in Exhibit 2 indicates that the monetary columns are for two dates; the left column for the close of business on December 31, 20X2 and the right column for the close of business on December 31, 20X1.

A balance sheet is not useful for day-to-day operations and therefore department managers seldom receive it. The financial health of a company is the responsibility of executives; they make the decisions to purchase expensive assets or borrow funds. Other readers of the balance sheet are investors, creditors, and others with a vested interest in a company's financial position.

Reading the Balance Sheet

The monetary amounts on the balance sheet do not reflect current market value of land, buildings, and other long-lived assets. A company's well-known *goodwill* does not appear on its balance sheet. The only time goodwill shows on a balance sheet is when a company is purchased at a value higher than the fair market value (FMV) of its assets (the excess over FMV is goodwill.)

All balance sheets are divided into the three major sections of assets, liabilities, and equity. Each section contains information that is valuable in evaluating the financial health of a company. This evaluation also uses ratio analysis and comparative analysis. To assist in this examination, the major sections are further subdivided. The asset section is subdivided into current assets, property and equipment, and other assets. The liabilities section is subdivided into current liabilities and long-term liabilities.

Common-Size Analysis

Common-size percentages are computed by dividing each amount on the balance sheet by total assets. It can be illustrated by the following formula:

$$\frac{\text{Dollar amount of line item on balance sheet}}{\text{Total Assets}}$$

Using Exhibit 2, the common-size percentage for the 20X2 line item *Cash* is computed as follows:

$$\frac{\$39{,}000}{\$275{,}000} = 14.2\%$$

This common-size result tells us that cash makes up 14.2 percent of the total assets. Continuing these calculations for the remaining assets will show what part each asset is of total assets. Since the total assets amount and the total liabilities and equity amount are identical, any line item in the liabilities and equity sections can also use the same divisor, except that the result is interpreted as showing what part each liability or equity is to the total liabilities and equity.

Comparative Analysis

Using a comparative analysis on a balance sheet is very popular and informative, especially when comparing the end of the current year with the end of the previous year, because this analysis reveals which items increased or decreased from the prior reporting date.

In Exhibit 2, the line item *Cash* decreased by $6,000 from the previous date. The increase or decrease effect is computed as follows:

Amount for current date	$39,000
Less: Amount for prior date	45,000
Difference	$ 6,000

A positive difference is an increase and a negative difference is a decrease. The increases or decreases may also be stated as a percentage of the prior date's amount; this percentage is computed by dividing the increase or decrease amount by the prior date's amount. Using Exhibit 2, the line item *cash* is analyzed as follows:

	20X2	20X1	Increace (Decrease)	Percentage
Cash	$39,000	$45,000	$(6,000)	(13.3%)

Cash has decreased 13.3 percent, computed by dividing the $6,000 decrease by the prior date's amount of $45,000. These increases and decreases are sometimes related. An increase in an asset may bring a decrease in another asset, or an increase in an asset may bring an increase in liabilities or equity; for example:

- Cash is down and accounts receivable are up. The change could be due to increased sales or a change in credit policy.
- Cash is up, marketable securities are down. The change could be the result of selling stocks or bonds to increase the cash position.
- Inventories are up, accounts payable are up. The liability has increased to increase an asset.
- Property and equipment are up and mortgages payable or notes payable are up. This is another case in which liabilities have increased to increase assets.
- Capital stock increases and cash or another significant asset increases. The corporation may have sold stock to increase its cash position or purchase property or equipment.
- Treasury stock increases and cash decreases. Cash was used to repurchase the company's own stock.
- Treasury stock decreases. The corporation may have sold its treasury stock to increase its cash position or purchase property or equipment.

In the case of Southern Fast Food, the obvious major changes and possible reasons for some balance sheet increases and decreases in Exhibit 2 are:

- Cash is down, accounts receivable are up. Cash was also used to buy back its own stock (see treasury stock below).
- Marketable securities have been completely sold. Proceeds might have been used to supplement the purchase of treasury stock.
- Property and equipment are significantly up. There are new liabilities in the form of a mortgage and notes payable.
- New capital stock was issued (sold). Proceeds may have been used to finance day-to-day operations, for a down payment to purchase significant assets, or to finance the increase in accounts receivable.
- Treasury stock increased. This action may have caused the decrease in cash or short-term investments (marketable securities).

Some of these answers will become more obvious when the statement of cash flows is analyzed.

Ratio Analysis

Balance sheet ratios are useful in evaluating:

- Liquidity—a company's ability to pay its short-term (current) debt.
- Solvency—a company's ability to pay all its debt (current and long-term).
- Asset management—a company's efficient and profitable use of its assets.

A full discussion of all the ratios used to analyze a balance sheet would require a chapter unto itself. Here we focus on *current ratio* and *acid-test ratio,* the two most popular and universal ratios used by executives, investors, creditors, and investment analysts to measure a company's liquidity position.

Current Ratio. The current ratio shows the relationship of current assets to current liabilities. The formula is:

$$\frac{\text{Current Assets}}{\text{Current Liabilities}}$$

Using Exhibit 2, the current ratio at the end of 20X2 is calculated as follows:

$$\frac{\text{Current Assets}}{\text{Current Liabilities}} = \frac{\$80{,}000}{\$104{,}000} = 0.77$$

Southern Fast Food has a current ratio that is 0.77 to 1.00, meaning that it has 77 cents of current assets for every dollar of current liabilities. Current ratios should be compared against prior periods or industry standards to make meaningful judgments. However, there is a definite weak liquidity position when a current ratio falls below 1.00. Further study is needed by the management of Southern Fast Food to determine corrective action. For example, selling its treasury stock and omitting future dividends would improve its liquidity ratio.

Acid-Test Ratio. The acid-test ratio, also called the *quick ratio,* is a more refined version of the current ratio, resulting in a more strict measurement of liquidity. This ratio excludes the less liquid assets of inventories and prepaid expenses. The formula is:

$$\frac{\text{Cash} + \text{Short-Term Investments} + \text{Receivables (net)}}{\text{Current Liabilities}}$$

In Exhibit 2, the acid-test ratio at the end of 20X2 is calculated as follows:

$$\frac{\$39{,}000 + \$0 + \$28{,}000}{\$104{,}000} = .64$$

Southern Fast Food has an acid-test ratio that is 0.64 to 1.00, meaning that it has 64 cents of the most highly liquid current assets for every dollar of current liabilities. Acid-test ratios should be compared against prior periods or industry standards to make an informed judgment.

Note the close results of the current ratio (0.77) and the acid-test ratio (0.64). In the hospitality industry, it is not unusual for the results of these ratios to be relatively close because inventories are a small part of current assets.

Statement of Cash Flows

The statement of cash flows (SCF) is the only statement that is prepared using only cash transactions. Its preparation is tedious and complex and its purpose is to report on cash receipts and cash paid out (disbursements). The period of time covered is identical to that of the income statement.

Department managers seldom receive the statement of cash flows. Managing cash is the responsibility of executives who make the decisions to purchase costly assets or to borrow funds. Other readers of the SCF are investors, creditors, and others with a vested interest in a company's sources and uses of cash.

Reading the SCF

The statement of cash flows is divided into three major sections of activities:

- Operating
- Investing
- Financing

Cash flow is the net result of cash receipts and cash payments. If the cash receipts exceed the cash payments, the result is labeled as *net cash provided by* (name of activities section). If the cash payments exceed the cash receipts, the result is labeled as *net cash used by* (name of activities section).

The SCF in Exhibit 3 starts with the three activities sections. The totals of each section are as follows:

Operating Activities	$ 17,200
Investing Activities	(41,200)
Financing Activities	18,000

The total of these three sections results in a decrease to cash of $6,000 for the current year for Southern Fast Food ($17,200 − $41,200 + $18,000).

With this background information, the SCF in Exhibit 3 can be easily read as follows:

- The beginning cash balance of $45,000 comes from the end of last year as shown on the balance sheet (Exhibit 2).
- The $6,000 cash decrease resulting from the three activities sections is subtracted from the beginning cash balance of $45,000 to arrive at $39,000, representing the ending cash balance at the end of the current year.

Exhibit 3 Southern Fast Food—Statement of Cash Flows

Statement of Cash Flows
Southern Fast Food, Inc.
For the year ended 12/31/X2

Cash Flows from Operating Activities:		
Net income		$ 9,000
Adjustments to reconcile net income to net cash flows from operating activities:		
Depreciation expense	$ 18,000	
Amortization expense	500	
Gain on sale of equipment	(1,000)	
Loss on sale of short-term investments	1,200	
Increase in accounts receivable	(9,500)	
Decrease in inventories	2,000	
Increase in prepaid expenses	(1,000)	
Decrease in accounts payable	(1,500)	
Increase in sales tax payable	800	
Decrease in accrued expenses	(1,300)	8,200
Net cash provided by operating activities		17,200
Cash Flows from Investing Activities:		
Proceeds from sale of equipment	6,000	
Proceeds from sale of short-term investments	3,800	
Purchase of equipment	(43,000)	
Down payment on purchase of land	(8,000)	
Net cash used in investing activities		(41,200)
Cash Flows from Financing Activities:		
Cash proceeds from note payable due 2/1/X4	30,000	
Proceeds from issuance of no-par capital stock	9,000	
Dividends declared and paid this year	(1,000)	
Purchase of treasury stock	(20,000)	
Net cash provided by financing activities		18,000
Increase (decrease) in cash for the year		(6,000)
Cash at the beginning of the year		45,000
Cash at the end of the year		$ 39,000

Supplemental Disclosures of Cash Flow Information

Cash paid during the year for:

Interest	$ 1,000
Income taxes	$ 2,000

Supplemental Schedule of Noncash Investing and Financing Activities

A parcel of land was purchased in December 20X2 as follows:

Acquisition cost of land	$ 40,000
Cash down-payment	8,000
Balance financed by mortgage	$ 32,000

Disclosure of Accounting Policy

For purposes of the statement of cash flows, the Company considers all highly liquid debt instruments purchased with a maturity of three months or less to be cash equivalents.

- The ending cash balance of $39,000 is verifiable because it must equal the cash balance at the end of this year as shown on the balance sheet (Exhibit 2).

The SCF is required to have footnotes that address certain topics:

- Cash used to pay for interest and income taxes.
- Cash used as down payments to purchase assets financed by a mortgage or note payable.
- Disclosure of accounting policy.

Cash Flows from Operating Activities

The purpose of the operating activities section is to report the net income on the *cash* basis. Either of two methods can be used to prepare this section—the direct method or the indirect method. The indirect method is the more popular procedure in the hospitality industry and is used in this chapter. Refer to the operating activities section in Exhibit 3 and examine the following for Southern Fast Food:

- The operating activities section starts with the net income from Exhibit 1 of $9,000. This net income was computed on the accrual basis, not on the cash basis.
- All the line items in this section are an accounting procedure used in the indirect method to adjust the $9,000 accrual basis net income to its true cash basis of $17,200.
- Unless you have an overwhelming interest in accounting procedures, you can focus on only the $17,200 total of the operating activities section; this will not dilute your reading of the SCF.

Cash Flows from Investing Activities

The purpose of the investing activities section is to report on cash used to purchase investments or long-lived assets and cash received from the sale of investments or long-lived assets.

This section does not involve gains or losses on sale of assets or the purchase cost of assets.

Investments bought or sold for cash may be short-term (marketable securities) or long-term. Long-lived assets generally involve cash transactions regarding property and equipment.

If an asset costing $100,000 is purchased with a $25,000 cash down payment and the balance of $75,000 is financed, then only the $25,000 will appear as cash paid out in this section. (Remember, the SCF reports only on *cash* in and *cash* out.)

If an asset is sold for $80,000 cash resulting in a $15,000 loss, then only the $80,000 will appear as cash received in this section.

Refer to the investing activities section in Exhibit 3 and examine the following for Southern Fast Food:

- Cash increased because equipment was sold for $6,000 *cash* and investments were sold for $3,800 *cash*. Any gain or loss is ignored in this section.

- Cash decreased because equipment was purchased for $43,000 cash and land was purchased with a down payment of $8,000 cash. (The financing of the land purchase is explained in the footnotes.)
- The cash flows from investing activities for Southern Fast Food results in a net cash decrease of $41,200.

Cash Flows from Financing Activities

The purpose of the financing activities section is to report on cash received or paid out relating to any equity or debt transactions, such as:

- Issuance of capital stock or bonds.
- Purchase or sale of treasury stock.
- Payment of dividends.
- Cash borrowings.
- Payment of principal portion of debt financing.

Refer to the financing activities section in Exhibit 3 and examine the following for Southern Fast Food:

- Cash increased by $30,000 from a cash loan.
- Cash increased by $9,000 from the issuance of capital stock.
- Cash decreased by $1,000 for the payment of dividends.
- Cash decreased by $20,000 for the purchase of treasury stock this year.
- The cash flows from financing activities for Southern Fast Food results in a net cash increase of $18,000.

Key Terms

absolute values—In the context of financial statements, amounts stated in a monetary format.

accountant's letter—A letter accompanying the financial statements explaining the level of service performed by a public accountant.

audit—The highest level of service performed by a public accountant. It is a comprehensive examination of the accounting records, including observation of physical inventories and confirmation of receivables and payables.

common-size analysis—A method that uses a common divisor to produce relative values. Also called vertical analysis.

comparative analysis—The comparison of absolute values against a prior period, a standard, or a budget. Also called horizontal analysis.

compilation—The lowest level of service performed by a public accountant in the preparation of financial statements. This service does not provide any level of assurance on the unaudited statements.

footnotes—Also called notes to the financial statements. These notes provide disclosures that supplement the contents of the statements and explain non-monetary items or events such as pending lawsuits and leases.

horizontal analysis—See comparative analysis.

prime cost—The sum of cost of sales plus payroll and related.

ratio analysis—A method to express the relationship between two numbers by dividing one by the other. Ratios serve as benchmarks and are useful in pointing to possible problem areas requiring investigation.

relative values—Amounts stated in a percentage format.

review—A level of service that is lower than that of an audit. It provides limited assurance that no material changes are necessary to the financial statements.

vertical analysis—See common-size analysis.

Review Questions

1. What specific items might be in the notes to the financial statements?
2. What are the differences between an audit, a review, and a compilation service in the preparation of financial statements?
3. Why is the net income amount on the income statement not representative of cash income?
4. What are the differences among common-size analysis, comparative analysis, and ratio analysis?
5. What are the purposes of the income statement, balance sheet, and the statement of cash flows?
6. What are the names and representations of the three subtotals of income and final total of income on the income statement?
7. What is meant by the term liquidity and which ratios are used to measure liquidity?
8. What are the purposes of the operating activities section, investing activities section, and financing activities section of the statement of cash flows?

Problems

Problem 1

Compute the *net sales, gross profit, operating income, income before income taxes,*and *net income* from the following information:

Income taxes	$ 4,000
Cost of sales	70,000
Non-operating losses	7,000
Sales	255,000

Payroll and related	82,000
Allowances and rebates	5,000
Depreciation and amortization	15,000
Other operating expenses	48,000

Problem 2

Compute the common-size percentages from the following partial income statement:

Sales	$ 425,000
Cost of sales	131,750
Payroll	106,250
Employee benefits	21,250

Problem 3

Compute the over/(under) budgetary variances using a comparative analysis from the following partial income statement:

	Budget	Actual
Sales	$ 420,000	$ 425,000
Cost of sales	134,750	131,750
Payroll	107,250	106,250
Employee benefits	20,250	21,250

Problem 4

Compute the food cost percentage, labor cost percentage, prime cost percentage, and profit margin ratio from the following condensed income statement:

Food sales	$ 425,000
Cost of food sales	131,750
Gross profit	293,250
Payroll	106,250
Employee benefits	21,250
Other operating expenses	130,750
Total operating expenses	258,250
IBIT	35,000
Income taxes	4,000
Net income	$ 31,000

Problem 5

Compute the current assets, property and equipment, other assets, total assets, current liabilities, long-term liabilities, equity, and total liabilities and equity from the following information:

Accounts payable	$ 11,000
Accounts receivable	4,000

Land	30,000
Taxes and other payables	7,000
Buildings and equipment, net of depreciation	80,000
Supplies inventory	1,000
Cash	34,000
Liquor license (net purchase cost)	4,000
Common stock issued	43,000
Food inventory	6,000
Retained earnings	58,000

Mortgage payable $40,000 of which $6,000 is due within 12 months of this balance sheet date.

Problem 6

Prepare a comparative analysis from the following partial balance sheet:

	Last Year End	This Year End	Change	% Change
Total Current Assets	$ 29,396	$ 46,550		
Total Assets	151,889	162,350		
Accounts Payable	15,300	25,400		

Problem 7

Compute the common-size percentages from the following partial balance sheet:

Cash	$ 36,500
Total Current Assets	46,550
Total Assets	162,350
Accounts Payable	25,400

Problem 8

Compute the current ratio and acid-test ratio from the following partial balance sheet:

Cash	$ 36,500
Short-term Investments	2,000
Accounts Receivable	1,450
Inventories	4,000
Prepaid Expenses	2,600
Total Current Assets	46,550
Total Assets	162,350
Accounts Payable	25,400
Total Current Liabilities	39,350
Long-term Liabilities	40,000
Total Liabilities	79,350
Total Equity	$ 162,350

Problem 9

What is the cash flow (increase or decrease in cash) for the period from the following information:

Cash used in operating activities	$ (30,000)
Cash provided by investing activities	90,000
Cash used by financing activities	(20,000)
Cash balance at beginning of year	15,000

Problem 10

Compute the cash provided or used for the operating activities section, investing activities section, and the financing activities section from the following information:

Sold equipment for $15,000 cash
Net income on the accrual basis is $65,000
Net income converted to a cash basis is $40,000
Issued common stock for $100,000 cash
Paid dividends in cash $8,000
Purchased land costing $200,000 with a $50,000 down payment and a mortgage of $150,000

Ethics Case

A privately held lodging company, Katymoe Properties, is a member of AH&LA. The company has been requested by the association to submit data to be used in developing industry statistics. However, the company has experienced a terrible business year and does not want to disclose that fact to anyone.

The company has cooperated in providing its operating results to AH&LA for the last 20 years and does not want to refuse at this time. Therefore, Martin Beebee, president of Katymoe, instructs the company's treasurer to calculate an average of the last five years and submit this average as the operating results for the recent year.

Because these numbers will be consolidated with data from hundreds of other lodging properties, the final statistics should not be affected.

1. Identify the stakeholders in this case.
2. Analyze and comment on any issues pertinent to this matter.

Appendix

Excerpts from Dave & Buster's 2001 Annual Report

DINING • DRINKS • DIVERSIONS

Dave & Buster's Inc.

2481 Manana Drive

Dallas, Texas 75220

www.daveandbusters.com

Raymond Cote and the Educational Institute of the American Hotel & Lodging Association wish to thank **Dave and Buster's, Inc.**, for generously granting us permission to reproduce the following excerpts from Dave and Buster's annual report for 2001.

Management's discussion and analysis of financial condition and results of operations Dave & Buster's, Inc.

(DOLLARS IN THOUSANDS)
Management's Discussion and Analysis of Financial Condition and Results of Operations discusses our consolidated financial statements, which have been prepared in accordance with generally accepted accounting principles. The preparation of these financial statements requires management to make certain estimates and assumptions that affect the amounts reported in the financial statements and accompanying notes. On an ongoing basis, management evaluates its estimates and judgements, including those that relate to depreciable lives, goodwill and debt covenants. The estimates and judgements made by management are based on historical data and on various other factors believed to be reasonable under the circumstances.

Management believes the following critical accounting policies, among others, affect its more significant judgements and estimates used in the preparation of its consolidated financial statements.

Depreciable lives – expenditures for new facilities and those which substantially increase the useful lives of the property, including interest during construction, are capitalized along with equipment purchases at cost. These costs are depreciated over various methods based on an estimate of the depreciable life, resulting in a charge to the operating results of the Company. The actual results may differ from these estimates under different assumptions or conditions. The depreciable lives are as follows:

PROPERTY AND EQUIPMENT	
Games	5 years
Buildings	40 years
Furniture, fixtures and equipment	5 to 10 years
Leasehold and building improvements	Shorter of 20 years or lease life
INTANGIBLE ASSETS	
Trademarks	Over statutory lives
Lease Rights	Over remaining lease term

Goodwill – is being amortized over 30 years. Whenever there is an indication of impairment, the Company evaluates the recoverability of goodwill using future undiscounted cash flows. Any resulting impairment loss could have a material adverse impact on our financial condition and results of operations, however an impairment charge was not considered necessary under FAS 121 as of February 3, 2002.

In June 2001, the Financial Accounting Standards Board issued Statements of Financial Accounting Standards No. 141, Business Combinations and No. 142, Goodwill and Other Intangible Assets ("Statements"), effective for fiscal years beginning after December 15, 2001. Under the new rules, goodwill and intangible assets deemed to have indefinite lives will no longer be amortized but will be subject to annual impairment tests in accordance with the Statements. Other intangible assets will continue to be amortized over their useful lives.

The Company will apply the new standards on accounting for goodwill and other intangible assets beginning in the first quarter of 2002. Application of the nonamortization provisions of the Statements is expected to result in an increase in income before tax of $349 ($.03 per diluted share) in 2002 as a result of nonamortization of existing goodwill. During the first quarter 2002, the Company will perform the required impairment test of goodwill as of February 3, 2002. Based on current analysis, the Company will record an expense to "Cumulative effect of a change in an accounting principle" of $4,541 net of income tax benefit of $2,555 ($.35 per diluted share), upon the adoption of the new standard.

Debt covenants – of the Company's facility agreement require compliance with certain financial covenants including a minimum consolidated tangible net worth level, maximum leverage ratio, minimum fixed charge coverage and maximum level of capital expenditures. The Company was in compliance with the covenants for the fiscal year ended February 3, 2002. The Company believes the results of operations for the fiscal year ending February 2, 2003 and thereafter would enable us to remain in compliance with the existing covenants absent any material negative event affecting the U.S. economy as a whole. However, the Company's expectations of future operating results and continued compliance with the debt covenants cannot be assured and our lenders' actions are not controllable by us. If the projections of future operating results are not achieved and the debt is placed in default, the Company would experience a material adverse impact on our reported financial position and results of operations.

Management's discussion and analysis of financial condition and results of operations

Dave & Buster's, Inc.

Fiscal 2001 Compared to Fiscal 2000

Total revenues increased to $358,009 for fiscal 2001 from $332,303 for fiscal 2000, an increase of $25,706 or 7.7%. New stores opened in fiscal 2001 increased revenues by $28,431. Revenues from comparable stores decreased by 2.8% in fiscal 2001. The decrease in comparable stores revenues is primarily attributed to the attacks on New York and Washington, D.C. on September 11th resulting in a decline in corporate events of 15.4%. Total revenues from licensing agreements were $537.

Costs of revenues increased to $66,939 for fiscal 2001 from $61,547 for fiscal 2000, an increase of $5,392 or 8.8%. The increase was principally attributed to opening four new stores during the year. As a percentage of revenues, cost of revenues were up .2% to 18.7% for fiscal 2001 versus 18.5% in fiscal 2000 due to freight costs and higher amusement costs associated with redemption, offset by lower food costs.

Operating payroll and benefits increased to $110,478 for fiscal 2001 from $101,143 for fiscal 2000, an increase of $9,335 or 9.2%. As a percentage of revenue, operating payroll and benefits were 30.9% in fiscal 2001, up .5% from 30.4% in fiscal 2000 due to higher store fixed labor and benefits.

Other store operating expenses increased to $106,971 for fiscal 2001 from $90,581 for fiscal 2000, an increase of $16,390 or 18.1%. As a percentage of revenues, other store operating expenses were 29.9% in fiscal 2001 as compared to 27.3% in fiscal 2000. The increase in other store operating expenses is due to increases in utilities, marketing and occupancy costs.

General and administrative expenses increased to $20,653 in fiscal 2001 from $20,019 for fiscal 2000, an increase of $634 or 3.2%. As a percentage of revenues, general and administrative expenses were 5.8% for fiscal 2001 and 6.0% for fiscal 2000.

Depreciation and amortization expense increased $2,977 to $28,693 in fiscal 2001 from $25,716 in fiscal 2000. As a percentage of revenues, depreciation and amortization increased to 8.0% from 7.7% for the comparable period due to new store openings.

Preopening costs decreased to $4,578 for fiscal 2001 from $5,331 for fiscal 2000, a decrease of $753 or 14.1%. As a percentage of revenues, preopening costs were 1.3% for fiscal 2001 as compared to 1.6% for fiscal 2000. This decrease is due to timing of store openings and only one store scheduled to open in fiscal 2002.

Interest expense-net decreased to $7,820 for fiscal 2001 from $8,712 for fiscal 2000. The decrease was due to lower interest rates in fiscal year 2001.

The effective tax rate for fiscal 2001 was 36.2% as compared to 36.4% for fiscal 2000 and was the result of a lower effective state tax rate.

Fiscal 2000 Compared to Fiscal 1999

Total revenues increased to $332,303 for fiscal 2000 from $247,134 for fiscal 1999, an increase of $85,169 or 34%. New stores opened in fiscal 2000 and in fiscal 1999 accounted for 91% of the increase. Revenues at comparable stores increased 3.6% for fiscal 2000. Increases in revenues were also attributable to a 2% overall price increase and a higher average guest check. Total revenues for fiscal 2000 from licensing agreements were $966.

Cost of revenues increased to $61,547 for fiscal 2000 from $45,720 for fiscal 1999, an increase of $15,827 or 35%. The increase was principally attributable to the 34% increase in revenues. As a percentage of revenues, cost of revenues were the same for fiscal 2000 and fiscal 1999 at 18.5%.

Operating payroll and benefits increased to $101,143 for fiscal 2000 from $76,242 for fiscal 1999, an increase of $24,901 or 33%. As a percentage of revenue, operating payroll and benefits decreased to 30.4% in fiscal 2000 from 30.9% in fiscal 1999 due to lower fixed labor costs, taxes and benefits offset by higher variable labor costs.

Other store operating expenses increased to $90,581 for fiscal 2000 from $65,292 for fiscal 1999, an increase of $25,289 or 39%. As a percentage of revenues, other store operating expenses were 27.3% of revenues in fiscal 2000 as compared to 26.4% of revenues in fiscal 1999. Other store operating expenses were higher due to higher marketing costs associated with the Company's 2000 marketing campaign.

General and administrative expenses increased to $20,019 for fiscal 2000 from $14,988 for fiscal 1999, an increase of $5,031 or 34%. The increase over the prior comparable period resulted from increased administrative payroll and related costs for new personnel, and additional costs associated with the Company's future growth plans. As a percentage of revenues, general and administrative expenses decreased to 6.0% in fiscal year 2000 from 6.1% in fiscal year 1999.

Depreciation and amortization expense increased to $25,716 for fiscal 2000 from $19,884 for fiscal 1999, an increase of $5,832 or 29%. The increase was attributable to new stores opened in fiscal 2000 and in fiscal 1999. As a percentage of revenues, depreciation and amortization decreased to 7.7% from 8.0% for the comparable prior period.

Management's discussion and analysis of financial condition and results of operations Dave & Buster's, Inc.

Preopening costs decreased to $5,331 for fiscal 2000 from $6,053 for fiscal 1999, a decrease of $722 or 12%. As a percentage of revenues, preopening costs were 1.6% for fiscal 2000 as compared to 2.4% for fiscal 1999. This decrease was due to the lesser number of new stores opened in 2000 compared to 1999.

Interest expense-net increased to $8,712 for fiscal 2000 from $3,339 for fiscal 1999. The increase was due to a higher average debt balance and higher interest rates in 2000 versus 1999.

The effective tax rate for fiscal year 2000 was 36.4% as compared to 36.7% for fiscal year 1999 and was the result of a lower effective state tax rate.

Liquidity and Capital Resources

Net cash provided by operating activities increased to $44,917 in 2001 compared to $36,678 in 2000 and $24,940 in 1999. Operating cash flows in 2001 increased primarily due to the timing of accounts payable disbursements. The increase in 2000 was attributable to improvement in profitability and timing of operational receipts and payments.

Cash used in investing activities was $25,727 in 2001 and $53,574 in 2000 compared to $73,798 in 1999. All investing expenditures are related to opening of new stores and normal recurring maintenance at previously existing stores.

Financing activities provided cash of $47,440 in 1999 and $16,984 in 2000 compared to a use of cash of $17,407 in 2001. Net use of cash by financing activities in 2001 was directly attributed to repayment of long-term debt of $41,648 offset by borrowings from long-term debt of $24,060. Net cash provided by financing activities in 2000 and 1999 was due to borrowings under long-term debt exceeding any repayments during each year.

The Company has a $110,000 senior secured revolving credit and term loan facility. The facility includes a five-year revolver and five- and seven-year term debt. The facility agreement calls for quarterly payments of principal on the term debt through maturity. Borrowing under the facility bears interest at a floating rate based on LIBOR (1.77% at February 3, 2002) or, at the Company's option, the bank's prime rate (4.75% at February 3, 2002) plus, in each case, a margin based upon financial performance. The facility is secured by all assets of the Company. The facility has certain financial covenants including a minimum consolidated tangible net worth level, a maximum leverage ratio, minimum fixed charge coverage and maximum level of capital expenditures. On November 19, 2001, the Company amended the facility to allow proceeds from sale/leaseback transactions to be applied to both the revolving credit and the term loans for a limited period. At February 3, 2002, $5,208 was available under this facility.

The Company has entered into an agreement that expires in 2007 to change a portion of its variable rate debt to fixed-rate debt. Notional amounts aggregating $51,255 are fixed at 5.44%. The Company is exposed to credit losses for periodic settlements of amounts due under the agreements if LIBOR decreases. A charge of $858 to interest expense was incurred in fiscal 2001 under the agreement.

The market risks associated with the agreements are mitigated because increased interest payments under the agreement resulting from reductions in LIBOR are effectively offset by a reduction in interest expense under the debt obligation.

The Company plans to open one new store during the fiscal year ended February 2, 2003. The preopening and construction costs of the new store will be provided from internal cash flow. Subsequent to the fiscal year ending February 2, 2003,the Company intends to open up to three stores per year, if adequate external financing can be secured to supplement internally generated cash flow.

Sale/Leaseback Transactions

During the year ended February 3, 2002, the Company completed the sale/leaseback of two stores (Atlanta and Houston) and the corporate headquarters in Dallas. Cash proceeds of $18,474 were received along with $5,150 in twenty year interest bearing notes receivable at 7 - 7.5%. The locations were sold to non-affiliated entities. No revenue or profit was recorded at the time of the transaction.

Upon execution of the sale/leaseback transactions, property costs of $27,360 and accumulated depreciation of $3,832 were removed from the Company's books resulting in a loss of $272 which was recognized in 2001 and a gain of $713 on one facility being amortized over the term of the operating lease.

Future operating lease obligations under the lease agreements are as follows: $2,917 in 2002, $2,957 in 2003, $2,997 in 2004, $3,037 in 2005, $3,078 in 2006 and $50,976 thereafter. Future minimum note payments and interest income associated with the sale/leasebacks at Houston and Atlanta are as follows: $488 in 2002, $488 in 2003, $488 in 2004, $488 in 2005 and $7,782 thereafter.

Management's discussion and analysis of financial condition and results of operations

Dave & Buster's, Inc.

Contractual Obligations and Commercial Commitments

The following tables set forth the Company's contractual obligations and commercial commitments (in thousands):

		PAYMENTS DUE BY PERIOD			
CONTRACTUAL OBLIGATIONS	TOTAL	1 YEAR OR LESS	2-3 YEARS	4-5 YEARS	AFTER 5 YEARS
Long-term debt	$ 90,396	$ 5,500	$ 19,700	$ 54,653	$ 10,543
Operating leases	344,633	19,474	37,614	36,566	250,979
Operating leases under sale/leaseback transactions	65,964	2,917	5,953	6,115	50,979
Total	$ 500,993	$ 27,891	$ 63,267	$ 97,334	$ 312,501

		AMOUNT OF COMMITMENT EXPIRATION PER PERIOD			
OTHER COMMERCIAL COMMITMENTS	TOTAL	1 YEAR OR LESS	2-3 YEARS	4-5 YEARS	AFTER 5 YEARS
Letters of Credit	$ 940	$ 940	$ —	$ —	$ —

Quarterly Fluctuations, Seasonality, and Inflation

As a result of the substantial revenues associated with each new Complex, the timing of new Complex openings will result in significant fluctuations in quarterly results. The Company expects seasonality to be a factor in the operation or results of its business in the future due to expected lower third quarter revenues due to the fall season, and expects higher fourth quarter revenues associated with the year-end holidays. The effects of supplier price increases are not expected to be material. The Company believes low inflation rates in its market areas have contributed to stable food and labor costs in recent years. However, there is no assurance that low inflation rates will continue or that the Federal minimum wage rate will not increase.

Market Risk

The Company's market risk exposure relates to changes in the general level of interest rates. The Company's earnings are affected by changes in interest rates due to the impact those changes have on its interest expense from variable-rate debt. The Company's agreement to fix a portion of its variable-rate debt mitigates this exposure.

"Safe Harbor" Statement Under the Private Securities Litigation Reform Act of 1995

Certain statements in this Annual Report are not based on historical facts but are "forward-looking statements" that are based on numerous assumptions made as of the date of this report. Forward looking statements are generally identified by the words "believes", "expects", "intends", "anticipates", "scheduled", and similar expressions. Such forward-looking statements involve known and unknown risks, uncertainties, and other factors which may cause the actual results, performance, or achievements of Dave & Buster's, Inc. to be materially different from any future results, performance, or achievements expressed or implied by such forward-looking statements. Such factors include, among others, the following: general economic and business conditions; competition; availability of capital; locations and terms of sites for Complex development; quality of management; changes in, or the failure to comply with, government regulations; and other risks indicated in this filing.

Market for the Company's Common Stock and Related Stockholder Matters

The Company's Common Stock is traded on the New York Stock Exchange ("NYSE") under the symbol DAB. The following table summarizes the high and low sales prices per share of Common Stock for the applicable periods indicated, as reported by the NYSE.

	FIRST QUARTER		SECOND QUARTER		THIRD QUARTER		FOURTH QUARTER	
Fiscal Year **2001**	$ 10.80	$ 7.75	$ 9.15	$ 7.61	$ 8.25	$ 5.45	$ 8.65	$ 6.10
Fiscal year 2000	$ 10.50	$ 6.25	$ 7.50	$ 6.00	$ 8.88	$ 6.06	$ 12.25	$ 7.56

As of April 17, 2002, there were 1,943 holders of record of the Common Stock.

Consolidated balance sheets Dave & Buster's, Inc.

IN THOUSANDS, EXCEPT SHARE AND PER SHARE AMOUNTS	FEBRUARY 3 2002	FEBRUARY 4 2001
Assets		
Current assets:		
Cash and cash equivalents	$ 4,521	$ 3,179
Inventories	25,964	21,758
Prepaid expenses	1,442	3,663
Other current assets	2,445	1,787
Total current assets	34,372	30,387
Property and equipment, net (Note 2)	258,302	260,467
Goodwill, net of accumulated amortization of $2,612 and $2,263	7,096	7,445
Other assets	9,364	5,576
Total assets	$ 309,134	$ 303,875
Liabilities and Stockholders' Equity		
Current liabilities:		
Current installments of long-term debt (Note 4)	$ 5,500	$ 4,124
Accounts payable	15,991	9,291
Accrued liabilities (Note 3)	11,085	7,050
Income taxes payable (Note 5)	5,054	3,567
Deferred income taxes (Note 5)	1,220	1,229
Total current liabilities	38,850	25,261
Deferred income taxes (Note 5)	8,143	7,667
Other liabilities	7,099	4,700
Long-term debt, less current installments (Note 4)	84,896	103,860
Commitments and contingencies (Notes 4, 6 and 11)		
Stockholders' equity (Note 7):		
Preferred stock, 10,000,000 authorized; none issued	—	—
Common stock, $0.01 par value, 50,000,000 authorized; 12,959,209 and 12,953,375 shares issued and outstanding as of February 3, 2002 and February 4, 2001, respectively	131	131
Paid in capital	115,701	115,659
Restricted stock awards	382	243
Retained earnings	55,778	48,200
	171,992	164,233
Less: treasury stock, at cost (175,000 shares)	1,846	1,846
Total stockholders' equity	170,146	162,387
Total liabilities and stockholders' equity	$ 309,134	$ 303,875

See accompanying notes to consolidated financial statements.

Consolidated statements of income

Dave & Buster's, Inc.

FISCAL YEAR IN THOUSANDS, EXCEPT PER SHARE AMOUNTS	2001	2000	1999
Food and beverage revenues	$ 181,358	$168,085	$ 121,390
Amusement and other revenues	176,651	164,218	125,744
Total revenues	358,009	332,303	247,134
Cost of revenues	66,939	61,547	45,720
Operating payroll and benefits	110,478	101,143	76,242
Other store operating expenses	106,971	90,581	65,292
General and administrative expenses	20,653	20,019	14,988
Depreciation and amortization expense	28,693	25,716	19,884
Preopening costs	4,578	5,331	6,053
Total costs and expenses	338,312	304,337	228,179
Operating income	19,697	27,966	18,955
Interest expense, net	7,820	8,712	3,339
Income before provision for income taxes and cumulative effect of a change in an accounting principle	11,877	19,254	15,616
Provision for income taxes (Note 5)	4,299	7,009	5,724
Income before cumulative effect of a change in an accounting principle	7,578	12,245	9,892
Cumulative effect of a change in an accounting principle, net of income tax benefit of $2,928	—	—	4,687
Net income	$ 7,578	$ 12,245	$ 5,205
Net income per share – basic			
Before cumulative effect of a change in an accounting principle	$ .58	$ .95	$ .76
Cumulative effect of a change in an accounting principle	—	—	.36
	$ .58	$ .95	$ .40
Net income per share – diluted			
Before cumulative effect of a change in an accounting principle	$ .58	$ .94	$ .75
Cumulative effect of a change in an accounting principle	—	—	.36
	$ .58	$ .94	$ .39
Weighted average shares outstanding			
Basic	12,956	12,953	13,054
Diluted	13,016	12,986	13,214

See accompanying notes to consolidated financial statements.

Consolidated statements of stockholders' equity

Dave & Buster's, Inc.

IN THOUSANDS	COMMON STOCK SHARES	COMMON STOCK AMOUNT	PAID IN CAPITAL	RESTRICTED STOCK AWARDS	RETAINED EARNINGS	TREASURY STOCK	TOTAL
Balance, January 31, 1999	13,069	$ 131	$ 114,621	$ —	$ 30,750	$ —	$ 145,502
Proceeds from exercising stock options	59	—	786	—	—	—	786
Tax benefit related to stock option exercises	—	—	252	—	—	—	252
Purchase of treasury stock	(175)	—	—	—	—	(1,846)	(1,846)
Net income	—	—	—	—	5,205	—	5,205
Balance, January 30, 2000	12,953	$ 131	$ 115,659	$ —	$ 35,955	$ (1,846)	$ 149,899
Amortization of restricted stock awards	—	—	—	243	—	—	243
Net income	—	—	—	—	12,245	—	12,245
Balance, February 4, 2001	12,953	$ 131	$ 115,659	$ 243	$ 48,200	$ (1,846)	$ 162,387
Amortization of restricted stock awards	—	—	—	139	—	—	139
Proceeds from exercising stock options	6	—	40	—	—	—	40
Tax benefit related to stock option exercises	—	—	2	—	—	—	2
Net income	—	—	—	—	7,578	—	7,578
Balance, February 3, 2002	12,959	$ 131	$ 115,701	$ 382	$ 55,778	$ (1,846)	$ 170,146

See accompanying notes to consolidated financial statements.

Consolidated statements of cash flows

Dave & Buster's, Inc.

FISCAL YEAR IN THOUSANDS	2001	2000	1999
Cash flows from operating activities:			
Net income	$ 7,578	$ 12,245	$ 5,205
Adjustments to reconcile net income to net cash provided by operating activities:			
Cumulative effect of change in an accounting principle	—	—	4,687
Depreciation and amortization	28,693	25,716	19,884
Provision for deferred income taxes	467	1,182	986
Restricted stock awards	—	243	—
Gain on sale of assets	(441)	—	—
Changes in assets and liabilities			
Inventories	(4,206)	(5,515)	(5,432)
Prepaid expenses	2,221	(1,559)	(361)
Other assets	(4,457)	(671)	(666)
Accounts payable	6,700	(2,577)	(1,827)
Accrued liabilities	4,035	2,192	1,073
Income taxes payable	1,487	3,567	—
Other liabilities	2,399	1,855	1,391
Net cash provided by operating activities	44,476	36,678	24,940
Cash flows from investing activities:			
Proceeds from sale/leasebacks	18,474	—	—
Capital expenditures	(44,201)	(53,574)	(73,798)
Net cash used in investing activities	(25,727)	(53,574)	(73,798)
Cash flows from financing activities:			
Purchase of treasury stock	—	—	(1,846)
Borrowings under long-term debt	24,060	131,292	50,000
Repayments of long-term debt	(41,648)	(114,308)	(1,500)
Proceeds from issuance of common stock, net	181	—	786
Net cash provided by financing activities	(17,407)	16,984	47,440
Increase (decrease) in cash and cash equivalents	1,342	88	(1,418)
Beginning cash and cash equivalents	3,179	3,091	4,509
Ending cash and cash equivalents	$ 4,521	$ 3,179	$ 3,091
Supplemental disclosures of cash flow information:			
Cash paid for income taxes	$ 2,590	$ 1,941	$ 4,188
Cash paid for interest, net of amounts capitalized	$ 7,261	$ 8,363	$ 3,455

See accompanying notes to consolidated financial statements.

Notes to consolidated financial statements Dave & Buster's, Inc.

IN THOUSANDS EXCEPT PER SHARE AMOUNTS

NOTE 1

Summary of Significant Accounting Policies

BASIS OF PRESENTATION – The consolidated financial statements include the accounts of Dave & Buster's, Inc. and all wholly-owned subsidiaries (the "Company"). All material intercompany accounts and transactions have been eliminated in consolidation. The Company's one industry segment is the ownership and operation of restaurant/entertainment complexes (a "Complex" or "Store") under the name "Dave & Buster's," which are principally located in the United States.

USE OF ESTIMATES – The preparation of financial statements in conformity with generally accepted accounting principles requires management to make certain estimates and assumptions that affect the amounts reported in the financial statements and accompanying notes. Actual results could differ from those estimates.

FISCAL YEAR – The Company's fiscal year ends on the Sunday after the Saturday closest to January 31. References to 2001, 2000 and 1999 are to the 52 weeks ended February 3, 2002 and to the 53 weeks ended February 4, 2001 and to the 52 weeks ended January 30, 2000, respectively.

INVENTORIES – Inventories, which consist of food, beverage and merchandise are reported at the lower of cost or market determined on a first-in, first-out method. Static supplies inventory is capitalized at each store opening date and reviewed periodically for valuation.

PREOPENING COSTS – The Company adopted Statement of Position 98-5 ("SOP 98-5"), "Reporting on the Costs of Start-Up Activities", in the first quarter of fiscal 1999. This accounting standard requires the Company to expense all start-up and preopening costs as they are incurred. The Company previously deferred such costs and amortized them over the twelve-month period following the opening of each store. The cumulative effect of this accounting change, net of income tax benefit of $2,928, was $4,687 in fiscal 1999.

PROPERTY AND EQUIPMENT – Expenditures for new facilities and those which substantially increase the useful lives of the property, including interest during construction, are capitalized. Interest capitalized in 2001, 2000 and 1999 was $892, $1,555 and $1,623, respectively. Equipment purchases are capitalized at cost. Property and equipment lives are estimated as follows: buildings, 40 years; leasehold and building improvements, shorter of 20 years or lease life; furniture, fixtures and equipment, 5 to 10 years; games, 5 years.

GOODWILL – Goodwill of $9,708 is being amortized over 30 years. Whenever there is an indication of impairment, the Company evaluates the recoverability of goodwill using future undiscounted cash flows. In June 2001, the Financial Accounting Standards Board issued Statements of Financial Accounting Standards No. 141, Business Combinations and No. 142, Goodwill and Other Intangible Assets ("Statements"), effective for fiscal years beginning after December 15, 2001. Under the new rules, goodwill and intangible assets deemed to have indefinite lives will no longer be amortized but will be subject to annual impairment tests in accordance with the Statements. Other intangible assets will continue to be amortized over their useful lives.

The Company will apply the new standards on accounting for goodwill and other intangible assets beginning in the first quarter of 2002. Application of the nonamortization provisions of the Statements is expected to result in an increase in income before tax of $349 ($.03 per diluted share) in 2002 as a result of nonamortization of existing goodwill. During the first quarter 2002, the Company will perform the required impairment test of goodwill as of February 3, 2002. Based on current analysis, the Company will record an expense to "Cumulative effect of a change in an accounting principle" of $4,541 net of income tax benefit of $2,555 ($.35 per diluted share), upon the adoption of the new standard.

DEPRECIATION AND AMORTIZATION – Property and equipment, excluding most games, are depreciated on the straight-line method over the estimated useful life of the assets. Games are generally depreciated on the 150%-double-declining-balance method over the estimated useful lives of the assets. Intangible assets are amortized on the straight-line method over estimated useful lives as follows: trademarks over statutory lives and lease rights over remaining lease terms.

INTEREST RATE SWAP AGREEMENTS – The Company adopted Statement of Financial Accounting Standards No. 133, Accounting for Derivative Instruments and Hedging Activities ("FAS 133") effective February 5, 2001. FAS 133 requires the Company to recognize all derivatives on the balance sheet at fair value. Derivatives that are not hedges must be adjusted to fair value through income. If the derivative is a hedge, depending on the nature of the hedge, changes in fair value of derivatives will either be offset against the change in fair value of the hedged assets, liabilities, or firm commitments through earnings or recognized in other comprehensive income until the hedged item is recognized in earnings. The ineffective portion of a derivative's change in fair value will be immediately recognized in earnings. During the year, the Company has entered into an agreement

Notes to consolidated financial statements Dave & Buster's, Inc.

that expires in 2007, to fix its variable-rate debt to fixed-rate debt (5.44% at February 3, 2002) on notional amounts aggregating $51,255. The market risks associated with the agreements are mitigated because increased interest payments under the agreement resulting from reductions in LIBOR are effectively offset by reduction in interest expense under the debt obligation.

The Company is exposed to credit losses for periodic settlements of amounts due under the agreements. A charge of $858 to interest expense was incurred in fiscal 2001 under the agreement.

INCOME TAXES – The Company uses the liability method which recognizes the amount of current and deferred taxes payable or refundable at the date of the financial statements as a result of all events that are recognized in the financial statements and as measured by the provisions of enacted tax laws.

STOCK OPTION PLAN – The Company elected to follow Accounting Principles Board Opinion No. 25, "Accounting for Stock Issued to Employees" ("APB 25") and related Interpretations in accounting for its employee stock options because the alternative fair value accounting provided for under SFAS No. 123, "Accounting for Stock-Based Compensation", requires use of option valuation models that were not developed for use in valuing employee stock options. Under APB 25, because the exercise price of the Company's employee stock options equals the market price of the underlying stock on the date of grant, no compensation expense is recognized.

REVENUE RECOGNITION – Food, beverage and amusement revenues are recorded at point of service. Foreign license revenues are deferred until the Company fulfills its obligations under license agreements, which is upon the opening of the Complex. The license agreements provide for continuing royalty fees based on percentage of gross revenues and are recognized when assured.

ADVERTISING COSTS – In accordance with SOP 93-7 "Reporting on Advertising Costs", all costs of advertising are recorded as expense in the period in which the costs are incurred or the first time the advertising takes place. For fiscal 2001 and 2000, such expenses are 3.7% and 3.3% of revenue, respectively.

TREASURY STOCK – During fiscal 1999, the Company's Board of Directors approved a plan to repurchase up to 1,000 shares of the Company's common stock. Pursuant to the plan, the Company repurchased 175 shares of its common stock for approximately $1,846 during fiscal 1999.

NOTE 2 Property and Equipment

Property and equipment consist of the following:

	2001	2000
Land	$ 6,706	$ 11,308
Buildings	34,232	56,023
Leasehold and building improvements	143,114	110,559
Games	79,673	69,970
Furniture, fixtures, and equipment	92,033	72,723
Construction in progress	3,711	17,914
Total cost	359,469	338,497
Accumulated depreciation	(101,167)	(78,030)
Total property and equipment	$ 258,302	$ 260,467

Notes to consolidated financial statements Dave & Buster's, Inc.

NOTE 3 Accrued Liabilities

Accrued liabilities consist of the following:

	2001	2000
Payroll	$ 2,393	$ 1,873
Sales and use tax	1,387	1,618
Real estate tax	2,620	1,873
Other	4,685	1,686
Total accrued liabilities	$ 11,085	$ 7,050

NOTE 4 Long-term Debt

In 2000, the Company secured a $110,000 senior secured revolving credit and term loan facility. On November 19, 2001, the Company amended its senior secured revolving credit and term loan facility to allow proceeds from sale/leaseback transactions to be applied to both the revolving credit and term loans. The facility includes a five-year revolver and five- and seven-year term debt. The facility agreement calls for quarterly payments of principal on the term debt through the maturity date. Borrowing under the facility bears interest at a floating rate based on LIBOR (1.77% at February 3, 2002) or, at the Company's option, the bank's prime rate (4.75% at February 3, 2002) plus, in each case, a margin based upon financial performance. The facility is secured by all assets of the Company. The facility has certain financial covenants including a minimum consolidated tangible net worth level, a maximum leverage ratio, minimum fixed charge coverage and maximum level of capital expenditures. At February 3, 2002, $5,208 was available under this facility. The fair value of the Company's long-term debt approximates its carrying value.

The Company has entered into an agreement that expires in 2007, to change a portion of its variable rate debt to fixed-rate debt. Notional amounts aggregating $51,255 are fixed at 5.44%. The Company is exposed to credit losses for periodic settlements of amounts due under the agreements if LIBOR decreases. A charge of $858 to interest expense was incurred in 2001 under the agreement.

NOTE 5 Income Taxes

The provision for income taxes is as follows:

	2001	2000	1999
Current expense			
Federal	$ 3,149	$ 5,077	$ 4,242
State and local	504	750	496
Deferred tax expense	646	1,182	986
Total provision for income taxes	$ 4,299	$ 7,009	$ 5,724

Notes to consolidated financial statements Dave & Buster's, Inc.

Significant components of the deferred tax liabilities and assets in the consolidated balance sheets are as follows:

	2001	2000	1999
Accelerated depreciation	$ 11,399	$ 9,474	$ 7,475
Preopening costs	(1,378)	—	—
Prepaid expenses	152	129	130
Capitalized interest costs	1,740	1,281	1,346
Total deferred tax liabilities	11,913	10,884	8,951
Worker's compensation	281	304	330
Leasing transactions	2,288	1,500	791
Other	(19)	184	116
Total deferred tax assets	2,550	1,988	1,237
Net deferred tax liability	$ (9,363)	$ (8,896)	$ (7,714)

Reconciliation of federal statutory rates to effective income tax rates:

	2001	2000	1999
Federal corporate statutory rate	35.0%	35.0%	35.0%
State and local income taxes, net of federal income tax benefit	3.1%	2.2%	2.1%
Goodwill amortization and other nondeductible expenses	1.0%	2.1%	2.2%
Tax credits	(4.3)%	(2.0)%	(1.9)%
Effect of change in deferred tax rate	—	(1.9)%	(2.4)%
Other	1.4%	1.0%	1.7%
Effective tax rate	36.2%	36.4%	36.7%

NOTE 6 Leases

The Company leases certain properties and equipment under operating leases. Some of the leases include options for renewal or extension on various terms. Most leases require the Company to pay property taxes, insurance and maintenance of the leased assets. Some leases have provisions for additional percentage rentals based on revenues; however, payments of percentage rent were minimal during the three-year period ended February 3, 2002. For 2001, 2000 and 1999, rent expense for operating leases was $19,469, $14,295 and $11,119, respectively. At February 3, 2002, future minimum lease payments required under operating leases are $22,391 in 2002; $21,892 in 2003; $21,675 in 2004; $21,368 in 2005; $21,313 in 2006 and $301,957 thereafter.

During the year ended February 3, 2002, the Company completed the sale/leaseback of two stores (Atlanta and Houston) and the corporate headquarters in Dallas. Cash proceeds of $18,474 were received along with $5,150 in twenty year interest bearing notes receivable at 7-7.5%. The locations were sold to non-affiliated entities. No revenue or profit was recorded at the time of the transaction

Upon execution of the sale/leaseback transactions, property costs of $27,360 and accumulated depreciation of $3,832 were removed from the Company's books resulting in a loss of $272 which was recognized in 2001 and a gain of $713 on one facility being amortized over the term of the operating lease.

Future operating lease obligations under the lease agreements are as follows: $2,917 in 2002, $2,957 in 2003, $2,997 in 2004, $3,037 in 2005, $3,078 in 2006 and $50,976 thereafter. Future minimum note payments and interest income associated with the sale/leasebacks at Houston and Atlanta are as follows: $488 in 2002, $488 in 2003, $488 in 2004, $488 in 2005 and $7,782 thereafter.

Notes to consolidated financial statements Dave & Buster's, Inc.

NOTE 7 Common Stock

In 1995, the Company adopted the Dave & Buster's, Inc. 1995 Stock Option Plan (the "Plan") covering 675 shares of common stock. In 1997, 1998 and 2001, the Company increased the shares of common stock covered by the Plan to 1,350, 2,350 and 2,950 respectively. The Plan provides that incentive stock options may be granted at option prices not less than fair market value at date of grant (110% in the case of an incentive stock option granted to any person who owns more than 10% of the total combined voting power of all classes of stock of the Company). Non-qualified stock options may not be granted for less than 85% of the fair market value of the common stock at the time of grant and are primarily exercisable over a three- to five-year period from the date of the grant.

In 1996, the Company adopted a stock option plan for outside directors (the "Directors' Plan"). A total of 150 shares of common stock are subject to the Directors' Plan. The options granted under the Directors' Plan vest ratably over a three year period. In 2001, the Company increased the shares of common stock subject to the Directors' Plan from 150 shares to 190 shares.

In 2000, the Company amended and restated the Dave & Buster's, Inc. 1995 Stock Incentive Plan to allow the Company to grant restricted stock awards. These restricted stock awards will fully vest at the end of the vesting period or the attainment of one or more performance targets established by the Company. Recipients are not required to provide consideration to the Company other than render service and have the right to vote the shares and to receive dividends. The Company issued in 2001 and 2000, 63.5 and 267 shares of restricted stock at a market value of \$6.45 – \$7.90 and \$6.75, respectively which vest at the earlier of attaining certain performance targets or seven years. The total market value of the restricted shares, as determined at the date of issuance, is treated as unearned compensation and is charged to expense over the vesting period. The charge to expense for the unearned compensation was \$139 and \$243 in 2001 and 2000, respectively.

Pro forma information regarding net income and earnings per common share is required by SFAS 123, and is used as if the Company had accounted for its employee stock options under the fair value method. The fair value for these options is estimated at the date of grant using a Black-Scholes option pricing model with the following weighted-average assumptions for 2001, 2000 and 1999, respectively: risk-free interest rates of 4.59%, 6.30%, and 5.39%; dividend yields of 0.0%; volatility factors of the expected market price of the Company's common stock of .650, .740, and .494; and a weighted-average life of the option of 3.2, 2.7, and 4.4 years.

The Black-Scholes option valuation model is used in estimating the fair value of traded options, which have no vesting restrictions and are fully transferable. In addition, option valuation models require the input of highly subjective assumptions including the expected stock price volatility. Because the Company's employee stock options have characteristics significantly different from those of traded options, and because changes in the subjective input assumptions can materially affect the fair value estimate, in management's opinion, the existing models do not necessarily provide a reliable single measure of the fair value of its employee stock options.

For purposes of pro forma disclosures, the estimated fair value of the options is amortized to expense over the option's vesting period. Because SFAS 123 requires compensation expense to be recognized over the vesting period, the impact on pro forma net income and pro forma earnings per common share as reported below may not be representative of pro forma compensation expense in future years.

The Company's pro forma information follows:

	2001	2000	1999
Net income, as reported	\$ 7,578	\$ 12,245	\$ 5,205
Pro forma net income	\$ 5,931	\$ 10,018	\$ 3,627
Basic net income per share, as reported	\$ .58	\$ .95	\$ .40
Pro forma basic net income per share	\$ .46	\$ .77	\$ .28
Diluted net income per share, as reported	\$ .58	\$ .94	\$ .39
Pro forma diluted net income per share	\$ .46	\$ .77	\$ .27

Notes to consolidated financial statements Dave & Buster's, Inc.

A summary of the Company's stock option activity and related information is as follows:

	2001		2000		1999	
	OPTIONS	WEIGHTED-AVERAGE EXERCISE PRICE	OPTIONS	WEIGHTED-AVERAGE EXERCISE PRICE	OPTIONS	WEIGHTED-AVERAGE EXERCISE PRICE
Outstanding – beginning of year	1,932	$ 14.78	1,666	$ 17.24	1,145	$ 16.82
Granted	1,233	$ 6.82	674	$ 7.49	734	$ 18.10
Exercised	(6)	$ 6.80	—	—	(59)	$ 12.88
Forfeited	(234)	$ 13.16	(408)	$ 12.77	(154)	$ 20.09
Outstanding – end of year	2,925	$ 11.56	1,932	$ 14.78	1,666	$ 17.24
Exercisable – end of year	1,178	$ 15.26	642	$ 17.37	516	$ 14.87
Weighted-average fair value of options granted during the year		$ 3.28		$ 3.96		$ 8.36

As of February 3, 2002, exercise prices for 2,925 options ranged from $6.10 to $25.32. The weighted-average remaining contractual life of the options is 7.6 years.

Under a Shareholder Protection Rights Plan adopted by the Company, each share of outstanding common stock includes a right which entitles the holder to purchase one one-hundredth of a share of Series A Junior Participating Preferred Stock for seventy five dollars. Rights attach to all new shares of common stock whether newly issued or issued from treasury stock and become exercisable only under certain conditions involving actual or potential acquisitions of the Company's common stock. Depending on the circumstances, all holders except the acquiring person may be entitled to 1) acquire such number of shares of Company common stock as have a market value at the time of twice the exercise price of each right, or 2) exchange a right for one share of Company common stock or one one-hundredth of a share of the Series A Junior Participating Preferred Stock, or 3) receive shares of the acquiring company's common stock having a market value equal to twice the exercise price of each right. The rights remain in existence until ten years after the Distribution, unless they are redeemed (at one cent per right).

NOTE 8 Earnings Per Share

The following table sets forth the computation of basic and diluted earnings per share:

	2001	2000	1999
Numerator – Net Income	$ 7,578	$ 12,245	$ 5,205
Denominator:			
Denominator for basic net income per share – Weighted average shares	12,956	12,953	13,054
Effect of dilutive securities – employee stock options	60	33	160
Denominator for diluted earnings per share – adjusted weighted average shares	13,016	12,986	13,214
Basic net income per share	$ .58	$ .95	$ .40
Diluted net income per share	$ .58	$ .94	$ .39

Notes to consolidated financial statements Dave & Buster's, Inc.

Options to purchase 1,529, 1,346 and 925 shares of common stock for 2001, 2000 and 1999, respectively, were not included in the computation of diluted net income per share because the options would have been antidilutive.

NOTE 9 Related Party Activity

During 2000, the Company was party to a consulting agreement with Sandell Investments ("Sandell"), a partnership whose controlling partner is a director of the Company. Sandell advises the Company with respect to expansion and site selection, market analysis, improvement and enhancement of the Dave & Buster's concept and other similar and related activities. Annual fees of $125 were paid to Sandell in 2000 and 1999, the maximum fee provided for under the agreement.

The Company was a party to a sale/leaseback transaction with Cypress Equities, Inc. for its San Diego, California location, whereby the Company received $8,000 in exchange for committing to lease payments of approximately $6,300 over 20 years with options for renewal. A director of the Company is the managing member of Cypress Equities, Inc. Payments to Cypress Equities, Inc. in 2001 and 2000 were $1,242 and $349, respectively.

NOTE 10 Employee Benefit Plan

The Company sponsors a plan to provide retirement benefits under the provision of Section 401(k) of the Internal Revenue Code (the "401(k) Plan") for all employees who have completed a specified term of service. Company contributions may range from 0% to 100% of employee contributions, up to a maximum of 6% of eligible employee compensation, as defined. Employees may elect to contribute up to 20% of their eligible compensation on a pretax basis. Benefits under the 401(k) Plan are limited to the assets of the 401(k) Plan.

NOTE 11 Contingencies

The Company is subject to certain legal proceedings and claims that arise in the ordinary course of its business. In the opinion of management, the amount of ultimate liability with respect to all actions will not materially affect the consolidated results of operations or financial condition of the Company.

NOTE 12 Quarterly Financial Information (unaudited)

FISCAL **2001**	FIRST	SECOND	THIRD	FOURTH
Total revenues	$ 88,210	$ 83,622	$ 81,371	$ 104,806
Income before provision for income taxes	4,834	2,675	(2,936)	7,304
Net income	3,084	1,707	(1,873)	4,660
Basic net income per share	$ .24	$ .13	$ (.14)	$ .36
Basic weighted average shares outstanding	12,953	12,954	12,956	12,957
Diluted net income per share	$ .24	$ .13	$ (.14)	$ .36
Diluted weighted average shares outstanding	13,068	13,028	12,956	12,992

FISCAL 2000	FIRST	SECOND	THIRD	FOURTH
Total revenues	$ 77,849	$ 77,566	$ 79,244	$ 97,644
Income before provision for income taxes	4,565	3,397	2,368	8,924
Net income	2,890	2,150	1,499	5,706
Basic net income per share	$ .22	$ .17	$ .12	$ .44
Basic weighted average shares outstanding	12,953	12,953	12,953	12,953
Diluted net income per share	$ .22	$ .17	$ .12	$ .44
Diluted weighted average shares outstanding	12,960	12,954	12,974	13,077

Report of independent auditors Dave & Buster's, Inc.

STOCKHOLDERS AND BOARD OF DIRECTORS
DAVE & BUSTER'S, INC.

We have audited the accompanying consolidated balance sheets of Dave & Buster's, Inc. as of February 3, 2002 and February 4, 2001, and the related consolidated statements of income, stockholders' equity and cash flows for each of the three years in the period ended February 3, 2002. These financial statements are the responsibility of the company's management. Our responsibility is to express an opinion on these financial statements based on our audits.

We conducted our audits in accordance with auditing standards generally accepted in the United States. Those standards require that we plan and perform the audit to obtain reasonable assurance about whether the financial statements are free of material misstatement. An audit includes examining, on a test basis, evidence supporting the amounts and disclosures in the financial statements. An audit also includes assessing the accounting principles used and significant estimates made by management, as well as evaluating the overall financial statement presentation. We believe that our audits provide a reasonable basis for our opinion.

In our opinion, the financial statements referred to above present fairly, in all material respects, the consolidated financial position of Dave & Buster's, Inc. at February 3, 2002 and February 4, 2001 and the consolidated results of its operations and its cash flows for each of the three years in the period ended February 3, 2002, in conformity with accounting principles generally accepted in the United States.

Ernst + Young LLP

Dallas, Texas
March 27, 2002

Index

Q

R

S

T

U

V

W